Understanding Intercultural Communication

Stella Ting-Toomey
California State University at Fullerton

Leeva C. Chung
University of San Diego

Instructor's Manual/Testing Program and
Interactive Student Study Guide Available

New York   Oxford
OXFORD UNIVERSITY PRESS

Oxford University Press, Inc., publishes works that further Oxford University's
objective of excellence in research, scholarship, and education.

Oxford   New York
Auckland   Cape Town   Dar es Salaam   Hong Kong   Karachi
Kuala Lumpur   Madrid   Melbourne   Mexico City   Nairobi
New Delhi   Shanghai   Taipei   Toronto

With offices in
Argentina   Austria   Brazil   Chile   Czech Republic   France   Greece
Guatemala   Hungary   Italy   Japan   Poland   Portugal   Singapore
South Korea   Switzerland   Thailand   Turkey   Ukraine   Vietnam

Published by Oxford University Press, Inc.
198 Madison Avenue, New York, New York 10016
http://www.oup.com

ISBN 978-0-19-533006-9

10 9 8 7 6

Printed in the United States of America
on acid-free paper

Dedication to Our Parents

獻給我最親愛的父母親

To my loving parents: Ting Chun Yen and Wang Shu Chin, this book is dedicated to you. For all your love, sacrifices, resilient spirit, and a lifetime of hard work—I thank you for teaching me caring, considerateness, and adaptability wherever I go. I love you and appreciate your "letting go" of me at a young age and letting me come to America and study. Whatever I've accomplished, I'm an extension of your love and gentle grace.

To my visionary parents: Chung Dai Tau and Pang Duk Wai, this book is dedicated to you—allowing me the freedom to find my voice, inspiring me through your creative energy, and teaching me to trust intuition, flowing with it, despite life's uncertainties. For all of your love—I thank you both.

Contents

Preface

This text, *Understanding Intercultural Communication*, is written for you to increase your knowledge and skills about intercultural communication. With increased globalization and demographic changes in U.S. society, it is inevitable that you will be communicating with people who are culturally different. Developing constructive, quality intercultural relationships can make life enriching and exciting to ourselves and to people around us.

This book is an introductory text designed for undergraduate students, teachers, and practitioners who are searching for a user-friendly text on the fundamentals of intercultural communication. With the lens of flexible intercultural communication, we are able to thread through an abundance of intercultural material with a very practical theme. This book emphasizes a strong value-orientation approach and its effect on intercultural communication. It also addresses the complex role of cultural-ethnic identity and its relationship to intercultural contacts in our increasingly pluralistic U.S. society.

This book is distinctive because of its well-balanced emphasis on both international/intercultural communication issues and U.S. domestic diversity issues. It is a text with many special hooks and original features. For example, it offers first-time students the following:

- A comprehensive *introduction* to all the important concepts of intercultural communication.

- A sound *knowledge base* of recent intercultural communication research areas.

- A practical entry into the world of culturally different others by hearing their voices and reading their real-life *intercultural examples.*

- *An Intercultural Toolkit* at the end of each chapter to remind students to practice flexible intercultural communication skills in everyday interactions.

- *Jeopardy* boxes to increase students' global, pop culture, and domestic diversity literacy.

- *Double Take* personal narratives and stories to connect abstract intercultural concepts with meaningful understanding.

- *Picture This* poems for students to visualize the intercultural experiences of culturally diverse others.

- *Snapshot* photos to transport students to culturally different communities where they will experience culture shock.

- *Know Thyself* mini-assessments and fun quizzes to motivate students to interact with the book in an enjoyable, active learning manner.

- *Active Dialogue* scenes to illustrate the dynamic intercultural message exchange process.

- Simple *Tables and Figures* to highlight various important intercultural and interethnic communication ideas.

- A well-designed *Instructor's Manual* with many active learning exercises and activities plus instructional tips for managing challenging topics in the intercultural classroom.

Three initial assumptions guided the development of this text. First, we wanted students to enjoy learning about the various concepts of intercultural communication. Second, we wanted to signal to the students that there is no one right way to practice intercultural communication—instead, there are multiple paths and risk-taking efforts to connect with culturally different others. Third, we wanted to have fun writing this book together—as a way of celebrating our friendship. As we approach the ending journey of writing this text, we believe that we have realized our goals with joy.

This book is organized in three parts. The first part lays the foundational frameworks and concepts of intercultural communication. The reasons for studying intercultural communication and practicing flexible intercultural skills are articulated. Major research areas, such as cultural value patterns (e.g., individualism-collectivism) and cultural-ethnic identity, are explored—especially through the reflections of many cultural voices and personal stories.

The second section emphasizes the process of intercultural communication. Topics such as developmental culture shock, language functions and culture, and diverse cultural verbal styles, as well as fun topics such as nonverbal space violations and cross-cultural hand gestures are discussed and accompanied with lively intercultural examples.

The third section focuses on intercultural-interpersonal relationship development contexts. Important factors such as E.S.P. (i.e., ethnocentrism, stereotypes, and prejudice) are discussed in depth. Practical knowledge and skills to manage intercultural conflict competently are proposed. Many animated conflict dialogues and interpersonal examples are used to illustrate the development of intimate intercultural relationships. The contemporary topic of the development of a hybrid, global identity is addressed through a new concept we coined as the "e.net individual." We discuss the impact of technology and pop culture and its effect on our shifting value patterns. Finally, a cornerstone theme, becoming an ethical intercultural communicator, rounds out the book. Throughout this book, personal stories, poems, snapshots, fun quizzes, ethical dilemmas, and practical toolkits are posed to invite students to engage in active learning to master the foundational concepts of intercultural communication. At the same time, we strive to give first-time students an accurate and enjoyable basic text to learn about intercultural communication. We want them to come away with a special appreciation for the mindful effort it takes to communicate across cultures. We hope we have succeeded in this endeavor. ✦

Acknowledgments

Crafting a book such as *Understanding Intercultural Communication* is more than the effort of two individuals. We are grateful to the many individuals who encouraged and motivated us to bring this work to fruition. First and foremost, we want to thank our many students who have contributed their voices and shared their intercultural experiences with us. Without their voices, this book would have been quite abstract. We also want to thank our colleagues at the California State University at Fullerton (CSUF) and the University of San Diego (USD) for providing a supportive environment in which to conduct our writing.

Second, we want to thank Claude Teweles, Publisher at Roxbury, for his enormous patience and sustained faith in us and the book. Thank you to Phong Ho, Carla Plucknett, Ann West, Jim Ballinger, Nina Hickey, and the entire production staff at Roxbury for their professional help and their determination to make this volume the "best" in the intercultural market. We also want to thank our reviewers for their detailed suggestions: Myrna Cornett-DeVito, Emporia State University; Robbin D. Crabtree, Fairfield University; Fernando Delgado, Minnesota State University, Mankato; Tina M. Harris, University of Georgia; Armeda C. Reitzel, Humboldt State University; Diana Rios, University of Connecticut; and Arvind Singhal, Ohio University. To Candice Thomas-Maddox, Ohio University, Lancaster, your encouraging comments and illuminating insights motivated us to bring this book to closure. To Alex Flecky, your keen eye and meticulous proofreading made the book more comprehensible and inviting. We appreciate all your detailed comments and astute suggestions. In addition, we extend our special appreciation to all our Portland Summer Institute of Intercultural Communication Workshop faculty, students, and staff for providing us with a nurturing environment in which to dialogue about intercultural communication issues.

We also want to thank the following individuals for their wonderful support throughout the writing of this book at CSUF: Grant Bardsley, Apryl Cato, Alejandro Jazan, Wei-Cheng Lin, Maureen Petta, Jennifer

Quinn, and Ana Marie Vargas. At USD, we want to thank Leanna Cummings, Thulan, Leeann Kim, Katie Moyce, Ashley Pendergrast, Jennifer Rall, Chad Tew, and Josette Turner. A very special thanks and kudos to Peter Lee, who helped us in preparing the tables and figures. Peter, without your gracious help and cheerful support, this project could not have made it to the finish line. We would also like to take this opportunity to acknowledge the warm support of many of our remarkable students, friends, and families.

From Stella Ting-Toomey: I extend my special thanks and appreciation to many of my students, who let me experiment and test many of the ideas in this book and so embrace "sideways learning" as a playful teaching tool. Your positive energy for learning and your willingness to stretch make me a better teacher every step of the way. I also thank the special individuals in my life who serve as my supportive network and cheering squads: Maria Chan-Sew, Ge Gao, Wintilo Garcia, Atsuko Kurogi, Peter Lee, Angela Nagao, John Oetzel, Shonna Ries, Ramona Rose, Amy Starr, Gloria Strasburger, Miki Yamashita, and especially Annette Bow—the "role model" of interpersonal and intercultural sensitivity.

I also want to mention the special men in my life: my husband, Charles, and my son, Adrian—your endless cheering, good humor, and unconditional support provide the cushion for this book. Without your love and understanding, this book would not have meant as much. I also want to mention my three special brothers—Tom, Henry, and Victor—to all three of you, I treasure your love, support, and your adventurous spirit. Although we are spread out in different corners of the world, you are all constantly in my warm thoughts.

From Leeva Chung: This book would not have been finished without the unfailing support of my colleagues at the University of San Diego (USD). I could not have asked for a more intellectual and collegial group to work with. To the Dean's office, thank you for the faculty research grants, which enabled me to find time to work on this project. Thank you to Charles, who always provided the advice I needed to hear; to Dan O'Hair, for the motivational advice; and Toni, for the space to keep it together. I also want to extend a special shout-out to my students at USD. Always engaged, you all give me the reason why I teach: the challenge and thrill of discovery. Your energy is contagious.

I would also be remiss if I did not mention my collaborative relationship with Stella. Life is truly amazing. From the point of teacher, advisor, mentor, and friend, she serves as my strongest advocate at every step of my professional journey. I am beyond grateful and blessed to have such a connection and an inspiring mentor as a role model, who embodies the definition of compassion, wisdom, and flexibility. The path we took together to accomplish this book was filled with many food breaks and moments of laughter and much focused energy, despite the constant pressure to "get it done." We ate well and we laughed well together!

In addition, lifting my spirits at each turning point of this journey were my friends, family, and ohana, both close and far. I am most thankful to my wild and crazy family, four generations who played a key role in this book, living vicariously through my writing highs and lows. You are all a special part of this accomplishment. To my dear friends and ohana, all who served as protectors when my soul needed soothing, who made me laugh and allowed me to be real, I count each of you as my special blessings. And more important, to Ngao—for your love and patience, keeping me in check and balanced.

To the very special women in my life: my beautiful sisters, Gheeva and Ghava, and my two resilient grandmothers—the four of you are a reflection of everything I am and everything I will become. Thank you for keeping me grounded and protecting me.

I would be remiss if I did not say anything about my professional relationship with Leeva, and, more important, our friendship. It has been more than ten years since Leeva was in my interpersonal communication graduate seminar class. We started off in a teacher-student, mentor-mentee relationship. Witnessing Leeva's professional development has been one of my life's true blessings. My second blessing was to work on the book with her. Our yin-yang styles complement each other. When I got exhausted working on the book, she picked up my spirits. When we faltered together, we tried to cheer each other up with many cups of Starbucks coffee and many bowls of Vietnamese *pho* (noodles). Our creativity sparked each other forward. She has been a special bright light in my meandering professional path. Although the writing of this book has been an exhilarating journey, the joy of our friendship has outweighed any stress from working on the manuscript.

As partners taking joy in our friendship and energized by our collaboration, we wish you a fascinating journey of intercultural discovery. ✦

About the Authors

Dr. Stella Ting-Toomey is a professor of human communication at California State University at Fullerton. She received her Ph.D. at the University of Washington in 1981. She teaches courses in intercultural communication, interpersonal conflict management, and intercultural communication training. Stella has published numerous books and articles on the topics of intercultural conflict competence, cross-cultural facework styles, and cultural and ethnic identity negotiation process. Her publications have appeared in the *International Journal of Intercultural Relations, Communication Monographs, Human Communication Research,* and *Communication Research,* among others. Three recent book titles are *Communicating Across Cultures* (Guilford), *Managing Intercultural Conflict Effectively* (Sage; with John Oetzel), and *Communicating Effectively with the Chinese* (Sage; with Ge Gao). Stella has held major leadership roles in international communication associations and has served on numerous editorial boards. She has lectured widely throughout the United States, Asia, and Europe on the theme of mindful intercultural conflict practice. She has also designed and conducted over 100 intercultural training programs for corporations, universities, and social service organizations. *Understanding Intercultural Communication* (coauthored with Leeva C. Chung) is her fourteenth book. Stella is an ardent Lakers basketball fan and she also plays the piano for fun and relaxation.

Dr. Leeva C. Chung is an associate professor at the University of San Diego (USD). She received her Ph.D. at the University of Oklahoma in 1998. At USD, she teaches in both the Department of Communication Studies and the Department of Ethnic Studies. As an interdisciplinary effort, she assisted in curriculum development and planning for the ethnic studies major. Leeva teaches courses in intercultural communication, ethnic identity, and small group theories, among others. Her research interests include cultural and ethnic identity, global identity, aging across cultures, and pop culture. She has published articles in the *Journal for Intercultural Communication Research, International Journal of Intercultural Relations, Communication Research Reports,* and *Communication Reports.* In the San Diego community, she serves as a founding member of the San Diego Asian

Film Foundation Festival. She also plays for the USD symphony and is a board member for the Organization for Chinese Americans.

Chapter 1

Why Study Intercultural Communication?

Chapter Outline

❑ Practical Reasons to Study Intercultural Communication
- Adapting to Global and Domestic Workplace Diversity
- Improving Multicultural Health Care Communication
- Engaging in Creative Problem Solving
- Enhancing Intercultural Relationship Satisfaction
- Deepening Self-Awareness
- Fostering Global and Intrapersonal Peace

❑ Intercultural Communication Flexibility
- Knowledge, Attitude, and Skills
- Flexible Intercultural Communication: Four Criteria

❑ Mastering Intercultural Communication Flexibility
- A Staircase Model
- Communicating Flexibly

As we enter the twenty-first century, direct contact with culturally differ-ent people in our neighborhoods, community, schools, and workplaces is an inescapable part of life. With immigrants and minority group members representing nearly 30 percent of the present workforce in the United States, practicing intercultural communication flexibility is especially critical in today's global world.

Flexible intercultural communication means managing cultural dif-ferences adaptively and creatively in a wide variety of situations. The underlying values of a culture (e.g., individual competitiveness versus group harmony) often shape communication expectations and attitudes. How we define a communication problem in a work team and how we approach the communication process itself are also likely to vary across cultures, ethnicities, situations, and individuals. For example, some cul-tural groups (e.g., German and Dutch work teams) may believe that addressing a workplace problem directly and assertively can be stimulat-ing and spark further new ideas. Other cultural groups (e.g., Chinese and Japanese work teams) may believe that approaching a conflict issue indi-rectly and tactfully can facilitate a more harmonious communication process.

With such layered complexity facing global and domestic diversity issues, we need to practice intercultural communication sensitivity when dealing with culturally different others. This chapter examines the rea-

sons why we should understand intercultural communication from a flexibility approach. This approach is developed in three sections. First, we offer several practical reasons why we should pay special attention to the study of intercultural communication. Next, we explain the necessary components and criteria of intercultural communication flexibility. Last, we present a staircase model to increase your communication flexibility in dealing with cultural and ethnic differences in everyday life.

Practical Reasons to Study Intercultural Communication

With rapid changes in the global economy, technology, transportation systems, and immigration policies, the world is becoming a small, intersecting community. We find ourselves having increased contact with people who are culturally different. In a global workforce, people bring with them different work habits and cultural practices. For example, cultural strangers may approach problem-solving tasks or nonverbal emotional expression issues differently. They may develop friendships and romantic relationships with different expectations and rhythms. They may also have different communication desires, goals, and emphases in an intercultural encounter process. In this twenty-first century global world, people are constantly moving across borders, into and out of a country. Neighborhoods and communities are changing. In what was once a homogeneous community, we may now find more diversity and cultural values in flux.

The study of intercultural communication is about the study of communication that involves, at least in part, cultural group membership differences. It is about acquiring the necessary knowledge and dynamic skills to manage such differences appropriately and effectively. It is also about developing a creative mind-set to see things from different angles without rigid prejudgment. There are indeed many practical reasons for studying intercultural communication. We offer six reasons here: global and domestic workforce diversity, multicultural health care, creative problem solving, intercultural relationship satisfaction, deepening self-awareness, and global and intrapersonal peace.

Adapting to Global and Domestic Workforce Diversity

To begin, do you know which companies have the most valuable global brands? Take a guess and then check out Jeopardy Box 1.1. Workplace diversity on the global level represents both opportunities and challenges to individuals and organizations. Individuals at the forefront of workplace diversity must rise to the challenge of serving as global employees and leaders. According to a recent international business trend report (*Training and Development*, 1999), three competencies that are essential in the global workplace in the twenty-first century are intercultural communication skills, problem solving, and global leadership. Intercultural communication skills are needed to solve problems, manage conflicts, and forge new visions as a dynamic global employee or leader.

Jeopardy Box 1.1 Top-Ten Most Valuable Global Brands by Dollar Value	
Brand Name	**Industry**
1. Coca-Cola	Beverages
2. Microsoft	Technology
3. IBM	Technology
4. General Electric	Diversified
5. Intel	Technology
6. Nokia (Finland)	Technology
7. Disney	Leisure
8. McDonald's	Food Retail
9. Marlboro	Tobacco
10. Mercedes (Germany)	Automobiles

Note: All U.S.-owned unless otherwise stated.
Source: Interbrand, http://www.bwnt.businessweek.com/brand/2003/index.asp (Retrieved February 1, 2004).

In this new era, it is inevitable that employees and customers from dissimilar cultures are in constant contact with one another—whether it is through face-to-face, cellular phone, or e-mail contacts. By the way, do you know which countries have the most Internet users? And which countries have the most cellular mobile phone subscribers? Take a guess and check out Jeopardy Box 1.2 and Jeopardy Box 1.3. As we communicate across the globe through various electronic or wireless media, flexible intercultural communication becomes critical in a global work environment.

In the domestic U.S. context, a *Workforce 2020* trend report indicates that four of every five new jobs in the United States are generated as a direct result of international business. Furthermore, 33 percent of U.S. corporate profits are derived from import-export trade (Judy & D'Amico, 1997). According to a recent U.S. Labor Bureau report, 350,000 U.S. individuals are currently working in overseas assignments. Although most U.S. international employees are considered technically competent, they may lack effective intercultural communication skills to interact productively in the new culture. Researchers estimate that the proportion of U.S. workers who fail in their global assignments (i.e., return prematurely) ranges from 10 percent to 45

Jeopardy Box 1.2	Top-Ten Countries With the Most Internet Users

Country

1. United States
2. Japan
3. China
4. Germany
5. United Kingdom
6. South Korea
7. Italy
8. Canada
9. France
10. India

Source: http://www.c-i-a.com/pr1202.htm (Retrieved January 23, 2004).

Jeopardy Box 1.3	Top-Seven Countries With the Highest Ratio of Cellular Mobile Phone Users

Country

1. Taiwan
2. Hong Kong
3. Singapore
4. New Zealand
5. South Korea
6. Australia
7. Japan

Source: Adapted from Madanmohan Rao, "Asia: Centre of the World"s Wireless Explosion." Institute for Media Communications Management. Copyright © 2003, Madanmohan Rao. http://www.electronicmarkets.org/files/cms/44.php (Retrieved January 25, 2004).

percent—with the highest failure rates associated with assignments in developing countries. This means that one in ten to nearly half of all U.S. employees sent overseas fail to accomplish their particular overseas assignments (Black, Gregersen, Mendenhall, & Stroh, 1999).

Even if we do not venture beyond our national borders, cultural diversity becomes a crucial part of our everyday work lives (see Snapshot 1.1). The study of intercultural communication on the U.S. domestic front is especially critical for several reasons. First, according to U.S. Census (2000) data, we are now a nation with increased multicultural complexities and nuances—of the nation's 281.4 million people, 69.1 percent are Whites/non-Hispanics, 12.5 percent are Latinos/Hispanics, 12.3 percent are African Americans/Blacks, 3.6 percent are Asian Americans, 0.9 percent are American Indians/Alaskan Natives, 0.1 percent are Native Hawaiians, and 2.4 percent report as mixed races. The most dramatic demographic change has occurred in the

Latino/a population, which has grown 58 percent over the last decade. California, New Mexico, and Texas are the three most racially diverse states in the United States. Conversely, Maine, Vermont, and New Hampshire are listed as the three most homogeneous states (check out Jeopardy Boxes 1.4 and 1.5).

Second, we are moving at an accelerated pace with increased foreign-born diversity in the nation. According to the U.S. census data for 2000, 28.4 million people representing 10.4 percent of the total U.S. population are foreign-born nationals.

Snapshot 1.1

In the twenty-first century, it is inevitable that people from different cultures will work side by side.

Among the foreign born, 51.0 percent were born in Latin America, 25.5 percent were born in Asia, 15.3 percent were born in Europe, and the remaining 8.1 percent were born in other regions of the world. The current and future generations in the United States include many individuals whose parents or grandparents were born in a Latin American or Asian region. Thus, the influence of multicultural customers is expanding in every industry. Automakers, retailers, banks, and media and entertainment industries have to learn to reach out to these multiethnic customers with increased intercultural sensitivity and skills.

Third, skilled and highly educated immigrants (especially in the areas of computer and engineering service industries) play a critical

---

Jeopardy Box 1.4 Top-Ten Most Racially/Ethnically Diverse States in the United States

1. California
2. New Mexico
3. Texas
4. New York
5. Hawaii
6. Maryland
7. Nevada
8. Arizona
9. New Jersey
10. Florida

Source: U.S. Census Bureau Data (2000).

Jeopardy Box 1.5 Top-Ten Most Racially/Ethnically Homogeneous States in the United States
1. Maine
2. Vermont
3. New Hampshire
4. West Virginia
5. Iowa
6. North Dakota
7. Montana
8. Kentucky
9. Wyoming
10. South Dakota
Source: U.S. Census Bureau Data (2000).

role in the U.S. advanced-technology industries. The payrolls of leading information technology (IT) companies such as Intel and Microsoft include "many highly skilled, foreign-born employees. In their absence it would be difficult for America to regain its global lead in IT" (Judy & D'Amico, 1997, p. 21). Many U.S. immigrants have contributed positively (historically and presently) to the social and economic development of the nation. The richness of cultural diversity in U.S. society has led to dramatic breakthroughs in the fields of physics, medicine, and technology.

Attention to diversity issues bolsters employee morale, creates an inclusive climate in the workplace, and sparks creative innovation. Many recruiting experts say that they are launching aggressive campaigns to recruit the top management candidates who have experience and skills in managing diversity issues, such as culture, race, gender, and age. Workplace trend reports indicate that losing an employee can cost up to four times an employee's salary. Losing a vital employee with significant ties to a multicultural or diverse community can cost many missed business opportunities and fruitful outcomes.

Improving Multicultural Health Care Communication

As borders continue to merge and divide, one area rich in conversation is the state of multicultural health care. When Liliana was giving birth to her daughter, the doctor was surprised that her husband, Senel, did not stand by Liliana. He did not coach her along or support her through the various stages of labor pain. In fact, he was not even in the delivery room to witness the delivery of a beautiful baby girl named Aryana. The doctor was quite perturbed and puzzled. Several months later, during a routine baby check-up, in chatting with Liliana, the doctor finally realized that Senel was not in the delivery room because of his Muslim faith and belief. For Muslims, birth comes through the "house" with a midwife in attendance, a very sacred place, and no man should be inside the room during baby delivery. Similarly, Native Indians in Belize and Panama also believe that the father should not be in the delivery room with the mother or the baby or else harm can come to both of them. If you were a trained nurse or health care professional, would you likely be aware of this religious tradition concerning childbirth?

Many immigrants and multicultural citizens have high expectations that health care workers will respect their personal beliefs and health care practices. This is not always the case. For example, Fadiman (1997) documents a case in which a Hmong child became brain-dead after doctors in Merced, California, continuously miscommunicated with the parents. The clash between traditional Hmong beliefs and the role of Western medicine resulted in a tragic incident.

Multicultural health care in this global age is an additional concern because of the aging population. Many must agonize over the rising cost of providing quality care to aging parents and grandparents. They also have to struggle with their own cultural and personal values of taking care of their aging parents at home or sending them away to a health care facility. Additionally, immigrants with limited English skills have to struggle to communicate with the hospital staff, nurses, or doctors to convey a simple message. Many immigrants also use their children as translators—which easily tips the balance between the parental role and the child's role in a status-oriented family system. Worse, even if the child speaks English fluently, she or he may not know how to translate all the medical terms or medication prescriptions for a parent.

In addition, different cultural beliefs and traditions surround the concept of "death." For many U.S. Americans, death is a taboo topic. Euphemisms are often used, such as "He is no longer with us," "She passed away peacefully," "She's in a better place," or "May he rest in peace." There are also a number of different cultural traditions in terms of burial practices. For example, the tradition among Orthodox Jews is to bury the deceased before sundown the next day and have postdeath rituals that last for several days. When Muslims approach death, they may wish to face Mecca, their holy city in Saudi Arabia, and recite passages from the Qur'an (Purnell & Paulanka, 2003). Some Mexicans hold an elaborate ceremony such as a *velorio*, which may appear like a big party; in fact, they are celebrating the person's life as she or he has actually lived it fully. Likewise, the Irish hold a *wake*, and they eat and drink and celebrate the person's bountiful life. However, if you do not subscribe to any of the foregoing rituals, you would likely find it odd that some of these groups actually laugh and sing and dance during painful periods of grieving.

Concepts such as ethnocentrism and ethnorelativism, cultural value patterns such as "doing" and "being," and intercultural conflict skills such as facework management and mindful reframing (as explored in the next few chapters) can serve as basic tools and conceptual building blocks for effective multicultural health care communication. Learning some of these basic concepts and skills can help professionals and service providers to launch their first steps toward practicing respectful intercultural attitudes and adaptive communication styles.

Engaging in Creative Problem Solving

Our ability to value different approaches to problem solving and mindfully move away from traditional "either/or" binary thinking can create and expand diverse options in managing team intercultural problems. According to creativity research (Sternberg, 1999), we learn more from people who are different from us than from those who are similar to us. At the individual level, creativity involves a process of taking in new ideas and of being thrown into chaos. If the uncertainty or chaos is managed with an open-minded attitude, team members can come up with a synergistic perspective that involves the best of all viewpoints. A **synergistic perspective** means combining the best of all cultural approaches in solving a workplace problem.

At the small-group level of research, results indicate that the quality of ideas produced in ethnically diverse groups has been rated significantly higher by experts than that in ethnically homogeneous groups (McLeod, Lobel, & Cox, 1996). Of course, culturally heterogeneous teams also have more conflicts or communication struggles than homogeneous work teams. However, if such conflicts are managed competently and flexibly, the outcome of heterogeneous team negotiations often results in a better quality product than that produced by a homogeneous team. Culturally and ethnically diverse teams have the potential to solve problems creatively because of several factors. Some of these factors include a greater variety of viewpoints brought to bear on the issue, a higher level of critical analysis of alternatives, and a lower probability of groupthink due to the heterogeneous composition of the group (Ting-Toomey & Oetzel, 2001).

A cultural synergistic approach to problem solving in heterogeneous teams often involves the core intercultural communication skills of mindful listening and careful perception checking. By mindfully listening to the diverse viewpoints articulated by members of different cultures, we can understand their cultural standpoints and expectations. In carefully perception checking the accuracy of our understanding, we can ensure that our interpretation of what we have heard is accurate. Through mindful dialogue with culturally different others in a team, we can learn to "bounce off" creative ideas that can incorporate the best of all cultural viewpoints.

Global managers and employees, international human resource groups, global product development teams, multiethnic customer service groups, international marketing and sales teams, multicultural counselors, and school teachers and advisors can all benefit from mastering intercultural communication competencies. Any individuals or groups who have to communicate on a daily basis with culturally diverse coworkers, clients, customers, or classmates can benefit from acquiring the awareness, knowledge, and skills of flexible intercultural communication.

Enhancing Intercultural Relationship Satisfaction

A meaningful life often entails deep relationship contacts with our families, close friends, and loved ones. However, with close contact often comes relationship disappointments and expectancy violations. If we already feel inept in handling different types of interpersonal relationships with people from our own cultural groups, imagine the challenges (plus, of course the rewards) of dealing with additional cultural factors in our intimate relationship development process. Interpersonal friction provides a sound testing ground for the resilience of our intimate relationships. According to expert researchers in interpersonal conflict (e.g., Cupach & Canary, 1997), it is not the *frequency* of conflict that determines whether we have a satisfying or dissatisfying intimate relationship. Rather, it is the *competencies* that we apply in managing our conflicts that will move the intercultural-intimate relationship onto a constructive or destructive path. Even if we do not venture out of our hometown, the places for people to meet, to socialize, and to date are changing. For example, in Guam, the Kmart store, which opened in 1996, changed the social life of Guamanians. Kmart is "the island's social center, its unofficial town square, a place where you never fail to run into a neighbor, a friend, or a cousin" ("Shopper Flock ..." 1999). When locals want to shop, they come early in the morning. If locals want to hang out and meet people, they come at night before the store closes at midnight.

Another interesting phenomenon is online dating, both domestically and globally. In the past, dating was considered to be a private affair. Now, online dating services, chat rooms, and services allow people to meet on the basis of criteria they find important. Some people may disclose their ethnicities, and some people may not, in the early stage of courtship and flirting. Brooks (2003) reports that 40 million U.S. individuals date online! With match.com and various dating services, the supply is definitely in demand in this Hook-Up Age. With the dramatic rise of intercultural marriages and dating relationships in the United States, intimate relationships are a fertile ground for culture shock and clashes. According to U.S. census data for 2000, the nation has more than 1.3 million racially mixed marriages. California is reported as the top-ranked U.S. state with a biracial heritage population of 1.6 million, followed by New York and Texas. A recent Gallup Poll revealed that more than twice as many U.S. teenagers of all races reported a willingness to date interracially as did teenagers in a similar poll in 1980. Teenagers are often more receptive to developing close friendships and dating relationships across all racial lines than their parents' or grandparents' generations.

Intimate personal relationships often involve friction because we have such high hopes and expectations riding on these exclusive relationships. Understanding the possible external and internal obstacles that affect an intimate intercultural relationship can increase our acceptance of our intimate partners. Intercultural relationship conflict, when managed competently, can bring about positive changes in a relationship. It allows the conflict partners to use the conflict opportunity to reassess the state of the relationship. It opens doors for the conflict individuals to discuss in-depth their wants and needs in a relationship.

On the topic of intercultural relationship satisfaction, for many U.S. adoptive families, which countries do you think most foreign-born adopted children come from? Take a guess and check out Jeopardy Box 1.6. The U.S. Census Bureau's very first profile of adopted children reveals that 1.6 million adopted kids under age 18 are now living in U.S. households. Although foreign adoptions are increasing and getting the most headlines, the report shows that 87 percent of adoptees from diverse ethnic-racial backgrounds under 18 were born in the United States. As more U.S. families are becoming families of color, the challenge is to grapple with issues of race and ethnicity. For example, Matt Plut and his wife adopted a 4-year-old African American boy. He recalls, "We are white parents. We don't know what it is like to grow up black in America. Looking back, I know I was a sheltered white person in a white community. I remember how my peers and everyone talked about race. It is not a comfortable feeling to know this is what you were taught" (as cited in MacGregor, 2002, p. E1). Other relevant and important issues include where to live and raise a biracial family, reaching out and making connections with those ethnically similar to the adopted child, and understanding the dilemmas and problems of a child's or adolescent's racial/ethnic identity development stages (see Chapter 4 and Chapter 11).

Culture-sensitive intercultural communication can increase relational and family closeness and deepen cultural self-awareness. The more that intercultural partners and family members get to know each other on a culturally responsive level, the more they can appreciate the differences and deep commonalities among them. The power of being

Jeopardy Box 1.6 Top-Ten Countries of Birth for Foreign-Born Adopted Children Under Age 18 in the United States

Country	Total	Percentage
1. South Korea	47,555	24
2. China	21,053	11
3. Russia	19,631	10
4. Mexico	18,201	9
5. India	7,793	4
6. Guatemala	7,357	4
7. Colombia	7,054	4
8. Philippines	6,286	3
9. Romania	6,183	3
10. Vietnam	4,291	2

Source: U.S. Census Bureau Data (2000).

understood on an authentic level can greatly enhance relationship quality, satisfaction, and personal insight.

Deepening Self-Awareness

The late Tupac Shakur once rapped: *"Words of wisdom, they shine upon the strength of a nation. Conquer the enemy, on with education. Protect thy self, reach with what you wanna do. Know thy self, teach with what we've been through"* (from Shakur's *2Pacolypse Now*, 1991).

As we systematically acquire the building-block concepts and skills to deal with cultural differences, this knowledge base should challenge you to question your own cultural assumptions and primary socialization process. We acquired our cultural beliefs, values, and communication norms often on a very unconscious level. Without a comparative basis, we may never question the way we have been conditioned and socialized in our primary cultural system. Cultural socialization, in one sense, encourages the development of ethnocentrism.

Ethnocentrism means seeing our own culture as the center of the universe and seeing other cultures as insignificant or even inferior (see Chapter 9). As Charon (2004) describes the development of ethnocentrism, "Groups develop differences from one another, so do formal organizations, communities, and societies. *Without interaction with outsiders, differences become difficult to understand and difficult not to judge.* What is real to us becomes comfortable; what is comfortable becomes right. What we do not understand becomes less than right to us" (p. 156).

Without sound comparative cross-cultural knowledge, we may look at the world from only one lens—i.e., our own cultural lens. With a solid intercultural knowledge base, we may begin to understand the possible value differences and similarities between our own cultural system and that of another cultural system. Intercultural knowledge can deepen our awareness of who we are, where we acquired our values in the first place, and how we make sense of the world around us. To increase our self-awareness, we need to be in tune with our own uncertainty and emotional vulnerabilities. We need to understand our own cognitive filters and emotional biases in encountering cultural or ethnic differences. Knowledge brings the power of new insights. New insights, however, can be at times disconcerting and threatening. Confusion is part of the intercultural discovery journey.

Fostering Global and Intrapersonal Peace

The need for global peace has never been more apparent. Look at the headlines in any international or local newspaper, and the top stories will include bombings and death tolls in Iraq, a nuclear threat in North Korea, and concerns over bioterrorism. The United States has never experienced terrorism so close at hand as on September 11, 2001, when almost 3,000 individuals perished in the attack on the World Trade Center and the Pentagon. The death toll includes individuals from many other countries, such as Australia, China, the Dominican Republic, El Salvador, Germany, Ireland, Israel, Japan, and Sweden (cnn.com).

To practice global peacemaking, we need to hold a firm commitment that considerations of fairness should apply to all identity groups. We need to be willing to consider sharing economic and social resources with the underprivileged groups to level the fear and resentment factors. We need to start practicing win-win collaborative dialogue with individuals or groups we consider as our enemies. We need to display a mindful listening attitude even if we do not like the individuals or agree with their ideas or viewpoints. In displaying our respect for the other nation or groups of individuals, we may open doors for more dialogues and deeper contacts. Human respect is a prerequisite for any type or form of intercultural or interethnic communication.

On the bright side, many active conflict peacemaking groups and efforts are under way. For example, in 1998, the late Joan Kroc established the Joan B. Kroc Institute for Peace and Justice at the University of San Diego (USD), with an endowment of $25 million. Joan Kroc envisioned a center where people could come together to make peace, study peace, and work for social justice. The mission of the institute is to establish harmony, safety, and hope in a context of mutual respect and fairness in international, national, and local communities through its peace studies, research, and outreach programs. After her recent death from illness, Kroc's estate gave USD and the University of Notre Dame two of the largest gifts ever given for the study of peace, which totaled $100 million. The $50 million USD endowment will establish the Joan B. Kroc School of Peace Studies, and the other $50 million will establish the Joan B. Kroc Institute for International Peace Studies at the University of Notre Dame. Through these peace centers, we can train more students and professionals in intercultural peace-building skills and nonviolent approaches to conflict.

Global peace-building is closely connected to intrapersonal peace-building. If we are at peace with ourselves, we will hold more compassion and caring for others around us. If we are constantly angry and fighting against ourselves, we will likely spread our anger and resentment to others. His Holiness the Dalai Lama made comments to this effect in a recent interview (see Double Take 1.1).

Double Take 1.1

As a Buddhist monk, I try to develop compassion within myself, not simply as a religious practice, but on a human level as well. To encourage myself in this altruistic attitude, I sometimes find it helpful to imagine myself standing as a single individual on one side, facing a huge gathering of all human beings on the other side. Then I ask myself, "Whose interests are more important?" To me it is quite clear that however important I may feel I am, I am just one individual while others are infinite in number and importance. . . .

Dalai Lama Interview, *Shambhala Sun*, September, 2003, p. 63.

Finally, let's go to Picture This 1.1 and read the lyrics by John Lennon. Perhaps by listening to this song, we can engage in some imaginative peace-building work in our everyday lives—with our loved ones, families, close friends, classmates, teachers, neighbors, coworkers, and cultural strangers that come our way.

Picture This 1.1

IMAGINE

Imagine there's no heaven,
It's easy if you try,
No hell below us,
Above us only sky,
Imagine all the people
Living for today . . .

☞

> *Imagine there's no countries,*
> *It isn't hard to do,*
> *Nothing to kill or die for,*
> *No religion too,*
> *Imagine all the people*
> *Living life in peace . . .*
>
> *Imagine no possessions,*
> *I wonder if you can,*
> *No need for greed or hunger,*
> *A brotherhood of man,*
> *Imagine all the people*
> *Sharing all the world . . .*
>
> *You may say I'm a dreamer,*
> *but I'm not the only one,*
> *I hope some day you'll join us,*
> *And the world will live as one.*

Source: Words and music by John Lennon. Copyright © 1971 (renewed 1999) LENONO. MUSIC. All rights controlled and administered by EMI BLACKWOOD MUSIC, INC. Used by permission.

In this section, we have discussed six practical reasons why the study of intercultural communication is such an important topic. With the knowledge and skills gained as an intercultural student, and with imagination and creativity, we hope that you will find yourself in many diverse settings applying this intercultural knowledge and these communication skills. We now turn to a discussion of the components and criteria of intercultural communication flexibility.

Intercultural Communication Flexibility

What is intercultural communication flexibility? How do we know that the individuals in the communication process have communicated inflexibly or flexibly? Intercultural communication flexibility has three content components—knowledge, attitude, and skills (see also Chapter 2). **Flexible intercultural communication** emphasizes the importance of integrating knowledge and an open-minded attitude and putting them into adaptive and creative practice in everyday communication. **Inflexible intercultural communication** stresses the continuation of using our own cultural values, judgments, and routines in communicating with culturally different others.

While inflexible intercultural communication reflects an ethnocentric mindset, flexible intercultural communication reflects an ethnorelative attitude. An **ethnocentric mindset** means staying stuck with our own cultural worldviews and using our own cultural values as the baseline standards to evaluate the other person's cultural behavior. An **ethnorelative mindset**, however, means to understand a communication behavior from the other person's cultural frame of reference. In an optimal state of ethnorelativism, a flexible mindset, an alert emotional awareness, and competent interaction behaviors come together and help us to become dynamic, flexible intercultural communicators. We first discuss the three components of flexible intercultural communication. We then discuss the four criteria for evaluating whether the cultural members in the process have behaved flexibly or inflexibly.

Knowledge, Attitude, and Skills

Knowledge here refers to the systematic, conscious learning of the essential themes and concepts in intercultural communication flexibility. Conscious learning can be developed through formal studying and informal immersion experiences. *Formal studying* can include taking classes in intercultural communication and ethnic-related studies. It includes attending intercultural communication seminars and diversity-related training. It could mean taking a foreign language class or a global history class. *Informal learning* experiences can include international traveling, studying abroad, volunteering for community service, and visiting ethnic neighborhoods, temples, or stores in our own backyard. It includes reading international newspapers and magazines. It could mean putting ourselves in constant contact with culturally different others and learning to be comfortable with the differences.

To digest the knowledge we have learned, we have to develop an open mindset and an attentive heart. **Attitude** can include both cognitive and affective layers. The cognitive layer refers to the willingness to suspend our ethnocentric judgment and readiness to be open-minded in learning about cross-cultural difference issues. The affective layer refers to the emotional commitment to engage in cultural perspective-taking and the cultivation of an empathetic heart in reaching out to culturally diverse groups. It also means we have spent time reflecting on our own identity and emotional vulnerability issues in dealing with the changes within our own affective state. A receptive and responsive attitude serves as the basis to push us forward to communicate adaptively with people from diverse cultural communities.

In developing cognitive and affective openness, we try to intentionally put on a new pair of "glasses" or "lenses" (i.e., the practice of ethnorelative thinking and empathy). A flexible intercultural attitude means engaging in ethnorelative thinking to understand someone else's behavior from her or his cultural point of view. From an ethnorelative lens, we put our ethnocentrism on hold and suspend our snapshot cultural judgments.

Skills are our operational abilities to integrate knowledge and a responsive attitude with adaptive intercultural practice. Adaptive communication skills help us to communicate mindfully in an intercultural situation. Many interaction skills are useful in promoting flexible intercultural communication. Some of these, for example, are value clarification skills, mindful tracking skills, attentive listening, verbal code-switching, nonverbal sensitivity skills, and intercultural conflict management tools (see the Intercultural Toolkit section at the end of each of the remaining chapters). These skills will be discussed under different topics in later chapters.

Flexible Intercultural Communication: Four Criteria

The criteria of communication appropriateness, effectiveness, adaptability, and creativity can serve as evaluative yardsticks of whether an intercultural communicator has been perceived as behaving flexibly or inflexibly (Spitzberg & Cupach, 1984; Ting-Toomey, 1999) in an interaction episode. A dynamic, competent intercultural communicator is one who manages multiple meanings in the communication exchange process—appropriately, effectively, adaptively, and creatively. All four criteria can also be applied developmentally to an individual who is attempting to increase her or his mastery of knowledge, an open attitude, and skills in dealing constructively with members of diverse cultures.

Appropriateness refers to the degree to which the exchanged behaviors are regarded as proper and match the expectations generated by the insiders of the culture. Individuals typically use their own cultural expectations and scripts to approach an intercultural interaction scene. They also formulate their impressions of a competent communicator on the basis of their perceptions of the other's verbal and nonverbal behaviors in the particular interaction setting. The first lesson in communication competence is to "tune in" to our own ethnocentric evaluations concerning "improper" dissimilar behaviors. Our evaluations of "proper" and "improper" behavior stem, in part, from our ingrained cultural socialization experiences. If your friend has never eaten with a knife and fork, this does not mean your friend lacks good manners. Perhaps your friend eats with chopsticks, hands, a spoon, or a combination of these.

To understand whether appropriate communication has been perceived, it is vital to obtain competence evaluations from the standpoint of both communicators and interested observers. It is also critical to obtain both self-perception and other-perception data. We may think that we are acting appropriately, but others may not concur with our self-assessment. Appropriate communication behaviors can be assessed through understanding the underlying values, norms, social roles, expectations, and scripts that govern the interaction episode. When we act appropriately in an interaction scene, our culturally proper behaviors can facilitate communication effectiveness. Instead of saying to your friend, "You are so weird!" you may ask him if he can teach you how to use a pair of chopsticks.

Effectiveness refers to the degree to which communicators achieve mutually shared meaning and integrative goal-related outcomes. Effective encoding and decoding processes lead to mutually shared meanings. Mutually shared meanings lead to perceived intercultural understanding. Interaction effectiveness has been achieved when multiple meanings are attended to with accuracy and when mutually desired interaction goals have been reached. Interaction ineffectiveness occurs when content or relational meanings are mismatched and intercultural noises and clashes jam the communication channels.

Communication effectiveness can improve task productivity. Productivity is closely related to outcome factors, such as the generation of new ideas, new plans, new momentum, and creative directions in resolving the intercultural problem. In an unproductive interaction episode, both sides feel that they have wasted their time and energy in being involved in the interaction in the first place. Both sides feel they have lost sight of the original goals in the stressful interaction episode. In a productive communication exchange, both sides feel that they have mutual influence over the communication process and that they have devoted positive energy in creating the constructive outcome.

Communication adaptability refers to our ability to change our interaction behaviors and goals to meet the specific needs of the situation. It implies behavioral flexibility in dealing with the intercultural miscommunication episode. It signals our mindful awareness of the other person's perspectives, interests, goals, and communication approach, plus our willingness to modify our own behaviors and goals to adapt to the interaction situation. By mindfully tracking what is going on in the intercultural situation, both parties may modify their nonverbal and verbal behavior to achieve a more synchronized communication process. In modifying their behavioral styles, polarized views on the intercultural content problem may also be depolarized or "softened."

Flexible intercultural communication requires us to communicate appropriately and effectively in different intercultural situations, which necessitates adaptation. By having an open-minded attitude that motivates our behaviors, we generate intercultural interest and curiosity in the intercultural relating process.

Last, **communication creativity** is one of the critical criteria for evaluating intercultural communication flexibility. To create is to produce something inventive through an imaginative lens and flexible skills. It takes a flexible mindset to combine the best practices of both cultures to arrive at a synergistic solution. It also takes a well-balanced heart to move beyond the practices of both cultures and utilize a third-culture approach to sensitively bridge the cultural differences. An individual with an open mindset is able to flex her or his communication muscles and can flow adaptively through a diverse range of intercultural situations.

Communication creativity requires us to be sensitive to the differences and similarities between dissimilar cultures. It also demands that we be aware of our own ethnocentric biases when making snapshot evaluations of other people's communication approaches. It also asks us to communicate appropriately, effectively, adaptively, and playfully in a culturally respectful manner.

Mastering Intercultural Communication Flexibility

To understand intercultural communication flexibility from a long-term developmental viewpoint, we present the staircase model to reinforce your learning and stretch your imagination.

A Staircase Model

Flexible intercultural communication can be conceptualized along the following stages (see Figure 1.1): (1) unconscious incompetence—the ignorance stage in which an individual is unaware of the communication blunders he has committed in interacting with a cultural stranger; (2) conscious incompetence—the stage in which an individual is aware of her incompetence in communicating with members of the new culture but does not do anything to change her behavior in the new cultural situation; (3) conscious competence—the stage when an individual is aware of his intercultural communication "nonfluency" and is committed to integrating the new knowledge, attitude, and skills into competent practice; and (4) unconscious competence—the stage when an individual is spontaneously practicing her intercultural knowledge and skills to the extent that the intercultural interaction process flows smoothly from an "out-of-conscious awareness" rhythm (Howell, 1982).

In the first stage, the **unconscious incompetence stage,** individuals have no culture-sensitive knowledge (nor do they have responsive attitudes or skills) to communicate competently with the host members of the new culture (see Snapshot 1.2). This is the cultural oblivi-

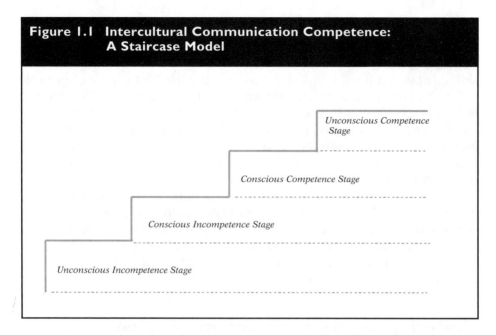

**Figure 1.1 Intercultural Communication Competence:
A Staircase Model**

*Unconscious Competence
Stage*

Conscious Competence Stage

Conscious Incompetence Stage

Unconscious Incompetence Stage

ousness stage or cultural ignorance stage. Cultural members operate from a total ethnocentric worldview. For example, Esteban, who is Cuban American, likes to tell racial jokes . . . about Cubans. He has been corrected and told it was inappropriate. In the second stage, the **conscious incompetence stage,** individuals have some notions (i.e., attitudinal openness) that they behave incompetently; however, they lack the knowledge or skills to operate adaptively in the new culture. They do, however, start questioning their own ethnocentric lens and communication habits. For example, Estaban still admits to telling racial jokes out of habit—although he is aware of his terribly offensive behavior.

Snapshot 1.2

*What stage do you think describes your positic
the staircase model of intercultural competence*

In the third stage, the **conscious competence stage,** individuals are actively pursuing new intercultural knowledge to improve their communication competencies. Given time and practice, they would probably move from the conscious semi-competence phase to the conscious full-competence phase. In the fully developed conscious competence phase, individuals are able to connect knowledge, a responsive attitude, and skills into competent applications. In the conscious competence stage, individuals try to stay in tune and be fully mindful of the communication process itself. They use an ethnorelative lens, rather than an ethnocentric lens, in interpreting what is going on in the intercultural encounter process.

For example, if we decide to spend time in Spain, we must learn new behaviors conscientiously, from *"el punto del sal"* (a Spanish custom that says one should not add salt to a meal until after tasting it, because you doubt the competency of the chef; the food should arrive at the table with the correct amount of salt) to "always wearing shoes or slippers inside the house" (bare or stocking feet are unseemly and improper, according to the Spanish culture). Becoming consciously competent can allow you to pick up everyday intercultural meaning and also practice competent intercultural behaviors.

The fourth stage, the **unconscious competence stage**, is the "mindlessly mindful" stage in which individuals move in and out of spontaneous yet adaptive communication with members of the new culture. They can code-switch effortlessly between the two different intercultural communication systems. Their effort appears to be very "seamless"—thus, the notion of "unconscious" competence. For example, once a person becomes conscious of the Spanish custom of always wearing shoes inside a Spanish house, with repeated practice it becomes a spontaneous habit—done without awareness. However, if the same person now travels to Japan, he has to now learn new rules of behaving (e.g., taking off his shoes before entering a traditional Japanese house and wearing a pair of nice, clean socks). Thus, in any intercultural situation, the most flexible intercultural communicators often rotate between the conscious competence stage and the unconscious competence stage. Through such rotation between stages, the flexible intercultural communicator is constantly updating his knowledge about cultural difference issues and refreshing his attitude in dealing with culturally diverse situations.

If an individual stays in the unconscious competence stage for too long without a humble attitude, cultural arrogance may set in without notice. The individual may easily fall back into the unconscious incompetence stage because of overconfidence or cultural condescension (see Figure 1.2).

Communicating Flexibly

A flexible communicator is a well-trained individual with a vast amount of knowledge in the domain of intercultural communication. She is able to make creative connections among cultural values, communication styles, and situational issues. She is also able to combine ideas and skills and use them flexibly and adaptively in a wide range of intercultural terrain.

A creative, flexible communicator practices both convergent and divergent thinking. **Convergent thinking** focuses on synthesis and

Figure 1.2 Intercultural Incompetence

analytical problem solving to reach a clearly defined outcome. **Divergent thinking,** on the other hand, emphasizes a fluid thinking pattern, the ability to switch from one perspective to another, connecting unrelated ideas in a meaningful fashion, and the ability to bring a new idea to completion (Csikszentmihalyi, 1996). Thus, a creative intercultural communicator is alert to systematic patterns in a culture and, at the same time, is able to see the individual variations and layered complexity within a culture.

A flexible communicator is also a mindful cultural scanner. To engage in a state of mindfulness, an individual needs to learn to (1) be open to new intercultural concepts and ideas; (2) be receptive to the fact that multiple lenses exist in framing an intercultural incident; and (3) be committed to or receptive to the multiple lenses when applying divergent cultural viewpoints in analyzing a miscommunication situation (Langer, 1989, 1997). Being open to new concepts requires a curious mindset and the suspension of immediate culture-centric judgment. Being receptive to multiple cultural lenses means being aware that there are multiple frames of explanation in making sense of an intercultural incident. Being committed to applying divergent cultural viewpoints means taking the time and patience to work out the cultural differences.

To be flexible intercultural communicators, we have to increase the complexity of our intercultural communication knowledge. We have to develop a keen sense of alertness on two fronts—one is increasing self-awareness as a cultural and unique being, and the other is increasing our awareness of others as complex cultural and unique beings. Furthermore, we have to develop a more layered sense of understanding by realizing that many cultural, ethnic, situational, and personal factors shape and, in turn, affect an intercultural miscommunication episode. We will lay out some of these ideas in the coming chapters.

Intercultural knowledge opens doors to the diverse richness and breadth of the human experience. It reveals to us multiple ways of experiencing, sensing, feeling, and knowing. It helps us to start questioning our own stance regarding issues that we once took for granted. It widens our vision to include an alternative perspective of valuing and relating. By understanding the worldviews and values that influence others' communication approaches, we can understand the logic that motivates their actions or behaviors.

In summary, this chapter discusses several reasons why we should study intercultural communication. It also covers the components and criteria of intercultural communication flexibility. Finally, the chapter ends with a discussion of a staircase learning model—from unconscious incompetence to unconscious competence—and the role of mindfulness in achieving intercultural communication flexibility. To be a dynamic, flexible intercultural communicator, you need to start practicing some of the ideas you have read in this chapter in your everyday intercultural encounters. Let the learning journey begin. ✦

What Is Intercultural Communication?

Chapter Outline

❏ Culture: A Learned Meaning System
  ● Surface-Level Culture: Popular Culture
  ● Intermediate-Level Culture: Symbols, Meanings, and Norms
  ● Deep-Level Culture: Traditions, Beliefs, and Values

❏ Understanding Intercultural Communication: A Process Model
  ● Intercultural Communication Process: Overall Characteristics
  ● Intercultural Communication: Meaning Characteristics

❏ Practicing Intercultural Process Thinking
  ● Process Consciousness: Underlying Principles

❏ Intercultural Toolkit: Recaps and Checkpoints

My buddies and I were hiking all over Europe and arrived in Italy craving a nice, yummy pizza. We went to a little restaurant and ordered beer and a pepperoni pizza. The pizza arrived, and, to our surprise, we got this pizza with grounded meat all over—not like the round-shaped, mouth-watering pepperoni's back home. I told the waiter that I didn't want the ground-meat pizza and asked him if he could get us a plain cheese pizza instead. The waiter looked very upset and walked away, huffing and puffing.

When he returned he came back with the restaurant cook. The cook looked really angry and started shouting at us in Italian and swinging his arms at us. I got really embarrassed—with all the other customers staring at us. We ended up keeping the ground-meat pizza and ordered another cheese pizza on the side. I found out much later that Italians take food and cooking very seriously. The Italian chef took the time to bake us a nice pizza, and, apparently he was offended that we complained about his cooking. Back home in the United States, sending food back to the kitchen seems to be a no big deal thing. Guess I really need to learn more about intercultural communication.

—Ethan, *College Student*

To *communicate adaptively with culturally different others, we have to understand the major characteristics that make up the intercultural communication process. Although both culture and communication reciprocally influence one another, it is essential to distinguish between the characteristics of the two concepts for the purpose of understanding the complex relationship between them. "Culture" is an elastic concept that takes on multiple shades of meaning. Similarly, the concept "communica-tion" is also dynamic and subject to multifaceted interpretations.*

In this chapter, we address the following two questions: What is cul-ture? What is the intercultural communication process? This chapter is developed in four sections: First, we define the three different layers of cul-ture. Next, we introduce a culture-based process model to help you under-stand the "big picture" of the intercultural communication process. Third, we outline general principles to help increase your understanding of the intercultural communication process. Last, we end the chapter with a set of recaps and checkpoints to guide you through your intercultural communication excursions.

Culture: A Learned Meaning System

What is culture? This question has fascinated scholars in various academic disciplines for many decades. As long ago as the early 1950s, Kroeber and Kluckhohn (1952) identified more than 160 different defi-nitions of the term **culture.** The study of culture has ranged from the study of its external architecture and landscape to the study of a set of implicit values to which a large group of members in a community sub-scribe. The term originates from the Latin word *cultura* or *cultus* as in *"agri culture,* the cultivation of the soil. . . . From its root meaning of an activity, culture became transformed into a condition, a state of being cultivated" (Freilich, 1989, p. 2).

To be a "cultivated" member of a cultural community, the implica-tion is that you understand what it means to be a "desirable and ideal" member of that particular system. It means you have acquired the meanings of "right" and "wrong" actions that produce particular con-sequences in that cultural environment. It means you have been nur-tured by the core values of that cultural community and understand what constitutes "desirable" and "undesirable" behaviors as sanc-tioned by members of that system.

Culture is basically a learned system of meanings—a value-laden meaning system that helps you to "make sense" of and explain what is going on in your everyday intercultural surroundings. It fosters a par-ticular sense of shared identity and solidarity among its group mem-bers. It also reinforces the boundary of "we" as an ingroup, and the "dissimilar others" as belonging to distant outgroups. *Ingroup identity* basically refers to the emotional attachments and shared fate (i.e., per-ceived common treatment as a function of category membership) that we attach to our selective cultural, ethnic, or social categories. *Outgroups* are groups from which we remain psychologically or emo-tionally detached, and we are skeptical about their words or intentions.

In sum, *culture* is defined in this book as *a learned meaning system that consists of patterns of traditions, beliefs, values, norms, meanings, and symbols that are passed on from one generation to the next and are shared to varying degrees by interacting members of a community.* Members within the same cultural community share a sense of traditions, worldviews, values, rhythms, and patterns of life. We explore some of the key definitional ideas of culture—popular culture, meanings, symbols, norms, values, beliefs, and traditions—in the following subsections.

Surface-Level Culture: Popular Culture

Culture is like an iceberg: The deeper layers (e.g., traditions, beliefs, values) are hidden from our view. We tend to see and hear only the uppermost layers of cultural artifacts (e.g., fashion, pop music). We can also witness the exchange of overt verbal and nonverbal symbols (see Figure 2.1). However, to understand a culture, or a person in a cultural community, with any depth, we have to match their underlying values coherently with their respective norms, meanings, and symbols.

It is the underlying set of cultural beliefs and values that drives people's thinking, reactions, and behaviors. Furthermore, to understand commonalities between individuals and groups, we have to dig deeper

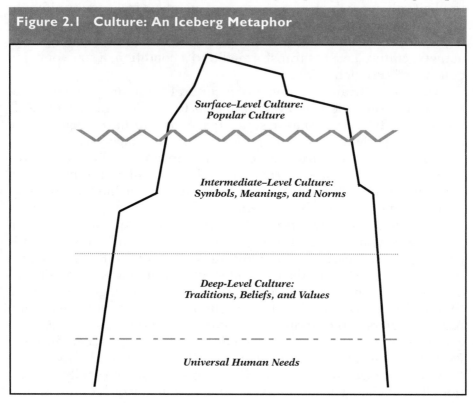

Figure 2.1 Culture: An Iceberg Metaphor

Surface–Level Culture:
Popular Culture

Intermediate–Level Culture:
Symbols, Meanings, and Norms

Deep-Level Culture:
Traditions, Beliefs, and Values

Universal Human Needs

into the level of universal human needs. Some universal human needs, for example, can include the needs for security, inclusion, love/connection, respect, control, and creating meaning. Even though people in diverse cultures are dissimilar in many ways, they are also alike in many aspects—especially in the deep levels of the needs for human respect, connection, and security. Unfortunately, using the analogy of the iceberg, individuals usually do not take the time or effort to discover the deeper layers of universal human needs and connections.

On the most surface level, we often learn about another culture via the representation of its popular culture (for further examples, see Chapter 12). Popular culture is often referred to as "those cultural artifacts, processes, effects, and meanings that are popular by definition, derivation, or general understanding" (Zelizer, 2001, p. 299). Popular culture covers a wide spectrum of mediums—from pop music to pop gadgets, from pop karaoke to pop icons, and from global TV shows to global hip-hop fashion.

Popular culture basically refers to cultural artifacts or systems that have mass appeal and that infiltrate our daily life. Popular images as portrayed in television, film, advertising, pop music, and even comic strips often reinforce cultural and gender ideologies in a society. However, the media actually do offer some positive images of ethnic roles (e.g., *The George Lopez Show* and *My Wife and Kids*) and strong female gender roles (e.g., *Alias* and *Buffy the Vampire Slayer*) that transcend stereotypic ethnic and gender roles. It is also important to remember that all popular media are businesses that aim for mass consumption and profit-generating outcomes. In this context, U.S. popular culture tends to dominate the global market (e.g., films like *The Matrix* and *Kill Bill*) and represents just the surface layer of U.S. commercial culture. Other films, such as *Titanic, Phantom Menace,* and *Indiana Jones,* promote sweeping adventures, romance, open frontiers, and a spirit of exploration—images that reinforce the notion of the United States as a carefree, action-packed, adventure-seeking culture. Beyond films, people also receive images of another country via newsmagazines and television shows. Do you actually know what are the most popular U.S. newsstand magazines? Take a guess and check out Jeopardy Box 2.1.

U.S.-exported television shows, such as *Sex in the City, The Sopranos, Friends,* and *Will & Grace,* reinforce the stereotypic notions of the United States as a free-sex, violence-prone, drug-prone, and fun-seeking culture. Furthermore, icons, such as Disneyland, McDonald's, Coca-Cola, and Nike brand names, in conjunction with pop music, television shows, and films that are exported and imported on a global level, are some prime popular culture examples. Some forms of popular culture have a direct correlation with the culture's underlying values and norms, but other forms of popular culture have been created for sheer entertainment purposes and profit-making objectives.

Jeopardy Box 2.1	Top-Ten Newsstand Magazines in the United States

Magazine	Issues Per Year (2002)
1. *Cosmopolitan*	(12)
2. *Family Circle*	(17)
3. *National Enquirer*	(52)
4. *Woman's World*	(52)
5. *Woman's Day*	(17)
6. *People*	(52)
7. *First for Women*	(17)
8. *Star*	(52)
9. *Glamour*	(12)
10. *Good Housekeeping*	(12)

Source: Audit Bureau of Circulations (February 2003) as cited in Ash (2004), p. 100.

Popular culture is often driven by an economic industry with a targeted audience in mind. Individuals consume a particular form of popular culture (e.g., CNN) as a way to be informed, entertained, and included in their cultural community. By commenting on the headline news as reported on CNN, for example, individuals have a common symbol to rally around and to trade reactions with one another. Of course, individuals can also resist the one-sided, "brainwashing" effect of a particular form of popular culture by staying away from it. The key to understanding surface-level culture is to realize that individuals on a global level do take away with them images of another culture based on surface-level encounters and fleeting images they witness on television or in sensational news coverage.

Boosting global appeal is another aspect of popular culture driven by economic interests. As the music industry continues to suffer a slump in revenue, music labels are finding alternative ways to achieve success. One such alternative is the combination of East meets West. Beyonce Knowles, of Destiny's Child, released her first solo album, titled *Dangerously in Love*. In her album, Beyonce included an Asian rendition of her song "Crazy in Love," featuring Vanness Wu. Vanness is one of the four members of the Taiwanese band F4. According to Fowler (2003), Vanness is more famous in the Asian market than Beyonce is in the United States. The record was produced in the studio, and the two performers never met. Other collaborations include David Bowie's song "Let's Dance," featuring the Indian Bollywood remix.

Although having some information is better than no information before we visit another culture, all of us need to remain vigilant in questioning the sources of where we receive our ideas or images about another culture. For example, the images we have acquired about Cuba, Iraq, the Palestinian state, or Russia are often derived from secondhand news media. We should ask ourselves questions such as the following: Who are the decision makers behind the production of all these popular images, icons, or sounds? Who are the targeted audience members? How are these stereotypic or sensationalized images being marketed and consumed by the audience?

To monitor our mindless consumption of popular culture images about a particular culture or ethnic group, we should ask ourselves: Have we ever had a meaningful conversation with someone directly from that particular culture concerning his specific cultural or personal standpoints? Do we actually know enough people from that particular culture who are able to offer us multiple perspectives to understand the diverse reality of that culture? Do we actually have any acquaintances or close friends from that group who could help us to comprehend their culture on both a broad and a deep level?

In other words, we need to be more watchful about how we process or form mental images about a large group of people under the broad category of "culture" or "race." Although we can travel in time to many far-flung places through the consumption of various media, we should remain mindful that a culture exists on multiple levels of complexity. Popular culture represents only one surface slice of the embedded richness of a culture.

On a deeper level of analysis, we may do well to think about the why, how, and what of the consumption of popular culture on the global level. In one sense, popular culture can serve as a hybrid cultural space that draws people together to coordinate diverse communication activities and to link marginal selves together. For more popular culture discussions, see Chapter 12.

Intermediate-Level Culture: Symbols, Meanings, and Norms

A **symbol** is a sign, artifact, word(s), gesture, or nonverbal behavior that stands for or reflects something meaningful. We use language as a symbolic system (with words, idioms, and phrases), which contains rich culture-based categories to organize and dissect the fluctuating world around us. Naming particular events (e.g., "formal gathering" versus "hanging out") via distinctive language categories is part of what we do in everyday communication activities. Expressions such as "Where there's a will there's a way" (a U.S. expression) or "The nail that sticks out gets hammered down" (a Japanese expression) reveal something about that culture's attitude toward self-determination or group-value orientation. Intercultural frictions often arise because of the ways we label and attach meanings to the different expressions or behaviors around us.

The **meanings** or interpretations that we attach to a symbol (e.g., a national flag or a nonverbal gesture), for example, can cue both objective and subjective reactions. People globally can recognize a particular country by its national flag because of its design and color. However, people of different cultural or ethnic backgrounds can also hold subjective meanings of what the flag means to them, such as a sense of pride or oppression. Other symbolic meaning examples can include the use of different nonverbal gestures across cultures. An animated "OK" nonverbal gesture sign from the United States, for example, with the thumb and forefinger signaling a circle, can mean money to the Japanese, a sexual insult in Brazil and Greece, a vulgar gesture in Russia, or zero in France.

Cultural norms refer to the collective expectations of what constitutes proper or improper behavior in a given interaction scene. For example, whether we should shake hands or bow to a new Japanese supervisor when being introduced reflects our sense of politeness or respect for the other individual in the scene. However, to enact a proper "getting acquainted" interaction script, we have to take the setting, interaction goal, relationship expectation, and cultural competence skills into account.

The **setting** can include the consideration of cultural context (e.g., the interaction scene takes place in Japan or the United States) or physical context (e.g., in an office or a restaurant). The **interaction goal** refers to the objective of the meeting—a job interview meeting is quite different from a chance meeting in a restaurant. A meeting to "show off" that you are an expert about the Japanese culture (therefore, you bow appropriately) is quite different from a chance meeting with a Japanese supervisor in an American restaurant (therefore, maybe a slight head nod will do). The **relationship expectation** feature refers to how much role formality/informality or task/social tone you want to forge in the interaction. Last, **cultural competence skills** refer to the cultural knowledge you have internalized and the operational skills you are able to apply in the communicating scene. For example, if you do not have a good knowledge of the different degrees of bowing that are needed in approaching a Japanese supervisor, you may make a fool of yourself and cause awkward interaction. You may end up with an improper performance in the "getting-acquainted bowing" scene. By not differentiating the different levels of bowing (e.g., lower bowing for supervisors and shallow bowing for low-ranking staff), you may have committed a cultural bump without conscious realization.

To understand a culture, we need to master the operational norms of a culture. However, beyond mastering the prescriptive rules of what we "should" or "should not do" in a culture, we need to dig deeper to understand the cultural logics that frame such distinctive behaviors. While norms can be readily inferred and observed through behaviors, cultural beliefs and values are deep-seated and invisible. Cultural traditions, beliefs, and values intersect to influence the development of collective norms in a culture.

Deep-Level Culture: Traditions, Beliefs, and Values

On a communal level, culture refers to a patterned way of living by a group of interacting individuals who share a common set of history, traditions, beliefs, values, and interdependent fate. This is known as the *normative culture* of a group of individuals. On an individual level, members of a culture can attach different degrees of importance to these complex ranges and layers of cultural beliefs and values. This is known as the *subjective culture* of an individual (Triandis, 1972). Thus, we can talk about the broad patterns of a culture as a group membership concept. We can also think about the culturally shared beliefs and values as subjectively subscribed by members of a group, demonstrating varying degrees of endorsement and importance.

Culturally shared traditions can include myths, legends, ceremonies, and rituals (e.g., celebrating Hanukkah or Thanksgiving) that are passed on from one generation to the next via an oral or written medium. It serves to reinforce ingroup solidarity, communal memory, cultural stability, and continuity functions. Culturally shared traditions can include, for example, the celebrations of birth, coming-of-age rituals, courtship rituals, wedding ceremonies, and seasonal change celebration rituals. They can also include spiritual traditions, such as in times of sickness, healing, rejuvenation, mourning, and funeral rituals for the dead.

Culturally shared beliefs refer to a set of fundamental assumptions or worldviews that people hold dearly to their hearts without question. These beliefs can revolve around questions as to the origins of human beings, the concept of time, space, and reality, the existence of a supernatural being, and the meaning of life, death, and the afterlife. Proposed answers to many of these questions can be found in the major religions of the world, such as Christianity, Islam, Hinduism, and Buddhism.

Peering into U.S. culture, do you know what are the top-five religions in the United States and which countries have the largest Christian and Jewish populations? Take a guess and check out Jeopardy Boxes 2.2 and 2.3. Do you know which are the top-five countries with respect to the largest Buddhist, Hindu, and Muslim populations? Take a guess and cross-check your answers with Jeopardy Box 2.4. People who subscribe to any of these religious philosophies tend to hang on to their beliefs on faith, often accepting the fundamental precepts without question. They also tend to draw from their deeply held beliefs to subscribe meanings and explanations for why certain things happen in the cosmic order of life itself.

Jeopardy Box 2.2 Top-Five Religions in the United States

United States Religions	Estimated Followers in Mid-2001
1. Christianity	159,030,000
2. Judaism	2,831,000
3. Islam	1,104,000
4. Buddhism	1,082,000
5. Hinduism	766,000

Source: *American Religious Identity Survey (2001)*.

Jeopardy Box 2.3 Top-Five Countries With Largest Christian and Jewish Populations

Top-Five Countries With Largest Christian Populations

Country
1. United States
2. Brazil
3. Mexico
4. China
5. Russia

Top-Five Countries With Largest Jewish Populations
1. United States
2. Israel
3. France
4. Canada
5. Russia

Source: *National Geographic's Concise Atlas of the World* (November 2003), p. 27.

Jeopardy Box 2.4 Top-Five Countries With Largest Buddhist, Hindu, and Muslim Populations

Top-Five Countries With Largest Buddhist Populations*
1. China
2. Japan
3. Thailand
4. Vietnam
5. Myanmar

Top-Five Countries With Largest Hindu Populations**
1. India
2. Nepal
3. Bangladesh
4. Indonesia
5. Sri Lanka

Jeopardy Box 2.4 Top-Five Countries With Largest Buddhist, Hindu, and Muslim Populations (continued)

☞ **Top-Five Countries With Largest Muslim Populations*****

    1. Indonesia
    2. Pakistan
    3. India
    4. Bangladesh
    5. Turkey

Source: * Ash (2004).
Source: **http://www.zackvision.com/weblog/archives/entry/000104.html (Retrieved January 25, 2004).
Source: *** http://www.nationmaster.com/encyclopedia/Muslim (Retrieved February 1, 2004).

Beyond fundamental cultural or religious beliefs, people also differ in what they value as important in their cultures. **Cultural values** refer to a set of priorities that guide "good" or "bad" behaviors, "desirable" or "undesirable" practices, and "fair" or "unfair" actions. Cultural values (e.g., individual competitiveness versus group harmony) can serve as the motivational bases for actions. For example, an Israeli psychologist, Shalom Schwartz (1992), believes that we should understand the underlying motivational values that drive human actions. Those motivational values or basic value needs include the following: satisfying biological needs, social coordination needs, and the survival and welfare needs of the group. From his various research studies in more than 50 countries, Schwartz has further identified 10 value clusters that motivate people to behave the way they do in different cultures.

These motivational value clusters or value types include the following: self-direction, stimulation, and hedonism; security, tradition, and conformity; power and benevolence; achievement, and universalism. Although self-direction, stimulation, and hedonism appear to reflect individualistic value tendencies, security, tradition, and conformity appear to reflect group-based, collectivistic value patterns. Power and benevolence seem to reflect whether individuals crave social recognition or deeper meaning in life. Achievement and universalism reflect whether individuals are ambitious and crave material success or whether they are universalistic-oriented in wishing for a world at peace and inner harmony. More important, Schwartz's research indicates that a clear structure of values does emerge in reflecting people's underlying needs. The value structure and the relationship between value types appear to be consistent across cultures. However, cultures vary in terms of how strongly or how weakly they endorse a particular cluster of values.

Furthermore, cultural values can serve as the explanatory logic for verbal and nonverbal behaviors. By understanding particular cultural value dimensions and orientations, we can meaningfully link some of those value patterns with different communication style issues (see Chapter 3 for a detailed discussion). Before you continue reading, fill out the brief survey in Know Thyself 2.1. After looking at the two sets of values, you should have a clearer picture of your instrumental values' emphasis and your terminal values' emphasis. Cultural values can also

---

Know Thyself 2.1 Instrumental Values and Terminal Values Preference Assessment

Instructions: First, rank order the following instrumental values (i.e., process values) with 1 = *most preferred value* to 10 = *least preferred value*. Please use all 10 numbers.

Overall, I believe it is very important for me to

_____ Act Responsibly

_____ Act Independently

_____ Behave Politely

_____ Behave Honestly

_____ Feel Connected With Others

_____ Think Logically

_____ Act With Self-Discipline

_____ Act With Ambition

_____ Behave in a Helpful Manner

_____ Behave in an Assertive Manner

Second, rank order the following terminal values (i.e., end goals) with 1 = *most preferred value*, to 10 = *least preferred value*. Please use all 10 numbers.

Overall, I believe it is very important for me to attain or experience the following life values and goals:

_____ A Sense of Accomplishment

_____ A Life With Inner Harmony

_____ An Exciting Life

_____ A Sense of True Belonging

_____ A Life With Social Recognition

_____ A Higher Spiritual Life

_____ A Happy Life

_____ A Secure Family Life

_____ An Adventurous Life

_____ A Meaningful Life

Reflection Probes: What are your top three instrumental values? What are your top three terminal values? What are the factors that shape your values preferences? Check out your value rankings with those of a classmate. Discuss the differences and similarities in your answers.

Source: Adapted from Rokeach (1973) and Schwartz (1992).

serve as guidelines or preferable modes of conduct in the pursuit of certain valued existential outcomes. These process values or path values are also known as *instrumental values*. Acting honestly or acting tactfully, acting ambitiously or acting modestly, and communicating assertively or nonassertively are some examples of instrumental values (Stringer & Cassidy, 2003).

Values can also serve as the preferable end states or goals to be met. The desired outcome values are known as *terminal values* (Rokeach, 1973). An exciting life, a comfortable life, and a life with tangible or spiritual accomplishment are some examples of terminal values. While members of different cultural/ethnic groups may hold similar desires for certain terminal values (e.g., family security, a meaningful life, a world at peace), they may differ in their interpretations and also the selection of instrumental paths in attaining those end goals. To understand various communication patterns in a culture, we have to understand the deep-rooted cultural values that give meanings to such patterns. An in-depth discussion of the contents of cultural values appears in Chapter 3.

Overall, culture is a complex frame of reference that consists of patterns of traditions, beliefs, values, norms, meanings, and symbols that are shared to varying degrees by interacting members of a community. Oftentimes, our ignorance of a different culture's worldviews or values can produce unintentional clashes between us and people of that culture. We may not even notice that we have violated another culture's norms in a particular communication scene. The result may worsen the intercultural misinterpretation process.

Understanding Intercultural Communication: A Process Model

Intercultural communication takes place when cultural group membership factors (e.g., cultural values) affect our communication process—on either an awareness or unawareness level (see Figure 2.2). For example, both individuals—A and B—can be aware that a cultural *faux pas* has been committed in the communication process, and both of them are in the "mutual alertness" state. They can then decide either to repair the mistake through verbal means (e.g., trying to clarify the misunderstanding or apologizing to each other) or to let it stand. They may also attribute the communication misstep to factors (e.g., personality flaws) other than culture-level factors and escalate the mistake to a confrontational conflict level. At the opposite end of the spectrum, neither communicator is aware that a cultural mistake has been made, and both are in the "mutual obliviousness" state. They are completely unaware that the seeds of intercultural discord have been sown. But,

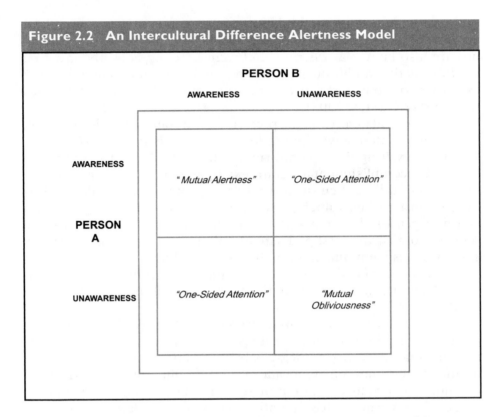

Figure 2.2 An Intercultural Difference Alertness Model

retrospectively, they may realize that something went terribly wrong and that subsequent repair work cannot salvage the damage.

Then there is the possibility that only A or only B is aware of the intercultural mistake, and the other person (the violator B or A) has no sense that a cultural mistake has been committed. Thus, there is a "one-sided attention" state to the overriding problematic intercultural situation. While one person is experiencing more and more frustration, the other conflict party is still paying no attention to the existing intercultural problem. This is probably the most common occurrence in many intercultural encounters. If both intercultural communicators continue to ignore culture-based factors that have an influence on their encounters, their incompetence in interpreting the other's behaviors may easily spiral into major escalatory conflicts.

Intercultural communication is often referred to as a symbolic exchange process between persons of different cultures. In the symbolic exchange process, intentions are inferred and culture-based interpretations are formed. To increase your alertness and attunement to the intercultural communication process, we identify the characteristics of the intercultural communication process in two subsections: the overall characteristics of the process and the specific meaning characteristics of the intercultural exchange process. Figure 2.3 is a

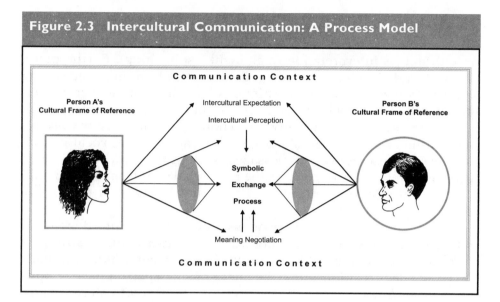

Figure 2.3 Intercultural Communication: A Process Model

graphic model that represents some of the key elements in an intercultural-based process model.

Intercultural Communication Process: Overall Characteristics

Intercultural communication is defined as *the symbolic exchange process whereby individuals from two (or more) different cultural communities negotiate shared meanings in an interactive situation.* The major components of this definition include the following concepts: symbolic exchange, process, different cultural communities, negotiate shared meanings, and an interactive situation.

In any intercultural encounter process, people use verbal and nonverbal messages to get their ideas across. The first component, **symbolic exchange,** refers to the use of verbal and nonverbal symbols between a minimum of two individuals to accomplish shared meanings. Although verbal symbols represent the digital aspects of our message exchange process, nonverbal symbols or cues (i.e., the smallest identifiable unit of communication), such as smiles, represent the analogical aspects of our message exchange process. Digital aspects of communication refer to the content information that we convey to our listener. The relationship between a digital cue (e.g., the word *angry*) and its interpretation is arbitrary. The word *angry* is a digital symbol that stands for an intense, antagonistic emotional state. The word itself, however, does not carry the feeling: It is people, as symbol users, who infuse the word with intense emotions.

In contrast, analogical aspects of communication refer to the "picturesque" meanings or the affective meanings that we convey through the use of nonverbal cues. Nonverbal cues are analogical because there exists a resemblance relationship between the nonverbal cue (e.g., a frown) and its interpretation (e.g., dislike something). Furthermore, although verbal cues are discrete (i.e., with clear beginning and ending sounds), nonverbal cues are continuous (i.e., different nonverbal cues flow simultaneously with no clear-cut beginning and ending) throughout the message exchange process. Though verbal messages always include the use of nonverbal cues, such as accents and vocal intonations, we can use nonverbal messages, such as touch, without words. As babies, we acquire or soak up the nonverbal cues from our immediate cultural environment before the actual learning of our native tongue.

The second component, **process,** refers to the interdependent nature of the intercultural encounter. Once two cultural strangers make contact and attempt to communicate, they enter into a mutually interdependent relationship. A Japanese businessperson may be bowing, and an American businessperson may be ready to shake hands. The two may also quickly reverse their nonverbal greeting rituals and adapt to each other's behavior. This quick change of nonverbal postures, however, may cause another awkward moment of confusion. The concept of process refers to two ideas: the transactional nature and the irreversible nature of communication (Watzlawick, Beavin, & Jackson, 1967).

The *transactional* nature of intercultural communication refers to the simultaneous encoding (i.e., the sender choosing the right words or nonverbal gestures to express his or her intentions) and decoding (i.e., the receiver translating the words or nonverbal cues into comprehensible meanings) of the exchanged messages. When the decoding process of the receiver matches the encoding process of the sender, the receiver and sender of the message have accomplished shared content meanings effectively. Unfortunately, more often than not, intercultural encounters are filled with misunderstandings and second guesses because of language problems, communication style differences, and value-orientation differences.

Furthermore, intercultural communication is an *irreversible* process because the decoder may form different impressions even in regard to the same repeated message. Once an encoder has uttered something to a decoder, he or she cannot repeat the same exact message. The encoder's tone of voice, interaction pace, or facial expression will not stay precisely the same. It is also difficult for any encoder to withdraw or cancel a message once the message has been decoded. For example, if a sender utters a remark such as "I have friends who are Japs!" and then quickly attempts to withdraw the message, this attempt cannot succeed because the message has already created a damaging impact on the receiver's decoding field. Thus, the intercultural communication process is irreversible (Barnlund, 1962).

The third component, **different cultural communities**, is defined as a broad concept. A **cultural community** refers to a group of interacting individuals within a bounded unit who uphold a set of shared traditions and way of life. This unit can refer to a geographic locale with clear-cut boundaries, such as a nation. This unit can also refer to a set of shared beliefs and values that are subscribed to by a group of individuals who perceive themselves as united even if they are dispersed physically. For example, many Jews, who are dispersed throughout the world, tend to perceive themselves as a united cultural community via their shared religious traditions and beliefs.

Broadly interpreted, a cultural community can refer to a national cultural group, an ethnic group, or a gender group. It is, simultaneously, a group-level concept (i.e., a patterned way of living) and an individual's subjective sense of membership or an affiliation with a group. The term *culture* here is used as a frame of reference or knowledge system that is shared by a large group of individuals within a perceived bounded unit. The "objective" boundaries of a culture may or may not coincide with national or political boundaries. The term can also be used on a specific level to refer to a patterned way of living by an ethnocultural group (i.e., an ethnic group within a culture).

Intercultural Communication: Meaning Characteristics

The fourth component, **negotiate shared meanings,** refers to the general goal of any intercultural communication encounter. In intercultural business negotiations or intercultural romantic relationships, a first level of concern is that we want our messages to be understood. When the interpretation of the meaning of the message overlaps significantly with the intention of the meaning of the message, we have established a high level of shared meanings in the communication process. The word *negotiate* indicates the creative give-and-take nature of the fluid process of human communication. For example, if both communicators are using the same language to communicate, they may ask each other to define and clarify any part of the exchanged message that is perceived as being unclear or vague.

Furthermore, every verbal and nonverbal message contains multiple layers of meanings. The three layers of meaning that are critical to our understanding of how people express themselves in a communication process are content meaning, relational meaning, and identity meaning.

Content meaning refers to the factual (or digital) information that is being conveyed to the receiver through an oral channel or other communication medium. When the intended content meaning of the encoder has been accurately decoded by the receiver, the communicators have established a level of mutually shared content meanings. Content meaning is usually tied to substantive discussion or issues (e.g., business contract details) with verifiable, factual overtones (i.e., "Did you or did you not say that?"). It also involves what is appropriate to say in a particular cultural scene. For example, in many Asian cultures, it is impolite to say "no" directly to a request. Thus, people from traditional Asian backgrounds will tend to use qualifying statements such as "I agree with you in principle; however . . ." and "Maybe if I finish studying and if you still want to borrow my lecture notes . . ." to imply a "no" or "maybe" answer. In most encounters, however, people are more aware of content meaning negotiation than relational or identity meaning negotiation.

Relational meaning offers information concerning the state of the relationship between the two communicators. Relational meaning is inferred via nonverbal intonations, body movements, or gestures that accompany the verbal content level. It conveys both power distance (e.g., equal-unequal) meanings and relational distance (e.g., friendly-unfriendly) meanings. For example, the professor says, "I want to talk to you about your grade in this class," which can be interpreted as either "You're in serious trouble—I can't believe you handed in such a sloppy paper!" or "I'm concerned about your grade in this class—let me know how I can help you." On the relational level, the professor's statement can be decoded as an intimidating-unfriendly request, or a caring-friendly statement. The comment can also be decoded with compliance or resistance by the recipient of the message. The relational meaning of the message often implies how the relationship between the communicators should be defined and interpreted. It is closely linked with identity meaning issues.

Identity meaning refers to the following questions: "Who am I and who are you in this interaction episode?" "How do I define myself in this interaction scene?" and "How do I define you in this interaction scene?" (Wilmot & Hocker, 1998). Identity meaning involves issues such as the display of respect or disrespect and identity approval or disapproval. Decoders typically infer identity meanings through the speaker's tone of voice, facial expressions, nonverbal postures, spatial distance, and selective word choices. Nonverbal tones or gestures, however, are highly culture dependent and are oftentimes easily misinterpreted.

For example, the statement "Komsu Mamuya, come over here!" can be rephrased as "Mr. Mamuya, when you have a minute, I would really like to talk to you" or "Komsu, don't you understand my English? I need to talk to you right now!" or "Dr. Mamuya, please, when you have some time, I would really appreciate your advice on this." These different statements indicate different shades of respect accorded to the addressee—depending on the tone of voice and whether the individual is addressed with her title or not—and also situational and cultural contexts.

The characteristics of content, relational, and identity meaning negotiation constitute the dynamic nature of the intercultural communication process. The process can take place in either a face-to-face or mediated situation through e-mail, cellular phone, or the teleconferencing context. Thus, the communication situation, the nature of the topical exchange, the relational features, the language use, and the cultural territory in which the exchange took place all have a profound influence on the symbolic exchange process itself.

The fifth component, an **interactive situation,** refers to the idea that every communication episode occurs in a relational context, a psychological context, and a physical context.

Throughout this book, we will use examples of intercultural acquaintance relationships, friendships, dating relationships, and business relationships to illustrate various intercultural communication processes. We also encourage you to think of additional examples and questions to clarify your own understanding of important concepts that affect the intercultural communication process. A **psychological context,** in turn, refers to our psychological interpretations (e.g., perceived formal versus informal context) and expectations of an interactive situation. Last, a **physical context** refers to the physical features (e.g., furniture or seating arrangement in a room) and layouts surrounding the interaction. We acquire the meanings to these situational features via the primary socialization process of our culture. The next section introduces a set of principles to guide you in your intercultural excursions.

Practicing Intercultural Process Thinking

The general goal of intercultural communication is to create shared meanings effectively—so that what I intended to say or imply is clearly understood by the culturally different other. Furthermore, intercultural communication does not happen in a vacuum. We have to develop a keen sense of adaptability and creativity in our intercultural relating process.

Process Consciousness: Underlying Principles

The following guidelines are presented to increase your conceptual understanding of the intercultural communication process. On an everyday intercultural communication level, we need to develop a keen sense of mindfulness of the following principles:

Principle 1: Intercultural communication often involves mismatched expectations that stem, in part, from cultural group membership differences. When we encounter miscommunication in an intercultural interaction process, we experience emotional frustration.

Some of the emotional frustration often stems, in part, from cultural differences, mismatched expectations, or ignorance. Intercultural miscommunication takes place when our cultural group membership factors affect, in part, our communication process on either an awareness or unawareness level.

The cultural membership differences can include deep-level differences, such as cultural worldview differences and value differences. Concurrently, they can also include the mismatch of applying different norms and expectations in a particular communication scene. In practicing mindful intercultural communication, we can develop an understanding of the valuable differences that exist between different cultural groups. At the same time, we also need to continuously recognize the commonalities that exist in all humans, across all cultures.

Principle 2: *Intercultural communication often involves varying degrees of biased intergroup perceptions.* Biased intergroup perceptions often involve overgeneralizations or stereotypes. The term *intergroup* means viewing the person as a representation of a group membership category and deemphasizing the person's unique attributes. Thus, from an intergroup lens, stereotyping involves an overestimation of the degree of association between stereotypic-psychological traits (e.g., cantankerous, grumpy) and group membership categories (e.g., elderly population). Moreover, stereotyping is also about creating self-fulfilling prophecies. We tend to see behavior that confirms our expectations even when it is absent, and we ignore vital information (e.g., knowledgeable, wise advice) when it is incongruous with our expectations.

When we communicate mindlessly, we do not notice the distinctive qualities of the cultural person with whom we are communicating. Rather, we fall back on our stereotypes to reduce our guesswork and, perhaps, emotional vulnerability level. Although the contents of our stereotypes can be positive or negative, rigidly typecasting selective members of a cultural group into "triangles" and "squares" can perpetuate inaccurate impressions and myths. If we are unwilling to question our rigidly held stereotypes, our intergroup relationships will stay only at a superficial level of contact. Stereotyping, together with an ethnocentric attitude and a prejudiced mindset, can often perpetuate misinterpretation spirals and intergroup conflict cycles.

Principle 3: *Intercultural communication involves the simultaneous encoding and decoding of verbal and nonverbal messages in the exchange process.* This is the key assumption to understanding the concept of "process" in intercultural communication. From a transactional model viewpoint, both intercultural communicators in the communication process are viewed as playing the sender and receiver roles. Both are responsible for synchronizing the conversational process and outcome. An effective encoding and decoding process leads to shared meanings. An ineffective encoding and decoding process by one of the two "transceivers" can lead to intercultural misunderstanding.

However, beyond the accurate encoding and decoding of messages on the content level, communicators need to cultivate additional sensitivity along multiple levels (such as relational, identity, and situational meanings) of intercultural understanding. Without a keen sense of cultural decoding competence, we are likely to misjudge our intercultural partners' intentions and find ourselves in serious trouble. Without a mindful sense of message encoding, we may say the wrong things in the wrong context and with bad timing. With mindful alertness, we can conscientiously choose words and behaviors that make dissimilar others feel affirmed, included, and listened to.

Principle 4: *Intercultural communication involves multiple goals, and the goals people have are largely dependent on how they define the interaction episode.* Echoing the various layers of meaning negotiation, three types of goals are important in an intercultural encounter process: content goals, relational goals, and identity goals. *Content goals* refer to external, substantive issues in the communication process. Some questions we may want to consider are these: What do we want to accomplish in the intercultural negotiation session? What are the content or instrumental interaction goals? What are the potential obstacles and the necessary steps to accomplish our goals effectively? For example, a clear content goal discussion can involve asking a professor to postpone the deadline of a group project or requesting a pay raise from your international boss. We need to think ahead in terms of the cultural or interpersonal obstacles that lie in the path of content goal attainment. We also need to decide whether we should pursue our content goals in an individualistic, assertive manner or in a relational, tactful manner.

Relational goals refer to the socio-emotional issues or relational role expectations that are involved in the intercultural negotiation session. We need to examine questions such as the following: What are my role expectations and the other person's role expectations in the intercultural encounter episode? What are the situational conditions that shape the dynamics of the role-encountering process? What are the behavioral requirements, and what is "off limits" in this intercultural interaction scene? A professor from a large power distance value culture (e.g., Iran) may expect more formality from students in the classroom setting. A professor from a small power distance value culture (e.g., the United States) may be more comfortable with informal discussions with her students in the classroom environment. However, the same Iranian professor may relax his or her role expectations at a student-sponsored picnic in the park. To be flexible communicators across cultural lines, we must recognize the interconnected nature of norms, roles, and situations.

Identity goals refer to the projected self-image or self-worth issues in the interaction scene. Identity goals can involve identity respect/disrespect or approval/disapproval postures. It can also be interpreted in connection with our desires to have our cultural, ethnic, gender, disability, professional, and personal images respected in the communication episode. The ability to project a desired self-image or "face" and to have this projected "face" be validated are critical skills in any intercultural negotiation session. *Face* is basically about identity respect issues and other consideration issues within and beyond the intercultural encounter process. In a mindful facework negotiation process, honoring others' face and helping others to save face are ways to manage favorable interactive identities across cultures.

Principle 5: *Intercultural communication calls for understanding and acceptance of diverse communication approaches and styles.* For example, in an intercultural conflict episode, parties often utilize different communication styles that are consistent with their culture-based values. For some cultures, a conflict with another party should be confronted directly and assertive steps should be taken to resolve the conflict in a clear win-lose direction. In other cultures, a conflict should be avoided at all costs to preserve relational harmony. Mutual face-saving and face-honoring moves may supersede the need to arrive at a clear win-lose resolution. In fact, conflict negotiators may want to cultivate the image of a win-win conflict process so that both parties can maintain some face, or dignity, before returning to their home cultures.

The cultural preferences for certain communication styles are, of course, mediated by many situational and relationship expectation factors. To embark on an inclusive communication approach, we need to learn to be flexible in our verbal and nonverbal styles in dealing with diverse groups. We also have to pay close attention to mediating factors—such as situational parameters and interaction goals—in shaping our different communication modes.

Principle 6: *Many intercultural encounters involve well-meaning culture bumps or clashes.* Individuals of different cultural communities have learned different interaction forms, for example, eye contact maintenance or avoidance, in everyday conversations. They also tend to use their own cultural scripts to evaluate the competencies of cultural strangers' behaviors. Many intercultural miscommunication episodes start off from culture bumps or clashes.

A **culture bump** is defined as a cultural violation on the behavioral level when our meanings do not overlap with one another in viewing the same behavior, which creates communication awkwardness or embarrassment (Archer, 1991). Let us look at Double Take 2.1.

In this particular story, even though David acted in an "unconscious incompetent" manner in the beginning, he caught his own culture bump and moved to the "conscious incompetent" stage to inquire

---

Double Take 2.1

In a Poly Sci[ence] class during a group discussion, I was sitting to the right of a man from Saudi Arabia. As I was talking to him, I placed my right ankle on my left knee. I noticed a definite change in his demeanor toward me. After class, I approached him and asked if I had done or said something that offended him. He told me that in the Arab culture, exposing the soles of your shoes while directly speaking to someone is tantamount to giving them "the finger." I apologized for my ignorance; he apologized for his ignorance of my ignorance. We ended up being friendly to one another for the remainder of the semester.

—David, *College Student*

---

about his own communication mistake. A culture bump often ends in more miscommunications and frustration when the two communicators continue to misinterpret each other's behavior as rude or even insulting. A culture bump is about violating another person's cultural norms without malicious intent. More often than not, we commit unintentional culture bumps in a new culture because we have not mastered the norms and the meaning fluency of that new system.

Well-meaning clash basically refers to misunderstanding an encounter in which people are actually behaving in a "socially skilled manner" and with "good intentions" according to the norms in their own culture (Brislin, 1993). Unfortunately, the behaviors that are considered proper or effective in one culture can be considered improper or ineffective in another culture. For example, using direct eye contact is considered a sign of respect in U.S. culture, whereas direct eye contact can signify disrespect in the Thai culture. The term *well-meaning* is used because no one in the intercultural encounter intentionally behaves obnoxiously or unpleasantly. Individuals are trying to be well mannered or pleasant in accordance with the politeness norms of their own culture. Individuals behave ethnocentrically—often without conscious realization of their automatic-pilot verbal or nonverbal routines.

Principle 7: Intercultural communication always takes place in a context. Intercultural communication does not happen in a vacuum, but is always context bound. Patterns of thinking and behaving are always interpreted within an interactive situation or context. To understand intercultural communication from a contextual viewpoint, we need to consider how the physical and psychological settings of the communicators establish the climate or mood of their interaction.

The physical setting can include furniture arrangement, props, color of the room, temperature of the room, and who is in the room. However, and more important, we have to understand the psychological or emotional meanings that are attached to the physical setting by the different cultural participants. Additionally, the expected roles of the participants, their relational distance, conversational topics, inter-action goals, implicit communication rules, and culture shock factors can all influence the interaction climate. Last, the degree of cultural knowledge, past cultural visiting experience, and competent perfor-mance of communication skills form the overall patterns of the com-munication context.

Principle 8: *Intercultural communication always takes place in embedded systems.* A system is an interdependent set of components that constitutes a whole and, simultaneously, influence each other. Our enculturation process (i.e., our primary socialization process at a young age) is influenced by both macro- and micro-level events in our cultural environment. On a macro level, we are programmed or enculturated into our culture via our family and educational systems, religious and political systems, and government and socioeconomic systems, as well as by the paramount influence of media in our every-day life.

On a micro level, we are surrounded by people who subscribe to similar worldviews, values, norms, and expectations. We are the recipi-ents and also the preservers of our culture via the daily messages that we trade. However, culture is not a static web. It is a dynamic, evolu-tionary process. Human beings are also not static individuals—they are changeable. In learning about another culture or dissimilar groups, we can expand our mental landscape and emotional horizon. Through the lens of another culture, we may be able to reinterpret our own iden-tity and culture with fresh visions and insights.

Intercultural Toolkit: Recaps and Checkpoints

In this chapter, we defined culture and intercultural communica-tion. In discussing the definition of culture, we explored the three lev-els of understanding a culture: surface-level, intermediate-level, and deep-level culture. In exploring the definition of intercultural commu-nication, we emphasized the importance of using a meaning-centered approach to look at the intercultural communication process. We also urged you to develop a strong "process consciousness" in dealing with cultural strangers.

More specifically, we would like you to build on what you've learned so far, keeping the following checkpoints in mind when, in the next chapter, you learn about the value dimensions of a culture:

- A flexible intercultural communicator emphasizes a process-focused approach to intercultural communication.

- A flexible intercultural communicator recognizes the sepa-rate, ethnocentric realities that divide individuals and groups.

- A flexible intercultural communicator is willing to suspend snapshot, evaluative judgments concerning culture-based verbal and nonverbal style differences.

- A flexible intercultural communicator can deal with ambiguities and paradoxes in uncertain intercultural situations.

- A flexible intercultural communicator can communicate appropriately, effectively, adaptively, and creatively through the use of a variety of constructive verbal and nonverbal communication skills. ✦

Chapter 3

What Are the Essential Cultural Value Patterns?

Chapter Outline

Nani Parales, a local Filipino American, works for the State Department in Hawaii. This department is made up of a diverse group of workers. Nani has been a supervisor for the past two years, in charge of ten clerks in her division. She sees herself as a caring supervisor. In this last year, Nani has made a point to get together with her employees and their families once a month outside of work—usually a fun lunch or brunch over the weekends. Her employees see her more as a family friend than a supervisor.

☞

☞ However, in the past two months, Nani has experienced increased frustration with several of her employees. Whenever she asks them to work on a project or to meet a deadline, they do not come through. They say "yes," but they do not take her requests seriously. Worse, they have even started to talk behind her back or give her an attitude. Nani now dreads going to work. She is feeling very uncomfortable—where did she go wrong? Maybe she has been too friendly with her employees. Maybe she is just not a competent boss. She also needs to do their year-end performance review reports. She does not want to write anything negative, but she will probably have to do so. All these things go against her values and her own caring self-image. What is your interpretation of her plight? What advice can you give Nani?

Identifying cultural and personal value differences provides us with a map to understand why people behave the way they do in a new cultural setting. It also sheds light on our own behavior and styles of communicating with people from diverse cultural communities. Cultural values form part of the content of our sense of self and answer this question: Who am I in this world? Our sense of self is infused with cultural, ethnic, gender, spiritual, professional, relational, and personal values.

This chapter asks the question, Can we identify some general value patterns of different cultures that will help us to cross cultural boundaries more effectively? The chapter is organized into five sections. We first explore the various functions of cultural value patterns. Second, we discuss the four value dimensions that are critical in influencing people's communication styles. Third, we examine four additional value orientations that affect individuals' cultural boundary-crossing journey. We then discuss dimensions of personality that may combine with cultural values in shaping people's communication styles. Last, we offer practical checkpoints to remind you to keep these diverse cultural value patterns in mind when crossing cultures.

Functions of Cultural Values

By peering into the window of another culture, intercultural knowledge can make individuals more reflective on their own ingrained cultural beliefs and values. By understanding where major cultural differences exist, learners can figure creative ways to harness the differences and to find common ground to work with individuals from diverse cultural groups.

Systematic cultural value analysis helps us to grasp the alternative paths that other cultures may prefer in their ways of thinking, valuing, and being. This section defines and explores some of the major functions of cultural value patterns.

Analyzing Cultural Values

Values are shared ideas about what is right or wrong, what is fair or unfair, what is important or not important. Although each of us has developed our unique set of values based on our socialization and life experience, there are also larger values at work on a cultural level. Cultural values are relatively stable and enduring—values protect a culture in times of crisis and stressful situations.

Cultural value patterns form the basic criteria through which we evaluate our own behaviors and the behaviors of others. They cue our expectations of how we should act and how others should act during an interaction. They serve as implicit guidelines for our motivations, expectations, perceptions, interpretations, and communicative actions. They set the emotional tone for interpreting the behavior of cultural strangers. Cultural value patterns serve many functions, including the identity meaning function, sense-making explanatory function, boundary regulation function, and adaptational function.

Identity Meaning Function

Cultural values provide the frame of reference to answer the most fundamental question of each human being: Who am I in this world? Cultural beliefs and values provide the anchoring points to which we attach meanings and significance to our complex identities. For example, in the larger U.S. culture, middle-class U.S. values often emphasize individual initiative and achievement. A person is considered "competent" or "successful" when he or she takes the personal initiative to realize and maximize his or her full potential. The result? Recognition and rewards (e.g., an enviable career, a six-digit salary, a coveted car, or a dream house) that are tangible and acknowledged by others. A person who can realize his or her dreams, while overcoming all odds, is considered to be a "successful" individual in the context of middle-class U.S. culture.

Valuing individual initiative may stem, in part, from the predominantly Judeo-Christian belief system in the larger U.S. culture. In this belief system, each person is perceived as unique, as having free will, and as responsible for his or her growth and decisions. The concept of being a "successful," "competent," or "worthwhile" person and the meanings attached to such words stem from the fundamental values of a given culture. The identity meanings we acquire within our culture are constructed and sustained through everyday communication.

Explanatory Function

Within our own group, we experience safety and acceptance. We do not have to constantly justify or explain our actions or values. Our commonly shared values are implicitly understood and celebrated via everyday communication rituals. With people of dissimilar groups, however, we have to be on the alert and may need to explain or defend our behaviors or underlying values with more effort.

When we interact with people from our own cultural group, we can mentally "fill in the blanks" and understand why people behave the way they do. However, when we communicate with people from another cultural group, we need mental energy to try to figure out why they behave the way they behave. We constantly have to perform anxiety-laden guessing games. We may be witnessing people using different public displays of affection or strange phrases; however, we may remain clueless in terms of why they communicate the way they do. Basically, we have not mastered the value-based explanatory system of that culture. We cannot come up with a reasonable guess or interpretative competence as to why people do certain "strange" things in that "strange" culture.

Boundary Regulation Function

Culture creates a comfort zone in which we experience ingroup inclusion and ingroup/outgroup differences. A shared common fate or a sense of solidarity often exists among members of the same group. For example, within our own cultural group, we speak the same language or dialect, we share similar nonverbal rhythms, and we can decode each other's nonverbal mood with more accuracy. However, with people from a dissimilar membership group, we tend to "stand out," and we experience awkwardness during interaction. The feeling of exclusion or differentiation leads to interaction ambiguity or anxiety (Brewer, 1991).

The boundary regulation function shapes our ingroup and outgroup attitudes in dealing with people who are culturally dissimilar. An *attitude* is a learned tendency that influences our behavior. Contrastive value patterns help us to form evaluative attitudes toward ingroup and outgroup interactions. **Ingroups** are groups with whom we feel emotionally close and with whom we share an interdependent fate, such as family or extended family, our sorority or fraternity, or people from our own cultural or ethnic group. **Outgroups,** on the other hand, are groups with whom we feel no emotional ties, and, at times, we may experience great psychological distance from them and even feel competitive against them—they can be our rival fraternity, our wartime enemy, or simply individuals who belong to another cultural or ethnic group.

Overall, we tend to hold favorable attitudes toward ingroup inter-actions because of our perceived value and behavioral similarities, and we hold unfavorable attitudes toward outgroup interactions because of our ignorance of their cultural values and norms. Furthermore, value patterns regulate ingroup consensus and set evaluative standards concerning what is *valued* or *devalued* within a culture. They provide a clear reward and punishment system that reinforces certain behaviors and sanctions other unacceptable behaviors over time.

Adaptational Function

Cultural values or principles facilitate the adaptation processes among the self, the cultural community, and the larger environment (i.e., the ecological habitat). Cultural values evolve due to people's desires and needs, and vice versa. When people adapt their needs and their particular ways of living in response to a changing habitat, cul-ture also changes accordingly. Surface-level cultural artifacts, such as fashion or popular culture, change at a faster pace than deep-level cul-tural elements, such as traditional beliefs, values, and ethics.

Triandis (1994) made the observation that ecologies in which sur-vival depends on hunting and fishing are different from ecologies in which survival depends on farming. In agricultural societies, for exam-ple, cooperation is often required. Farmers need to cooperate in order to work together digging irrigation canals or constructing storage barns. As a result, socialization in such cultural communities empha-sizes dependability and cooperation. Thus, culture rewards certain behaviors that are compatible with its ecology and sanctions other behaviors that are mismatched with the ecological niche of the culture.

In sum, cultural values serve the identity meaning, explanatory, boundary regulation, and adaptation functions. Communication, in essence, serves as the major hook that links the various channels (e.g., family socialization, educational institution, religious/spiritual institu-tion) of value transmission systems in a coherent manner. Drawing from the various functions of cultural values as discussed above, we can now turn to explore the core value patterns that shape the intercultural communication process.

Analyzing Cultural Value Dimensions

Cultural value analysis highlights the potential differences and similarities of value patterns between cultural groups. Despite the dif-ficulties in generalizing about the diverse values in heterogeneous cul-tures such as India and the United States, it is possible and in fact imperative to engage in such cultural value assessments. Mindful value comparison on a cultural group membership level acts as a critical first step toward better understanding of potential cultural differences and similarities.

This section introduces the cultural value analysis concept and examines four value dimensions: the key value dimension of individualism/collectivism and the other three value dimensions of power distance, uncertainty avoidance, and femininity-masculinity.

Discovering Cultural Values

Based on the comparative studies of a wide range of cultures throughout the world, specific value patterns in different cultures have been uncovered by researchers in the areas of anthropology, cross-cultural psychology, sociology, international management, linguistics, and intercultural communication. Cultural values form the implicit standards by which we judge appropriate and inappropriate behaviors in a communication episode. They are the contents of self that drive our thoughts, emotions, and everyday decision-making processes. They serve to shape the motivation to explain human behavior.

However, cultural value patterns such as individualism and collectivism exist as general value tendencies on a cultural level of analysis. Cultural-level tendencies, however, do not explain the behaviors of all members in a single culture. Family socialization, individual life experience, popular culture, and immigration or intergroup contact experience will all have differential effects on the value formation processes of an individual in a society. If two cultures (e.g., Vietnam and the United States) differ on a value dimension (e.g., collectivism), it does not necessarily mean that a particular Vietnamese person is bound to be collectivistic and a particular U.S. American, individualistic. It only implies that the average tendencies of the two cultures—on a group membership level—differ in terms of the value characteristics. However, within each culture, wide variations exist on the individual level of analysis. Although we can say that a majority of individuals in the United States subscribe to some form of individualistic values, we should also recognize that some individuals in the United States have strong interdependent tendencies. Likewise, even though we can say that a majority of individuals in Vietnam subscribe to some form of group-based values, we should also pay close attention to the fact that some individuals in Vietnam have strong "I-identity" attributes. The more pluralistic or "loose" the culture, the more we may find diverse individuals subscribing to diverse norms and belief systems in that culture. Before we discuss the four value dimensions at the cultural level of analysis, let's look at Know Thyself 3.1. Take a few minutes to complete it before you continue reading.

Your honest answers to the four situations should provide some insight into your personal values. Your responses basically reflect how

Know Thyself 3.1   Discovering Personal Value Dimensions

Instructions: The following scenarios reflect four dilemmas. Each situation gives two decision-making alternatives. Use your gut-level reaction and check the answer that you consider best reflects your honest decision under the circumstances.

1. You have two hours to prepare for an examination for one class and an oral report that you and several fellow students will present in another class. The exam score is your own; the oral report earns a group grade. Both are worth 25 percent of your grade in each class. In the two hours, you can only do one well. What should you do?
   a. _____ Study hard for the exam—it reflects your individual achievement.
   b. _____ Prepare for the group report—do not let down your team members.

2. You are deeply in love with a romantic partner from a different cultural background. However, your parents do not approve of him or her because they think it's hard enough to make a relationship work even if the person is from the same culture. What should you do?
   a. _____ Tell your parents to respect your dating choice and decision.
   b. _____ Tell your partner to be patient and try to understand your parents' viewpoint.

3. Your next-door neighbors are partying loudly again and it's already 1:00 a.m. You have an important job interview scheduled for the early morning. You really want to have a good night's sleep so that you can wake up refreshed in the morning. What should you do?
   a. _____ Tell your neighbors to stop the partying.
   b. _____ Grin and bear it. You really don't like conflict, and you hope the noise level will die down eventually.

4. Your nephew really enjoys playing with dolls and your niece really enjoys playing with tanks and soldiers. Your sister asks you for advice. Should she be worried about her two kids and their playing habits? What would you say?
   a. _____ Don't worry. There's nothing wrong with boys playing with dolls and girls playing with tanks.
   b. _____ You're right to be concerned. It seems like the kids are confused about their sex-role identity. You should observe them more closely.

Scoring: If you put a check mark on the (a) answers, the answer keys are as follows: *(1a) individualistic, (2a) small power distance, (3a) weak uncertainty avoidance,* and *(4a) "feminine" patterns.*

If you put a check mark on the following (b) answers, your answers are reflective of the following: *(1b) collectivistic, (2b) large power distance, (3b) strong uncertainty avoidance,* and *(4b) "masculine" patterns.*

If you have checked some (a) answers and some (b) answers, your values are reflective of a mixed set of value patterns. Review and label your own answers now.

Interpretation: Please continue to read your text under the "Analyzing Cultural Value Dimensions" section for further value interpretations.

your individual values shape your interpretations of the four situations. Keep your responses in mind as you read the remainder of this section.

Identity: Individualism-Collectivism Value Pattern

In reviewing your answer to situation one about "solo versus group achievement," if you checked (1a), your value pattern tends toward the "I-identity" end of the spectrum. If you checked (1b), your value pattern tends toward the collectivistic or "we-identity" end of the spectrum. Hofstede (1991, 2001) derived four cultural variability dimensions in his large-scale study of a U.S. multinational business corporation. The corporation has subsidiaries in 50 countries and three regions (the Arabic-speaking countries, East Africa, and West Africa). All together, 116,000 managers and employees in this worldwide corporation were surveyed twice. On the basis of the results, Hofstede (1991) delineated four organizational value patterns across a diverse range of cultures.

The first and most important dimension that shapes our sense of self is the individualistic-collectivistic value pattern. The other three cultural variability dimensions are power distance, uncertainty avoidance, and femininity-masculinity. We should note that Hofstede's four cultural value dimensions are related to business organizational values in different cultures. He also argues that ethnic and religious groups, gender, generation, social class, and social structure assert a strong influence on the value patterns within a particular culture. The four value dimensions should be viewed as a first systematic research attempt to compare a wide range of cultures on an aggregate, group level.

Before you continue to read on, since individualism-collectivism is such an important intercultural value theme, please fill out the brief assessment in Know Thyself 3.2 and find out your value tendency preference. Do you subscribe more to individualistic or collectivistic value tendencies? The individualism-collectivism value dimension has received consistent attention from both intercultural researchers and cross-cultural psychologists (Gudykunst & Ting-Toomey, 1988; Triandis, 1995). Intercultural scholars have provided evidence that the value patterns of individualism and collectivism are pervasive in a wide range of cultures. Individualism and collectivism can explain some of the basic differences and similarities concerning communication behavior between clusters of cultures.

Basically, **individualism** refers to the broad value tendencies of a culture in emphasizing the importance of individual identity over group identity, individual rights over group rights, and individual needs over group needs. Individualism promotes self-efficiency, individual responsibility, and personal autonomy. In contrast, **collectivism** refers to the broad value tendencies of a culture in emphasizing

Know Thyself 3.2 Assessing Your Individualism and Collectivism Value Tendencies

Instructions: The following items describe how people think about themselves and communicate in various situations. Let your first inclination be your guide and circle the number in the scale that best reflects your overall value. The following scale is used for each item:

4 = **SA** = *Strongly Agree*
3 = **MA** = *Moderately Agree*
2 = **MD** = *Moderately Disagree*
1 = **SD** = *Strongly Disagree*

	SA	MA	MD	SD
1. Act assertively to get what you want.	4	3	2	1
2. Be sensitive to the needs of others.	4	3	2	1
3. Be competitive and move ahead.	4	3	2	1
4. Blend in harmoniously with the group.	4	3	2	1
5. Act on independent thoughts.	4	3	2	1
6. Be respectful of group decisions.	4	3	2	1
7. Value self-reliance and personal freedom.	4	3	2	1
8. Consult family and friends before making decisions.	4	3	2	1
9. Be sensitive to the majority views in a group.	4	3	2	1
10. Voice my personal opinions when everyone else disagrees.	4	3	2	1

Scoring: Add up the scores on all the odd-numbered items and you will find your individualism score. *Individualism* score: _____ . Add up the scores on all the even-numbered items and you will find your collectivism score. *Collectivism* score: _____ .

Interpretation: Scores on each value dimension can range from 5 to 20; the higher the score, the more individualistic and/or collectivistic you are. If all the scores are similar on both value dimensions, you are a bicultural value person.

Reflection Probes: Take a moment to think of the following questions: Do your values reflect your family of origin's values? How have your values changed over time? What can you do to achieve greater understanding of people from a different value system?

the importance of the "we" identity over the "I" identity, group rights over individual rights, and ingroup needs over individual wants and desires. Collectivism promotes relational interdependence, ingroup harmony, and ingroup collaborative spirit (see Table 3.1).

Individualistic and collectivistic value tendencies are manifested in *everyday family, school,* and *workplace interaction.* Individualism pertains to societies in which ties between individuals are loosely linked

Table 3.1   Value Characteristics in Individualistic and Collectivistic Cultures

Situations	Individualistic Cultures	Collectivistic Cultures
General:	"I" Identity	"We" Identity
Family:	Nuclear Family	Extended Family
Relationship:	Privacy Regulation	Relational Harmony
School:	Individual Competition	Teamwork
Workplace:	Personal Competence	Ingroup Emphasis
Communication:	Direct Communication Patterns	Indirect Communication Patterns
Personality Equivalence:	Independent Self	Interdependent Self

and everyone is expected to look after himself or herself and his or her immediate family. Comparatively, collectivism refers to societies in which ties between individuals in the community are tightly intertwined. Group members view their fate as interdependent with one another. Although they will look after the welfare of ingroup members, they also expect their ingroup members to look after their interests and concerns throughout their lifetimes. If you were collectivistic, what would be your reaction to the popular U.S. television host Dr. Phil? His popularity is due to his straightforward advice, such as "Just do it!" or "Why are you not making your own decisions? You are not your parents!" Will this kind of advice help you with your decisions or confuse you somewhat?

Hofstede's (1991, 2001) research reveals that factors such as national wealth, population growth, and historical roots affect the development of individualistic and collectivistic values. For example, wealthy, urbanized, and industrialized societies are more individualistically oriented, whereas the poorer, rural, and traditional societies are more collectivistically oriented. However, there are some exceptions, especially in East Asia, where Japan, South Korea, Taiwan, Hong Kong, and Singapore appear to retain collectivism in spite of industrialization.

Individualism is a cultural pattern that is found in most northern and western regions of Europe and in North America. More specifically, high individualism has been found in the United States, Australia, Great Britain, Canada, the Netherlands, New Zealand, Italy, Belgium, Denmark, and Sweden. *Collectivism* is a cultural pattern common in Asia, Africa, the Middle East, Central and South America, and the Pacific islands. Though less than one-third of the world population resides in cultures with high individualistic value tendencies, a little more than two-thirds of the people live in cultures with high collectivistic value tendencies (Triandis, 1995). High collectivistic value tendencies have been found in Guatemala, Ecuador, Panama, Venezuela, Colombia, Indonesia, Pakistan, Costa Rica, and Peru (Hofstede, 1991).

The *top individualist values* emphasized are freedom, honesty, social recognition, comfort, hedonism, and personal equity. The *top collectivist values* are harmony, face-saving, filial piety (respecting parents' wishes), equality in the distribution of rewards among peers (for the sake of group harmony), and fulfillment of others' needs (Triandis, 1995). For example, let's check out the following story: Larimer (2000) interviewed sports philosopher Dr. Mitsunori Urushibara to discuss the enormous pressure on Japanese athletes to bring home gold medals during the Olympics. According to Dr. Urushibara, a Japanese star swimmer was left off the current Olympic team because she lost in the last Olympics in 1998. According to him, the concept of team is compared to an old-fashioned village, where a mayor lords over the other villagers. As a communal-based relationship develops, the star swimmer should have known what to do for the village. She should bring honor and recognition to the village, not shame or failure. Her every success and failure reflects on the entire town or village. Because of the village mentality, failure is not an option. Failure or losing a game involves shame and insult of the entire family, clan, or village. It causes the entire village to "lose face" on the world stage.

Overall, researchers have found that different layers of individualism (e.g., emphasizing personal need in the United Kingdom or immediate family need in Sweden) and collectivism (e.g., emphasizing work group need in Singapore or caste need in India) exist in different cultures. For each culture, it is important to determine the group with which individuals have the closest identification (e.g., their family, their corporation, their religion). For example, for the Vietnamese, it is the extended family; for the Japanese, the corporation; and for the Irish, the Roman Catholic Church, and so on.

In addition, *gender differences* exist in adherence to individualistic or relational-based values. U.S. males generally have been found to adhere more to individualistic values than to communal-based values. U.S. females generally have been found to subscribe to communally oriented values. However, compared with females in other collectivistic societies, such as Italy and Mexico, U.S. females are still fairly individualistic in their orientation. In their gender identity formation, U.S. males emphasize self-identity separation and competition, whereas U.S. females emphasize other-identity support and relational connection. Gendered groups in many cultures appear to differ in their preferences for individualistic or collectivistic value tendencies.

Our discussion of value patterns appears to be on two opposite poles of a continuum. In reality, many of you probably hold an integrative set of values, such as I-identity *and* we-identity patterns across a diverse range of situations. The key is that the more you are attuned to analyzing your own value patterns and those of culturally different others, the more you increase your cultural value awareness quotient. In addition to the individualism-collectivism dimension, another important value dimension is the dimension of power distance.

Power: Small-Large Power Distance Value Pattern

In reviewing your answer from Know Thyself 3.1 to situation two about intercultural dating, if you checked (2a), your value pattern tends toward the small power distance pole. If you checked (2b), your value pattern tends toward the large power distance pole. The power distance value dimension refers to the extent to which individuals subscribe to the ideology of equal power distributions and the extent to which members adhere to unequal power distributions in an interaction episode, within an institution or within a society. Small power distance scores are found, for example, in Austria, Israel, Denmark, New Zealand, Ireland, Sweden, and Norway. Large power distance scores are found, for example, in Malaysia, Guatemala, Panama, the Philippines, Mexico, Venezuela, and Arab countries (Hofstede, 1991).

People in **small power distance cultures** tend to value equal power distributions, equal rights and relations, and equitable rewards and punishments on the basis of performance. People in **large power distance cultures** tend to accept unequal power distributions, hierarchical rights, asymmetrical role relations, and rewards and punishments based on age, rank, status, title, and seniority. For small power distance cultures, equality of personal rights represents an ideal to strive toward in a system. For large power distance cultures, respect for power hierarchy in any system is a fundamental way of life (see Table 3.2).

In *small power distance family situations*, children may contradict their parents and speak their mind. They are expected to show self-initiative and learn verbal articulateness and persuasion skills. Parents and children work together to achieve a democratic family decision-making process. In *large power distance family situations*, children are expected to obey their parents. Children are punished if they talk back or contradict their parents. The value of respect between unequal status members in the family is taught at a young age. Parents and grandparents assume the authority roles in the family decision-making process.

In *small power distance work situations*, power is evenly distributed. Subordinates expect to be consulted, and the ideal boss is a resourceful democrat. In *large power distance work situations*, the power of an organization is centralized at the upper-management level. Subordinates expect to be told what to do, and the ideal boss plays the benevolent autocratic role. Although the United States scores on the low side of power distance, it is not extremely low. Hofstede

Table 3.2 Value Characteristics in Small and Large Power Distance (P.D.) Cultures

Situations	Small P.D. Cultures	Large P.D. Cultures
General:	Emphasize Interpersonal	Emphasize Status-Based Equality Difference
Family:	Children May Contradict Parents	Children Should Obey Parents
Relationship:	Younger People Are Smart	Older People Are Wise
School:	Teachers Ask for Feedback	Teachers Lecture
Workplace:	Subordinates Expect Consultation	Subordinates Expect Guidance
Communication:	Informal Communication Patterns	Formal Communication Patterns
Personality Equivalence:	Horizontal Self	Vertical Self

(1991) explains that "U.S. leadership theories tend to be based on subordinates with medium-level dependence needs: not too high, not too low" (p. 42).

Small power distance during interaction can create misunderstanding and confusion. Negotiating power distance often leads to levels of anxiety and frustration. For example, suppose you have an intercultural teacher who wants you to call him by his first name. He is friendly and open to class discussion, and he does not mind sharing personal stories related to different intercultural topics. Perhaps you and the class feel very comfortable. But one day, when you get the result of a class project, you notice your team did not do well at all; your teacher made two full pages of evaluative notes commenting on the strengths and weaknesses of the project. You and your team get very upset with your teacher. Your reaction may be due to the negotiation of different power distance expectations. Believing that your teacher is so "friendly" and "easy to talk to," you'll also likely expect that he will go "easy" on the grading. These are preconceived stereotypes associated with small power distance value patterns. As soon as the teacher plays the large power distance role of an evaluative instructor (and from his perspective he is being a responsible teacher), it may leave you to think that this "friendly, open" teacher is actually quite "mean" and "picky" toward the entire group.

Uncertainty: Weak-Strong Uncertainty Avoidance Value Pattern

In reviewing your answer from Know Thyself 3.1 to situation three about "neighborhood conflict," if you checked (3a), your value pattern tends toward the weak end of the uncertainty avoidance continuum. If you checked (3b), your value pattern tends toward the strong end of the uncertainty avoidance continuum. Uncertainty avoidance refers to the extent to which members of a culture do not mind conflicts or uncertain situations and the extent to which they try to avoid those uncertain situations. **Weak** (or **low**) **uncertainty avoidance** cultures encourage risk taking and conflict-approaching modes. **Strong** (or **high**) **uncertainty avoidance** cultures prefer clear procedures and conflict-avoidance behaviors. Weak uncertainty avoidance scores, for example, are found in Singapore, Jamaica, Denmark, Sweden, Hong Kong, Ireland, the United Kingdom, and the United States. Strong uncertainty avoidance scores, for example, are found in Greece, Portugal, Guatemala, Uruguay, Belgium, El Salvador, and Japan (see Table 3.3).

Table 3.3 Value Characteristics in Weak and Strong Uncertainty Avoidance (U.A.) Cultures		
Situations	**Weak U.A. Cultures**	**Strong U.A. Cultures**
General:	Uncertainty Is Valued	Uncertainty Is a Threat
Family:	Dynamic and Changing	Reinforce Family Rules
Relationship:	High Mobility	Low Mobility
School:	Challenges Are Welcome	Routines Are Welcome
Workplace:	Encourage Risk Taking	Encourage Clear Procedure
Communication:	Conflict Can Be Positive	Conflict Is Negative
Personality Equivalence:	High Tolerance for Ambiguity	Low Tolerance for Ambiguity

While members in weak uncertainty avoidance family situations prefer informal rules to guide their behavior, members in high uncertainty avoidance family situations tend to prefer formal structure and formal rules. Rules and laws are established to counteract uncertainties in social interaction. In *weak uncertainty avoidance family situations*, roles and behavioral expectations are actively negotiated. Children are given more latitude to explore their own values and morals. In *strong uncertainty avoidance family situations*, family roles are clearly established and family rules are expected to be followed closely. In *weak uncertainty avoidance work situations*, there is a greater tolerance of innovative ideas and behavior. Conflict is also viewed as a natural part of organizational productivity. In *strong uncertainty avoidance work situations*, there is a greater resistance to deviant and innovative ideas. Career mobility is high in weak uncertainty avoidance cultures, whereas career stability is a desired end goal in strong uncertainty avoidance cultures.

Hofstede (1991) uses the following statements to represent the basic characteristics of *strong uncertainty avoidance organizations:* (1) most organizations would be better off if conflict could be eliminated; (2) it is important for a manager to have at hand precise answers to most of the questions that subordinates may raise about their work; and (3) when the respective roles of the members of a department become complex, detailed job descriptions are essential. Members of strong uncertainty avoidance organizations tend to score high on these statements; members of weak uncertainty avoidance organizations tend to score low on them.

Sex Roles: Feminine-Masculine Value Pattern

In reviewing your answer from Know Thyself 3.1 to situation four about toys preference, if you checked (4a), your value pattern tends toward the "feminine" value pole. If you checked (4b), your value pattern tends toward the "masculine" value pole. Distinctive female and male organizational behavior differences are found on the feminine-masculine value dimension. **Femininity** pertains to societies in which social gender roles are fluid and can overlap—that is, whatever a woman can do, a man can do; likewise, both women and men are supposed to be modest, observant, and tender, and they are concerned with the ecological quality of their environment (Hofstede, 1991). **Masculinity** pertains to societies in which social gender roles are clearly complementary and distinct. Namely, men are supposed to be assertive, masculine, tough, and focused on task-based accomplishment and material success, whereas women are supposed to be more modest, feminine, tender, and concerned with the quality of life (Hofstede, 1991).

"Feminine" cultures emphasize flexible sex role behaviors and "masculine" cultures emphasize complementary sex-role domains. Sweden, Norway, the Netherlands, Denmark, Costa Rica, Yugoslavia, and Finland, for example, have high femininity scores. Comparatively, Japan, Austria, Venezuela, Italy, Switzerland, Mexico, and Ireland, for example, have high masculinity scores. The United States ranks 15th on the masculine scale (i.e., closer to the masculine value pattern) out of the 50 countries and three regions studied (Hofstede, 1998).

Historical roots and family socialization processes concerning gender roles shape the development of the feminine-masculine dimension. In "feminine" families, both boys and girls learn to be caring and concerned with both facts and feelings. In "masculine" families, boys learn to be assertive, tough, and ambitious, but girls learn to be nurturing and relational-based. "Feminine" families stress the importance of quality-of-life issues. "Masculine" families are achievement and success oriented. A "feminine" workplace merges male and female roles flexibly. A "masculine" workplace differentiates male and female roles clearly. A "feminine" organization tends to emphasize quality of work life and family balance issues above and beyond business performance, whereas a "masculine" organization tends to emphasize the important role of business performance and gross profits (see Table 3.4). By implication, when one communicates in a "feminine" organizational culture, one should be sensitive to the flexible sex-role norms and roles in that workplace. When one communicates in a "masculine" organizational culture, one should be mindful of the norms and rules of complementary sex-role behaviors in the system. In working for a "feminine" organization, one should be more mindful of the importance of quality of work/life balance issues. In working for a "masculine" culture, one should focus more on business achievements and tangible results-based performance.

Cultural values are deposits of wisdom that are passed from one generation to the next. Simultaneously, they also can serve as cultural blinders to alternative ways of thinking, feeling, motivating, and relating. Even though cultural values serve many useful functions, such as those of identity maintenance, explanatory, and group solidarity functions, they also reinforce various habitual practices and norms of communicating.

Table 3.4 Value Characteristics in "Feminine" and "Masculine" Cultures		
Situations	**"Feminine" Cultures**	**"Masculine" Cultures**
General:	Flexible Sex Roles	Complementary Sex Roles
Family:	Emphasize Nurturance	Emphasize Achievement
Relationship:	Both Take Initiatives	Males Take Initiatives
School:	Social Adjustment Is Critical	Academic Performance Is Critical
Workplace:	Work in Order to Live	Live in Order to Work
Communication:	Fluid Gender Communication	"Masculine" Toughness and "Feminine" Softness
Personality Equivalence:	Overlapped Gender Roles	Clear Masculine-Feminine Gender Roles

Additional Value Orientation Patterns

Before proceeding to our discussion about the four additional value orientations, take a few moments to answer the questions in Know Thyself 3.3.

Know Thyself 3.3   Discovering Personal Value Orientations

Instructions: Read each set of statements and check (a), (b), or (c) in each set. The check means the statement sounds very much like your own value preference.

1. _____ a. I feel useless if I am not doing something constructive every day.

   _____ b. I prefer to enjoy life with my full five senses present in each waking moment.

   _____ c. Developing an inner understanding of who I am is more important than any other tangible accomplishment.

2. _____ a. I believe we, as human beings, have a great deal of decision-making power in how we shape and manage our life's destiny.

   _____ b. In my everyday life, I strive to live simply and flow with it, which is closer to the natural world.

   _____ c. I believe that no matter how much we try to plan and control things, a variety of forces operate beyond us and direct our destiny.

3. _____ a. I tend to keep lists of schedules and tasks that I need to accomplish today and tomorrow.

   _____ b. I tend to "go with the flow." Worrying about the past or future is a waste of my time and energy.

   _____ c. I tend to respect older people for their life experience and wisdom.

4. _____ a. I feel very uncomfortable when an acquaintance stands too close to me.

   _____ b. While I don't like people standing too close to me, I can tolerate it and not get too stressed out.

   _____ c. I actually enjoy people standing close to me. I can be quite at ease when conversing with them.

Scoring: Your answers to the above statements should increase your awareness of your personal value orientation preferences.

Scoring Interpretation:

1a = Doing	1b = Being	1c = Being-in-Becoming
2a = Controlling	2b = Harmonizing	2c = Yielding
3a = Future	3b = Present	3c = Past
4a = High Privacy	4b = Medium Privacy	4c = Low Privacy

You may want to circle and label all your answers. You will get an initial review of your personal value orientations.

Interpretation: Please continue to read your text under the "Additional Value Orientation Patterns" section for further interpretations.

Value Orientations: Background Information

On the basis of their research on Navajo Indians, Latino/as, and European Americans in the Southwest, Kluckhohn and Strodtbeck (1961) proposed a set of universal questions that human beings consciously or unconsciously seek to answer. In addition, the famous cross-cultural anthropologist Edward T. Hall (1966, 1983) also emphasized the study of time and space in conjunction with understanding issues in culture and communication. These intercultural experts observed that human beings in all cultures face this set of common human problems or existential questions. Of the set of proposed questions, the following four questions are the most relevant to our understanding of complementary value patterns: (1) What do people consider as meaningful or worthwhile in their everyday activity? (activity value orientation); (2) What is the relationship between people and nature? (destiny, people-nature relation value orientation); (3) What is the time focus of human life? (temporal value orientation); and (4) How do people structure their everyday spatial arrangements? (spatial value orientation).

The value orientations approach assumes that the above questions are universal ones and that all human beings seek answers to these inquiries. The answers or solutions to these questions are available in all cultures. However, some cultures have a stronger preference for one particular set of answers than for others. The solutions represent the cumulative wisdom or survival mechanisms of a particular culture passed from one generation to the next. The range of potential solutions to these four questions is shown in Figure 3.1.

Figure 3.1: Four Value Orientation Patterns

ORIENTATION	RANGE		
MEANING	Doing (Action-Oriented)	Being-in-Becoming (Inner Development)	Being (Emotional Vitality)
DESTINY	Controlling Nature (Mastering)	Harmony with Nature (Flow)	Subjugation to Nature (Yielding)
TIME	Future-Oriented (Schedule-Bound)	Present-Oriented (Here-and-Now)	Past-Oriented (Tradition-Bound)
SPACE	Privacy-Centered	Moderate Privacy	Communal-Centered

Source: Adapted from Strodbeck (1961) and Kohls (1996).

Meaning: Doing-Being Activity Value Orientation

What do people consider as meaningful—doing or being—in this particular cultural community? The activity orientation further asks: Is human activity in the culture focused on the doing, being, or being-in-becoming mode? The **"doing" solution** means achievement-oriented activities. The **"being" solution** means living with emotional vitality. The **"being-in-becoming"** mode means living with an emphasis on spiritual renewal and connection.

Middle-class African Americans, Asian Americans, Latino/a Americans, and European Americans focus on a "doing" or an achievement-oriented solution, but Native Americans tend to focus on the "being-in-becoming" mode (Sue & Sue, 1990). However, the "doing" preference is manifested quite differently among the European American, African American, Chicano/a, Asian American, and Latino/a American groups.

For example, a "doing" solution among African Americans and Chicano/as means to fight against adversity and to combat racism through social achievements and activism for the good of the community. The "doing" mode among Asian and Latino/a immigrants in the United States is typically associated with working hard and making money to fulfill basic obligations toward family and extended family networks. A "doing" mode among European Americans is the focus on tangible accomplishments for personal satisfaction.

Furthermore, traditional Africans and African Americans also display a "being" solution for living. They attach positive meanings to a sense of aliveness, emotional vitality, and openness of feelings. African American culture is infused with "a spirit (a knowledge that there is more to life than sorrow, which will pass) and a renewal in sensuousness, joy, and laughter. This symbol has its roots in African culture and expresses the soul and rhythm of that culture in America" (Hecht, Collier, & Ribeau, 1993, p. 103). Likewise, Latino/a Americans emphasize the "being" vitality solution. Many traditional Latino/as subscribe to the "being" mode of activity, which means enjoying the moment to the fullest. Shared celebrations and recreation with close friends and family members often form a sacred part of a Latino/a's lifestyle.

For many traditional Native American groups, the preferred choice is the "being-in-becoming" mode. Many Native American cultures are oriented toward religious and spiritual preservation. They are concerned with spiritual well-being more than material well-being. Spiritual self-renewal and enrichment are much more important to them than tangible gains and losses. It is also critical to remember that there are 505 federally recognized tribes with 252 different languages. Because each tribe has its own traditions, beliefs, and values, the term "Native American" is a broad-based one.

Destiny: Controlling-Yielding People-Nature Value Orientation

The destiny value orientation asks this question: Is the relationship between people and the natural (or supernatural) environment one of control, harmony, or subordination? Many middle-class European Americans tend to believe in mastery and control over the natural environment. By *controlling their environment*, they can also increase their productivity and efficiency in accumulating material security and personal comfort. If something goes wrong in a system or organization, they believe they can fix it, change it, or master it. For example, when seven crew members perished in the space shuttle Columbia disaster, individuals who endorse a strong "controlling" solution believed that the disaster could have been prevented if only the mechanical flaw were detected earlier and fixed accordingly.

Buddhist cultures, such as those of Bhutan, Laos, Thailand, and Tibet, tend to emphasize strongly the *harmony-with-nature* or *"flowing" value solution*. Their outlook on life tends to emphasize spiritual transformation or enlightenment rather than material gain. Many ethnocultural groups (such as African, Asian, Latino/a, and Native American) in the United States tend to believe in living harmoniously with nature. Many Native American groups, for example, believe that what is human, what is nature, and what is spirit are all extensions of one another. We should learn to live harmoniously with one another because we are all creatures of the same universe.

In contrast, many Polynesian cultures, Middle Eastern cultures, and Indian cultures subscribe to the *subjugation-to-nature* or *"yielding" value solution*. Natural disasters such as earthquakes, volcano eruptions, and floods may have contributed to their belief that nature is a powerful force that is beyond the control of individuals (see Snapshot 3.1). The best way to deal with nature is to pay respect to it and act humbly in the face of cataclysmic external forces. Individuals who endorse a strong "yielding" value solution would tend to believe that the Columbia tragedy was predestined and the fate of the seven crew members was sealed from the beginning. Or, think of fires that burned in Southern California during the Fall of 2003. They destroyed over a million acres of land, and over 3,500 houses were burned down or destroyed. But some families and individuals refused to leave their property despite being in danger. Some of them believed they were in the hand of fate or "Mother Nature." All together, 24 lives were lost in those raging fires ("San Diego Wildfires," 2004).

After experiencing centuries of tragedies, wars, and natural disasters, generations of people who have lived in similar disaster-prone cultural communities tend to be more fatalistic in their cultural beliefs. For them, the destiny of life is to "submit" to the supernatural forces that shape their life cycles. These individuals may try their best to meet certain life goals and dreams; however, in the back in their minds, they also believe the power of a supernatural force or fate can strike anytime, anywhere. One current example is people of the swamplands in Louisiana. According to Rick Bragg (2002), generations of families have lived on a tiny island in Louisiana, the Isle de Jean Charles. Currently, only 230 individuals remain there because the surrounding water is swallowing this island. It is sinking, and people have watched water rising onto gardens, baseball sandlots, and backyards. Residents, however, have no intention of leaving. They would rather live ankle deep in the muddy waters than abandon a place they have been living in for generations. They would rather yield to Mother Nature and let fate take over than use a more controlling or action-oriented attitude by moving away from their beloved community.

When tornadoes hit, it is difficult to control "Mother Nature."

Take another example: East Indian culture, which emphasizes the *law of karma*. **Karma** involves fatalism, which has shaped the Indian philosophical view of life over the centuries. In its simplest form, the law of karma states that happiness or sorrow is the predetermined effect of actions committed by the person either in a present life or in one of his or her numerous past lives. Things do not happen because we make them happen. Things happen because they are *destined* to happen. We can only try so much, and then we should "yield" to our fate or karma.

The implication of this value orientation is that although some individuals believe in gaining control over their environment, others believe in the importance of living harmoniously or submissively in relationship to their natural habitat. People who tend to believe in controlling nature would have a stronger sense of the "self-over-nature" approach in dealing with their surroundings. People who tend to subscribe to the "self-with-nature" or "self-under-nature" viewpoint would have a more harmonious or fatalistic approach in dealing with their outer surroundings.

When individuals from different "people-nature" solutions come together, intercultural problems may arise. Individuals from one cultural group are eager to "fix" the environment with huge projects by building dams, levees, and reservoirs, but another cultural group may be deeply offended because the action may provoke the anger of the spirits that inhabit the river being dammed or the terrain being inundated. Flexible adjustment and cultural sensitivity are needed for both cultural parties to reach common ground in their collaborative efforts.

Time: Future-Past Temporal Value Orientation

The time-sense orientation asks this question: Is the temporal focus in the culture based on the future, present, or past? The **future-oriented time sense** means planning for desirable short- to medium-term developments and setting out clear objectives to realize them. The **present-oriented time sense** means valuing the here and now, especially the interpersonal relationships that are unfolding currently. The **past-oriented time sense** means honoring historic and ancestral ties plus respecting the wisdom of the elders.

Those who subscribe to the future value solution (e.g., middle-class European Americans) tend to deemphasize the past, move forward boldly to the immediate future, and strongly emphasize the importance of "futurism" (e.g., the glorification of the youth culture and devaluation of aging). Latino/a Americans tend to have a strong affective response to the present experience. Asian immigrants and Native Americans tend to revere the past.

Many Africans and African Americans tend to embrace a combination of past-present value solution. For many Africans and African Americans, people and activities in the present assume a higher priority than an external clock schedule (Asante & Asante, 1990). As Pennington (1990) observed, "Time is conceived [for Africans] only as it is related to events, and it must be experienced in order to make sense or to become real. The mathematical division of time observed by Westerners has little relevance for Africans" (p. 131). In traditional African societies, people tend to emphasize that something is experienced only at the present moment and that the past and the ancestors are indispensable in giving meaning to one's present existence. Likewise, the larger French culture has been classified as reflecting the "past-present" value solutions. For African Americans and the French, the past looms as a large historical canvas with which to understand the present.

In addition, for many Vietnamese American immigrants, their past profoundly influences their present identities. Many first-generation Vietnamese Americans believe in the Buddhist precepts of karma and rebirth. They believe that an individual life cycle is predetermined by good and evil deeds from a previous life. Their hope is to achieve eventual spiritual enlightenment. Oftentimes, ancestors are worshiped for four generations after death.

Many Mexican Americans, in contrast, prefer to experience life and people around them fully in the present. This outlook may be derived from the influence of a traditional cultural belief in the concept of "limited good." In fact, this is the belief that "there is only so much good in the world and, therefore, only so much good is possible in any one person's life" (Locke, 1992, p. 140). Experiencing the rhythms of life in the present and temporarily forgetting about the day's worries is a learned cultural art. Living life fully and relating to family and friends through meaningful connections make intuitive sense to many traditionally oriented Mexicans or Mexican Americans (Hecht, Ribeau, & Sedano, 1990).

A potential clash can develop between members of business groups with different time orientations, for example, between members who favor a "past-present" focus and members who favor a "future" focus. Business members from the first group want to view everything from the company's history and tradition, but members from the latter group want to bypass the past and plan ahead efficiently for an immediate future. Individuals with a "past-present" focus have a long-term view of time, whereas individuals with a "future" focus have a short-term to medium-term view of time.

Space: Privacy-Communal Spatial Value Orientation

Space and time are boundary regulation issues because we, as humans, are territorial animals. Our primary identities are tied closely with our claimed territories. The spatial value orientation question asks: What is the spatial value emphasis in this particular culture—*high spatial privacy, moderate,* or *low*? On a psychological level, this value orientation also addresses the issue of cross-cultural psychological privacy.

When our territories (e.g., extending from our home down to our personal space) are "invaded," our identities perceive threats and experience emotional vulnerability. Protective territory or sacred space satisfies our needs for human security and inclusion. *Proxemic studies* examine the functions and regulation of interpersonal space in different cultures. Claiming a space for oneself means injecting one's sense of identity or personhood into a place. For instance, we often use object markers, such as a book, coat, and backpack, to mark or claim our favorite chair or table in a classroom, coffee shop, movie theater, or library.

What constitutes appropriate personal distance for one cultural group can be perceived as crowding by another group. The average conversational distance or personal space for European Americans is approximately 20 inches—which means relatively high spatial privacy need. For some Latin American and Caribbean cultural groups (e.g., Costa Ricans, Puerto Ricans, Bahamians, and Jamaicans), however, the average personal space is approximately 14 to 15 inches. For the Saudi, the ideal conversational distance between two individuals is approximately 9 to 10 inches—which means relatively low spatial privacy need.

When Arabs overstep the personal spatial boundary of European Americans, they are often considered rude and intrusive. However, Arab negotiators frequently find European Americans to be aloof, cold, and standoffish. Personal space often serves as a hidden dimension of intercultural misunderstanding and discomfort (Hall, 1966). For high spatial privacy people, the need for a well-defined personal space is strong. This personal space marks a protective territory (see more detailed discussions in Chapter 8), which they will defend strongly. Low spatial privacy people may have come from a family or cultural region that is high in population density. Thus, they are used to "crowding" or spatial intrusion in social interaction settings. Although members of all cultures engage in the claiming of space for themselves or for the collective effort, the experience of spaciousness and crowdedness and the perception of space violation vary from one culture to the next. Concepts of territory and identity are intertwined because we usually invest lots of time, emotion, energy, and self-worth in places that we claim as our primary territories.

Spatial regulation is an unconscious nonverbal behavior that reflects larger, underlying cultural values. However, different spatial privacy needs may cause more unintentional culture clashes because of their pervasive influence in our everyday lives. From proxemic conversational distance issues to a powerful means of marking ingroup and outgroup boundaries, these spatial privacy needs all reflect personal to communal territorial claims and defensiveness. In Chapter 8, we will take up some of these fascinating nonverbal concepts. Taken together, we believe that these four additional value orientations— meaning, destiny, time, and space—all shape our outlook on intercultural verbal and nonverbal communication.

Individual Socialization Development

Beyond cultural-ethnic group membership values, individuals develop distinctive personal identities due to unique life histories, experiences, and personality traits. We develop our personal identities—our conception as a unique individual or a "unique self"—via our observations of role models around us and our own drives, relational experiences, cultural experiences, and identity construction. To examine individualism-collectivism on an individual level of analysis, Markus and Kitayama (1991) coined the terms *independent construal of self* and *interdependent construal of self*. Before you read on, take a few minutes and fill out the brief survey in Know Thyself 3.4. The survey is designed to find out how you generally think of yourself and your connection with members of groups to which you belong.

Know Thyself 3.4 Assessing Your Independent Versus Interdependent Self-Construal Traits

Instructions: Recall how you generally feel and act in various situations. Let your first inclination be your guide and circle the number in the scale that best reflects your overall impression of yourself. The following scale is used for each item:

4 =	YES!	=	*strongly agree—IT'S ME!*
3 =	yes	=	*moderately agree—it's kind of like me*
2 =	no	=	*moderately disagree—it's kind of not me*
1 =	NO!	=	*strongly disagree—IT'S NOT ME!*

	YES!	yes	no	NO!
1. Feeling emotionally connected with others is an important part of my self-definition.	4	3	2	1
2. I believe I should be judged on my own accomplishments.	4	3	2	1
3. My family and close relatives are important to who I am.	4	3	2	1
4. I value my personal privacy above everyone else's.	4	3	2	1
5. I often consult my close friends for advice before acting.	4	3	2	1
6. I prefer to be self-reliant rather than depend on others.	4	3	2	1
7. My close friendship groups are important to my well-being.	4	3	2	1
8. I often assume full responsibility for my own actions.	4	3	2	1
9. I enjoy depending on others for emotional support.	4	3	2	1
10. My personal identity is very important to me.	4	3	2	1

Scoring: Add up the scores on all the even-numbered items and you will find your independent self-construal score. *Independent Self-Construal* score: _____. Add up the scores on all the odd-numbered items and you will find your interdependent self- construal score. *Interdependent Self-Construal* score: _____.

Interpretation: Scores on each personality dimension can range from 5 to 20; the higher the score, the more independent and/or interdependent you are. If the scores are similar on both personality dimensions, you are a biconstrual personality individual.

Reflection Probes: Take a moment to think of the following questions: Have your self-construals changed throughout the years? What factors shape your independent or interdependent self-construals? Do you like your own independent and/or interdependent self-construals? Why or why not?

Source: Scale adapted from Gudykunst et al. (1996).

Independent Versus Interdependent Self-Construal

The terms *independent self-construal* and *interdependent self-construal* (Markus & Kitayama, 1991, 1994) refer to the degree to which people conceive of themselves as separate or connected to others, respectively. The **independent construal of self** involves the view that an individual is a unique entity with an individuated repertoire of feelings, cognitions, and motivations. Individuals with high independent self-construals tend to view themselves as distinct and unique from others and from the context. They use their own abilities and ideas as motivational bases rather than the thoughts and feelings of others. People who have high independent self-construals value personal achievement, self-direction, and competition. When communicating with others, high independents believe in striving for personal goals, being in control of their environment, and expressing their needs assertively. Independent self-construal types tend to predominate in individualistic cultures or ethnic groups (Gudykunst et al., 1996).

The **interdependent construal of self,** on the other hand, involves an emphasis on the importance of fitting in with relevant others and ingroup connectedness (Markus & Kitayama, 1991). People who have high interdependent self-construals strive to fit in with others, act in a proper manner, value conformity, and emphasize relational connections. When communicating with others, individuals with interdependent self-construals aim for relational harmony, avoid direct conflicts, and interact in a diplomatic, tactful manner. Interdependent self-construal types tend to predominate in collectivistic cultures or ethnic groups (Gudykunst et al., 1996).

Independent-self individuals tend to be found in individualistic societies, and interdependent-self individuals tend to be located in collectivistic societies. People of independent self-construal value the ideals, goals, motivations, and identity negotiation process of an "unencumbered self." In comparison, people of interdependent self-construal value the ideals, goals, motivations, and emotions of a "connected self." This connected self binds the person to his family, extended family, reference group, neighborhood, village, or caste group. While the independent self emphasizes the basis of the individual as the fundamental unit of interaction, the interdependent self emphasizes relationship or the ingroup as the basic focus of social interaction.

Horizontal Versus Vertical Self-Construal

Before you continue reading, fill out the Know Thyself 3.5 assessment. The survey assesses your horizontal versus vertical personality tendency. Parallel to the above self-construal idea, we can examine power distance from an individual level of analysis. Individuals and their behaviors can be conceptualized as moving toward either the "horizontal self" or the "vertical self" end of the spectrum.

Know Thyself 3.5   Assessing Your Horizontal Versus Vertical Personality Traits

Instructions: Recall how you generally feel and act in various situations. Let your first inclination be your guide and circle the number in the scale that best reflects your overall impression of yourself. The following scale is used for each item:

4 = **YES!** =	*strongly agree*—**IT'S ME!**	
3 = yes =	*moderately agree*—it's kind of like me	
2 = no =	*moderately disagree*—it's kind of not me	
1 = **NO!** =	*strongly disagree*—**IT'S NOT ME!**	

	YES!	yes	no	NO!
1. I generally obey my parents' rules without question.	4	3	2	1
2. I believe in respecting people's abilities—not their age or rank.	4	3	2	1
3. I believe teachers should be respected.	4	3	2	1
4. I respect people who are competent—not their roles or titles.	4	3	2	1
5. I believe people who are older are usually wiser.	4	3	2	1
6. I believe all people should have equal opportunities to compete for what they want.	4	3	2	1
7. I think older siblings should take care of their younger siblings.	4	3	2	1
8. I believe families should encourage their children to challenge their parents' opinions.	4	3	2	1
9. I value the advice of my parents or older relatives.	4	3	2	1
10. I respect parents who encourage their children to speak up.	4	3	2	1

Scoring: Add up the scores on all the even-numbered items and you will find your horizontal self score. *Horizontal Self* score: _____. Add up the scores on all the odd numbered items and you will find your vertical self score. *Vertical Self* score: _____.

Interpretation: Scores on each personality dimension can range from 5 to 20; the higher the score, the more horizontal and/or vertical you are. If the scores are similar on both personality dimensions, you have both personality traits.

Reflection Probes: Think of your own family system some more. Do your parents encourage you to speak up and express your emotions? Do they enforce family rules flexibly or strictly? Do you like all the family rules? Or do you rebel against them? Discuss your family socialization experience and family rules with a classmate.

Individuals who endorse **horizontal self-construal** prefer informal-symmetrical interactions (i.e., equal treatment) regardless of people's position, status, rank, or age. They prefer to approach an intercultural problem directly and use impartial standards to resolve the problem. In contrast, individuals who emphasize **vertical self-construal** prefer formal-asymmetrical interactions (i.e., differential treatment) with due respect to people's position, titles, life experiences, and age. They apply a "case by case" standard to assess the right or wrong behaviors in accordance with the roles occupied in the hierarchical network.

The different power distance personality types mean that people will seek different kinds of relationships, and when possible, "convert" a relationship to the kind with which they are most comfortable. Thus, a professor from a horizontal-based self-construal may convert a professor-student relationship to a friend-friend relationship, which may well confuse a student from a vertical-based self-construal (Triandis, 1995), who expects a larger power distance in professor-student interaction.

Internal Versus External Locus of Control

Let's check out whether you prefer to control your destiny, or you yield to your fate. Fill out the brief assessment in Know Thyself 3.6.

Know Thyself 3.6   Assessing Your Internal Versus External Locus of Control

Instructions: Recall how you generally feel and act in various situations. Let your first inclination be your guide and circle the number in the scale that best reflects your overall impression of yourself. The following scale is used for each item:

4 = YES!	=	*strongly agree*—IT'S ME!
3 = yes	=	*moderately agree*—it's kind of like me
2 = no	=	*moderately disagree*—it's kind of not me
1 = NO!	=	*strongly disagree*—IT'S NOT ME!

	YES!	yes	no	NO!
1. I believe I'm the master of my own destiny.	4	3	2	1
2. I generally yield to my luck or fate in doing things.	4	3	2	1
3. I am driven by my own motivation and effort.	4	3	2	1
4. "Mother Nature" is usually in charge, and wins.	4	3	2	1
5. I am in charge of my own future and planning.	4	3	2	1
6. I believe it is difficult to transcend fate.	4	3	2	1
7. I believe personal willpower can conquer everything.	4	3	2	1

☞

☞

Know Thyself 3.6 Assessing Your Internal versus External Locus of Control (*continued*)				
8. I do my best and then let fate take over.	4	3	2	1
9. I believe I have complete control of what will happen tomorrow.	4	3	2	1
10. Life is unpredictable—the best we can do is to flow with our fate.	4	3	2	1

Scoring: Add up the scores on all the odd-numbered items and you will find your internal locus of control score. *Internal Locus of Control* score: _____. Add up the scores on all the even-numbered items and you will find your external locus of control score. *External Locus of Control* score: _____.

Interpretation: Scores on each locus of control can range from 5 to 20; the higher the score, the more internal and/or external you are. If the scores are similar on both personality dimensions, you subscribe to both personality traits.

Reflection Probes: Think of the major decisions in your life (e.g., where to go to college, where to live, buying a car, or whom to date), and reflect on the following questions: Where did you learn your self-determination attitude? Or where did you learn your yielding attitude? How do you think your locus of control attitude influences your everyday decision making? What do you think are some of the strengths and limitations of being a high-internal locus of control person or a high-external locus of control person?

Locus of control reflects the destiny value orientation (control vs. yielding) on the cultural level. In terms of the locus of control personality dimension, there are two personality types: internal and external (Rotter, 1966). Internal locus of control individuals have a strong mastery-over-nature tendency, and external locus of control individuals have a strong yielding-fatalistic tendency.

Individuals with **internal locus of control** tend to emphasize free will, individual motivation, personal effort, and personal responsibility over the success or failure of an assignment. In comparison, individuals with **external locus of control** emphasize external determinism, karma, fate, and external forces shaping a person's life happenings and events. Internal locus of control is parallel to the notion of mastery over nature (i.e., controlling value), and external locus of control is parallel to the notion of subordination to nature (i.e., yielding value). Internal-locus individuals believe in the importance of free will and internal control of one's fate. External-locus individuals believe in trying their best and then letting fate take over.

Some individuals plan their actions in terms of the internal locus of control tendency, and others contemplate their life events along the external locus of control tendency. Perceived control of one's destiny exists in varying degrees in an individual, across situations and across cultures (Rotter, 1966). In terms of gender socialization differences, for example, males tend to endorse internal locus of control, and females tend to endorse external locus of control in a wide variety of cultures (Smith, Dugan, & Trompenaars, 1996). The translation is that males in many cultures are more motivated by internal drives and a doing/fixing approach, and females tend to be more contextual and being-oriented in their attempt to flow with their external environment.

To engage in competent identity-support work, we have to increase our awareness and accuracy levels in assessing others' group membership and personal identity issues. There are many more identities (e.g., e.net, social class, sexual orientation, age, disability) that people bring into an interaction. However, for the purposes of this interculturally focused book, we shall emphasize cultural and ethnic identity issues and their relationship to communication.

Intercultural Toolkit: Recaps and Checkpoints

This chapter has reviewed eight value patterns that we (the authors) believe can explain some major differences and similarities that exist between clusters of cultures on a global level. The four value dimension patterns are individualism-collectivism, power distance, uncertainty avoidance, and feminine-masculine. The additional four value orientations are meaning, destiny, time, and space value patterns.

We have also identified distinctive personality types that carry their own unique stamps in their communication styles. We will be using these eight cultural value patterns and some of the unique personality styles to discuss and explain a variety of intercultural communication behaviors and relationships in the next few chapters.

To start off, to be a flexible intercultural communicator at the values clarification level, here are some recommended guidelines and skills:

- When entering a new culture, learn to practice the mindful O-D-I-S method. The mindful O-D-I-S method refers to mindful observation, description, interpretations, and suspending ethnocentric evaluations.

- Rather than engaging in snapshot, negative evaluations, O-D-I-S analysis is a slowing-down process that involves learning to *observe* attentively—the verbal *and* nonverbal signals that are being exchanged in the communication process. Skipping the mindful observation process when confronted with different patterns of behavior often leads to biased interpretations and ineffective intercultural communication.

- After patient mindful observation, we should then try to *describe* mentally and in behaviorally specific terms (e.g., "She is not maintaining eye contact with me when speaking to me" or "He is standing about six inches from me while we're conversing") what is going on in the intercultural interaction. Description is a clear report of what we have observed, including a minimum of distortion. It also means refraining from adding any evaluative meaning to the observed behavior.

- Next, we should generate *multiple interpretations* (e.g., "Maybe from her cultural value framework, eye contact avoidance is a respectful behavior; from my cultural perspective, this is considered a disrespectful sign") to make sense of the behavior we are observing and describing. Interpretation is what we think about what we see and hear. The important thing to keep in mind is that there can be multiple interpretations (e.g., "she is shy," "she is just doing her cultural thing," or "she is being disrespectful") for any description of an observed behavior.

- We may decide to respect the differences and *suspend* our ethnocentric evaluation. We may also decide to engage in open-ended evaluation (e.g., "I understand that eye contact avoidance may be a cultural habit of this person, but I still don't like it because I feel uncomfortable in such interaction") by acknowledging our discomfort with unfamiliar behaviors. Evaluations are positive or negative judgments (e.g., "I like the fact that she is keeping part of her cultural norms" or "I don't like it because I've been raised in a culture that values the use of direct eye contact") concerning the interpretation(s) we attribute to the behavior.

- Additionally, learn to observe a wide range of people in a wide range of situations in the new cultural setting before making any premature generalizations about the people's behavior in that culture. For example, we may want to observe a wide variety of people (and in a wide range of contexts) from this cultural group to check if eye contact avoidance is a cultural custom or an individual trait. ✦

Chapter 4

What Are the Keys to Understanding Cultural and Ethnic Identities?

Chapter Outline

What does it mean to be Black? . . . My mom worked long hours and she worked so very hard all her life so that she could send me to a private school. I did in fact have some Black friends but not as many as I would have liked. Does this mean I don't consider myself Black? NO! Not at all. I see myself as Black and I love being Black. But I don't know much of Black history. What I know is just the surface, and what I NEED to know is the core. What makes me sad is, I am considered to be the White girl in my family. It saddens me because they don't know my struggle deep inside. Yes, I wish I were strong in being more "ethnic," but I'm not and that scares me. Am I blind? Do I not have a place in this society?

—Lanitra, *College Student*

> **I** was quite naive growing up and not knowing all the hardships of my ethnic and cultural background. After going to college, I started immersing myself in learning about my ethnic traditions and history and getting to know myself more. I have now taken courses that deal with Chicanos and Mexican Americans. I have just now begun to accept the balance between the two. I find myself calling myself an Americanized Mexican.
>
> —Rafael, *College Student*

Individuals acquire and develop their identities through interaction with others in their cultural group. Through interaction with others on a daily basis, we acquire the meanings, values, norms, and styles of communicating. The above two scenarios highlight two very common questions we ask ourselves: Who am I? and Who are you? The struggle to answer both questions is profoundly influenced by our cultural socialization, family socialization, and acculturation and identity change processes. For many, the result is a struggle between an individual's perception of being "different" coupled with the inability to blend with both the mainstream culture and the ethnic heritage group. Although culture plays the larger role in shaping our view of ourselves, it is through multiple channels that we acquire and develop our own ethics, values, norms, and ways of behaving in our everyday lives. For example, through the direct channel of family, values and norms are transmitted and passed on from one generation to the next. Parents teach their children about right and wrong and teach acceptable or unacceptable ways of behaving through the words they use and through their role-modeling actions.

This chapter is organized into five main sections. We first explore the theme of family and gender socialization. We then discuss the content and salience (i.e., degree of importance) of cultural-ethnic identity issues. Third, we address the underlying factors that influence immigrants' acculturation process. We then explain two ethnic identity development models. Finally, we offer recaps and checkpoints for increasing your cultural self-awareness and cultural other-validation skills.

Family and Gender Socialization

Children in their early years internalize what to value and devalue, what to appreciate and reject, and what goals are important in their culture through the influence of their family system. Additionally, teenagers and young adults may be influenced, to a certain extent, by the pervasive messages from the popular culture and the contemporary media scenes. It is through pervasive cultural value patterns—as filtered through family and media systems—that persons define meanings and values of identities, such as ethnicity, gender, and identity types.

The term **identity** is used in this chapter as the reflective self-conception or self-image that we each derive from family, gender, cultural, ethnic, and individual socialization processes. It is acquired via our interaction with others in particular cultural scenes. Identity refers to our reflective views of ourselves and of other perceptions of our self-images—at both the social identity and the personal identity levels. Before you continue reading, fill out the Know Thyself 4.1 survey. The survey assesses how much your social and personal identities influence your everyday communication.

Know Thyself 4.1   Assessing the Importance of Your Social and Personal Identities

Instructions: The following items describe how people think about themselves and communicate in various situations. Let your first inclination be your guide and circle the number in the scale that best reflects your overall value. The following scale is used for each item:

$$4 = SA = \textit{Strongly Agree}$$
$$3 = MA = \textit{Moderately Agree}$$
$$2 = MD = \textit{Moderately Disagree}$$
$$1 = SD = \textit{Strongly Disagree}$$

	SA	MA	MD	SD
1. My group memberships (e.g., ethnic or gender) are important when I communicate with others.	4	3	2	1
2. My personality usually comes across loud and clear when I communicate.	4	3	2	1
3. I am aware of my own ethnic background or social roles when I communicate.	4	3	2	1
4. My personality has a stronger influence on my everyday interaction than any social roles.	4	3	2	1
5. I am aware of ethnic or gender role differences when I communicate.	4	3	2	1
6. I tend to focus on the unique characteristics of the individual when I communicate.	4	3	2	1
7. Some aspects of my ethnic or social roles always shape my communication.	4	3	2	1
8. I believe I can make a clear distinction between people's personal identity and social identity.	4	3	2	1

☞

**Know Thyself 4.1   Assessing the Importance of your
                              Social and Personal Identities (*continued*)**

☞   9. I prefer to see people as people and not in   4   3   2   1
            social role categories.

     10. My unique self is more important to me than   4   3   2   1
            my ethnic or cultural role self.

Scoring: Add up the scores on all the odd-numbered items and you will find your
social identity score. *Social Identity* score: _____. Add up the scores on all the
even- numbered items and you will find your personal identity score. *Personal Identity* score: _____.

Interpretation: Scores on each identity dimension can range from 5 to 20; the
higher the score, the more social and/or personal you are. If all the scores are similar on both identity dimensions, you emphasize the importance of both social and
personal identities in your everyday communication process.

Reflection Probes: In the first encounter with a stranger, do you usually try to
understand the social role identity or personal identity of the stranger? Why? Do
you primarily share your social role identity or personal role identity information
with a stranger? What factors (e.g., work situations, classroom situations, or attraction) usually prompt you to exchange either more social role data or more
personal identity data in your communication process?

Social identities can include cultural or ethnic membership identity, gender identity, sexual orientation identity, social class identity,
age identity, disability identity, or professional identity. **Personal identities,** however, can include any unique attributes that we associate
with our individuated self in comparison with those of others. In
collectivistic group-oriented cultures, for example, people may be
more concerned with communal or social-based identity issues. In
individualistic cultures, however, people may be more concerned with
individuation-based personal identity issues. Regardless of whether we
may or may not be conscious of these identities, they influence our
everyday behaviors in a generalized and particularized manner.

In this section, we explore some important ideas about family and
gender socialization processes. In the next section, we discuss cultural
and ethnic identity formation processes.

Family Socialization and Interaction Patterns

Family is the fundamental communication system in all cultures.
People in every culture are born into a network of family relationships.
First and foremost, we acquire some of the beliefs and values of our
culture via our primary family system. The rules that we acquire in
relating to our parents, grandparents, siblings, and extended families
contribute to the initial blueprint of our formation of role, gender, and
relational identities.

For example, through our family socialization process, we learn to deal with boundary issues, such as space and time. We also learn to deal with authority issues, such as gender-based decision-making activities (e.g., who did what household chores) and power dynamics (e.g., which parents or siblings held what power status). We also acquire the scripts for emotional expressiveness or restraint, as well as for nonverbal eloquence or stillness within our family system.

Families can be defined in many ways. Among them are traditional family, extended family, blended family, and single family. The **traditional family,** for example, consists of a husband-wife, father-mother pair with a child or children, a father working outside the home, and a homemaker-mother. In the United States, the traditional family is never the standard except for upper- and middle-class white heterosexuals. Historically, most U.S. families have had at least two wage earners. The **extended family,** on the other hand, consists of extended kinship groups, such as grandparents, aunt and uncles, cousins, and nieces and nephews. For example, Native Americans, Hawaiians, and Filipino families often include extended family networks that contain several households. These integrative households include parents, children, aunts, uncles, cousins, and grandparents. The **blended family** refers to the merging of different family systems from previous marriages. The **single family** refers to a household headed by a single parent. In many U.S. households, parents are single, and men and women can be single parents to their children.

We can also think of two possible family types in the family decision-making process: the personal family system and the positional family system. Some of the major characteristics of the **personal family system** include the emphasis on personal, individualized meanings, negotiable roles between parents and child, and the emphasis on interactive discussions within the family (Bernstein, 1971; Haslett, 1989). Democratic families try to emphasize different family members as unique individuals. Democratic parents are consultative in their decision-making process. They hold family meetings to solicit input in major family decision issues. They are explicit in their communication styles, and they encourage experimentation and individual initiative in their children. They try to foster individualistic and small power distance value patterns in the family system. They act more like friends to their children than authority figures (Guerrero Andersen, & Afifi, 2001).

Comparatively, the **positional family system** emphasizes communal meanings, ascribed roles and statuses between parents and child, and family rule conformity. Positional families emphasize the importance of holding the hierarchical power structure in the family exchange process. Individuals have different status-based authority and responsibilities in a positional family system. Authoritarian parents, from a positional family framework, are demanding and directive. They expect their children to obey family rules without question. They do not believe in explaining the reasons behind their disciplinary actions to their children (Guerrerro et al., 2001, p. 304). Many positional family systems exist in collectivistic, large power distance cultural regions (see Table 4.1).

Table 4.1	Characteristics of Personal Versus Positional Family Systems	
Personal Family System	**Positional Family System**
Individualized Meanings	Communal Meanings
Democratic Decision Making	Authoritarian Decision Making
Negotiable Roles	Conventional Roles
Children Can Question	Children Should Obey
Small Power Distance	Large Power Distance

Some of the collectivistic, large power distance themes in many Latino/a American family structures are *familism, personalism, hierarchy, spiritualism*, and *fatalism* (Ho, 1987). Briefly, **familism** refers to the deep commitment to family ties in the Latino/a family system. An individual's sense of self-worth and security is essentially drawn from the support of his or her family. The family is the strongest glue that holds together all social activities. During good times or crises, the family members' welfare and also the family name and reputation should always come first. **Personalism** refers to the inner qualities of a person that earn respect and social recognition from others. Maintaining self-respect and upholding one's dignity are essential to a Latino/a self-conception and self-presentation. *Hierarchy* refers to generational hierarchy and gender role hierarchy. **Generational hierarchy** means showing respect for older individuals in the family—parents for grandparents, children for parents, and younger siblings for older siblings. **Gender hierarchy** means traditional status role differences between males and females—with the male playing the dominant breadwinning role and the female playing the household nurturing role. The term *hierarchy* also applies to distinctive social class difference and differential treatments between upper-class families and lower-class families. In many societies, social class differences outweigh many other factors in shaping one's communication style and outlook. **Spiritualism** refers to the religious and spiritual convictions of many Latino/a Americans. Last, **fatalism** refers to the "being" attitude of some Latino/a Americans in perceiving their external environment with acceptance and resignation.

As a result of our interaction with our family and peers, we directly and indirectly acquire the various value patterns in our culture.

Although no single family can transmit all the value patterns in a culture, families who share similar cultural and ethnic ties do have some family value patterns in common. Family serves as the primary value socialization channel that creates a lasting imprint in our communicative behavior. It also cues our perceptions and interpretations concerning appropriate gendered-based interpersonal behaviors.

Gender Socialization and Interaction Patterns

The gender identities we learned as children affect our communication with others. They affect how we define ourselves, how we encode and decode gendered messages, how we develop intimate relationships, and how we relate to one another. Gender identity, in short, refers to the meanings and interpretations we hold concerning our self-images and expected other-images of femaleness and maleness.

For example, females in many cultures are expected to act in a nurturing manner, to be more affective, and to play the primary caregiver role. Males in many cultures are expected to act in a competitive manner, to be more emotionally reserved, and to play the breadwinner role. The orientations toward femaleness and maleness are grounded and learned via our own cultural and ethnic practices. Children learn appropriate gender roles through rewards and punishments they receive from their parents in performing the "proper" or "improper" gender-related behaviors. In the United States, feminine-based tendencies, such as interdependence, cooperation, and verbal relatedness, are often rewarded in girls, whereas masculine-based tendencies, such as independence, competition, and verbal assertiveness, are often promoted in boys.

Gender researchers observe that young girls and boys learn their gender-related behaviors in the home and school and in childhood games. For example, in the United States, girls' games (e.g., playing house, jump rope) tend to involve either pairs or small groups. The girls' games often involve fluid discussion about who is going to play what roles in the "playing house" game, for example, and usually promote relational collaboration. Boys' games (e.g., baseball, basketball), on the other hand, involve fairly large groups and have clear objectives, distinct roles and rules, and clear win-lose outcomes. The process of playing, rather than the win-lose outcome, is predominant in girls' games in the larger U.S. culture (Maltz & Borker, 1982; Tannen, 1994). From such research observations, one researcher (Wood, 1997) concludes that girls' games enable U.S. females to form the expectations that communication is used to create and maintain relationships and respond to others' feelings empathetically rather than for individual competitiveness. In contrast, boys' games prompt U.S. males to form the expectations that communication is used to achieve some clear outcomes, attract and maintain an audience, and compete with others for the "talk stage."

Moving beyond the U.S. cultural context, to illustrate, in traditional Mexican culture, child-rearing practices also differ significantly in socializing girls and boys. At the onset of adolescence, the difference between girls and boys becomes even more markedly apparent. The female is likely to remain much closer to home and to be "protected and guarded in her contact with others beyond the family. . . . The adolescent male, following the model of his father, is given much more freedom to come and go as he chooses and is encouraged to gain much worldly knowledge and experience outside the home" (Locke, 1992, p. 137). Gender identity and cultural-ethnic identity intersect and form part of an individual's composite self-conception.

Our gender identities are created, in part, via our communication with others. They are also supported and reinforced by the existing cultural structures and practices.

Cultural-Ethnic Identity Formation

Our family scripts and gender role expectations influence our evaluations of how females or males "should" or "should not" behave in a given situation. In addition, cultural and ethnic identities that we acquired during childhood and adolescent years influence whom we befriend, what holidays to celebrate, what language or dialect we are comfortable with, and what nonverbal styles we are at ease with in communicating with others.

In being aware of our multifaceted self-conception, we can also develop a deeper awareness of the complex, multifaceted identities of culturally different others. We begin our discussion with cultural identity.

Cultural Identity Conceptualization

All individuals are socialized within a larger cultural membership group. For example, everyone born and/or raised in the United States has some sense of being an "American" (in this book, to avoid ambiguity, we shall use the term "U.S. American"). However, minority group members or biracial members may need to answer the question "Where are you from?" more often than mainstream White Americans. Let's look at Gitanjali's (1994, p. 133) musing in Double Take 4.1.

Alternatively, if you are very comfortable with your own cultural identities, and more important, if you look like everyone else in the mainstream culture, you may not even notice the importance of your cultural membership badge until someone asks you: "What is your nationality?" or "Where do you come from?" in your overseas travels.

Before you continue, fill out the brief assessment in Know Thyself 4.2. This brief survey explores your sense of identification with the larger U.S. culture.

Double Take 4.1

Interview Excerpts:

What is your nationality?

I don't know.

I wish I had a dollar for every time someone asked that question.

What is your nationality?

Maybe it's just an obsession.

Yeah, maybe it's you!

What is your nationality?

My mother's a Zebra and my father's a Martian.

So, what's your nationality? Is it a secret?

Know Thyself 4.2 Assessing the Degree of Importance of Your Cultural Identity and Marginal Identity

Instructions: Recall how you generally feel and act in various situations. Let your first inclination be your guide and circle the number in the scale that best reflects your overall impression of yourself. The following scale is used for each item:

4 = **YES!** =	*strongly agree—***IT'S ME!**
3 = yes =	*moderately agree—it's kind of like me*
2 = no =	*moderately disagree—it's kind of not me*
1 = **NO!** =	*strongly disagree—***IT'S NOT ME!**

	YES!	yes	no	NO!
1. It is important for me to identify closely with the larger U.S. culture.	4	3	2	1
2. I do not feel a sense of belonging at all to the larger U.S. culture.	4	3	2	1
3. I usually go by the values of the overall U.S. culture.	4	3	2	1
4. I feel very confused about my membership in the larger U.S. society.	4	3	2	1
5. I feel very comfortable identifying with the larger U.S. society.	4	3	2	1
6. I often feel lost concerning my cultural membership.	4	3	2	1

☞

☞

Know Thyself 4.2	**Assessing the Degree of Importance of Your Cultural Identity and Marginal Identity (*cont.*)**			

	4	3	2	1
7. The overall U.S. culture is an important reflection of who I am.	4	3	2	1
8. I feel anxious thinking about cultural membership issues.	4	3	2	1
9. I am an "American," period.	4	3	2	1
10. I feel like I live on the borderline of the larger U.S. society.	4	3	2	1

Scoring: Add up the scores on all the odd-numbered items and you will find your U.S. cultural identity score. *U.S. Cultural Identity* score: _____. Add up the scores on all the even-numbered items and you will find your marginal cultural identity score. *Marginal Cultural Identity* score: _____.

Interpretation: Scores on each identity dimension can range from 5 to 20; the higher the score, the more cultural and/or marginal you are. If the scores are similar on both identity dimensions, you have a mixed identity pattern: that means sometimes you feel very "American," and sometimes you feel confused about your cultural identity membership.

Reflection Probes: Take a moment to think of the following questions: What does it mean to be an "American"? Do you think your answers would be very similar or very different from your family members? How so? For the most part, how would you label your cultural or ethnic self? Do you have a strong sense of pride or confusion about your cultural identity? Why? Compare your answers with those of a classmate.

Source: Scale adapted from Ting-Toomey, Yee-Jung, Shapiro, et al. (2000).

We acquire our cultural group memberships through the guidance of primary caretakers and peer associations during our formative years. Furthermore, physical appearance, racial traits, skin color, language usage, self-appraisal, and other-perception factors all enter into the cultural identity construction equation. The meanings and interpretations that we hold for our culture-based identity groups are learned via direct or mediated contacts (e.g., mass media images) with others. **Cultural identity** is defined as the emotional significance that we attach to our sense of belonging or affiliation with the larger culture. To illustrate, we can talk about the larger Brazilian cultural identity or the larger Canadian cultural identity. To understand cultural identity more specifically, we need to discuss two issues: value content and cultural identity salience. **Value content** refers to the standards or expectations that people hold in their mindset in making evaluations. One way to understand the content of cultural identity is to look at the value dimensions that underlie people's behavior. Though there are many value content dimensions on which cultural groups differ, one dimension that has received consistent attention from intercultural researchers around the world is individualism-collectivism (see Chapter 3). In order to negotiate mindfully with people from diverse cultures, it is critical that we understand the value contents of their cultural identities.

Cultural identity salience refers to the strength of affiliation we have with our larger culture. Strong associations of membership affiliation reflect high cultural identity salience. Weak associations of membership affiliation reflect low cultural identity salience. The more strongly our self-image is influenced by our larger cultural value patterns, the more we are likely to practice the norms and communication scripts of the dominant, mainstream culture. Salience of cultural identity can operate on a conscious or an unconscious level. We should also clarify here that the concept of "national identity" refers to one's legal status in relation to a nation, but the concept of "cultural identity" refers to the sentiments of belonging or connection to one's larger culture. To illustrate, as an immigrant-based society, residents in the United States may mix some of the larger cultural values with those of their ethnic-oriented values and practices. To negotiate cultural and ethnic identities mindfully with diverse cultural-ethnic groups, we need to understand in depth the content and salience of cultural *and* ethnic identity issues.

Ethnic Identity Conceptualization

Let's go back and review the two opening scenarios, which reflect complex problems when looking at ethnic identity. An individual who is associated with a particular ethnic group may not actually behave in accordance with her or his ethnic norms or behaviors, such as Lanitra in the first scenario. In other words, skin color does not automatically guarantee ethnic ingroup membership. In the second scenario, Rafael tried hard to understand the complexity of his ethnic identity. Although many ethnic minority Americans strive hard to be "Americans," they are constantly reminded by the media or in actual interactions that they are not part of the fabric of the larger U.S. society. Before you continue reading, complete the brief scale in Know Thyself 4.3. By checking out your scores, you should have a better understanding of your identification with your ethnic heritage group.

Ethnic identity is "inherently a matter of ancestry, of beliefs about the origins of one's forebears" (Alba, 1990, p. 37). Ethnicity can be based on national origin, race, religion, or language. For many people in the United States, ethnicity is based on the countries from which their ancestors came (e.g., those who can trace their ethnic heritage to an Asian or a Latin American country). Most Native Americans—descendants of people who settled in the Western Hemisphere long before Columbus, sometime between 25,000 and 40,000 years ago—

Know Thyself 4.3 Assessing the Degree of Importance of Your Ethnic Identity and Bicultural Identity

Instructions: Recall how you generally feel and act in various situations. Let your first inclination be your guide and circle the number in the scale that best reflects your impression of yourself. The following scale is used for each item:

4 = YES!	=	*strongly agree—IT'S ME!*
3 = yes	=	*moderately agree—it's kind of like me*
2 = no	=	*moderately disagree—it's kind of not me*
1 = NO!	=	*strongly disagree—IT'S NOT ME!*

	YES!	yes	no	NO!
1. I have spent time to find out more about my ethnic roots and history.	4	3	2	1
2. I subscribe to both sets of values: my ethnic values and the larger U.S. cultural values.	4	3	2	1
3. My family really emphasizes where our ancestors came from.	4	3	2	1
4. I have close friends from both my ethnic group and the larger U.S. culture.	4	3	2	1
5. My family practices distinctive ethnic traditions and customs.	4	3	2	1
6. The values of my own ethnic group are very compatible with the larger U.S. cultural values.	4	3	2	1
7. I feel a sense of loyalty and pride about my own ethnic group.	4	3	2	1
8. It is important for me to be accepted by both my ethnic group and the overall U.S. culture.	4	3	2	1
9. The ethnic group I belong to is an important reflection of who I am.	4	3	2	1
10. I feel comfortable identifying with both my ethnic heritage and the overall U.S. culture.	4	3	2	1

Scoring: Add up the scores on all the odd-numbered items and you will find your ethnic identity score. *Ethnic Identity* score: _____. Add up the scores on all the even-numbered items and you will find your bicultural identity score. *Bicultural Identity* score: _____.

Interpretation: Scores on each identity dimension can range from 5 to 20; the higher the score, the more ethnic and/or bicultural you are. If all the scores are similar on both identity dimensions, you have a mixed ethnic/bicultural identity pattern: that means at the same time you identify closely with your ethnic heritage, you also identify closely with the larger U.S. culture.

Reflection Probes: Take a moment to think of the following questions: Are the values of your ethnic group compatible or incompatible with the larger U.S. cultural values? How do you reconcile the differences? Do most of your friends see you as an American or see you as a member of a particular ethnic group? Which way do you like to be perceived? Why? Compare your answers with those of a classmate.

Source: Scale adapted from Ting-Toomey, Yee-Jung, Shapiro, et al. (2000).

can trace their ethnic heritage based on distinctive linguistic or religious practices.

While new forensic technologies (DNA typing) open up opportunities for ethnic ancestry research (e.g., Zuni ancestors came from Japan), many African Americans still may not be able to trace their precise ethnic origins, or traditional ways of living, because of pernicious slavery codes (e.g., a slave could not marry or meet with an ex-slave; it was forbidden for anyone, including Whites, to teach slaves to read or write) and the uprootedness forced on them by slaveholders beginning in the 1600s (Schaefer, 1990). Last, many European Americans may not be able to trace their ethnic origins precisely because of their mixed ancestral heritage. This phenomenon stems from generations of intergroup marriages (say, Irish American and French American marriages, or mixed Irish/French American and Polish American marriages, and the like) starting with their great grandparents or grandparents.

Ethnicity, of course, is based on more than one's country of origin. It involves a subjective sense of belonging to or identification with an ethnic group across time. To understand the significance of someone's ethnicity, we also need to understand the ethnic value content and the ethnic identity salience of that person's ethnic identity in particular. For example, with knowledge of the individualism-collectivism value tendencies of the originating countries, we can infer the *ethnic value content* of specific ethnic groups. Most Asian Americans, Native Americans, and Latino/a Americans, for example, who identify strongly with their traditional ethnic values, tend to be group-oriented. Those European Americans who identify strongly with European values and norms (albeit on an unconscious level) tend to be oriented toward individualism. African Americans might well subscribe to both collectivistic and individualistic values—in blending both ethnic African values and assimilated U.S. values—for purposes of survival and adaptation.

Beyond ethnic value content, we should address the issue of ethnic identity salience. The role of *ethnic identity salience* is linked closely with the intergroup boundary maintenance issue across generations (e.g., third-generation Cuban Americans in the United States). Ethnic identity salience is defined as the subjective allegiance and loyalty to a group—large or small, socially dominant or subordinate—with which one has ancestral links (Edwards, 1994). Ethnic identity can be sustained by shared objective characteristics, such as shared language or religion. It is also a subjective sense of "ingroupness" whereby individuals perceive themselves and each other as belonging to the same ingroup by shared historical and emotional ties. However, for many ethnic minority group members living in the larger U.S. society, a constant struggle exists between the perception of their own ethnic identity issue and the perception of others' questioning of their ethnic heritage or role. Oftentimes, this results in a sense of both ethnic and cultural rootlessness. Let's take a look at Elaine Kim's story (1996, p. 357) in Double Take 4.2. She recounted her visit to Korea, the birthplace of her parents.

Double Take 4.2

Because I spent my early years living as something of a freak within mainstream American society, I decreed that there was no way to be "Asian" and "American" at the same time. I often longed to be held securely within the folds of a community of "my people." Like many other Asians born in the United States, I was changed forever when I visited Korea at the age of twenty—when I saw my relatives for the first time.

Finding myself among so many people similar to me in shape and color made me feel as though I came from somewhere and that I was connected in a normal way to other people instead of being taken as an aberration, a sidekick, or a mascot, whose presence was tolerated [only] when everyone was in a good mood.

But like other U.S.-born Asians, I came to understand that there is no ready-made community, no unquestioned belonging, even in Korea. For as soon as they heard me speak or saw me grin like a fool for no reason, as soon as they saw me launch down the street swinging my arms, as soon as they saw me looking brazenly into people's eyes when they talked, they let me know that I could not possibly be "Korean." . . .

—Elaine Kim, 1996

Thus, ethnic identity has both objective and subjective layers. Ethnicity is, overall, more a subjective phenomenon than an objective classification. Although a political boundary (e.g., delimiting Chechnya—formerly the Chechno-Ingush Autonomous Soviet Socialist Republic—from Russia) can change over generations, the continuation of ethnic boundaries is an enduring, long-standing phenomenon that lasts in the hearts and minds of its members. Ethnicity is basically an inheritance wherein members perceive each other as emotionally bounded by a common set of traditions, worldviews, history, heritage, and descent on a psychological and historical level.

By understanding how we define ourselves and how others define themselves ethnically and culturally, we can communicate with culturally different others with more sensitivity. We can learn to lend appropriate self-conception support in terms of ethnic and cultural identity issues. Uncovering and supporting others' self-conceptions requires mindful identity-support work. Moving beyond general cultural and ethnic identity issues, many majority-minority group identity models have been developed to account for the identity change process of immigrants and minority group members. We first discuss some of the underlying factors that affect immigrants' acculturation experiences and then explore two models of ethnic-cultural identity developmental processes.

Group Membership: Intercultural Boundary Crossing

The journey for immigrants, from identity security to insecurity and from familiarity to unfamiliarity, can be a turbulent or exhilarating process. The route itself has many ups and downs and twists and turns. In such a long, demanding journey, an incremental process of identity change is inevitable. This section explains immigrants' acculturation experiences and explores some of the key factors that shape immigrants' outlooks concerning their adopted homeland.

Defining Acculturation and Enculturation

The intercultural **acculturation** process is defined as the degree of identity change that occurs when individuals move from a familiar environment to an unfamiliar one. Intercultural acculturation, however, does not happen overnight. It is a gradual identity transformation process. The larger the difference between the two cultures, the higher the degree of identity vulnerability immigrants will experience in the new culture. Do you know which are the top three countries with the highest percentage of immigrants? Do you know which are the top three countries of origins for U.S. immigrants who arrived in the year 2000? Take a guess, and check out Jeopardy Box 4.1 and Jeopardy Box 4.2.

Jeopardy Box 4.1 Top-Ten Countries With the Highest Estimated Net Number of Immigrants per 1,000 Population	
Country	Estimated net number of immigrants per 1,000 population
1. Singapore	25.8
2. Qatar	17.5
3. Kuwait	14.0
4. San Marino	11.1
4. Afghanistan	10.3
5. Luxembourg	9.1
6. Monaco	7.8
7. Eritrea	7.3
8. Jordan	6.8
9. Andorra	6.7
10. United States	3.3

Note: In countries using latest year for which data is available.
Source: U.S. Census Bureau International Data Base (2000).

Jeopardy Box 4.2 Top-Ten Countries of Origin of U.S. Immigrants	
__Country__	__Immigrants in 2000__
1. Mexico	173,919
2. China	45,652
3. Philippines	42,474
4. India	42,046
5. Vietnam	26,747
6. Nicaragua	24,029
7. El Salvador	22,578
8. Haiti	22,364
9. Cuba	20,831
10. Dominican Republic	17,537

Source: U.S. Census Bureau International Data Base (2000).

The immigrant group comprises those who generally have voluntarily moved across cultural boundaries, but those in the refugee group often have involuntarily done so (for reasons of political, religious, or economic oppression). Unlike tourists and sojourners, immigrants and refugees usually aim for a permanent stay in their adopted country. Although there are some similar adaptation patterns (e.g., initial stress and culture shock) in these diverse groups, very different motivational patterns guide these newcomers' means and goals of adaptation.

The term **acculturation** refers to the incremental identity-related change process of immigrants and refugees in a new environment (Redfield, Linton, & Herskovits, 1936) from a long-term perspective. The change process of immigrants (hereafter, the term *immigrants* will also include refugees) often involves subtle change to overt more extensive change. Acculturation involves the long-term conditioning process of newcomers in integrating the new values, norms, and symbols of their new culture, and developing new roles and skills to meet its demands. Let's take a look at Double Take 4.3.

Double Take 4.3

I was thinking about those factors we discussed in class about what makes an immigrant's stay successful. Being raised in a family [whose members] are all immigrants from Iran, I feel somewhat closely related to what other immigrants have to experience. My grandparents had to learn to adapt to living in a completely different world from [the place] they still call home. I am not so sure that either set of my grandparents was too successful. They came to America in their early 70s, so they were retired. But my grandparents on my mom's side had to leave a lot of their material belongings behind, because there was a revolution in Iran and they had little time to leave the country. So not only did they have to adjust to living in a new culture, but they [also] had ☞

to adjust to losing most of their material possessions. I think that resilience and flexibility are two huge factors that my maternal grandmother [is] still working on to this day.

Growing up, I never really saw her try to learn about American culture. She felt more comfortable speaking with Persian friends, finding Persian stores, watching or listening to her Persian programs on television and radio. I am not saying that my grandmother has been wrong for doing these things, but I am noticing that she does not really have much interest in making her permanent stay here "successful."

My maternal grandfather, on the other hand, took ESL classes at night at the local high school and learned to make his way around a grocery store, speaking with the cashiers and knowing the exact change to give them. He was definitely more motivated to adjust to this huge change. Support networks have been really crucial to my grandmother's life. My father helped her

apply for a green card. Family friends who also came from Iran years earlier gave her a sense of security and comfort. There is an Iranian television station in Los Angeles where she can find out all about the news of America as well as Iran. She watches it all day long. I can hear the TV on sometimes at 3:00 a.m. And she gets so excited telling me the latest news she has heard.

This is a part of my life that really separated me from the rest of my classmates from elementary school until now . . . the feeling of being different and not quite fitting in with the rest of the kids. The question: What does it mean to live a successful immigrant experience in this country? It can mean so many different things to so many different people. The answer also depends on so many factors. I can see that in their unique yet separate ways, my grandparents [are] quite successful in adapting to this new culture. They use different strategies to deal with the changes surrounding them.

—Zahra, *College Student*

Enculturation, on the other hand, often refers to the sustained, primary socialization process of strangers in their original home (or natal) culture wherein they have internalized their primary cultural values. For example, a U.S. immigrant born in Iran would be *enculturated* into an Iranian identity, but slowly *acculturated* into U.S. culture (in some amount) once she or he immigrates. The same immigrant can be a *bicultural* individual if she or he relates strongly to both cultures (see the section on "Ethnic-Cultural Identity Change Process"). Let's take a look at a follow-up story by Laleh in Double Take 4.4, which is about her own ethnic identity struggles.

What do you think of Laleh's story? Have you ever thought about physical appearance and ethnic identity belongingness and exclusion issues? Have you ever felt excluded because you do not look mainstream enough? Beyond physical appearance, of course, many factors influence the immigrants' acculturation experience—from self-identification factors, to systems-level factors (e.g., receptivity of the host culture), to individual-level factors (e.g., individual expectations), and also interpersonal-level factors (e.g., formation of social networks).

Double Take 4.4

I have always been reminded of how different I am. . . . This is how minorities are visible. It is interesting how the definition of an "American" can be so clear-cut to some and totally unclear to others. Anyway, in this American culture, it seems so easy for people to determine who is NOT an American or at least not American enough.

To tell you a story, . . . some time ago I had planned to get a nose job. I knew exactly why I wanted to change my nose: it was a typical Persian big nose. I used to be so self-conscious about my nose that I would walk behind everyone so that they could not see my profile if I were standing side by side with them.

Both my parents are in support of me getting a nose job, but I have always been so hesitant to actually go through with the procedure. I realized if I do so, I would be erasing an ethnic identity that should be kept as a part of me.

—Laleh, *College Student*

Social Identity

Social identity is one key factor to examine when looking at identity with regard to group membership. As discussed earlier, *social identities* consist of cultural or ethnic membership identity, gender identity, sexual orientation identity, social class identity, age identity, disability identity, or professional identity. With regard to ethnic identity, social identity consists of two important elements. The first is knowledge of social group membership. According to Tajfel (1978), self-concept comes from the knowledge we have of our social group membership. The second element is emotional significance. If an individual places a high value on the emotional significance of group membership, the result is a positive self-concept.

Alba (1990) and Waters (1990) studied the link between ethnic identity and group membership. According to Alba (1990), individuals having weak ethnic identities with the group have a greater tendency to marry out of their ethnic group than individuals with strong ethnic identities. The main reason is that individuals with weaker ethnic identities are perceived as less ethnic and share more things in common with the dominant society than individuals who strongly identify with their ethnic group.

Regarding European Americans who live in suburban communities in the United States, Waters (1990) was very interested in their ethnic choices. She pointed out that among European Americans, ethnicity is more symbolic. This symbolic identity "fulfills the need to be from somewhere. An ethnic identity is something that makes you both special and simultaneously part of a community. It can come to you involuntarily through heredity, and at the same time, it is a personal choice " (p. 150). European Americans can choose to be individuals apart from their ethnic heritage group, or they can choose to claim themselves as "Irish Americans," "German Americans," or "French/Scottish Americans."

Ethnic differences appear to be strongest among those generations closest to the immigrant experience. Ethnic differences weaken, or became less distinct, among those farther down the generational line. As each generation is removed from the original immigrants, erosion of ethnic linkage naturally results. However, for some ethnic groups in the United States, such as African Americans, personal choice is not a factor. Ethnic individuals can be "marked" or "assigned" into categories ascribed by other groups on the basis of physical characteristics. Ethnicity is generally not a voluntary choice for all groups because it can be imposed. Orbe (1998), for example, has developed a theory called the **co-culture theory.** He claims that African Americans, because of their position in the larger U.S. society, develop a complex ethnic-cultural standpoint. He contends that in each society, "a hierarchy exists that privileges certain groups of individuals: In the United States these groups include men, European Americans, heterosexuals, the able-bodied, and [the] middle and upper class" (p. 11). He also goes on to explain the different broad communication strategies that minority group members use to deal with their everyday surroundings: assimilation, accommodation, and separation. **Assimilation** refers to communication strategies that adopt the majority culture's view. **Accommodation** refers to interaction strategies that combine both majority and co-culture views. Last, **separation** refers to communication strategies that emphasize separation, such as intraethnic networking or showcasing the strengths and pride of one's own ethnic group.

In sum, social identity explains individual behavior with regard to group membership. It is really about how different groups perceive their own and others' group membership identity issues. It is also about marking ingroup/outgroup boundaries as well as majority/minority group relations issues.

Systems-Level Factors

Systems-level factors are those elements in the host environment that influence newcomers' adaptation to the new culture (Y. Y. Kim, 1988, 2001, 2003). In this section, we shall emphasize the need and responsibility of both the host society and the immigrants to learn from each other—to create an inclusive, pluralistic cultural community.

From the findings of existing adaptation research, the following four observations can be made. First, the host culture's socioeconomic conditions influence the climate of adaptation (Puentha, Giles, & Young, 1987). When the host culture is economically sound, members appear to be more tolerant and hospitable toward newcomers. When the socioeconomic conditions are poor, strangers become the scapegoats for local economic problems. For example, newcomers are often perceived as competing for scarce resources, such as new jobs and promotion opportunities, and taking away the job opportunities of cultural insiders.

Second, a host culture's attitudinal stance on "cultural assimilation" or "cultural pluralism" produces a spillover effect on institutional policies (as well as on attitudes of the citizenry) toward newcomers' adaptation processes (Kraus, 1991). The main effect of cultural assimilation demands that strangers conform to the host environment (e.g., as urged by the U.S. "English Only" movement). In contrast, the cultural pluralist stance encourages a diversity of values (e.g., as supported by Canadian "multicultural" policies), providing strangers with wider latitude of norms from which to choose in their newfound homeland.

In a society that perpetuates assimilation, ethnic identity formation is strongly influenced by the dominant group's values. In a pluralistic society, ethnic identity formation rests on the choices between maintaining the customs of the heritage culture and inventing a new identity. In an assimilationist society, immigrants are often expected to conform quickly to local cultural practices. In a pluralistic society, immigrants are given more leeway to acquire the fund of knowledge and skills needed in adapting to the new culture. Societies with an assimilationist stance tend to be more intolerant of newcomers' retention of traditions and customs of their own heritage. Societies with a pluralist stance tend to display more tolerant attitudes and acceptance toward immigrants' ethnic traditions and practices.

Third, local institutions (e.g., schools, places of work, social services, and mass media) serve as firsthand contact agencies that facilitate or impede the adaptation process of sojourners and immigrants. Following the prevailing national policies, local institutions can either greatly facilitate strangers' adaptation process (e.g., via language help programs or job training programs) or produce roadblocks to the newcomers' adaptive experience. At public schools, varying degrees of receptivity and helpfulness of teachers toward immigrant children can either help the children to feel "at home" or leave them to "sink or swim." Whether the attitudes of local children in the classrooms are favorable or unfavorable can also produce a pleasant or hostile climate for these immigrant children during their vulnerable adaptive stages. Getting used to a strange language, unfamiliar signs, and different expectations and norms of a new classroom can be overwhelming for recent immigrant children.

Fourth, the host culture's meaning definition concerning the role of "strangers" can profoundly influence sojourners' and immigrants' initial adaptation process. Whether members of the host culture perceive strangers as nonpersons, intruders, aliens, visitors, or guests will influence their attitudes and behaviors toward the strangers. Members of host cultures that view outsiders as intruders are likely to be hostile to them, whereas host nationals who use an adoptive family metaphor for the incorporation of newcomers are likely to display positive sentiments toward them. Thus, some host nationals may offer proactive help, as opposed to reactive resistance, to the adaptation process of newcomers.

While some cultures make greater distinctions between insiders and outsiders, some groups have built-in mechanisms to facilitate the socialization of newcomers. Immigrants are marginalists to a new culture. They often need help and coaching to learn the inner workings of a culture. To the extent that insiders of a new culture treat the newcomers with dignity, inclusion, and respect, they experience identity confirmation and connection. To the extent that newcomers or minority members (including second- or third-generation families) are long treated as borderline persons (e.g., by asking third-generation Sansei Japanese Americans where they came from and when will they return "home"—when their home culture is right here in the United States), they experience identity frustration and dislocation.

The combined systems-level factors can create either a favorable or an unfavorable climate for the newly arrived strangers. Obviously, the more favorable and receptive the cultural climate toward the arrival of strangers, the easier it is for the strangers to adapt to the new culture (Y. Y. Kim, 2003; 2004). The more help the newcomers receive during the initial cultural adaptation stages, the more positive are their perceptions of their new environment.

Individual-Level Factors

For immigrants, the permanent residence status evokes a mixture of affective and work-related stressors. Immigrants often also have more family worries and identity dislocation problems than do short-term sojourners. The sense of "no return" (i.e., for immigrants) versus "transitory stay" (i.e., for sojourners) produces different motivational drives for newcomers to acquire the new core rituals, symbols, and scripts suited to their new setting.

Acculturation research indicates that many immigrants have uprooted themselves due to a mixture of "push" factors (e.g., political and economic reasons) and "pull" factors (e.g., the host culture's economic opportunities). Many immigrants were forced to depart from their home countries because of cultural, religious, or political persecution as well as economic strains there. By immigrating, they strive to create better opportunities for themselves and their families. Additionally, the new culture's attractions ("pull" factors) include better chances for personal advancement and better job opportunities, greater educational opportunities for the children, an improved quality of life for the family, a better standard of living, and democratic cultural values (Ward, Bochner, & Furnham, 2001). In sum, the motivational orientations of people leaving their homelands can greatly affect their expectations and behaviors in the new culture.

Newcomers' cultural knowledge and interaction-based knowledge about the host culture serve as other critical factors in their adaptation process. Cultural knowledge can include information about the following: cultural and ethnic diversity history, geography, political and economic systems, religious and spiritual beliefs, multiple value systems, and situational norms. Interaction-based knowledge can include language, verbal and nonverbal styles, diversity-related communication issues (e.g., regional, ethnic, and gender differences within a culture), and various problem-solving styles.

Fluency in the host culture's language, for example, has been found to have a direct positive impact on sociocultural adaptation, such as developing relationships with members of the host culture (Ward & Kennedy, 1993). In contrast, language incompetence has been associated with increased psychological and psychosomatic symptoms (e.g., sleeplessness, severe headaches) in immigrants to the United States from India (Krishnan & Berry, 1992). Beyond language fluency, interaction-based pragmatic competence, such as knowing "when to say what appropriately, under what situations," is critical in adapting to a new environment.

Additionally, demographic variables, such as age and educational level, have also been found to affect adaptational effectiveness, and younger children have an easier time adapting to the new culture than adults. Individuals with higher educational levels tend to adapt more effectively than do individuals with lower educational levels (Ward, 1996, 2004; Ward et al., 2001). We should note here that most of the cited studies are based on sojourners' and immigrants' experiences in the settings of Australia, Canada, and the United States. Thus, the research conclusions summarized in this chapter are reflective of acculturation norms in individualistic cultures more than in collectivistic cultures.

Interpersonal-Ethnic Media-Level Factors

Interpersonal-level factors can include relational face-to-face network factors (e.g., social network), mediated contact factors (e.g., use of mass media) (Y. Y. Kim, 2001), and interpersonal skills factors.

A supportive social network serves as a buffer zone between a newcomer's threatened identity, on the one hand, and the unfamiliar environment, on the other. Overall, studies of immigrants' network patterns have yielded some interesting findings. Ethnic-based social and friendship networks provide critical identity support during the initial stages of immigrants' adaptation process. This observation is based on the idea that if ethnic clusters or niches in the ethnic community are strong and available as a supportive network, then the immigrant may find supportive role models. Established individuals from the same or a similar ethnic background can serve as successful role models. They can also provide identity and affective support because they have gone through a similar set of culture shock experiences. These "established locals" can engage in appropriate and effective identity-validation messages (e.g., "I went through the same confusion and loneliness when I got here") that instill hope and confidence in the newly arrived immigrants or sojourners.

Research indicates that the more a newcomer participates in dominant cultural group activities, the more favorable his or her attitudes toward the host culture. These contact networks are often viewed as the "healing webs" that nurture the adaptive growth and inquiry process of newcomers. Both close ties (e.g., relatives, close friends) and weak ties (e.g., acquaintanceships with neighbors, schoolteachers, grocers) provide important identity and informational support functions. In fact, it has been speculated that oftentimes the latter connections may help newcomers to locate their first jobs or solve their everyday problems (Adelman, 1988; Granovetter, 1973).

Ethnic media (e.g., ethnic publications and broadcasts) also play a critical role in the initial stages of immigrants' adaptation. Due to language barriers, immigrants tend to reach out to ethnic newspapers, magazines, radio, and TV programs when such media resources are available in the local community. Ethnic media tend to ease the loneliness and adaptive stress of the new arrivals. The familiar language and images are identity-affirming and offer newcomers a sense of comfort and identity connection in the unfamiliar environment.

On the other hand, research indicates that the host media (e.g., radio and television) do play a critical educational role in providing a safe environment for newcomers to learn the host language and socialization skills (Y. Y. Kim, 2001). Overall, the mass media's influence on newcomers' adaptation process is broad, but not deep. The influence of personal relationship networks, in comparison, is deep, but not broad. Through the mass media (especially television), immigrants receive a smorgasbord of information concerning a broad range of host national topics, but without much informational depth. In contrast, through personal network contacts, newcomers learn about the host culture from a smaller sample of individuals, revolving around a narrower range of topics, but with more depth and specific personal perspectives.

In any successful intercultural learning process, members of the host culture need to act as the gracious hosts, and newcomers need to act as the willing-to-learn guests. Without collaborative effort, the hosts and the new arrivals may end up with great frustrations, miscommunications, and identity misalignments.

Ethnic-Cultural Identity Change Process

Immigrants and ethnic minority group members, in the context of intergroup relations, tend to be keenly sensitive to the intersecting issues of ethnicity and culture. For ethnic minority members, the perceived imbalanced power dimension within a society often leads them to draw clear boundaries between the dominant "power holder" group and the nondominant "fringe" group (Orbe, 1998). The one model that seems to capture the essence of immigrants' adaptation process is that of Berry and associates' fourfold identity typological model (Berry, Kim, & Boski, 1987).

Ethnic-Cultural Identity Typological Model

To understand how ethnic individuals see themselves in relation to both their ethnic group and the society at large, ethnic and cultural identity salience can be viewed as a fourfold model that emphasizes an individual's adaptation options toward ethnic identity *and* larger cultural identity maintenance issues (see Figure 4.1).

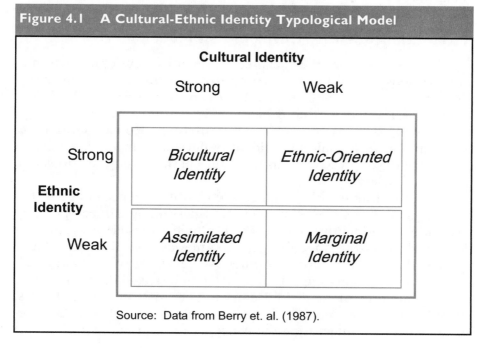

Figure 4.1   A Cultural-Ethnic Identity Typological Model

	Cultural Identity	
	Strong	**Weak**
Ethnic Identity — Strong	*Bicultural Identity*	*Ethnic-Oriented Identity*
Ethnic Identity — Weak	*Assimilated Identity*	*Marginal Identity*

Source: Data from Berry et. al. (1987).

According to Berry (1994, 2004), immigrants who identify strongly with ethnic traditions and values and weakly with the values of the dominant culture subscribe to the traditionally based or *ethnic-oriented identity* option. These individuals emphasize the value of retaining their ethnic culture and avoid interacting with the dominant group. As a result, there is an implication of a higher degree of stress that occurs through contact with the dominant group. Other individuals who identify strongly with ethnic tradition maintenance, and at the same time incorporate values and practices of the larger society, internalize the *bicultural identity* or integrative option. Integrated individuals feel comfortable being a member of both cultural groups.

Individuals who identify weakly with their ethnic traditions and values and identify strongly with the values and norms of the larger culture tend to practice the *assimilated identity* option. Finally, individuals who identify weakly with their ethnic traditions and also weakly with the larger cultural worldviews are in the *marginal identity* state. They basically have disconnected ties with both their ethnic group and the larger society and often experience feelings of ambiguity, invisibility, and alienation.

For example, a second-generation Asian American or Latino/a American can commit to one of the following four ethnic-cultural identity salience categories: Asian or Latino/a primarily, American primarily, both, or neither (Chung & Ting-Toomey, 1999; Espiritu, 1992). Systems-level, individual, and interpersonal factors, added together, have a net influence on immigrants' adaptive experience and identity change process.

Racial-Ethnic Identity Development Model

Alternatively, from the racial-ethnic identity development framework, various models have been proposed to account for racial or ethnic identity formation of African Americans (e.g., Cross, 1978, 1995), Asian Americans (e.g., Sue & Sue, 1999), Latino/a Americans (e.g., Ruiz, 1990), and European Americans (e.g., Rowe, Bennett, & Atkinson, 1994). Racial-ethnic identity development models tend to emphasize the oppressive-adaptive nature of intergroup relations in a pluralistic society.

From this framework, racial-ethnic identity salience concerns the development of racial or ethnic consciousness along a linear, progressive pathway of identity change. For example, Cross (1971, 1991) has developed a five-stage model of African American racial identity development that includes pre-encounter (stage 1), encounter (stage 2), immersion-emersion (stage 3), internalization (stage 4), and internalization-commitment (stage 5). Helms and her associates (e.g., Helms, 1993; Parham & Helms, 1985) have amended and refined this five-stage model (i.e., integrating the concept of *worldview* in each stage) into four stages: pre-encounter, encounter, immersion-emersion, and internalization-commitment (see Figure 4.2).

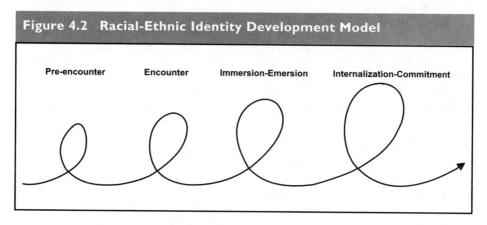

Figure 4.2 Racial-Ethnic Identity Development Model

Pre-encounter   Encounter   Immersion-Emersion   Internalization-Commitment

The *pre-encounter* stage is the high cultural identity salience phase wherein ethnic minority group members' self-concepts are influenced by the values and norms of the larger culture. In this stage, individuals are naive, unaware of being ethnic group members. They may define themselves as Canadian, American, or Australian. The *encounter stage* is the marginal identity phase, in which new racial-ethnic realization is awakened in the individuals because of a "racially shattering" event (e.g., encountering racism) and minority group members realize that they cannot be fully accepted as part of the "White world." The *immersion-emersion stage* is the strong racial-ethnic identity salience phase, in which individuals withdraw to the safe confines of their own racial-ethnic groups and become ethnically conscious. Last, the *internalization-commitment stage* is the phase in which individuals develop a secure racial-ethnic identity that is internally defined and at the same time are able to establish genuine interpersonal contacts with members of the dominant group and other multiracial groups. One example we use to highlight the stages is a true story that happened to one of us (see Double Take 4.5).

With the increase in minority groups living in the United States, the question of identification with group membership is an important concern. The range of issues, as we have shared with you, is enormous. One of the common threads is trying to figure out who we are in the context of a culturally pluralistic nation. How can we all learn to get along? How can we reconcile our own identity struggle and search processes? How do all these identity struggles manifest themselves in our everyday stereotyping process and ethnocentric views? How can we utilize the dynamic tensions and the best of different worldviews from diverse cultural groups to construct a meaningful "U.S. American" culture? These are important issues that await us in our development to be ethical intercultural communicators in the twenty-first century.

Double Take 4.5

Although my high school consisted of primarily black and Asian students, I felt more comfortable hanging around with white kids, who made up of 7 percent of the school. I am Chinese American, but at the time, I thought I was white. I befriended a girl named Susan. She was from the South and we became fast friends. In our senior year, Susan and I had to debate each other in our civics class about controversial topics. By the end of the debate, unknown to me, Susan was very angry at my "controversial stance" comments.

I remember sitting down after the last of the three topics. I heard her say, "Well, if you don't like it here and you have a problem with the rules of our country, you need to go back to where you came from!" I looked across at her and started to laugh at our mutual friend named Dana. Dana was black. I said, "Ha ha, Dana, she is talking about you!" She said, "Oh, no way, girl! She ain't talking about me, she's talking about you!" I turned to Susan and asked her if she was talking to me. She said yes, that if I did not like it here I should just pack my suitcase and go back to where I belong.

I was stunned into complete silence. I was born in America. I considered myself to be American. My friends were mostly white. What more did I have to do? But at that particular moment, I realized that I was the "other," foreign and an outsider to this country. I could dye my hair, wear the trendy clothes, speak the language, but I would NEVER be accepted as fully American. I never spoke to Susan again. When I graduated, I went to college and minored in ethnic studies. I took classes that helped me reconcile my conflict and the internal battle of who I am . . . , and what is the history of Chinese and Asian Americans in the United States. I learned Mandarin. I took a semester off and went to China, traveled around to "find myself." I came back and even worked in a Chinese restaurant for two years.

What I learned from all of my experiences is that although I will never be perceived as fully Chinese or American, I am normal. I accept this as my reality. I work on my identity every day, challenging myself to represent and express both voices.

—Leeva, *College Teacher*

Intercultural Toolkit: Recaps and Checkpoints

To understand the person with whom you are communicating, you need to understand the identity domains that she deems as important. For example, if the person strongly values her cultural membership identities, you need to find ways to validate and be responsive to those cultural identities; or if the person strongly values her personal identity above and beyond a certain cultural membership, you need to uncover ways to affirm her positively desired personal identity. We can discover identity issues that are desirable to the individuals in our everyday intercultural encounters through practicing the following communication skills:

- *Mindful listening:* Mindful listening demands that we pay thoughtful attention to both the verbal and nonverbal messages of the speaker before responding. It means listening attentively with all our senses and checking responsively for the accuracy of our meaning decoding process on multiple levels. We have to learn to listen responsively, or *ting* (the Chinese word for listening means "attending mindfully with our ears, eyes, and a focused heart"), to the sounds, tones, gestures, movements, nonverbal nuances, pauses, silence, and identity meanings in a given intercultural situation. Mindful listening essentially involves a fundamental shift of perspective. It means taking into account not only how things look from my identity perspective but also how they look and feel from the other's identity perspective.

- *Mindful paraphrasing skills:* Paraphrasing skills refer to two characteristics: (1) verbally summarizing the content meaning of the speaker's message in your own words; and (2) nonverbally echoing back your interpretation of the emotional meaning of the speaker's message. The verbal summary, or restatement, should reflect your tentative understanding of the speaker's content meaning, such as "It sounds to me that . . ." and "In other words, you're saying that . . ." You can also try to paraphrase the emotional meaning of the speaker's message by echoing back your understanding of the affective tone that underlies the speaker's message.

- *Perception-checking skills:* Perception-checking statements are designed to help us make sure we are interpreting the speaker's nonverbal and verbal behavior accurately during a culture bump episode. Perception-checking statements usually end up with a clarifying question-type format. It is a double-checking questioning skill that should be used judiciously and in a culture-sensitive manner. It can be used when we are unsure whether we are reading the meaning of the nonverbal or verbal message accurately. Culture-sensitive perception-checking statements involve either indirect or direct perceptual verification questions. For example, an indirect perceptual statement can be "From your puzzled facial expression, maybe I'm not making myself very clear. I apologize for that confusion. When I mentioned that I need the report by early next week, I meant at the latest by Tuesday by 5:00 p.m. Do you have any questions about the deadline? [pause]" Perception checking is part of mindful observation and mindful listening skills. It should be used cautiously, especially in accordance with the particular topic, relationship, timing, and situational context.

• *Identity validation skills:* When a person perceives authentic and positive identity validation, she will tend to view self-images positively. When a person perceives identity rejection, she will tend to view self-images negatively. Positive identity validation is typically expressed through verbal and nonverbal confirming messages. Confirming communication involves recognizing others with important group-based and person-based identities, responding sensitively to other people's mood and affective states, and accepting other people's experiences as real. Disconfirmation, however, is the process through which individuals do not recognize the existence of the others, do not respond sensitively to cultural strangers, and do not accept others' experiences as valid.

Of all the operational skills, identity validation is a major skill to master in flexible intercultural communication practice. By paying attention to the cultural stranger and mindfully listening to what he has to say, we signal our intention of wanting to understand the multi-layered identity of the stranger. By conveying our respect and acceptance of group-based and person-based differences, we encourage intercultural trust, inclusion, and connection. Through active verbal and nonverbal confirmation skills, we reaffirm the intrinsic worthiness of the dissimilar other. In learning from people who are culturally different, both hosts and new arrivals can stretch their identity boundaries to integrate new ideas, expand affective horizons, and respect diverse lifestyles and practices. ✦

Chapter 5

What Is Culture Shock?

외국인 전용 설명실(外國人 專用 說明室)
Observatory Room for Foreigners

Chapter Outline

When I first arrived in Madrid, Spain, last year to study for a semester, I strolled around the streets googly-eyed and fascinated with everything around me. But then as the weeks went by, I started to feel foreign. Stupid. Unwelcome. Inexperienced. The intimidating Spanish women strutted about, confident as ever, and looked at my friends and me as pathetic and ignorant twenty-something's.

Over time, however, I learned to adapt more to the new culture, language, and values. After a while, the glares became smiles, and many people even mistook me for a native (Spanish women dye their hair blonde, and I was getting pretty fluent in Spanish). I suppose everything is uncomfortable, at first, in such a situation. We step out of our comfort zone and into a world of uncertainty. In the end, it's all about how willing we are to take some risks, move beyond our comfort zone, and try to stretch ourselves.

—L. Holst, *College Student*

Millions *of U.S. Americans cross cultural boundaries every year to work, to study, to engage in government service, and to volunteer their time in global humanitarian work. Likewise, millions of international students, cultural exchange teachers, artists, scientists, and business people come to the United States to learn, to teach, to perform, to experiment, and to conduct business. When individuals move from their home cultures to a new culture, they take with them their cultural habits, familiar scripts, and interaction routines. For the most part, these old cultural habits may produce unintended clashes in the new culture.*

Culture shock is about the stress and the feeling of disorientation you experience in a new culture. If you are temporarily visiting (sojourning to) a new culture for the first time, it is likely that you will experience some degree of cultural shock. Even if you do not plan to go overseas to work in the next few years, international classmates and coworkers may be sitting right next to you—working side by side with you. By learning more in depth about their culture shock experiences, you may develop new knowledge, display more respectful attitudes, and learn to apply more flexible intercultural skills in communicating with your international coworkers or classmates. This chapter asks three questions: What is culture shock? Can we track meaningful patterns of the intercultural adjustment process? What are some creative strategies we can use when we are crossing cultural boundaries and encountering culture shock problems?

This chapter is divided into four sections. We first address the role and definition of culture shock. We then explain a W-shaped intercultural adjustment model that many sojourners or international students find useful. Third, we explore the concept of reentry culture shock. Finally, we present a set of recaps and checkpoints in your intercultural toolkit to guide you through your international discovery journey.

Understanding Culture Shock

Culture shock is an inevitably stressful and disorienting experience. Let's check out the story in Double Take 5.1.

Double Take 5.1

Three American universities accepted my undergraduate applications—one in Hawaii, one in Ohio, and one in Iowa. Because I had no clue as to how one university differed from another, I wrote down the names of the universities on three pieces of paper and asked my then 9-year-old brother, Victor, to pick one with his eyes closed. He picked Iowa. I decided fate had called me to the University of Iowa. Iowa City, in those days, was an all-White campus town. The University was huge—spread out and cut off by a river running through it. I was one of the first group of international students being admitted to the University from Asia.

Life was composed of a series of culture shock waves in my first few months there. From overdressing (I quickly changed my daily skirts to jeans to avoid the question: "Are you going to a wedding today?") to hyper-apprehension (e.g., the constant fear of being called upon to answer questions in the "small power distance" classroom atmosphere). I experienced intense homesickness at times. The months flew by quickly, however.

—Stella, *College Instructor*

People encounter culture shock whenever they uproot themselves from a familiar setting and move to an unfamiliar one (e.g., relocating from Beijing, China, to Kansas City, Kansas, or making the transition as a high school senior to a college freshman). Because culture shock is unavoidable, just how we manage culture shock will determine the adaptive process and outcome.

Culture shock is, first and foremost, an emotional experience, that is, intense emotions are involved to a high degree; then comes behavioral confusion and cognitive (i.e., thinking pattern) disorientation. Both short-term sojourners and long-term immigrants can experience culture shock at different stages of their adaptation. Sojourners, such as cultural exchange students, businesspersons, diplomats, journalists, military personnel, and Peace Corps volunteers, often play temporary resident roles with a short to medium span of stay. Immigrants, however, are often viewed from the role of a permanent resident and are treated quite differently by the new cultural hosts. For immigrants' adaptation and identity change processes, see Chapter 4. This section covers the definitional characteristics of culture shock, discusses the pros and cons, and describes the factors that affect the culture shock experience.

Culture Shock: Defining Characteristics

Before you read this section, work through Quick Poll 5.1 and check out your culture shock index when you encounter an unfamiliar environment.

Quick Poll 5.1
Recall the last time you traveled to an entirely new place or an unfamiliar environment. Think of that initial experience and put a check mark by the words that best capture your feelings:

Awkward	_____	Bizarre	_____
Disoriented	_____	Energized	_____
Excited	_____	Exhausted	_____
Embarrassed	_____	Surprised	_____
Alive	_____	Anxious	_____
Insecure	_____	Intense	_____
Challenged	_____	Rewarded	_____

Culture shock basically refers to a stressful transitional period when individuals move from a familiar environment into an unfamiliar one. In this unfamiliar environment, the individual's identity appears to be stripped of all protection. Previously familiar cues and scripts are suddenly inoperable in the new cultural setting. Let's check out a brief story in Double Take 5.2.

Double Take 5.2

I've been an international student here for almost one year now. I've experienced culture shock in many different ways. One incident I remembered clearly was that when I first arrived, Americans always liked to ask me, "How are you?" I learned quickly that I should say "Fine!"

However, one time I was really in a bad mood—because I was struggling with many of my classes. When an American classmate asked me, "How are you?" I answered "Not so good at all because. . . ." I barely finished my answer, and I could see I had violated some communication norm. My American classmate's face dropped, and she quickly moved on, saying, "Got to go, see you later!" Those early weeks were really tough and confusing. My textbook English did not prepare me to communicate properly with my American friends.

—Yemi, *College Student*

For many international students or sojourners, the previously familiar cultural safety net has all of a sudden vanished. Communication scripts have changed. From how to say a proper "hello" to how to say a proper "goodbye" in the new culture, every interaction moment could create unintentional awkwardness or stress. Unfamiliarity creates perceived threat, and perceived threat triggers fear and emotional vulnerability.

Oberg (1960), an anthropologist, actually coined the term *culture shock* nearly five decades ago. He believed that culture shock produces an identity disorientation state, which can bring about tremendous stress and pressure on the well-being of an individual. Culture shock involves (1) a sense of identity loss and identity deprivation with regard to values, status, profession, friends, and possessions; (2) identity strain as a result of the effort required to make necessary psychological adaptation; (3) identity rejection by members of the new culture; (4) identity confusion, especially regarding role ambiguity and unpredictability; and (5) identity powerlessness as a result of not being able to cope with the new environment (Furnham, 1988). An identity disorientation state is part of the culture shock experience.

In fact, Ward, Bochner, and Furnham (2001) discuss the *ABC's of culture shock* in terms of the affective, behavioral, and cognitive disorientation dimensions. Affectively, sojourners in the initial culture shock stage often experience anxiety, bewilderment, confusion, disorientation, and perplexity as well as an intense desire to be elsewhere. Behaviorally, they are at the confusion stage in terms of the norms and rules that guide communication appropriateness and effectiveness. They are often at a loss in terms of how to initiate and maintain smooth conversations with their hosts and how to uphold themselves in a proper manner with the proper nonverbal cadences. Cognitively, they lack cultural interpretive competence to explain many of the "bizarre" behaviors that are occurring in their unfamiliar cultural settings.

Culture shock is sparked by the anxiety that results from "losing all our familiar signs and symbols of social discourse. These signs or cues include a thousand and one ways in which we orient ourselves to the situations of daily life: when to shake hands and what to say when we meet people, when and how to give tips" (Bochner, 1986, p. 48). Despite having repeated practice in these interactions in our own culture, we are not aware of its taken-for-granted significance until we are away from our culture. When we start feeling very inept in the new cultural environment and when our peace of mind is jolted all of a sudden, we start realizing the importance of intercultural learning and intercultural competence skills.

Culture Shock: Pros and Cons

Culture shock can have both positive and negative implications. Its negative implications include the following: psychosomatic problems (e.g., headaches, stomachaches) due to prolonged stress, affective upheavals consisting of feelings of loneliness, isolation, depression, and drastic mood swings, interaction awkwardness due to the inability to perform optimally in the new language and nonverbal postures, and cognitive exhaustion due to difficulties in making accurate attributions.

On the other hand, culture shock, if managed effectively, can have the following positive effects on the newcomer: a sense of well-being and heightened positive self-esteem, emotional richness and enhanced tolerance for ambiguity, behavioral competence in social interaction, cognitive openness and flexibility, and an enhanced optimism about self, others, and the everyday surroundings. Culture shock creates an environment and an opportunity for the individuals to experiment with new ideas and coping behaviors. It forces the individuals to stretch beyond the usual boundaries of thinking and experiencing.

Approaching Culture Shock: Underlying Factors

The following factors have been found to influence why people manage their culture shock experience differently: motivational orientations, personal expectations, cultural distance, sociocultural adjustment, psychological adjustment, and personality attributes.

Sojourners' *motivational orientation* to leave their home countries and enter a new culture has a profound influence on their culture shock attitudes. Individuals with voluntary motivations (e.g., Peace Corps volunteers) to leave a familiar culture and enter a new cultural experience tend to manage their culture shock experience more effectively than do individuals with involuntary motivations (e.g., refugees). Furthermore, sojourners (e.g., international students) encounter less conformity pressure than do immigrants because of their temporary visiting role. Host cultures often extend a more friendly welcome to sojourners than to immigrants or refugees. Thus, sojourners tend to perceive their overall international stay as more pleasant and the local hosts as more friendly than do immigrants or refugees.

Personal expectations have long been viewed as a crucial factor in the culture shock management process. Expectations refer to the anticipatory process and predictive outcome of the upcoming situation. Two observations have often been associated with such expectations: The first is that realistic expectations facilitate intercultural adaptation, and the second is that accuracy-based positive expectations ease adaptation stress (Ward, 1996). Individuals with realistic expectations are better prepared psychologically to deal with actual adaptation problems than are individuals with unrealistic expectations. Furthermore, individuals with positive expectations tend to create a positive self-fulfilling prophecy in their successful adaptation (e.g., you think this is a great relocation move, and your thinking affects your positive actions); negative expectations tend to produce the opposite effect.

Past research (Ward et al., 2001) indicates that most international students tend to carry positive expectation images concerning their anticipated sojourn in the new culture. Overall, realistic and positively oriented expectancy images of the new culture can help to facilitate intercultural adaptation for both business and student sojourners. Expectations influence newcomers' mindsets, sentiments, and behaviors. A positively resilient mindset helps to balance the negative stressors that a newcomer may encounter in his or her adaptive efforts.

Overall, sojourners tend to encounter more severe culture shock when the cultural distance between their home cultures and the host society is high. **Cultural distance** factors can include differences in cultural values, language, verbal styles, nonverbal gestures, learning styles, decision-making styles, and conflict negotiation styles, as well as in religious, sociopolitical, and economic systems. Interestingly, however, when sojourners expect that the cultural distance is low, they may actually encounter more intercultural frustrations. These individuals become less culturally astute in dealing with the hosts from a perceived similar language/cultural background (e.g., U.S. Americans dealing with Britons in Britain; Spaniards in Spain dealing with Mexicans in Mexico). Due to this "assumed similarity" factor, both guests and hosts may gloss over the cultural difference dimension. They may overlook the vast differences in political or business practices. They may start using disparaging remarks in attacking the personality traits of their new cultural hosts and ignore any nuanced cultural difference that may exist. Both hosts and guests may encounter more frustrations without realizing that they are caught up in a very understated culture clash spiral.

Sociocultural adjustment refers to the ability to fit in and execute appropriate and effective interactions in a new cultural environment (Ward et al., 2001). It can include factors such as the quality or quantity of relations with host nationals and the length of residence in the host country. International students, for example, reported greater satisfaction with their host culture when host nationals took the initiative to befriend them. It has also been revealed that international students' friendship networks typically consist of the following patterns: (1) a primary, monocultural friendship network that consists of close friendships with other compatriots from similar cultural backgrounds (e.g., German international students developing friendship ties with other European students); (2) a bicultural network that consists of social bonds between sojourners and host nationals, whereby professional aspirations and goals are pursued; and (3) a multicultural network that consists of acquaintances from diverse cultural groups for recreational activities (Furnham & Bochner, 1982). Research further indicates that greater sociocultural adjustment and social support in the new cultural environment are associated with lower levels of depression and hopelessness in international students (see Know Thyself 5.1). Overall, culture-specific knowledge, language fluency, more extensive contact with host nationals, and a longer period of residence in the host culture are associated with lower levels of sociocultural difficulty in the new culture (Ward, 1996). In addition, the host culture's receptivity to new arrivals, the degree of cultural conformity expected, and the current political climate of open-door versus closed-door attitudes toward international students and visitors can also either facilitate or create roadblocks to sojourners' sociocultural adjustment process.

Know Thyself 5.1   Assessing Your Social Support Circle

Think of a stressful situation in which you have made a major transition (e.g., from high school to college; from an old job to a new job; from home to living on your own), read each item, and circle **T = True** or **F = False**. In this new environment, you actually have friends or acquaintances

1. To listen to and talk with you whenever you feel lonely   T or F
   or depressed.

2. To reassure you that you are supported and cared for.   T or F

3. To explain things and to make your situation clearer   T or F
   and easier to understand.

4. To spend some quiet time with you whenever you do   T or F   ☞
   not feel like going out.

☞

Know Thyself 5.1   Assessing Your Social Support Circle (*cont.*)

5. To explain and help you understand the local culture
   and communication issues.   T or F
6. To provide necessary information to help orient you
   to your new surroundings.   T or F
7. To help you interpret things that you don't really understand.   T or F
8. To tell you about available choices and options.   T or F
9. To show you how to do something that you didn't know
   how to do.   T or F

Scoring: Add up all your answers on TRUE. ***Decoding:*** 1–3 = low social support; 4–6 = moderate social support; 7–9 = high social support.

Interpreting: The higher your score, the greater your social support circle. The greater the social support circle, the easier it is for you to adjust to your transitional phase in a new environment.

Adapted from: Ong (2000). "The Construction and Validation of a Social Support Scale for Sojourners: The Index of Sojourner Social Support." Unpublished master's thesis, National University of Singapore, as cited in Ward et al. (2001), p. 89.

Psychological adjustment refers to feelings of well-being and satisfaction during cross-cultural transitions (Ward et al., 2001). (See Table 5.1). Chronic strain, low self-esteem, and low mastery have a direct effect on adjustment depression. As cultural distance widens and stress level increases, newcomers need to use different strategies to deal with such differences. According to research, there are two types of coping strategies: primary and secondary (Chang, Chua, & Toh, 1997; Cross, 1995).

Table 5.1 Characteristics of Sociocultural Adjustment Versus Psychological Adjustment	
Sociocultural Adjustment	**Psychological Adjustment**
Relationship Management	Stress Management
Network-Related	Psychologically-Related
Relationship Quality	Perceptual Interpretation
Host Culture Receptivity	Intrapersonal Control
Reaching Out	Digging In
Sociocultural Climate	Cognitive Reframing

Primary strategies are behavioral actions that aim to avoid or change the intrusive incidents in the stressful environment. For example, as a junior college student abroad, you purposely avoid taking all the German-speaking classes and, instead, you take all the English-speaking classes in the International Program in Munich, Germany.

Secondary strategies are more cognitive than behavioral—they involve changing perceptions and appraisals of the stressful events or situations. For example, you start to talk yourself into taking more German-speaking classes because you realize that one of your program goals is to master the German language. Overall, the primary strategies imply changing the situation to tailor to one's self-interest goal, whereas the secondary strategies imply changing one's thinking pattern to adapt to the environment. Research indicated that the use of secondary coping strategies (i.e., acceptance and positive reinterpretation) is associated with lower levels of perceived stress and fewer symptoms of depression in East Asian students in Singapore. Primary strategies, in contrast, did not assert a direct effect on perceived stress (Ward, 2004). Thus, cognitive reframing appears to soften the psychological stress level for East Asian students who are attempting to adapt to a collectivistic cultural environment. The nature of the stressful event and the degree of control and success that the students can assert on the distressing situation may explain this interesting finding.

In regard to *personality attributes*, such personality traits as high tolerance for ambiguity (i.e., high acceptance of ambiguous situations), internal locus of control (i.e., inner-directed drives and motivations), personal flexibility, and mastery can contribute to general good adjustment and positive psychological well-being. Interestingly, Ward (2004) also suggests a "cultural fit" proposition, which emphasizes the importance of a good match between personality types (e.g., extraversion and introversion) of the sojourners and the host cultural norms. For example, we can speculate that independent-self sojourners may be more compatible with individualistic cultural norms, whereas interdependent-self sojourners may be more compatible with collectivistic cultural norms. The synchronized match between a particular personality type and the larger cultural norms produces a "goodness of fit" and possibly cultivates a positive adaptive experience for the visiting residents.

Managing Culture Shock: Initial Tips

The fundamental need for newcomers in an unfamiliar culture is addressing the sense of emotional insecurity and vulnerability. The more competent newcomers are at managing their identity threat level, the more they are able to induce effective adaptation outcomes.

New arrivals can defuse their perceived threat and, hence, anxiety level by (1) increasing their motivations to learn about the new culture; (2) keeping their expectations realistic and increasing their familiarity concerning the diverse facets of the new culture (e.g., conducting culture-specific research through readings and diverse accurate sources, including talking with people who have spent some time in that culture); (3) increasing their linguistic fluency and learning why, how, and under what situations certain phrases or gestures are appropriate, plus understanding the core cultural values linked to specific behaviors; (4) working on their tolerance for ambiguity and other flexible personal attributes; (5) developing strong ties (close friends) and weak ties (acquaintanceships) to manage identity stress and loneliness; and (6) being mindful of their interpersonal behaviors and suspending ethnocentric evaluations of the host culture.

Intercultural Adjustment: Developmental Patterns

The term **intercultural adjustment** has been used to refer to the short-term and medium-term adaptive process of sojourners in their overseas assignments. Tourists are different from sojourners in that tourists are visitors whose length of stay exceeds 24 hours in a location away from home and who have traveled for voluntary, recreational holiday-enjoyment purposes. Sojourners, on the other hand, are temporary residents who voluntarily go abroad for a set period of time that is usually related to task-based or instrumental purposes. Both tourists and sojourners can, of course, experience culture shock—especially when the country they visit is very different from their own (see Snapshot 5.1). In fact, do you know which are the top worldwide tourist destinations? Take a guess and then check out Jeopardy Box 5.1. Where do you think most tourists to the United States come from (i.e., their countries of origin)? What do you think are the top-three tourism cities in the United States? Take a quick guess and check out Jeopardy Box 5.2 and Jeopardy Box 5.3. A tourist, while visiting another country, can be a welcome guest, a nuisance, or a downright intruder in a sacred land. Tourists, their hosts, and businesses/service providers all weave together interdependently to form impressions, to trade, and to share some memorable moments through brief encounters and amusing contacts.

Sojourners, however, are typically individuals who commit to a temporary residential stay in a

Snapshot 5.1

Do these fish egg bowls look appetizing?

Jeopardy Box 5.1 Top-Ten Worldwide Tourist Destinations, 2003

Country

1. France
2. Spain
3. United States
4. Italy
5. China
6. United Kingdom
7. Austria
8. Mexico
9. Germany
10. Canada

Source: World Tourism Organization (June 2004) http://www.world-tourism.org/news-room/Releases/2004/june/data.htm (Retrieved June 25, 2004).

Jeopardy Box 5.2 Top-Ten Countries of Origin of Visitors to the United States, 2003

Country

1. Canada
2. Mexico
3. United Kingdom
4. Japan
5. Germany
6. France
7. South Korea
8. Italy
9. Australia
10. The Netherlands

Source: U.S. Department of Commerce, Office of Travel and Tourism Industries (2004). http://ti-dev.eainet.com/view/f-2003-203-001/index.html?ti_cart_cookie=20040707.210407.18294 (Retrieved June 1, 2004).

Jeopardy Box 5.3 Top-Ten Tourism Cities in the United States, 2003

City	State
1. New York	New York
2. Los Angeles	California
3. Miami	Florida
4. Orlando	Florida
5. San Francisco	California
6. Oahu/Honolulu	Hawaii
7. Las Vegas	Nevada
8. Washington, DC	(Metro)
9. Chicago	Illinois
10. Boston	Massachusetts

Source: U.S. Department of Commerce, Office of Travel and Tourism Industries (2004). http://ti-dev.eainet.com/view/f-2001-45-561/index.html?ti_cart_cookie=20040307.002823.18497 (Retrieved February 1, 2004).

new culture as they strive to achieve both their instrumental and socio-emotional goals. *Instrumental goals* refer to task-based goals that sojourners would like to accomplish during their stay in a foreign country. *Socio-emotional goals* refer to relational, recreational, and personal development goals during their sojourning experience. Thus, a Peace Corps volunteer might take an overseas assignment for a year or two for both task and personal enrichment purposes. A business person might accept an international posting for between three and five years. A missionary might go for a longer period, and military personnel are often posted overseas for shorter "tours of duty." Each year, for example, over 1.3 million students worldwide choose to study outside their countries. There are approximately 586,000 international students right now, studying in different U.S. colleges with the explicit aim of getting their college degrees here. They also bring $12 billion into the U.S. economy via out-of-state tuition and living expenses. In fact, do you know where most of the international students come from? Take a guess and check out Jeopardy Box 5.4. Do you know what are the top-pick countries for U.S. student-abroad programs? Take a guess and check out Jeopardy Box 5.5.

Jeopardy Box 5.4 Top-Ten Countries of Origin of International Students to the United States, 2002/2003

Country
1. India
2. China
3. Republic of Korea
4. Japan
5. Taiwan
6. Canada
7. Mexico
8. Turkey
9. Indonesia
10. Thailand

Source: *NAFSA: Association of International Education Fact Sheet* (2003). http://opendoors. iienetwork.org (Retrieved September 1, 2003).

Indeed, most of the international students come from communal-oriented cultures, such as India, China, South Korea, Japan, and Taiwan. There are also approximately 11 percent or 154,168 U.S. students nationwide who embark on a one-year study abroad program. The favorite study abroad destinations of U.S. college students are the United Kingdom, Italy, Spain, France, and Mexico. These students cited personal growth, new perspectives on world affairs, and career enhancement as some of the reasons for why they opt to go abroad to study. Beyond instrumental goals, international exchange sojourners

Jeopardy Box 5.5 Top-Ten Study Abroad Locations for U.S. College Students, 2002

<u>Country</u>
1. United Kingdom
2. Italy
3. Spain
4. France
5. Mexico
6. Australia
7. Germany
8. Ireland
9. Costa Rica
10. China

Source: http://www.iie.org, Institute of International Education (Retrieved September 1, 2003).

also pursue socio-emotional goals or fun activities, such as developing new friendships with the local students and hosts, visiting local marketplaces and museums, and learning about local histories, sports, and folk crafts.

In the remainder of this section, we explore the developmental models of the short- to medium-term adjustment process of sojourners. By understanding the developmental phases of intercultural adjustment, we can increase our competencies in dealing with our own and others' change process.

The U-Curve Adjustment Model

A number of researchers have conceptualized the sojourners' adjustment process from various developmental perspectives. An interesting consequence of these stage-oriented descriptive models centers on whether sojourners' adaptation is a U-curve or a W-curve process. In interviewing over 200 Norwegian Fulbright grantees in the United States, Lysgaard (1955) developed a three-phase intercultural adjustment model that includes (1) initial adjustment, (2) crisis, and (3) regained adjustment: The (1) is the optimistic or elation phase of the sojourners' adjustment process, the (2) is the stressful phase, when reality sets in and the sojourners are overwhelmed by their own incompetence, and the (3) is the settling-in phase, when sojourners learn to cope effectively with the new environment.

Drawing from the above ideas, Lysgaard (1955; see also Nash, 1991) proposed the U-curve model of the sojourners' adjustment process, suggesting that sojourners pass through an initial honeymoon phase, then experience a "slump" or stressful phase, and finally pull themselves back up to an effective phase in managing their assignments abroad. In extending the U-curve model, Gullahorn and Gullahorn (1963) proposed a six-stage W-shaped model, with successive honeymoon, hostility, humorous, at-home, reentry culture shock, and resocialization stages. Expanding the ideas of Gullahorn and Gullahorn, we have developed the following seven-stage revised W-shaped adjustment model to explain sojourners' short-term to medium-term adjustment process (see Figure 5.1).

Figure 5.1   Revised W-Shaped Adjustment Model

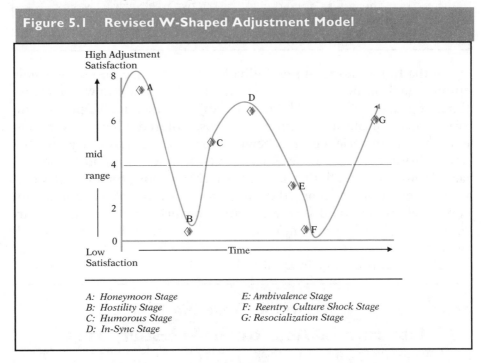

A: *Honeymoon Stage*
B: *Hostility Stage*
C: *Humorous Stage*
D: *In-Sync Stage*

E: *Ambivalence Stage*
F: *Reentry Culture Shock Stage*
G: *Resocialization Stage*

The Revised W-Shaped Adjustment Model

The revised W-shaped adjustment model consists of seven stages: the honeymoon, hostility, humorous, in-sync, ambivalence, reentry culture shock, and resocialization stages. The model applies especially to international students' experience abroad. Take a look first at Double Take 5.3 and check out the experience abroad of one college student, Laleh.

Double Take 5.3
Intercultural Adjustment—Honeymoon Stage

W-Shaped Model
Narrative. . . .

I feel like I went through several of the stages of culture shock while I

was doing a Junior [Year] Abroad study program in Spain. The *honey-*

☞

moon stage was great. This was right when I got there. I thought that everything was wonderful. I didn't really miss being at home because I was doing so many new and exciting things. I was traveling through the south of Spain, who would ever think that there was something better than that? I was having such a good time and didn't really seem to even notice that I was so far away. I thought that Spain was a great place. I wasn't able to see any of the downfalls. I would practice my Spanish with as many people as I could find. It was a very exciting time. I would say that this period lasted for about two weeks, while I was traveling through Spain.

—Laleh, *College Student*

In the **honeymoon stage,** individuals are excited about their new cultural environment. This is the initial landing phase in which everything appears fresh and exhilarating. Sojourners perceive people and events through pleasantly tinted (or "rose-colored") lenses. Nonetheless, they do experience mild bewilderment and perplexity about the new culture; they also experience bursts of loneliness and homesickness. However, overall, they are cognitively curious about the new culture and emotionally charged up at meeting new people. They may not completely understand the verbal and nonverbal behaviors that surround them, but they are enjoying their initial "friendly" contacts with the locals.

Check out the story in Double Take 5.4.

Double Take 5.4
Intercultural Adjustment—Hostility Stage

Then the *hostility stage* hit. I think that the turning point was the first night when I was at my senora's house. This experience was a huge shock to me. The apartment that I was living in was about a sixth of the size of my house. I was sharing a room that was the size of a shoebox. Needless to say I was really unhappy, at first. The minute that I got there it really hit me that I was living in another country for a long time without my family. To make things even worse, the room had no windows. All I wanted to do was go home. I didn't want to be in this little apartment with some woman that I didn't know, who didn't speak a word of English. I immediately called my dad crying. I told him that I wanted to come home and that I wasn't going to stay in Spain for a whole semester. After about a half an hour of listening to me whine and cry, my dad told me that I had to stay because he knew that that was what I really wanted and that this was just a bump in the road. He told me that I would get used to things and that everything would be all right. I thought that he had gone crazy.

The following few weeks were full of ups and downs. I was in an environment [in which] I didn't know what to do. I didn't even know where to buy the basic things that I needed. I felt like I was in a whole other world that didn't exist to me before. I had to learn how to take public transportation, which is something that I had never done before. After countless times of get-

☞ | ting on the wrong bus, I finally fig- | able to put together only the most
ured it out. I would get frustrated | basic of sentences.
because I wasn't able to express
what was going on, because I was | —Laleh, *College Student*

In the *hostility stage,* sojourners experience major emotional upheavals. This is the serious culture shock stage in which nothing is working out smoothly. This stage can occur rapidly right after the glow of the honeymoon phase is over and reality sets in sooner than expected. At this stage, sojourners experience a major loss of self-esteem and self-confidence. They feel incompetent and emotionally drained in many areas. Many of these sojourners can either become very aggressive or hostile in the new culture or become totally withdrawn. Anderson (1994), for example, identifies four types of "culture shockers" as follows: (1) the early returnees—those who tend to use aggressive or passive aggressive strategies to deal with the "hostile" environment and exit prematurely back to their home cultures; (2) the time servers—those who are doing a minimally passable job with minimal host contact and who are emotionally and cognitively "serving their time," but eagerly looking forward to returning home; (3) the adjusters—those who are slowly adjusting and doing a moderately effective job and are learning to mix with the host members to pursue their instrumental goals; and (4) the participators—those who are committed to adjust in an optimal manner and participate fully in their new culture and who take advantage of both instrumental and socio-emotional learning in the new environment.

The "early returnees" tend to use either *fight* or *pounce* strategies and blame all the problems on the new culture. They constantly use their own cultural standards to compare and evaluate the local practices and customs. They are operating from a highly ethnocentric state. The "time servers," on the other hand, tend to use *flee* or *avoidance* strategies. They use either physical avoidance or psychological withdrawal strategies to avoid interacting with host members. They also tend to engage in wishful thinking strategies and counting the days until they can go home. The "adjusters" tend to use segmentation strategies to function adaptively in the new culture. Although they make progress in pursuing their task-related goals, they have not grown or stretched in the socio-emotional domain. The "participators," on the other hand, use active commitment strategies to realign their identities with the new culture. They try to connect their newly acquired knowledge with skillful practice. They are committed to using an ethnorelative lens to view things from the other culture's frame of reference. With the help of supportive networks, incremental goal progression, and emotional resilience, many of the sojourners can pull themselves out from the hostility stage and arrive at the recovery curve.

Now let's check out Double Take 5.5, the humorous stage description.

Double Take 5.5
Intercultural Adjustment—Humorous Stage

The *humorous stage* was a little bit more enjoyable. I did have many times when I found myself doing something wrong and was able to laugh at myself. Once I was able to laugh about it and not worry so much about what I was doing, I felt a lot better. However, I still haven't gotten the hang of the whole kissing on both cheeks when you meet. I will still offer them my hand and they will be leaning in to kiss me. It is like an awkward first date goodbye. I do not think that I fully experienced that **in-sync stage**. I feel like I became more accustomed to what was going on, but I was never completely comfortable with many of the "strange" cultural situations. The longer I stayed there the more I got used to things. However, I was still wishing that things could have been more like home. I never understood why you couldn't just go in somewhere and order a nice turkey sandwich. There were little things that would get on my nerves on a daily basis, but I was able to work through them. I guess I became more in-sync with what was going on around me. I knew what I needed to do to get what I wanted, which was a big accomplishment.

—Laleh, *College Student*

At the **humorous stage,** sojourners learn to laugh at their cultural *faux pas* and start to realize that there are pros and cons in each culture—just as there are both good and evil people in every society. They experience a mixture of stress-adaptation-growth emotions (Y. Y. Kim, 1988, 2004), such as small frustrations and small triumphs. They are able to compare both their home and host cultures in realistic terms, and they no longer take things as seriously as in the hostility stage. They can now take a step backward and look at their own behavior and reactions objectively. Taskwise, they are making progress in attaining their instrumental goals (e.g., achieving their MBA degree or acquiring new business skills). They are beginning to form new friendships and social networks. These sojourners eventually arrive at the next stage.

At the **in-sync adjustment stage,** sojourners feel "at home" and experience identity security and inclusion. The boundaries between outsiders and insiders become fuzzier, and the sojourners experience social acceptance and support. They are now easily able to "make sense" of the "bizarre" local customs and behaviors. They may well be able to converse in the local language with flair, even catching some verbal jokes and puns and perhaps responding with a one-up joke.

They may now even act as role models or mentors to incoming sojourners from their home cultures. During the in-sync adjustment stage, sojourners develop a sense of trust and empathy and a wide spectrum of other positive emotions. They become much more creative and adaptive in the new environment. They are capable of making appropriate choices in connection with any new situations that may arise. Just as they arrive at a "comfort level" of their sojourn, however, they have to get ready to pack their bags and go home.

Let's check out Laleh's ambivalent feelings in Double Take 5.6.

Double Take 5.6
Intercultural Adjustment—Ambivalence Stage

I had two different experiences with the *ambivalence stage*. When I was leaving to come home for Christmas, I had a feeling like I hadn't accomplished everything that I wanted to. Which was why I decided to stay for another semester. There were so many things that I still wanted to do, and I felt that if I didn't stay for another semester that I would be cheating myself out of more wonderful cultural experiences. The second experience that I had with the ambivalence stage was quite different. When it was getting to the end of the second semester, I was totally ready to go home. I was ready to get out of there three weeks before school was over. I was tired of not being able to communicate like I wanted to. I had all my bags packed and [was] ready to take off and share all my wonderful stories with my family and friends.

—Laleh, *College Student*

In the **ambivalence stage,** sojourners experience grief, nostalgia, and pride, with a mixed sense of relief and sorrow that they are going home. They recall their early awkward days in the new culture, and they all count the new friends they have made since then. They also look forward eagerly to sharing all their intercultural stories with their family members and old friends back home. They finally say goodbye to their newfound friends and their temporarily adopted culture.

At the **reentry culture shock stage,** sojourners face an unexpected jolt (see the "Reentry Culture Shock" section that follows). Because of the unanticipated nature of reentry shock, its impact is usually much more severe, and returnees usually feel more depressed and stressed than they did with entry culture shock. There is a sharp sense of letdown (e.g., their friends or family members have no interest in hearing all their wonderful intercultural stories) and identity disjunction: The greater the distance (i.e., on the cultural values and communication dimensions) between the two cultures, the more intense the reentry shock. By now, though, most sojourners have become resourceful and resilient individuals. They can recycle some of the commitment strategies they used abroad to pull themselves through to the next stage.

In the **resocialization stage,** some individuals (i.e., the resocializers) may quietly assimilate themselves back to their old roles and behaviors without making much of a "wave" or appearing different from the rest of their peers or colleagues. They bury their newly acquired ideas and skills together with the snapshots in their photo albums and try not to look at them again. Looking at these pictures can only cause identity dissonance and disequilibrium. Other individuals (i.e., the alienators) can never "fit back" into their home cultures again. They are always the first to accept an overseas assignment. They feel more alive abroad than at home. These alienators may eventually become global nomads who claim the world as their home rather than any single place as their base culture. Finally, yet other individuals (i.e., the transformers) are the ones who act as agents of change in their home organizations or cultures. They mindfully integrate their new learning experience abroad with what is positive in their own culture. They apply multidimensional thinking, enriched emotional intelligence, and diverse angles to solve problems or to instigate change for a truly inclusive learning organization.

Transformers are the change agents who bring home with them a wealth of personal and cultural treasures to share, actively and responsibly, with colleagues, friends, and families. They do so with interpersonally sensitive skills—something they have learned in the foreign environment. They have no fears of acting or being perceived as "different"; they now have a "taste" of what it means to be "different" (however, this taste of difference is qualitatively different from the "difference" that many minority members experience in their everyday lives). They are comfortable in experiencing the identity double-swing process, for example, individualist and collectivist, low context and high context. They are more compassionate and committed than before about social injustice issues and human rights issues on a global scale. Transformers are the individuals who have acquired (and are always in the process of acquiring) mindfulness, compassion, and wisdom.

Culture Shock: Peaks and Valleys

In sum, the revised W-shaped adjustment model basically emphasizes the following characteristics, which can influence the progress of the sojourners' identity change process: (1) They need to understand the peaks and valleys, and positive and negative shifts, that constitute identity change in an unfamiliar environment, realizing that the frustration-and-triumph roller-coaster ride is part of the change-and-growth process. (2) They need to be aware and keep track of their instrumental, relational, and identity goals in the new culture; success in one set of goals (e.g., making new friends) can affect triumph in another set of goals (e.g., newfound friends can help to solve a school-related problem). (3) They need to give themselves some time and space to adjust; they should keep a journal to express their daily feelings and random thoughts, and they should also keep in touch with people in their home culture via letters, faxes, and e-mail. (4) They need to develop both strong ties (meaningful friendships) and weak ties (functional social connections, e.g., with supportive teachers, caring counselors, or friendly grocers) to cushion themselves and seek help in times of crisis. (5) They need to reach out to participate in the host culture's major cultural events—art and music festivals, parades, local museums, or national sports—and immerse themselves in this once-in-a-lifetime experience and learn to enjoy the local culture as much as possible.

The patterns of the revised W-shaped adjustment model consist of back-and-forth looping movements within and between stages. Length of sojourn, alone or with family, degree of adaptation commitment, degrees and types of communication competence (e.g., linguistic competence), first-time visit versus repeated visit, and realistic versus unrealistic goals are some other factors that will propel either progressive or regressive loops along the W-shaped model.

Church (1982) and Ward (2004), in reviewing the literature on these developmental models, comment that both the U-curve and W-shape models appear to be too general and do not capture the dynamic interplay between sojourners' and host nationals' factors in the adjustment process. In addition, sojourners adapt and learn at different rates. The support for both models is based on one-time cross-sectional data (i.e., one-time surveys of sojourners) rather than longitudinal data (i.e., collection of surveys at different points during sojourners' two-year adjustment). More controversial is the debate as to the initial phase (i.e., the *honeymoon stage*) of adjustment. Recent research (Osland, 1995; Rohrlich & Martin, 1991) indicates that international students and managers both tend to experience severe identity shock (i.e., the *hostility stage* comes very early, side by side with the fleeting honeymoon stage) in the early phase of their sojourn abroad. However, the overseas stressors also motivate them to become more resourceful and resilient in their search for new knowledge and skills in managing the alien environment.

Despite some of the limitations of the developmental models, their positive implications are that they offer us a developmental portrait of the culture shock experience, illustrate that the culture shock process is filled with peaks and valleys, and contribute to a holistic understanding of the psychological, affective, and identity changes in the new arrivals. Additionally, in the W-shaped model, we are made aware of the importance of understanding the role of *reentry culture shock.*

Reentry Culture Shock

The phenomenon of reentry culture shock has received increased attention from intercultural researchers (Martin, 2004; Martin & Harrell, 1996; Sussman, 1986). Reentry shock involves the realignment of one's new identity with a once familiar home environment. After living abroad for an extensive period of time, reentry culture shock is inevitable.

Let's check out Kari's reentry feelings in Double Take 5.7.

Double Take 5.7

I had problems readapting after spending a year in Italy. I have been feeling stuck in this reentry period for a little longer than normal. I feel like there is no one else who feels like I do, everyone else seems to transition effortlessly. But in a way, I feel bad for those people. I think that the reason that I feel the way I do is because I absorbed so much when I was there. I completely opened myself up to whatever new culture I came across, and this had a direct impact on how I look at things. . . . Though I seem to be temporarily stuck in the depression phase of it all, I would rather feel like this than to have let the experience pass me by with no impact at all.

—Kari, *College Student*

This identity realignment process can sometimes be more stressful and jolting than entry culture shock because of the unanticipated nature of one's own identity change and the accompanying change of one's friends and family.

Reentry Culture Shock: Surprising Elements

According to research (e.g., Osland, 1995), the often unanticipated, surprising elements that affect reentry culture shock include the following:

1. sojourners' identity change—the newly acquired values, emotions, cognitions, role statuses, managerial methods, and behaviors are, surprisingly, not a "good fit" with the once familiar home culture;

2. sojourners' nostalgic and idealized images of their home culture—sojourners tend to remember the positive aspects of their culture and forget its negative aspects during their experience abroad, and thus, the reentry reality often produces a strong jolt;

3. sojourners' difficulty in reintegrating themselves into their old career pathway or career roles because of their new cultural lenses;

4. sojourners' letdown in their expectations as to close ties with family members and friends who have become more distant because of the long separation;

5. family and friends' lack of interest in listening to the sojourning stories of the returnee and their growing impatience with her or him;

6. the home culture's demand for conformity and expectations for old role performance;

7. the absence of change in the home culture (e.g., the old system or workplace looks stale and boring in comparison with the overseas adventure), or too much change (e.g., political or corporate upheavals), which can also create immense identity disjunction for the recent returnees.

Thus, reentry culture shock can be understood from three domains: the returnees' readiness to resocialize themselves in the home environment, the degree of change in the returnees' friendship and family networks, and the home receptivity conditions. Sussman (1986) recommends that on the individual level, awareness of change should be a major component of reentry training as individuals face a wide range of psychological and environmental challenges. Pusch and Loewenthall (1988) further recommend that preparation for a successful return should include (1) the recognition of what sojourners are leaving behind and what they have gained in their assignments abroad; (2) the emotional costs of transition; (3) the value of worrying (i.e., anticipating and preparing for difficulties that may occur); (4) the need for support systems and ways to develop them; and (5) the necessity of developing one's own strategies for going home.

Resocialization: Different Returnees' Profiles

Adler (1997) identifies three profiles of returnee managers in relationship to the specific transition strategies they employ: resocialized returnees, alienated returnees, and proactive returnees. *Resocialized returnees* are the ones who do not recognize having learned new skills in the new culture. They are also psychologically distant from their international experience. They try to use the fit-back-in strategy and resocialize themselves quietly into the domestic corporate structure. They typically rate their reentry experience as quite satisfactory.

The *alienated returnees*, on the other hand, are aware of their new skills and ideas in their experience abroad. However, they have difficulty in applying their new knowledge in the home organizations. Rather, they try to use the "distance-rejective" strategy of being onlookers in their home culture. Of all the three types, they are the most dissatisfied group.

The *proactive returnees* are highly aware of changes in themselves and the new values and skills they have learned overseas. They try to integrate the new values and practices learned from the sojourning culture into the home culture and develop an integrated outlook in their reentry phase. While abroad, the proactive managers tend to use proactive communication to maintain close ties with the home organization via formal and informal means. They also have a home-based mentor to look after their interests and pass on important corporate information. Their mentor keeps the home-based headquarters informed of the sojourner's achievements while abroad.

Proactive managers might report the acquisition of the following skills in their assignments abroad: alternative managerial skills, tolerance of ambiguity, multiple reasoning perspectives, and ability to work with and manage others. They further report that the new skills improve their self-image and self-confidence. Not surprisingly, returnees who receive validation (e.g., promotions) from their bosses and recognition from their colleagues report higher reentry satisfaction than do returnees who receive no such validation or recognition (Adler, 1997).

Intercultural Toolkit: Recaps and Checkpoints

In this chapter, we explored the pros and cons of culture shock as we crossed cultural boundaries. We then explained some of the factors of why people manage culture shock differently.

We also talked about the developmental ups and downs of culture shock and suggested tips to manage culture shock adaptively. Last, we emphasized the importance of paying attention to reentry culture shock issues.

Overall, here are some practical tools for managing sojourners' culture shock effectively:

- Newcomers should realize that culture shock is an inevitable experience that most people encounter when relocating from a familiar environment to an unfamiliar one. Culture shock is induced because of perceived threat and emotional vulnerability in the unpredictable environment.

- New arrivals should understand that culture shock arises because of the unfamiliar environment, which is saturated with unfamiliar cues. Developing a supportive ethnic-based friendship network and easing themselves into the new setting slowly can help to restore the identity equilibrium state.

- Sojourners and immigrants should realize that part of the culture stress is due to their sense of acute disorientation with respect to unfamiliar norms and scripts in the new culture. Thus, making an effort to establish contacts with members of the host culture and learning to communicate with them can increase local knowledge and reduce such feelings of vulnerability. Likewise, the more members of the host culture extend a helping hand and the more they attempt to increase their familiarity with the new arrivals, the more they can increase the newcomers' sense of security and inclusion.

- Culture shock is induced partly by an intense feeling of incompetence. By seeking out positive role models or mentors, newcomers may be able to find reliable and competent cultural translators in easing the initial and developmental phases of their adaptation.

- Newcomers should realize that culture shock is a transitional affective phase of stress that ebbs and flows from high to low intensity. New arrivals need to hang on to a resilient sense of humor and emphasize the positive aspects of the environment rather than engaging in prolonged concentration on its negative aspects, realizing that these "growing pains" may lead to long-term personal and professional growth and development. ✦

Chapter 6

What Is the Relationship Between Language and Culture?

Chapter Outline

❑ Human Language: Distinctive Features
- Arbitrariness
- Abstractness
- Meaning-Centeredness
- Creativity

❑ Understanding Multiple Language Rules
- Phonological Rules
- Morphological Rules
- Syntactic Rules
- Semantic Rules
- Pragmatic Rules

❑ Understanding Diverse Language Functions
- The Cultural Worldview Function
- The Cognitive Formation Function
- The Social Reality Function
- The Group Identity Function
- The Social Change Function

❑ Intercultural Toolkit: Recaps and Checkpoints

Around the world, languages are disappearing. Native speakers of many indigenous cultures are dying off. Indigenous ethnic languages cannot compete with English—since English usage is pervasive throughout media, pop culture, and global technology. However, there are some cultural groups who are trying to reinvigorate their languages, despite the constraints.

Tribe leaders in Oklahoma, for example, are teaching young children Cherokee, legislation in South Africa is considering a bill to promote the equal use of 9 of its 11 official indigenous languages, and in Hawaii, there is an ambitious effort to bring the native Hawaiian language back from the brink of extinction. Many cultural activists all want to salvage the remnants of their cultures.

—Burns, *San Diego Union Tribune*
Septmeber 28, 2003

Indigenous people *refers to groups who are rooted to a particular place by history, traditions, legends, rituals, and language. According to expert linguists, an indigenous language dies every two weeks. For example, the*

Ariaal of Kenya, the Chipaya of Bolivia, and the Penan of Malaysia are endangered people with vanishing languages (Davis, 1999, August). With the death of a language comes the death of a people's way of thinking, living, and relating, their traditions, way of folklore, legacies, and centuries of irreplaceable knowledge and wisdom.

We use language to communicate, to agree and disagree with people, to make and decline requests, or to enforce politeness and defuse tension. Language frames our perceptions and interpretations of everyday events that are happening in our cultural community. It is a taken-for-granted aspect of our cultural lives. Without language, we cannot make sense of the cultural world around us. We cannot pass on the wisdom of our culture from one generation to the next.

We acquire meanings for words (e.g., competition, harmony) or phrases (e.g., love is a battlefield) via the value systems of our culture. Though language can easily create misunderstandings, it can also clarify misunderstandings and reduce friction. The "linguistic categories" we use in our everyday lives serve as a kaleidoscope that captures the multiple realities in our culture.

Language labels or the naming process highlights particular aspects of social reality that are deemed important or unimportant in our sociocultural lives. Language stretches our imagination to think of what is possible and what is going on in other cultures. It can transpose us to imagine a peaceful solution or violent act that would heal or destroy a relationship.

In this chapter we explore the relationships among language, perception, and culture. We will discuss different cultural-based verbal communication styles. This chapter is organized into four main sections: The first section explores the basic features of human language; the second section presents the multilayered rules of language; the third section examines the different functions of languages across cultures; and the last section offers checkpoints of how to deal with language difficulties when crossing cultural boundaries.

Human Language: Distinctive Features

Language is an arbitrary, symbolic system that names feelings, experiences, ideas, objects, events, groups, people, and other phenomena. Language is also governed by the *multilayered rules* developed by members of a particular sociocultural community. Although broad similarities exist among languages, tremendous variations remain in the sounds, written symbols, grammar, and nuances of meaning of an estimated 6,700 language varieties across worldwide cultures. This section examines the four distinctive features of language: arbitrariness, abstractness, meaning-centeredness, and creativity. The next section examines the multilayered rules of language usage in relationship to culture.

Arbitrariness

Human language is arbitrary in phonemic (i.e., sound unit) and graphic representation (i.e., alphabet or characters). Language is viewed as an arbitrary, symbolic system because the words that are strung together have no innate meaning. It is people in a speech community who attach meanings to words that they use in their everyday lives. For example, the word "kissing" has no real meaning in its sounds and letters, yet in English we interpret these sounds and letters as having a particular intimate meaning. Even sign language, as "spoken" by deaf people, is symbolic in nature. There are many different sign language varieties (e.g., American, British, and Chinese).

By the age of three months, infants have already acquired intonations or sounds similar to those changes in pitch heard in adult exclamations and questions. Through continuous reinforcement, children learn to retain sounds that are most familiar to their ears and tongues and drop off other nonessential sounds. In any culture, children first acquire speaking and comprehending skills, then reading and writing skills. While all children have the capacity to utter all the sounds in all languages, this linguistic competence tapers off as they reach puberty.

This explains why non-native speakers, even those fluent in English, appear to speak with a strange quality or an "accent." Russians, for example, even though rigorously trained to speak English, will still give themselves away when they pronounce the letter "t" in English. The Russian "t" is pronounced by contact between the tip of the tongue and the upper teeth. Native speakers of English pronounce "t" by making contact between the tongue, just back of its tip, and the upper gum ridge. Similarly, the French do not pronounce "h" if a word in English begins with "h," such as *hot dog* or *help*.

Can an accent be turned on or turned off? In the acting industry, it can. According to Griffen (2003), Latino/a actors are using their accents to their advantage by hiring dialect coaches. Learning a new dialect will provide more roles, and thus, more work. Dialect coaches are training Latino/a and non-Latino/a actors to use a variety of Latin American dialects. The cost for this coaching is approximately $100 for an hour-long session. An additional popular session is to learn to speak in "bland neutral American" voices.

Familiar sounds and words often create a comfort zone when we travel abroad. Unfamiliar sounds and signs often create confusion and puzzlement. When we hear and speak our own language, we often view our language as orderly and making perfect sense. However, when we hear non-native speakers speaking together, we often view the sound of that "foreign language" as nonsensical and random. Language is basically a subjective system that is created by humans to communicate, to reach out to each other, to bond, and to satisfy human survival needs.

Abstractness

Language, however, also allows humans to engage in abstract thoughts or hypothetical thinking. Because of this unique feature, we can plan for our intercultural trip, we can daydream, and we can fantasize about the infinite possibilities of our potential experience abroad. Our ability to use different linguistic categories to imagine ourselves in different locations, in different time zones, and in different social interaction scenes is truly a unique, human language feature.

We can also use language to remember the past, to comment about the present, and to anticipate the future. The more we move away from concrete, external phenomena, the more we engage in the process of language abstraction. In many instances, language creates intercultural friction because it is such an abstract, imprecise instrument. We can use language to negotiate conflict, reduce tension, and evoke peace and human connection.

Conversely, during the language negotiation process, we may provoke more conflict and misunderstanding. We may use words like *trust, reliable, unreliable, fair, unfair,* and *compromise* in a culturally-nuanced manner. Oftentimes, the use of such broad-based words can carry different meanings to the individuals who hold different experiential and cultural contexts for those words.

By *experiential context* we mean the experiential field of the person to whom the message is directed. For example, Kieran has very negative feelings for the word *compromise* because it makes him think of "moral compromise." Ahmed's intent when using *compromise* was the behavioral compromise of give-and-take. As a result, Kieran could misinterpret Ahmed's meaning, which may make the conflict situation more complex. By *cultural context* we mean the cultural field of the person to whom the message is intended. Again, using the same example, individualists (Kieran) for the most part tend to use the word "compromise" as task-based midpoint agreement; however, collectivists (Ahmed), perceive the term *compromise* as "relational give-and-take concessions." Furthermore, when we use language to cover a wide range of people or events, we start moving to the level of overgeneralizations and stereotypes. We hope that when we use terms such as *individualists* and *collectivists* in this book, you will realize that we are talking about general patterns of different cultures derived from empirical research data. And we ask that you keep in mind the important individual variations that exist within each culture.

Luckily, though, we can also use language to clarify our meaning and actual intentions when we feel that our communication process is jammed. When we perceive that the use of our language causes stress in our intercultural interaction, we may want to force ourselves to go "down the ladder" of symbolic abstraction—to use more specific words to comment on the perceived behaviors or incident. Likewise, we should also develop a sense of cultural sensitivity when we communicate with individuals from a linguistic system that values indirect, ambiguous communication styles.

Meaning-Centeredness

To understand a cultural stranger's language usage, we have to acquire both linguistic and interpretive competencies. The concept of "meaning" is tied closely to how we interpret the incoming verbal message. To truly understand what someone is saying, we need to understand five levels of meaning: discourse meaning, communicative meaning, relational meaning, situational meaning, and conventional meaning. **Discourse meaning** refers to both the denotative and connotative meaning of the word. Denotative meaning refers to objective, dictionary meaning, and connotative meaning refers to subjective, informal meaning (see next section on "Understanding Diverse Language Functions"). For example, the question "Are you flirting with me?" can conjure both objective and subjective interpretations from the standpoint of the receiver or decoder.

Communicative meaning refers to the intention and goal behind the discourse utterance. What is his or her intention when saying that? Why did he or she say that? To understand accurately the intention behind the verbal utterance, we have to understand the layers of relational meaning, situational meaning, and conventional meaning.

Relational meaning refers to relational distance and intimacy, and **situational meaning** refers to the physical and social context in which the utterance is made. If you have a close relationship with someone or you are attracted to that particular cultural stranger, a verbally flirtatious act can be fun and welcoming. However, if the verbal flirtation is inappropriate to the relationship and situation, you can actually view this as a sexual harassment overture. To understand a verbal utterance with accuracy and cultural sensitivity, we have to really master the conventional meaning as derived from the cultural context.

Thus, the **conventional meaning** of words refers to the needed coordination between verbal message usage and the expectations or norms of the cultural context. When is it appropriate to flirt and not to flirt? Who is the initiator of a verbal flirtation in this cultural community? What are the verbal/nonverbal routine and sequences when we engage in a playful, yet effective and appropriate, flirting exchange? In any interpersonal or intercultural communication, we should pay close attention to the unintended meanings behind the words we use.

Creativity

Language creativity is an underrated achievement of our human species. As indicated in the above discussion, people in all cultures have the capacity to talk about things far away in time and space (i.e., the displacement feature), to say things they have never said before by a mere reconfiguration of words in their native tongues (i.e., the productivity feature), and to use language (e.g., via oral history, epic poems, parables, or stories) to pass on their heritage and wisdom from one generation to the next (i.e., the traditional transmission feature). We can even use language to comment on the use of language itself, which serves the self-reflexivity function of human language. For example, we can say, "Let's use more precise language in this paragraph so that students can grasp the key point."

By the time children with normal language development patterns reach their fourth birthday, they have already internalized the exceedingly complex structure of their native tongue. Add a couple more years, and children will possess the entire linguistic system, allowing them the ability to utter and understand sentences they have never heard before. Parents do not have to teach their children every sentence in their language system. Humans have the creative potential to transform the basic recipes of their language system into infinite ways of communicating and expressing themselves.

Thus, it also means that individuals can garner their creative potential to use language mindfully for mutual collaboration and understanding. Alternatively, they can use language to disseminate hate-filled propaganda, engage in conflict, wage war, and engender destruction. Language can simultaneously be a hacking and a healing instrument—it can be used to "cut down" or degrade others' primary identities, but it can also be used mindfully to uplift and support their desired group-based or personal identities. The bottom line is that language is the key to the heart of a culture. Let's check out Picture This 6.1—an original poem, "Words," by Win Garcia, a college instructor.

What do you think of the poem? Can you relate to the words? Can you visualize his experience? Can you picture the hurting image of the word *wetback* versus the healing image of the word *love*?

Understanding Multiple Language Rules

Do you know what are the top-three languages spoken by most inhabitants of the world? What are the top-three official languages spoken in most countries? Take a guess and check out Jeopardy Box 6.1 and Jeopardy Box 6.2. All languages are constructed with words or symbols that are arranged in patterned ways, that is, they are rule governed. Most native speakers, however, cannot articulate clearly the rules of their own language because they use it daily on an unconscious

Picture This 6.1

WORDS
by Win Garcia

All their words were weapons
and they were aimed at me
"Wetback" was the chosen word
that others shot at me

I can feel the humiliation
I do remember the pain
how could an entire nation, I thought,
call me by an evil name?

Now the tide has shifted
for many of us "meek,"
we seem to be uplifted
by our refusal to be weak

I see their offspring walk about
attempting to hold on,
to their ideal of "sameness"
that is forever gone

Though I sometimes reminisce
about those painful years,
the words for me are different now
they range from "sir" to "dear"

I know that words are weapons
for many I have heard,
there are no needs for weapons here
only needs for loving words

Source: From Win Garcia, "Words" (an original poem). Copyright © 2004 by Win Garcia. Reprinted by permission.

competence level. We introduce the following rules of language here: phonology, morphology, syntactics, semantics, and pragmatics.

Jeopardy Box 6.1   Top-Ten Most Widely Spoken Languages Worldwide

Country (Language)	Approximate Number of Speakers
1. Chinese (Mandarin)	874,000,000
2. Hindustani*	426,000,000
3. Spanish	358,000,000
4. English	341,000,000
5. Bengali	207,000,000
6. Arabic#	206,000,000
7. Portuguese	176,000,000
8. Russian	167,000,000
9. Japanese	125,000,000
10. German	100,000,000

Notes: * = Hindi and Urdu are essentially the same language: Hindustani. As the official language of Pakistan, it is written in modified Arabic script and called Urdu. As the official language of India, it is written in the Devanagari script and called Hindi.
= includes 16 variants of the Arabic language.
Source: Adapted from Ash (2002), p. 100.

Jeopardy Box 6.2   Top-Ten Languages Officially Spoken in the Most Countries

Language	Countries
1. English	57
2. French	33
3. Arabic	23
4. Spanish	21
5. Portuguese	7
6. Dutch	5
7. German	5
8. Chinese/Mandarin	3
9. Danish	3
10. Italian	3
11. Malay	3

Note: Many countries have more than one official language—in Canada, for example, both English and French are officially recognized.
Source: Adapted from Ash (2002), p. 100.

Phonological Rules

The **phonological rules** (or **phonology**) of a language refers to the different accepted procedures for combining phonemes. **Phonemes** are the basic sound units of a word. For example, some of the phonemes in English are [k], [sh], and [t]. Native speakers of English, for example, may possess an intuitive sense of how to utter these sounds, such as *kiss, shy,* and *try;* however, they may not be able to articulate the how and why of the phonetic rules for producing these sounds. Although the English language has 45 phonemes, other languages have a range of phonemes spanning anywhere between 15 and 85.

Linguistically speaking, everyone who communicates speaks with an accent because **accent** means the inflection or tone of voice that is taken to be characteristic of an individual. Our inflection and tone of voice are unique. For example, law enforcement agencies sometimes use electronic equipment to generate "voiceprints" made from recordings of suspects' speech. These voiceprints can be used to help confirm the identities of the suspects because, like fingerprints, voiceprints are highly individualized.

Members of subcultures who are native speakers of the same language can also be identified as having accents. In such cases, the distinctive accents can be attributed to shared group membership. Many Bostonians, for example, claim that they can differentiate the Italian, Irish, and Jewish groups in their city by the way they articulate their /o(r)/ vowel sound (e.g., in words like "short" and "corn"). In casual speech situations, Italian Bostonians are the highest users of the /a(r)/ substitute sound (so that "short" sounds like "shot"—with no "r" sound), next are the Boston Irish, and then Jewish Bostonians. Ethnically distinct speech often indicates group solidarity. To a large degree, our accented speech pattern is reflective of our community group membership.

Unfortunately, we are sometimes very harsh on others and ourselves concerning accents. For example, a study conducted by Markley and Healy (2003) found that hiring decisions are sometimes based on how the job interviewer feels about the applicant's accent. In our personal life, our accent has a profound effect on how we relate to others.

Morphological Rules

The term **morphological rules** (or **morphology**) refers to how combinations of different sounds make up a meaningful word or part of a word (e.g., "new" and "com-er" form "new-com-er"). Phonemes combine to form morphemes, which are the smallest units of meaning in a language. In English and many other European languages, morphemes that are required by grammar are often put at the end of words as suffixes (i.e., "is going" and "is sleeping" contain the morpheme "ing," which indicates that an activity is currently in progress).

In Swahili, the grammatical information indicating verb tense appears at the beginning as a prefix (*law* = "to go," and *nlaw* = "is going"; or *sun* = "to sleep," and *nsun* = "is sleeping"). Again, languages develop different rules on the basis of cultural conventions that are passed down from one generation to the next.

Syntactic Rules

The **syntactic rules** (or **syntactics**) of a language refer to how words are sequenced together in accordance with the grammatical practices of the linguistic community. The order of the words helps to establish the meaning of an utterance. It is also reflective of the cultural notions of causality and order.

In English grammar, for example, explicit subject pronouns are used to distinguish self from other (e.g., "I cannot give you your gift because it is not ready"). In Chinese grammar, explicit pronouns, such as "I" and "you," are deemphasized. Instead, conjunctive words, such as "because" (*yinwei*), "so" (*suoyi*), and "then" (*juo*), appear early in the sentence to pave the way for the rest of the story. For example, the following statement illustrates this point: "*Because* of so many projects all of a sudden piling up, *so* the report has then not been handled properly, *then* we're now one week behind the deadline." Chinese syntax establishes a context and contingent conditions and then introduces the main point, but English syntax establishes the key point and then lays out the reason (Young, 1994). Likewise, in Spanish, at least four conjugations address the past tense, whereas English is a "matter-of-fact" language with fewer ways to address the past tense. The syntactic rules of a language—in interaction with the cultural value system—assert tremendous power on people's thinking and reasoning patterns within a culture.

Imagine that you are a translator or an interpreter of one language to another. You will have to pay extra attention to adjust one grammatical structure in one language to another grammatical form in the other language. Translation usually refers to the transference process of writing from the original language to the translated language. Interpretation usually refers to the oral transference process from the original language source to the translated source. For instance, when translating from the Danish language into Zulu, the interpreter has to make adjustments for the lack of a distinctive verbal tense in the Danish language. Rather, this person would have to use different intonations and shadings to indicate whether something had happened, is happening, or will likely happen.

Semantic Rules

The **semantic rules (semantics)** of a language concern the features of meaning we attach to words. Words themselves do not have self-evident meanings. It is people within a cultural community who consensually establish shared meanings for specific words and phrases. For example, *pretty* has a feature of (female), and *handsome* has a feature of (male). If we combine pretty with the (male) feature, such as "pretty boy" (or "handsome woman"), the concept takes on a whole range of different meanings (Chaika, 1989).

Beyond mastering the vocabulary of a new language, we need to master the appropriate cultural meaning features that are indicated by different word pairings. Without such cultural knowledge, we may have the right vocabulary but an inappropriate meaning association system (see Snapshot 6.1). Non-native speakers may think they are complimenting a boy by saying "What a pretty boy!" without realizing that although the sentence structure is accurate, the semantic field is misconstrued.

Snapshot 6.1

What is your interpretation of this sign?

In any language, two levels of meaning exist: denotative meaning and connotative meaning. A word's *denotative meaning* is its dictionary definition from an objective, public stance. *Connotative meaning* is the informal grasp that we have of particular words and phrases, and these meanings are relatively subjective and personal. Words such as *holiday, commitment,* and *justice* can hold both objective and subjective meanings. For instance, the objective meaning of *commitment* is "the state or an instance of being obligated or emotionally compelled." Camilla's connotation of the word *commitment* in the context of her relationship with Charles may include the presumption of marriage, whereas when Charles says, "I'm committed to you, Camilla," his subjective meaning includes an exclusive dating relationship with no intention of marriage.

An *idiom* is an informal expression that has a meaning that is quite different from the usual meaning of the words. There is a lack of idiomatic equivalence between cultures. For example, expressions such as "shooting the breeze," "taking care of business," "a low blow," "pull someone's leg," "you can't have your cake and eat it too," "raining cats and dogs," "until hell freezes over" are English idiomatic phrases. Translation problems and jokes that involve different semantic misunderstandings abound at the global level: "Things come alive with Pepsi" has been translated into German as "Pepsi can pull you back from your grave!" and General Motors' car "Chevy Nova" has been translated into Spanish as *no va,* which means "It doesn't go." Intercultural misunderstandings occur when we decode the literal meanings of the words but not the culturally specific meaning of the message. The challenge for translators is to understand the specific intention and meaning of the idiomatic expression and to appropriately adjust the meaning with regard to the cultural context of the other language.

Pragmatic Rules

The **pragmatic rules (pragmatics)** of a language refer to the contextual rules that govern language usage in a particular culture. Pragmatics concerns the rules of "how to say what to whom and under what situational conditions" in a speech community (Hymes, 1972). Let's look at the incident (adapted from Cushner & Brislin, 1996) in Double Take 6.1.

Double Take 6.1
A Brazilian Party Scene

A. J. Peterson worked in the human relations department of a large cosmetics store that was expanding into Brazil. A. J. had considerable influence concerning who should be granted interviews for available high-level positions. A. J. was at a party one evening with a Brazilian woman, Sonja, whom A. J. had known for a year. A. J. felt at ease and relaxed with Sonja, and he felt he could tell her jokes and make observations about Brazilian life.

During the party, Sonja smiled and approached A. J., saying "I'd like to introduce you to one of my very good friends who is smart and competent. She is thinking of going back to work, having worked part-time and raised her children on her own. She is very interested in hearing more about your company." A. J. replied cheerfully, "Sounds good. I look forward to meeting her. I just hope she doesn't try to hustle me!"

Sonja was visibly upset by this comment. She excused herself as politely as she could and did not speak with A. J. for the rest of the evening. A. J. was mystified and clueless in terms of why Sonja had reacted this way.

If A. J. asked your help to understand the Brazilian party's communication episode, how would you analyze the intercultural interaction? Your analysis could include any of the following possible explanations: (1) Sonja was testing A. J. to see if he was interested in her—A. J.'s enthusiasm to meet another woman annoyed her; (2) Sonja felt that A. J. and her friend would make a good match—however, A. J. did not show enough enthusiasm; (3) In Brazil, the politeness norm is to pay attention to single women standing by themselves—A. J. did not show enough cultural sensitivity; (4) Sonja interpreted A. J.'s remark as offensive and insulting.

What would be your analysis? You can answer either number (1), (2), (3), or (4). However, if you choose (4), congratulations! A. J.'s remark (i.e., "I just hope she doesn't try to hustle me!") was negatively interpreted by Sonja. The word *hustle* can have at least two meanings. A. J. had undoubtedly been to many parties at which people had asked him to use his influence in getting their friends a job. He used the idiomatic term *hustle,* as in the context of "being hustled or hassled for a job," in a very informal, American English way. However, *hustle* also means to "make romantic or sexual advances" toward someone. Sonja must have thought that this was the meaning A. J. had in mind. She probably felt that the remark sounded sexist and patronizing.

A. J. and Sonja have two language problems here: the semantic problem and the pragmatic problem. The semantic problem is due to the different meaning interpretations of the word *hustle.* The pragmatic problem is that Sonja perceived A. J.'s remark as out of context and insulting. Pragmatic rulers are about culturally relevant, contextual rules in the art of using language.

Pragmatic rules basically concern the cultural expectations of how, when, where, with whom, and under what situational conditions certain verbal expressions are preferred, prohibited, or prescribed in a speech community. A **speech community** is defined as a group of individuals who share a common set of norms and rules regarding appropriate communication practices (Carbaugh, 1996; Philipsen, 1996). For example, the large power distance values found in many of the traditional Filipino families basically dictate that the father must be head of the family and initiate major conversational topics, the mother must take care of the children around the dinner table, and the children must respect and obey the wishes of their father. There are clear pragmatic rules that shape who says what to whom and how in traditional Filipino dinner table conversations.

What can A. J. do now? After hearing your language analysis, A. J. may want to use a perception check with Sonja. He may want to approach Sonja and apologize for any unintended rudeness. He may ask Sonja for clarity—why she acted so upset at the party. He may also take the initiative to indicate his newfound awareness that the word *hustle* was the root of the confusion. If A. J. approaches Sonja with an open-minded attitude, it is likely that Sonja will be receptive to his explanation and apology.

We have identified five rules of human language and illustrated these rules with ample cultural examples. Linguistic rules give rise to the diverse functions of languages across cultures and answer the question of why language plays such a critical role within each culture. Language is an integral part of both a sense of identity and the mindset that goes with it.

Understanding Diverse Language Functions

Cultural value orientations drive language usage in everyday lives. For example, if a culture has a high individualism value index (e.g., Ireland and New Zealand), words and phrases such as "I," "me," "my goal," "my opinion," "self-help," and "self-service" tend to appear as part of everyday parlance. If a culture has a high collectivism value index (e.g., Guatemala and Nigeria), phrases such as "our work team," "our goal," "our future together," and "we as a group" are part of the everyday lexicon.

In this section, we identify the diverse functions of languages across cultures as the cultural worldview function, the cognitive formation function, the social reality function, the group identity function, and the social change function.

The Cultural Worldview Function

To understand a culture deeply, we have to understand the language of a cultural group. To understand language in context, we have to understand the fundamental worldview that drives particular language usage in particular circumstances. **Worldviews** refer to our larger philosophical outlook or ways of perceiving the world and how this outlook, in turn, affects our thinking and reasoning patterns. American English, for example, tends to emphasize explicit categorical words such as "absolutely," "certainly," and "positively" to signal precision and decisive actions. And in most cases, the "I" is placed at the beginning of a sentence. In contrast, Japanese speakers use more implicit and ambiguous words. Instead of appearing to be assertive, they use more qualifiers such as "maybe," "perhaps," "probably," and "excuse me," or "sorry" at the beginning of a sentence in substitution for the explicit use of the "I" pronoun in an up-front manner.

Intercultural experts have proposed two worldviews that divide the Western and Asian cultures: the linear worldview and the relational worldview (Stewart & Bennett, 1991). A *linear worldview* emphasizes rational thinking that is based on an objective reality. A relational worldview emphasizes holistic or connected thinking that is based on a contextual reality. The language systems of the linear worldview tend to emphasize either facts and figures or models and theories by using two reasoning patterns: inductive and deductive reasoning. **Inductive reasoning** refers to the importance of facts and evidence to make a claim. Facts are important because they are objective. A claim is not valid until proven with concrete facts and tangible figures. The U.S. American reasoning process has been identified as following an inductive reasoning pattern. **Deductive reasoning,** on the other hand, refers to the primacy of conceptual models and theories and then a move to specific points of implications, however, still via the linear, step-by-step logic of reasoning. The European style of reasoning has been identified as reflective of a deductive reasoning pattern (Stewart & Bennett, 1991). (See Table 6.1).

Table 6.1	Linear Worldview and Relational Worldview: A Comparison	
Linear Worldview	**Relational Worldview**
Rational Thinking	Connected Thinking
Objective Reasoning	Context-Based Reasoning
Facts and Evidence	Context and Relationship
Polarized Interpretation	Continuum Interpretation
Analytical Dissecting Mode	Holistic Big-Picture Mode
Tangible Outcome	Long-Term Relational Outcome

The *relational worldview* reflects a holistic reasoning pattern. The relational, complementary worldview is reflective of the Chinese language. Chinese thinking avoids using the polarized ends (e.g., good-evil, black-white, young-old) to comprehend the nature of the universe. Instead, the Chinese pay attention to the quality of the continuum or spectrum of emotions (e.g., "not too bad," "I like," "I very like," "I not too like"), which in English are polarized (e.g., *like* and *dislike*). Thus, words such as "tolerable" and "intolerable" would likely be expressed in Chinese through the use of moderately expressed emotions such as tolerable—"a little bit like," "very like," "a little bit not like," "don't like," "problematic like," and "dislike." Thus, the Chinese use correlational reasoning notions that are deeply embedded in the Chinese worldview and are manifested via the Chinese language system.

The Cognitive Formation Function

Extending the ideas in the previous section, language serves as a mediating link between our cultural worldviews, on one hand, and thinking patterns, on the other. Benjamin Whorf (1952, 1956), drawing from the work of his mentor, Edward Sapir (1921), has tested the "language is a shaper of ideas" hypothesis. By comparing the Hopi Indian language with European languages, Whorf (1952) found that language is not merely a vehicle for voicing ideas but also "the shaper of ideas." He further emphasized that the grammatical structure of a language shapes and constitutes one's thought process. This grammatical structure is entirely culture-based and, as such, language, thinking, and culture are integral parts of a mindset system.

Whorf cited several examples from the Hopi language: (1) The Hopi language does not possess a discrete past-present-future grammatical system as in most European languages; instead, it has a wide range of present tenses that concern the validity of the verbal statement the speaker is making, such as "I know that she is sleeping at this very moment" or "I am told that she is sleeping." (2) The Hopi language does not use a cyclic noun, such as "days" or "years," in the same manner as countable quantities, such as eight women or eight men; instead, it emphasizes the concept of "duration" when conceiving time. Thus, the Hopi equivalent for the English statement "They stayed eight days" is "I know that they stay until the seventh day." (3) English speakers tend to use spatial metaphors in their sentences (e.g., "time is up," "She's really on top of things," or "I'm running low"), but the Hopi language tends to emphasize events that are happening in the here and now.

Speakers of European languages believe time is a commodity that occurs between fixed points and that can be measured. Time is wasted or saved. The Hopi Indian, however, has no such belief about time but instead "thinks of it in terms of events. Plant a seed—and it will grow. The span of time in which the growing takes place is not the important thing but rather the way in which the event of growth follows the event of planting . . . the sequence of events [is emphasized]" (Farb, 1973, p. 209).

By linking cultural worldview and thought pattern together, one achieves the Sapir-Whorf hypothesis, also known as the *linguistic relativity hypothesis*. The grammars of different languages constitute separate conceptual realities for members of different cultures. We experience different thoughts and sensations via our linguistic systems. For example, the structure of the future tense in Spanish tells us a great deal about the notion of the future in Spain. In Spanish, statements made about the future signal probability rather than certainty. A Spanish speaker will prefer the statement "I may go to the office" (*"Puedo ir a la oficina"*) instead of "I will go to the office" to indicate the probability of an action in the future rather than the certainty of that action. The future, for many Spanish-speaking people, represents an unknown in time and space: Many things can happen later this afternoon or tomorrow; they are beyond the control of individuals. Thus, the use of a "probability" statement seems to fit logically with their overall cultural reasoning system.

After reviewing extensive studies on the Sapir-Whorf hypothesis, Steinfatt (1989) concluded that though the *weak* form (i.e., language helps to shape our thinking patterns) of the linguistic relativity hypothesis received some support, no conclusive evidence can be drawn to support the *strong* form (i.e., language completely determines our thinking patterns). Edward Sapir and Benjamin Whorf were trailblazing pioneers in linking language with culture, and as such, they left a major contribution to the study of intercultural communication.

The Social Reality Function

Language acts as a gatekeeper in naming and selecting what is considered "news" or "real" in our social environment. We use particular language categories to name and label our everyday moments in our sociocultural environment. The vocabularies from different cultures direct members' attention to the things that are important in their social experiences. For instance, the diversity of words for *karma* and *reincarnation* in the culture of India, and for *good* and *evil* spirits in many Native American cultures, emphasize the importance of karmic fate and spiritual worlds in these various cultural settings. The many words for expressing gratitude in the Greek and Arab worlds play a prominent role in these people's habitual ways of greeting and approaching others as cultural beings. People's linguistic thoughts and their habitual ways of perceiving in their cultural settings are highly interdependent.

Everyday language in a culture serves as a prism through which individuals interpret "meaningful" versus "meaningless" events out there. For example, in Mexico, Spanish words such as *machismo* (i.e., masculinity, physical strength, sexual attraction), *marianismo* (i.e., a woman's submissiveness, dependence, gentleness, and remaining a virgin until marriage), *respeto* (i.e., showing proper respect for authority, such as parents and elders), and *familismo* (i.e., the importance of family and the extended family network) are part of everyday parlance. These words infiltrate individuals' perceptions and beings, and they are used as yardsticks to measure self and others' role performance (see Picture This 6.2).

Picture This 6.2

YO SOY
by Karisma Rodriguez, 20, UCLA English Major

Puerto Rican's aren't Mexican
And Mexican's aren't Cubans
One comes from a democracy
The other's a "territory"
And that one's a commie
But they are all alive in me
And they are all "America"

☞

America's in me
You shake your head
And laugh your arrogance at me
It's your ignorance
You must have the word confused
With the United States
Don't be so quick to judge . . .

Back to the races now
Back to where we grew from, and how

They talk of their families
Particular to their culture
Mother and Father's religions
Whose is older?
But no one baptized me
I'm a free "thinker"
Not a soldier

And if you smelled the comida
You'd know you were home

I'll take the taquitos, fajitas
Tostadas sin carnitas
Just . . . not meat, please!

I'm a vegetarian
I've got ideals

For reals, man
Some things I can't condone
What's a Latina sin carne?
A green Latina!
A tree-hugging,
Gringa.
Wow, that's clever
But here's something even better

☞

What's a Latina without familia?
There's the question that unsettles. . . .

A winner
A failure

A question
"An exception"

A fighter who cries
And a loser who laughs

A writer who dances in two tongues
And then sticks out her leguna

A student forever I'll be
Long after the University graduates me

A performer
A reformer
Anything I want to be
Latinismo's in me.

Individuals perceive and simultaneously judge others' proper or improper behaviors via their use of habitual linguistic symbols. Thus, language permeates our social experience and ultimately shapes our cultural and gendered expectations and perceptions.

The Group Identity Function

Language represents a rallying point for evoking group sentiment and shared identity. Language serves the larger cultural-ethnic identity function because it is an emblem of group solidarity. In speaking a common tongue, members signal ingroup linkage and outgroup differentiation. The core symbols and linguistic categories of a group often express ethnic and nationalistic sentiment. By virtue of its powerful and visible symbolism, language maintenance issues are worth fighting and dying for—from many ethnic groups' perspectives.

For example, the disputes between Anglophones and Francophones over the use of English or French in Canada's Quebec province and the heated debates over whether Pidgin and Ebonics (i.e., Hawaiian English and Black English) are languages or dialects in the United States reflect the significant role of the group membership function of language. For example, in Hawaii, *Da Jesus Book* (i.e., the *New Testament Bible*) was written for the specific use of local Hawaiian people to use in church. A very popular section, from Corinthians, talks about love. In an English version of the Bible, the passage reads:

> *Love is patient and kind; it is not jealous or conceited or proud; love is not ill-mannered or selfish or irritable; love does not keep a record of wrongs; love is not happy with evil, but is happy with the truth. Love never gives up; and its faith, hope, and patience never fail.*
> —I Corinthians 13: 4–7:
> Today's
> English Version, p. 1674

When translated in *Da Jesus Book*, the passage reads:

> *Wen you get love an aloha, you can handle all kine pilikisa an hang in dea long time. You get good heart fo help da odda peopo. . . . Wen you get love an aloha, you no need talk big. You no mo big head. You no ack pilau kine . . . but you feel plenny good inside wen you tell da trut. Wen you get love an aloha, you can hang in dea fo everyting. You know everyting goin come okay bumbye. You can stand strong everytime.*
> —Numba I Fo Da Corint Peopo 13:
> 4–7:
> Aloha, p. 463

Well, what do you think of the above translation? Do you understand some of the words while getting totally confused by other words? Many may argue that such a book is offensive; but others will argue that to appeal to local Hawaiians who speak pidgin, the text gives them a strong connection and insight to the passage. Words such as *pilikisa* ("troubles"), *odda* ("other"), *peopo* ("people"), *pilau kine* ("hot headed," "awful"), *plenny* ("plenty"), and *bumbye* ("if . . . then clause") allow the local Hawaiian natives to visualize the love passage with more relevance because it is in their own meaning context.

Some cultural members develop enormous membership loyalty and pride in speaking their native tongue, but other members derive tremendous flexibility in their ability to code-switch. Code-switching means switching to another language or dialect to increase or decrease intergroup distance. For example, many African Americans have developed different verbal strategies to deal with the stigma attached to

Black English (or Ebonics) by the dominant group. Black English is "a distinctive language . . . evolving from [a] largely West African pidgin form" and "is governed by rules with specific historical derivations" (Hecht, Collier, & Ribeau, 1993, pp. 84–85). For instance, in Black English, subject nouns are followed by a repeated pronoun ("My sister, she . . ."), statements omit the verb form "to be" ("It dat way") to strategically imply a one-time occurrence, or include it ("It bees dat way") to imply multiple occurrences; questions omit the word do ("What it come to?"); and context clarifiers are used instead of a different verb tense ("I know it good when he ask me") (Hecht, Collier, & Ribeau, 1993; Wyatt, 1995). Many African Americans are able to code-switch; using mainstream American English in formal or work-related settings, then switching to Black English with familiar others in casual settings for the purpose of forging group identity and connection.

In another example, in the group-oriented Indian culture, when one asks for a Hindu's name, one will first receive the person's caste identity, then a village name, and finally a personal name (Bharati, 1985). In the Chinese, Japanese, Korean, and Vietnamese cultures, the family name always precedes the personal name, which signals the importance of family identity over personal identity. Thus, a person named Jin-Ah Kim in the English form of address is referred to as Kim Jin-Ah in the Korean form of address. Likewise, in the culture of Bali, a personal name is a nonsense syllable that is almost never used; instead, the name used is related to family role relations (e.g., the second born of family *X*, mother of *Y*, grandfather of *Z*). In sum, individuals construct their identities through "naming," and in turn their naming and labeling process shapes how they view themselves and others.

On purely linguistic grounds, all languages are created equal. However, in all linguistic struggles, both within and between languages, a fierce competition exists

> Not between languages themselves but, rather, between language communities or linguistic "interest groups." It is perhaps a good idea here to remake the point that neither languages nor dialects can be compared in terms of "better" or "worse" and that the strong preferences for given varieties, which have always existed, are based upon sociopolitical considerations; central here are the dominance and prestige of speakers. (Edwards, 1994, pp. 205–206)

Matters of power, then, interlock with perceptions to form attitudes toward different language varieties in the larger cultural context. For example, mainstream American English (AE) is preferred over Black English in work settings because AE is spoken by European Americans, who are considered to be the dominant power holders (i.e., individuals who control corporate or governmental resources) in U.S. society. The language struggle, in sum, is a sociopolitical power scuffle.

The Social Change Function

Twenty years ago, we did not have words like *cyberspace, cyberliteracy, infomercials, spamming,* and *text-messaging.* We now have those words at our fingertips. As innovative social beings, we are the creators of the social tool of human language. We are also at times trapped by the habits of our own linguistic system.

Let's do Quick Poll 6.1 here before you read on.

Quick Poll 6.1

Using your gut-level response, whom do you picture when you read the following words? Circle your answer quickly.

Businessman?	Man	Woman
Nurse?	Man	Woman
Chairman?	Man	Woman
Girl Friday?	Man	Woman
Mailman?	Man	Woman
Librarian?	Man	Woman
Fireman?	Man	Woman
Stewardess?	Man	Woman
Freshman?	Man	Woman
Mankind?	Man	Woman

Though some people may assume that women are included in such male generic terms as *chairman* and *mankind,* research has demonstrated conclusively that "masculine generics are perceived as referring predominantly or exclusively to men. When people hear them, they think of men, not women" (Wood, 1997, p. 152). For example, the use of male generic language in English—words such as *businessman, chairman,* or *fireman* used in Western society—tends to elevate men's experience as more valid and make women's experience less prominent. To the extent that the language of a culture makes men appear more visible and concurrently makes women seem invisible, the perceptions generated from such biased language usage create biased thinking. By flexibly changing some of our linguistic habits (e.g., changing *chairman* to *chairperson, fireman* to *firefighter, mankind* to *humankind*), we can start transforming our thinking patterns through the use of gender-equitable terms.

More important, language has a carryover effect on our expectations, and hence perceptions, of what constitutes proper or improper gendered role behaviors. Research indicates that "women who use assertive speech associated with masculinity are judged as arrogant and uppity, while men who employ emotional language associated with femininity are often perceived as wimps or gay. . . . Polarized thinking about gender encouraged by our language restricts us from realizing the full range of human possibilities" (Wood, 1997, p. 160). Language can indeed imprison us because it influences our way of perceiving the world "out there."

Fortunately, language can also set us free—that is, if we are willing to mindfully change our language habits and preconceived biased notions about different identity groups. We have discussed how linguistic sexism occurs when women are devalued and made invisible through the constant use of masculine-based generic words to include both males and females (e.g., using *spokesman* rather than *spokesperson*, and using the generic *he* to imply both female and male). To combat linguistic sexism, for example, you can commit yourself to removing sexist language usage from all of your everyday communication. You can practice and reinforce nonsexist language patterns until they become habitual. You can use reconstruction or substitution (e.g., change *founding fathers* to *founders*) to replace verbal sexism. In sum, you can use your imaginative capacity to reframe your male-generic verbal habits with gender-neutral words in both public and private conversations.

Beyond language habit change, two interesting trends are taking place in both international and U.S. social scenes. On the international language change scene is the issue of language borrowing. Edwards (1994) points out that in Germany, for example, teenagers "wear die jeans" and that "even the French grudgingly acknowledge the appeal of *le drugstore* and *le weekend* . . . [and] English words [are] integrated into Japanese, [such as] *hamu tosuto* for a 'toasted ham sandwich,' [or] *apaato* for "apartment" (p. 77). In Latin America, foreign name brands have integrated into everyday Spanish (Bianchi & Sama, 2003). The result? You can't tell the product from the brand. For example, when people want a pack of razors, they ask for "Gillettes"; if they want a whirlpool bath, they ask for a "Jacuzzi." Language borrowing can indicate an added status, a necessary convenience, or a signal of ingroup connection. Domestically, with an increase in the popularity of rap music, English is now up for grabs. Called this new "bilingual" English, this is a way for street kids, or the music industry, to promote the inclusion of the slang and jargon of rap music into everyday vocabulary.

To close this section, let's check out how much social change has occurred in your Internet linguistic literacy. Do you know what the following abbreviations AKF, FWIW, GAL, KISS, LOL, or YHM stand for in cyberspace? Check out the answers in Jeopardy Box 6.3.

Jeopardy Box 6.3 Abbreviated Internet Language

AFK:	Away From Keyboard
BBL:	Be Back Later
BRB:	Be Right Back
BST:	But Seriously Though
BTW:	By The Way
CUL:	See You Later
F2F:	Face To Face
FWIW:	For What It's Worth
GAL:	Get A Life
GIGO:	Garbage In, Garbage Out
GMTA:	Great Minds Think Alike
GTG:	Got To Go
IME:	In My Experience
IMO:	In My Opinion
IMHO:	In My Humble Opinion
IOW:	In Other Words
JAM:	Just A Minute
KISS:	Keep It Simple, Stupid
LOL:	Laughing Out Loud
NP:	No Problem
OMG:	Oh My Gosh
POS:	Parent Over Shoulder
RTFM:	Read the F****** Manual
R.U.	Are You
TIA:	Thanks In Advance
TNX:	Thanks
TPTB:	The Powers That Be
TTYL:	Talk To You Later
WRT:	With Regards To
YHM:	You Have Mail

Intercultural Toolkit: Recaps and Checkpoints

In this chapter, we've explored the diverse functions and rules of languages across cultures. More specifically, we've identified four distinctive language features: arbitrariness, abstractness, meaning-centeredness, and linguistic creativity. In addition, we've also explored the five functions of the relationship between language and culture: cultural worldview, cognitive formation, social reality, group identity, and social change functions. We offer some checkpoints here for you to communicate flexibly when you are using your native language (e.g., English) in communicating with a non-native English-speaking audience. To be flexible verbal communicators, try to practice the following guidelines:

- *Understand languaculture.* Have a basic grasp of the features of the languaculture that you will be encountering. The word *languaculture* emphasizes the necessary tie between language and culture (Agar, 1994). The features of a particular language, from syntactic rules to semantic rules, reflect a speaker's worldviews, values, and premises concerning different functions and ways of speaking.

- *Practice verbal tracking.* Pay close attention to the content meaning of the message. Remember that everyone speaks with an accent. Move beyond the accent and track the intended content meaning of the speaker. Next, scan for relational and identity meanings. Be sensitive to the transposition or mixing of rules from the native language to the non-native language. Try to connect cultural value issues that underlie different speaking styles.

- *Practice verbal patience.* Develop verbal empathy and patience for non-native speakers from a different culture. We can, for example, speak slowly and in simple sentences and allow for comprehension pauses. We can also try to use verbal restatements—through the use of different words or phrases—to convey the same intended content meanings. We need to refrain from using any culture-specific idiomatic expressions to avoid cultural misunderstandings.

- *Use probing questions.* Use culture-sensitive probing questions to check whether the message is received accurately. Paraphrase and perception check in accordance with the proper timing and the setting of the situation, and ask for feedback responses when appropriate.

- *Use multiple modes of presentation.* Use visual restatements, such as pictures, graphs, gestures, or written summaries, to reinforce your points. Likewise, if you sojourn to another country and are using a second language, use similar strategies to cross-check for understanding of the meaning of the message from your target audience.

- *Master the cultural pragmatic rules.* Understand the importance of pragmatic rules in language usage—you can be linguistically fluent in another culture but still act like a cultural fool if you do not master the appropriate norms of speaking in a particular cultural context.

This chapter has covered the distinctive features, rules, and functions of human language. The next chapter extends the notion of language and culture in more detail. Intercultural miscommunications often occur because individuals use cultural-laden linguistic habits to communicate and interpret each other's verbal messages. Fortunately, by staying flexible in our intercultural verbal decoding process, we may be able to catch our own verbal mistakes or comprehension mistakes and use language mindfully to promote better intercultural understanding. ✦

Chapter 7

What Are the Major Differences in Intercultural Verbal Styles?

Chapter Outline

When [getting] home from class, it might be normal for most people to grab something to eat and drink. However, as a quadriplegic, I am unable to do many things myself. So I wait for an opportunity when someone else gets a drink, and I might suggest that I would like one too. If no one makes a move for a snack, I might just mention that I'm kind of hungry, instead of openly asking for something to eat. There are so many small things that people have to do for me that I become frustrated and embarrassed to ask. It seems rude to be continually interrupting the routine of others to get things for myself; especially what seem to be small things but become huge when you are unable to do them for yourself.

—Tony, *College Student*

Intercultural frustrations often arise because of verbal communication style differences. When disabled individuals communicate with nondisabled individuals, they often experience emotional vulnerability or stress. Though some disabled individuals tend to not want to overimpose on other people for help, other nondisabled individuals tend to hold *negative stereotypes of disabled people as too "oversensitive or easily offended." Because of intercultural communication incompetence, even routine conversations can become very frustrating and stressful.*

More important, our intercultural ineptness or ignorance often clutters our ability to communicate mindfully with the disabled or with culturally different others. One of the first steps toward developing more mindful verbal communication with dissimilar others is to develop a keen awareness of those verbal style differences. Our mindless versus mindful interpretations of those differences can ultimately influence the quality of our intercultural or intergroup relationship developments. This chapter is organized in five sections. First, we introduce the low-context and high-context communication framework. Second, we discuss four cross-cultural verbal style differences: direct and indirect styles, complementary, animated and understated styles, formal and informal verbal styles, and cultural attitudes toward talk and silence. Third, we take a further look at everyday intercultural conversation processes, especially the important concept of self-disclosure. Fourth, we discuss different modes of cross-cultural persuasion. We close the chapter by summarizing key points and offering practical checkpoints to improve intercultural conversation flexibility.

Intercultural Low-Context and High-Context Communication Framework

In this section, we discuss the low-context and high-context communication framework and present some lively, comparative dialogue examples.

Defining Low-Context and High-Context Communication

Hall (1976) claimed that human interaction, on the broad level, can be divided into low-context and high-context communication systems. In **low-context communication,** the emphasis is on how intention or meaning is best expressed through explicit verbal messages. In **high-context communication,** the emphasis is on how intention or meaning can best be conveyed through the context (e.g., social roles or positions) and the nonverbal channels (e.g., pauses, silence, tone of voice) of the verbal message (see Table 7.1). Furthermore, the structure of the language system itself may be more low-context in expression or high-context in verbal implication.

The English and German language systems, for example, tend toward a more direct, low-context mode, but the Arabic and Spanish language systems tend toward a more status-based, high-context verbal mode (see Table 7.2).

Table 7.1	Low-Context Communication (LCC) and High-Context Communication (HCC): Verbal Patterns	
LCC Patterns		**HCC Patterns**
Individualistic Values		Collectivistic Values
Linear Logic		Spiral Logic
Direct Verbal Style		Indirect Verbal Style
Matter-of-Fact Tone		Understated or Animated Tone
Informal Verbal Style		Formal Verbal Style
Verbal Assertiveness or Talkativeness		Verbal Reticence or Silence

Table 7.2   Country Examples of Low-Context and High-Context Communication

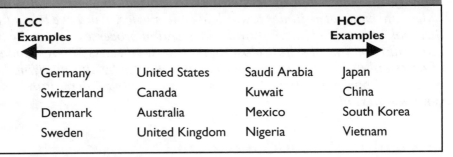

LCC Examples				HCC Examples	
Germany	United States	Saudi Arabia	Japan		
Switzerland	Canada	Kuwait	China		
Denmark	Australia	Mexico	South Korea		
Sweden	United Kingdom	Nigeria	Vietnam		

To do a quick check, do you know what are the top-three countries that have the most English, Germanic, Arabic, and Spanish speakers, respectively? Take a quick guess, and check out the answers in Jeopardy Boxes 7.1, 7.2, 7.3, and 7.4.

Jeopardy Box 7.1   Top-Ten Countries With the Most English-Language Speakers

Country	Approximate Number of Speakers*
1. United States	237,320,000
2. United Kingdom	58,090,000
3. Canada	18,218,000
4. Australia	15,561,000
5. Ireland	3,720,000
6. South Africa	3,700,000
7. New Zealand	3,338,000
8. Jamaica[#]	2,460,000
9. Trinidad and Tobago[#^]	1,245,000
10. Guyana[#^]	764,000

Notes: *People for whom English is their mother tongue.
#Includes English Creole.
^Trinidad English.
Source: Adapted from Ash (2002), p. 101.

Jeopardy Box 7.2 Top-Ten Countries With the Most German-Language Speakers

Country	Approximate Number of Speakers*
1. Germany	75,080,000
2. Austria	7,444,000
3. Switzerland	4,570,000
4. United States	1,850,000
5. Brazil	910,000
6. Poland	500,000
7. Canada	486,000
8. Kazakhstan	460,000
9. Russia	350,000
10. Italy	310,000

Note: *People for whom German is their mother tongue.
Source: Adapted from Ash (2002), p. 101.

Jeopardy Box 7.3 Top-Ten Countries With the Most Arabic-Language Speakers

Country	Approximate Number of Speakers*
1. Egypt	65,080,000
2. Algeria	26,280,000
3. Saudi Arabia	20,920,000
4. Morocco	18,730,000
5. Iraq	17,490,000
6. Yemen	17,400,000
7. Sudan	17,320,000
8. Syria	14,680,000
9. Tunisia[#]	6,710,000
10. Libya	4,910,000

Note: *People for whom Arabic is their mother tongue.
#Another 2,520,000 people speak Arabic-French, and 300,000 speak Arabic-English.
Source: Adapted from Ash (2002), p. 100.

Jeopardy Box 7.4 Top-Ten Countries With the Most Spanish-Language Speakers

Country	Approximate Number of Speakers*
1. Mexico	91,080,000
2. Colombia	41,880,000
3. Argentina	35,860,000
4. Spain[#]	29,860,000
5. Venezuela	23,310,000
6. United States	20,720,000
7. Peru	20,470,000
8. Chile	13,640,000
9. Ecuador	11,760,000
10. Dominican Republic	8,270,000

Notes: *People for whom Spanish is their mother tongue.
Castilian Spanish.
Source: Adapted from Ash (2002), p. 101.

In general, **low-context communication (LCC)** refers to communication patterns of direct verbal mode: straight talk, nonverbal immediacy, and sender-oriented values (i.e., the sender assumes the responsibility to communicate clearly). In the LCC system, the speaker is expected to be responsible for constructing a clear, persuasive message that the listener can decode easily. In comparison, **high-context communication (HCC)** refers to communication patterns of indirect verbal mode: self-humbling talk, nonverbal subtleties, and interpreter-sensitive values (i.e., the receiver or interpreter of the message assumes the responsibility to infer the hidden or contextual meanings of the message) (Ting-Toomey, 1985). In the HCC system, the listener or interpreter of the message is expected to "read between the lines," to accurately infer the implicit intent of the verbal message, and to decode the nonverbal subtleties that accompany the verbal message.

Low-Context and High-Context Communication Examples

Low-context communication is illustrated by the following dispute between two European American neighbors in Active Dialogue 7.1.

Active Dialogue 7.1

BELLA (knocks on her neighbor's screen door): Excuse me, it's past 11 o'clock already, and your loud music and dancing around are really disturbing my sleep. Please stop your jumping and banging around immediately! I have an important job interview tomorrow morning, and I want to get a good night's sleep. Some of us do need to pay rent!

HAYDEN (resentfully): Well, this is the only time I can rehearse! I have an important audition coming up tomorrow. You're not the only one that is starving, you know. I also need to pay my rent. Stop being so petty!

BELLA (frustrated): I really think YOU'RE being VERY ANNOYING and INTRUSIVE! There is an apartment noise ordinance, you know. And if you don't stop banging around immediately, I'm going to file a complaint with the apartment manager and he could evict you. . . .

HAYDEN (sarcastically and turning up the music louder): Whatever! Do what you want. I'm going to practice as I please. Don't bother to ask for my autograph when I become a big-time Hollywood star!

In contrast, the following interaction in Active Dialogue 7.2 involving two Japanese housewives illustrates their use of *high-context communication*.

Active Dialogue 7.2

MRS. KUROGI: Hello, Mrs. Yamashita . . . Your son Toji is entering his high school karaoke contest, isn't he? I envy you, because you must be so proud of his talent. You must be looking forward to his future as a pop singer. . . . I'm really impressed by his enthusiasm—every day, he practices so hard, for hours and hours, until late at night. . . .

MRS. YAMASHITA: Oh, I'm so sorry . . . Toji is just a beginner in karaoke singing. We don't know his future yet. . . . He is such a silly boy singing so late. We didn't realize you can hear all the noise next door. I'll tell him to stop right away. I'm so sorry about all your trouble, it won't happen again.

In Active Dialogue 7.1, Bella and Hayden spell out everything that is on their minds with no restraints. Their interaction exchange is direct, to the point, bluntly contentious, and full of face-threat verbal messages. Active Dialogue 7.1 represents one possible low-context way of approaching a disagreement. Although the example represents an unproductive scenario, Bella and Hayden might actually turn their dialogue around and obtain a more productive outcome by identifying their common interests (e.g., urgency of the job search or rent payment due) and exploring other constructive options (e.g., closing the windows or practicing in another room). They can use the strengths of low-context, "explicit talk" in dealing with the disagreement openly and nonevaluatively.

In Active Dialogue 7.2, Mrs. Kurogi has not directly expressed her concern over Toji's singing with Mrs. Yamashita because she wants to preserve face and her relationship with Mrs. Yamashita. Mrs. Kurogi uses indirect hints and nonverbal signals to get her point across. However, Mrs. Yamashita correctly "reads between the lines" of Mrs. Kurogi's verbal message and apologizes appropriately and effectively before any real conflict can bubble to the surface. Active Dialogue 7.2 represents one possible high-context way of approaching a disagreement. In high-context disagreement scenarios, even minor disagreement is perceived as a major face-threat situation if the *face*, or *social self-image*, of the contending parties is not supported. From the high-context communication viewpoint, minor disagreement can easily turn into a major conflict if face-threatening and face-saving issues are not dealt with competently. However, if Mrs. Kurogi were the neighbor of Hayden in Active Dialogue 7.1, Hayden might not be able to "read between the lines" of Mrs. Kurogi's verbal and, more important, nonverbal message. Hayden might be clueless that a disagreement was already simmering between them. Hayden might actually take Mrs. Kurogi's verbal message literally as a compliment—and continue late-night practices!

Mrs. Kurogi and Mrs. Yamashita are practicing the high-context interaction style frequently used in Japanese society, but Bella and Hayden are using the low-context communication style more commonly employed in U.S. society. Overall, low-context interaction emphasizes direct talk and individual-centered expressions. High-context interaction, in comparison, stresses indirect talk and a round-about way of expression. Let's look at another story by Kate, a college student. She offers an account of her parents on their honeymoon; though they are both European Americans, the following story in Double Take 7.1 illustrates interesting male-female communication style differences.

Double Take 7.1

Shortly after getting married, my parents took a trip to Hawaii. They checked into the Royal Hawaiian Hotel, which they both considered to be a huge splurge. My father said that my mom seemed to be very excited to be there—until they got to the room. Apparently, he sensed something was wrong with his wife, but he could not imagine what it could be.

He asked her if she liked the room and she assured him that everything was wonderful. About 5 minutes later, she started looking out the window and asked, "I wonder what the view would look like a few stories up." My dad sensed that something was wrong so he asked her again if she like the room. Once again, she said that the room was perfect and that she was thrilled to be there.

A few minutes later, my mom posed another subtle question: "Do you think they forgot to clean this room? It smells smoky in here. . . ." My dad said [that] at this point, he finally realized my mom really didn't like the room and wanted to change the room. So he said, "Let's change the room." To this my mom replied, "Okay, if that is what you want to do."

—Kate, *College Student*

When Kate asked her mother about this situation, her mom recalled that she jumped at the chance when her husband offered to switch rooms. Because he was taking her on such a wonderful vacation, her mom felt it was not her place to complain directly about the room. Meanwhile, Kate's dad recalled that he never fully understood why his wife never came right out and said what was on her mind. If Kate's dad and mom had known about low-context and high-context communication styles, they might have been better prepared for this early miscommunication during their honeymoon period. Research actually indicates that males tend to be more low-context in their communication style, and females tend to be more high-context in their communication approach. Males in the U.S. culture tend to emphasize clarity in conversations, and females tend to emphasize not hurting other's feelings or imposing on others (Ting-Toomey, 1988).

Low-Context and High-Context Verbal Style Comparisons

Before you continue reading, let's do Quick Poll 7.1 to check out your verbal style preference.

Quick Poll 7.1
Check off any of the following behaviors that you find irritating or frustrating when you interact with individuals who talk that way.

Not answering questions directly: _____

Talking bluntly: _____

Insisting on calling you Ms. or Mr.: _____

Making a request directly: _____

Using lots of silence in conversation: _____

Talking about themselves constantly: _____

Speaking slowly: _____

Speaking really fast: _____

Asking personal questions: _____

Speaking softly: _____

Speaking loudly: _____

Constantly apologizing: _____

Why did you find some of the verbal behaviors irritating? Where did you acquire your own verbal habits or rituals? What cultural or personal values influence your verbal styles? Do you notice any verbal style differences between females and males in your culture? How so? Do you communicate very similarly in different situations? Or do you switch your verbal styles to adapt to different interaction situations?

Although **low-context communicators** tend to emphasize direct verbal style, animated conversational tone, informal verbal treatment, and talkativeness, **high-context communicators** tend to value indirect verbal style, understated or exaggerated conversational tone, formal verbal treatment, and emphasis on the importance of silence. We compare low-context and high-context verbal style differences in this section.

Direct and Indirect Verbal Styles

Mannerism of speaking, or verbal style, frames *how* a message should be interpreted or understood. Of the four styles of verbal interaction, the research evidence for the direct-indirect verbal style dimension is the most extensive and persuasive.

This stylistic pair, direct and indirect verbal styles, can be thought of as straddling a continuum. Individuals in all cultures use all of these verbal styles to a certain degree, depending on assumed identities, intentions, interaction goals, relationship types, and the situation. However, in individualistic cultures, people tend to encounter more situations that emphasize direct talk. In contrast, in collectivistic cultures, people tend to encounter more situations that emphasize the use of indirect talk.

The direct and indirect styles differ in how they reveal the speaker's intentions through tone of voice and the straightforwardness of the content in the message. In the **direct verbal style,** verbal statements tend to reveal the speaker's intentions with clarity and are enunciated with a forthright tone of voice. In the **indirect verbal style,** verbal statements tend to camouflage the speaker's actual intentions and are carried out with a softer tone. For example, the overall U.S. American verbal style often calls for clear and direct communication. Phrases such as "be very clear," "don't beat around the bush," and "what is the point" are some examples. In contrast, in a verbal request situation, U.S. Americans tend to use a straightforward form of request, but Koreans tend to ask for a favor in a more roundabout and implicit way to sound not so imposing or demanding. The Koreans are not the only indirect group. Let's demonstrate a pair of contrastive "airport ride request" scenes in Active Dialogues 7.3 and 7.4 between two Irish Americans and two Latinas:

Active Dialogue 7.3

IRISH AMERICAN 1: We're going to the Orange Bowl in Miami this weekend.

IRISH AMERICAN 2: What fun! I wish I were going to the game with you. How long are you going to be there? [If she wants a ride, she will ask.]

IRISH AMERICAN 1: Three days. By the way, we may need a ride to the airport. Do you think you can take us?

IRISH AMERICAN 2: Sure. What time?

IRISH AMERICAN 1: 10:30 p.m. this coming Saturday.

IRISH AMERICAN 2: All right. No problem.

Active Dialogue 7.4

LATINA 1: We're going to the Orange Bowl in Miami this weekend.

LATINA 2: What fun! I wish I were going to the game with you. How long are you going to be there?

LATINA 1: Three days. [I hope she'll offer me a ride to the airport.]

LATINA 2: [She may want me to give her a ride.] Do you need a ride to the airport? I'll take you.

LATINA 1: Are you sure it's not too much trouble?

LATINA 2: It's no trouble at all.

Here we see that in the Latina conversation such requests for help are likely to be implied rather than stated explicitly and directly. Indirect requests can help both parties to save face and uphold smooth harmonious interaction. When Latina 2 detects a request during a conversation with Latina 1, she can choose to either offer help explicitly, or pretend not to acknowledge the request, or she can actually apologize, saying that she would like to take Latina 1 to the airport, but she's sorry she has to attend another party that night.

Thus, if Latina 2 with the high-context communication style decides not to acknowledge the implicit request, she might even subtly change the topic of conversation. Consequently, if Latina 1 discerns the cues from Latina 2, she will then subtlety drop the indirect request. An implicit understanding generally exists between two high-context communicators. They do no need to overtly state their request or use an overt "no" to, in their opinion, hurt the feelings of the other high-context collectivist.

Intercultural misunderstanding, however, becomes highly probable when the Latina communicates with the Irish American. They each rely on their own cultural scripts to inform them of what to expect in the interaction. Let's look at Active Dialogue 7.5 of the "airport ride request" dialogue, this time between a Latina and an Irish American (adapted from Gao & Ting-Toomey, 1998, p. 77).

Active Dialogue 7.5

LATINA: We're going to the Orange Bowl in Miami this weekend.

IRISH AMERICAN: What fun! I wish we were going to the game with you. How long are you going to be there?

LATINA: Three days. [I hope she'll offer me a ride to the airport.]

IRISH AMERICAN : [If she wants a ride, she'll ask me.] Well, have a great time.

LATINA: [If she had wanted to give me a ride, she would have offered it. I'd better ask somebody else.] Thanks. I'll see you when I get back.

Thus, we see that while the Latina verbal model emphasizes indirect verbal style or implicit request, the Irish American model emphasizes direct verbal style and explicit request. Because neither person has any knowledge of high-context and low-context communication differences, they may misunderstand each other. Similarly, many Asian conversation contexts do not make negative responses, such as "No," or "I disagree with you," or "I cannot do it." Instead, they use apologetic expressions, delayed decisions, or indirect expressions, such as "I'm so sorry, I'll not be able to see you off at the airport because of my cousin's birthday . . ." or "Let me check my calendar and hope that I'll make it. I'll call you later." In business conversations, some other Asian verbal messages could be "I kind of agree with you in principle; however, please understand my difficulties . . ." or "I sympathize with your difficulties; unfortunately . . ." Intercultural conversation bumps can easily spiral upward to become intercultural conflicts if we lack the knowledge and skills of code switching between direct and indirect communication styles when we construct our own messages and interpret others' messages. Becoming flexible intercultural communicators means mastering the art of verbal and nonverbal code switching without too much stress or pressure.

Complementary, Animated, and Understated Verbal Styles

The terms *animated* and *understated* refer to the rhythms, emotional expressiveness, and intensity of tone of voice that accompany the verbal content message. The **complementary style** refers to a matter-of-fact tone in delivering your verbal message—nothing more, nothing less. If the message is clearly delivered, we believe we are effective communicators. In comparison, the more *animated* the conversational style, the more it conveys emotional expressiveness and emotional vitality. The more *understated* the conversational style, the more emotional restraint or stoicism is displayed in the conversation pattern.

For example, though mainstream American conversation follows a complementary style approach, French conversation often follows an interruption-punctuation verbal pattern in the context of well-established relationships. This "continuous interruption" in French conversation often baffles U.S. Americans. However, from the French perspective, the interruption-punctuation pattern reflects "spontaneity, enthusiasm, and warmth, a source of unpredictability, interest and stimulation, a call for participation and pleasure. They are the ties that bind and that bring the conversants closer together" (Carroll, 1987, p. 37). The more animated the conversation, the more pleasure the French derive from the conversation. Compare that with the British conversational style.

The British prefer to practice using understatements and "good-mannered" conversation to make a point. For the British, emotional self-restraint means restraint in verbalizing one's feelings; it means ideally not showing them at all. The British distinguish between "*having* emotions and *showing* them; the former is natural and unavoidable, but the latter is entirely a matter of self-discipline—of which you can never have too much as far as the British are concerned" (Storti, 2001, p. 37).

Of course, there are ethnic verbal style variations in terms of animated or expressive verbal styles. As an example, distinctive differences between African Americans' and European Americans' verbal styles exist within our domestic culture. Kochman (1990) notes that among African Americans and European Americans, public presentations are a regular cause of communicative conflict. African American presentations tend to be more emotionally animated and demonstrative than the more verbally straightforward European American presentation.

If the conversational patterns of people from different cultural or ethnic groups at some point annoy you, think about the stylistic level of conversation. Although the British are indirect in comparison with U.S. Americans, the Japanese would not find them to be in the least bit indirect. All cultural characterizations and comparisons are in the eye of the beholder more than with the behavior of the beheld—these are relative differences between cultural and ethnic groups, not absolute differences. By understanding such differences, we can learn to accept or even to adapt to some of the culture-based verbal style differences.

Informal and Formal Verbal Styles

The **informal verbal style** emphasizes the importance of informality, casualness, and role suspension in verbal communication. The **formal verbal style,** on the other hand, emphasizes the importance of upholding status-based and role-based interaction that reflects formality and large power distance. Let's do Quick Poll 7.2 here. The former emphasizes the importance of casual or horizontal interaction, whereas the latter stresses proper or hierarchical-based interaction. The informal style emphasizes the importance of respecting unique, personal identities in the interaction. The formal style emphasizes the importance of honoring prescribed power-based membership identities.

Quick Poll 7.2

How do you usually greet the following people in your everyday life? Do you address them by their first names or their titles plus last names? Circle the usual ways you address them in your cultural-ethnic community:

Your Teachers:	First Name? or Title with Last Name?
Your Parents' Close Friends:	First Name? or Title with Last Name?
Your Doctors:	First Name? or Title with Last Name?
Your Close Friends' Parents:	First Name? or Title with Last Name?
Job Interviewers:	First Name? or Title with Last Name?
Your Neighbors:	First Name? or Title with Last Name?
Restaurant Servers:	First Name? or Title with Last Name?
Siblings or Cousins:	First Name? or Title with Last Name?

Those who engage in status-oriented verbal interaction use specific vocabularies and paralinguistic features to accentuate the status distance of the role relationships (e.g., in parent-child interaction, superior-subordinate relations, and male-female interaction in many Latin American cultures). Although low-context cultures tend to emphasize the use of the formal verbal style, high-context cultures tend to value the status-based verbal style.

For example, Okabe (1983), in commenting on the Japanese language, contends that English is an individual-centered language whereas Japanese is a status-oriented language. Okabe also observes that U.S. Americans tend to treat other people with informality and casualness. They tend to "shun the formal codes of conduct, titles, honorifics, and ritualistic manners in their interaction with others. They instead prefer a first-name basis and direct address. They also strive to equalize the language style between the sexes. In sharp contrast, the Japanese are likely to assume that formality is essential in their human relations. They are apt to feel uncomfortable in some informal situations" (p. 27). In other words, the Japanese tend to uphold the proper roles, with the proper words, in the appropriate contexts to create a predictable interaction climate.

The mode of speaking, in short, reflects the overall values and norms of a culture. The cultural modes of speaking in many speech communities reflect the hierarchical social order, family socialization, asymmetrical role positions, and power distance values of the different cultures.

Before you continue to read the next section, fill out the brief survey in Know Thyself 7.1. The survey is designed to help you assess your attitudes toward talkativeness versus silence.

Know Thyself 7.1	Assessing Your Attitudes Toward Talkativeness Versus Silence

Instructions: Recall how you generally communicate in various situations. Let your first inclination be your guide and circle the number in the scale that best reflects your communication pattern in your everyday life. The following scale is used for each item:

4 = SA = *Strongly Agree*
3 = MA = *Moderately Agree*
2 = MD = *Moderately Disagree*
1 = SD = *Strongly Disagree*

	SA	MA	MD	SD
1. I enjoy talking in all kinds of social situations.	4	3	2	1
2. In my family, silence is respected.	4	3	2	1
3. Talking about a problem makes you think more clearly.	4	3	2	1

☞

☞

Know Thyself 7.1   Assessing Your Attitudes Toward Talkativeness Versus Silence (*continued*)

4. Silence is sometimes more powerful than words.	4	3	2	1
5. I like people who talk a lot.	4	3	2	1
6. I enjoy people who use silence to listen.	4	3	2	1
7. Talking is the glue that holds people together.	4	3	2	1
8. I like people who are on the quiet side.	4	3	2	1
9. In my family, almost everyone enjoys talking.	4	3	2	1
10. In my cultural or ethnic community, silence speaks louder than words.	4	3	2	1

Scoring: Add up the scores on all the odd-numbered items and you will find your talkativeness score. *Talkativeness* score: _____. Add up the scores on all the even-numbered items and you will find your silence score. *Silence* score: _____.

Interpretation: Scores on each communication dimension can range from 5 to 20; the higher the score, the more talkative and/or quiet you are in your communication behaviors. If all the scores are similar on both communication dimensions, you value both talkativeness and silence equally.

Reflection Probes: Take a moment to think of the following questions: Where did you learn your communication habits? Is your family a "talkative" family or a "silent" family? What do you think of people who talk a lot? What do you think of people who seem to use silence a lot in their everyday conversations? Do your cultural or ethnic groups respect "talkativeness" or "silence"?

Beliefs Expressed in Talk and Silence

The Korean proverb "empty wagons make the most noise" illustrates the importance of silence as opposed talkativeness in many Asian collectivistic cultures. Silence can oftentimes say as much as words. Although silence occurs in interaction contexts in cultures around the world, how silence is interpreted and evaluated differs across cultures and between persons. Hall (1983) claims that silence, or *ma*, serves as a critical communication device in many Native American and Asian communication patterns. *Ma* is much more than pausing between words; rather, it is like a semicolon that reflects the inner pausing of the speaker's thoughts. Through *ma*, interpersonal understanding is made possible in many high-context cultures.

While silence may hold strong contextual meanings in high-context cultures, prolonged silence is often viewed as "empty pauses" or "ignorant lapses" in the Western rhetorical model. From the high-context perspective, silence can be the essence of the language of superiority and inferiority, affecting such relationships as teacher-student, male-female, and expert-client. The process of refraining from speaking can have both positive and negative effects. In some situations, notably in many Native American collectivistic cultures, those who must themselves be quiet also expect quiet from others.

For example, the concept of silence occupies a central role in the Apache culture in the United States (Basso, 1970). Silence is appropriate in contexts where social relations between individuals are unpredictable and involve high levels of ambiguity. In this culture, individuals also prefer silence in situations in which role expectations are unclear. Members of the Navajo and Papago Indian tribes exhibit similar silent behavior under the same conditions as the Apache. In France people tend to engage in animated conversations to affirm the nature of their established relationships; in the absence of any such relationship, silence serves the French as a neutral communication process. This is why in the elevator, in the street, or on the bus, people don't talk to each other readily in France. This is a seemingly inexhaustible source of misunderstanding between the French and U.S. Americans, especially because "these rules are suspended under exceptional circumstances and on vacation (and therefore on the train, on the plane). . . . U.S. Americans often feel rejected, disapproved of, criticized, or scorned without understanding the reason for this hostility" (Carroll, 1987, p. 30). With strangers, the French and many Native American groups generally preserve formal distance by means of silence. In contrast, European Americans tend to use talk to "break the ice" and reserve silence for their most intimate relationships.

Intercultural miscommunication can thus often occur because of the different priorities placed on talk and silence by different groups. Silence can serve various functions, depending on the type of relationship, the interactive situation, and the particular cultural beliefs held. Silence can also serve as a powerful means of sharing or persuasion.

Intercultural Conversation Process: Self-Disclosure

Both the willingness to reveal something about yourself and the willingness to pay attention to the other person's feedback about you are necessary to build a trusting intercultural relationship. We discuss an important communication concept in this section: self-disclosure.

Self-Disclosure: Verbal Revealment Versus Concealment

Let's take a look at the sharing process by Grant in Double Take 7.2.

In any relationship, verbal revelation and concealment act as critical gatekeepers in moving a relationship to greater or lesser intimacy. Verbal self-disclosure often follows a *trust-risk dilemma*. To trust someone, you have to be willing to take some risks to share some unique information about yourself. Through taking the risk, you may also

---

Double Take 7.2

I'm half Caucasian and half Chamoro (from my mom's Guamanian side). I was born and raised in Orange County, California. I am an openly homosexual individual who is active in helping my campus community through the Lesbian Gay Bisexual Alliance as well as helping out in other ethnic organizations on campus. I enjoy reaching out to assist my community to learn about lesbian and gay and cultural issues. . . .

I grew up in an intercultural environment; my father is white and my mother is part of the API community. In front of my father, I was expected to behave like an "All-American boy." But around my mother's family, I was expected to play the role of the "All-Chamoro boy." At my home with my father and mother, there was one way of living and acting, but around my grandparents, there was an alternative identity to play—which parallels my homosexuality.

—Grant, *College Student*

---

have established an initial trusting cycle in the interpersonal relationship. However, you may also have to worry about your friend betraying the exclusive information you have just shared. Thus arises the trust-risk dilemma—to tell or not to tell.

Before continuing with this section, fill out the Know Thyself 7.2 self-disclosure survey. The survey is designed to help you understand your degree of readiness for self-disclosure to strangers versus best friends.

Know Thyself 7.2 Assessing Your Readiness to Self-Disclose to Strangers Versus Best Friends

Instructions: Recall how you generally feel and communicate in various situations. Let your first inclination be your guide and circle the number in the scale that best reflects your overall impression of yourself. The following scale is used for each item:

4 = SA =	*Strongly Agree*	
3 = MA =	*Moderately Agree*	
2 = MD =	*Moderately Disagree*	
1 = SD =	*Strongly Disagree*	

Generally speaking, I readily disclose to *strangers* about the following topics:

	SA	MA	MD	SD
1. My interests and hobbies.	4	3	2	1
2. My goals and dreams.	4	3	2	1
3. My work or study situations.	4	3	2	1
4. How much money I make.	4	3	2	1
5. My political opinions.	4	3	2	1

Know Thyself 7.2 Assessing Your Readiness to Self-Disclose to Strangers Versus Best Friends (*continued*)

6. My racial beliefs and viewpoints.	4	3	2	I
7. My dream dates.	4	3	2	I
8. Conflicts with family members.	4	3	2	I
9. My feelings about my face.	4	3	2	I
10. My feelings about my body.	4	3	2	I
11. My positive qualities that I really like.	4	3	2	I
12. My own negative personality traits.	4	3	2	I

Generally speaking, I readily disclose to my *best friends* about the following topics:

	SA	MA	MD	SD
1. My interests and hobbies.	4	3	2	I
2. My goals and dreams.	4	3	2	I
3. My work or study situations.	4	3	2	I
4. How much money I make.	4	3	2	I
5. My political opinions.	4	3	2	I
6. My racial beliefs and viewpoints.	4	3	2	I
7. My dream dates.	4	3	2	I
8. Conflicts with family members.	4	3	2	I
9. My feelings about my face.	4	3	2	I
10. My feelings about my body.	4	3	2	I
11. My positive qualities that I really like.	4	3	2	I
12. My own negative personality traits.	4	3	2	I

Scoring: Add up the scores on all the "strangers" disclosure items and you will find your strangers disclosure score. *Strangers Disclosure* score: _____. Add up the scores on all the "best friends" items and you will find your best friends disclosure score. *Best Friends Disclosure* score: _____.

Interpretation: Scores on each self-disclosure dimension can range from 12 to 48; the higher the score, the more you are ready to self-disclose to strangers and/ or best friends on a variety of topics. If the scores are similar on both item sets, you are very balanced in your readiness to self-disclose to both strangers and best friends.

Reflection Probes: Check out your two scores with a classmate. Interview each other and ask each other the following questions: Where did you learn your self-disclosure habits? Do you come from a low self-disclosive family or a high self-disclosive family? How do you feel about people who self-disclose too much? How do you feel about people who self-disclose too little?

Source: Scale adapted from Barnlund (1989).

Here **revealment** or openness refers to the disclosure of information concerning the different facets of the public self (e.g., interest, hobbies, political opinions, career aspirations) and/or the private self (e.g., deep family issues, identity, self-image and self-esteem issues); **concealment** or closedness refers to the lack of disclosure or sharing of exclusive information about either the public self or the private self. The term **public self** refers to those facets of the person that are readily available and are easily shared with others; the term **private self,** on the other hand, refers to those facets of the person that are potentially communicable but are not usually shared with others (Barnlund, 1975).

Barnlund (1975) found that the Japanese tend to have a relatively small layer of public self and a relatively large layer of private self. In contrast, his research revealed that U.S. Americans have a larger layer of public self and a smaller layer of private self. Sharing information concerning either the public or the private self is conducted through relational openness. The Japanese were found to be more guarded as to disclosing their inner attitudes and private feelings and desires. In comparison, U.S. Americans are more responsive in disclosing information of a personal, private nature.

Self-disclosure is one of the key factors in developing a personalized relationship in any culture or ethnic group. **Self-disclosure** is the deliberate process of revealing significant information about oneself that would not normally be known. Two social psychologists, Altman and Taylor (1973), have developed *social penetration theory,* which explains the two dimensions of self-disclosure: breadth and depth. The *breadth* of self-disclosure refers to the number of topics a person is willing to share with others. When two friends meet for drinks or a meal, the number of topics is typically large. Issues can range from travel plans, to dating experiences, to school and work updates. The *depth* of self-disclosure refers to the level of intimacy or emotional vulnerability a person is willing to reveal in her or his conversation exchange process. For example, when two close friends talk about their interracial dating experiences, the depth of disclosure usually consists of intimate details, the high and low points, concerns, frustrations, family reactions, and exhilaration points. The same topic may be covered on a more superficial level with an acquaintance or coworker. Thus, you may also converse on similar topics with acquaintances or coworkers but really go to more deep and intimate levels—revealing your fears, worries, pride, or joy—with selective close friends. Fill out the "Who am I?" questions in Know Thyself 7.3, and rank order your answers from 1 = *less important* to 10 = *most important*. Share whatever you want to share with a classmate. What influences your self-disclosure process? Do you come from a high self-disclosive family or a low self-disclosive family? How did your classmate's self-disclosure process influence your self-disclosure pattern in the conversation?

Know Thyself 7.3 Who Am I?

Instructions: Let your first inclination be your guide and complete your gut-level answer on each question. Next, review your answers and rank order your answers from #10 to #1 (please use all 10 numbers)

#10 = This Particular Identity Is *Extremely Important to Me*
#1 = Comparatively, This Particular Identity Is *Less Important to Me*

	Answer	Rank
Who am I? I am . . .	_____	_____
Who am I? I am . . .	_____	_____
Who am I? I am . . .	_____	_____
Who am I? I am . . .	_____	_____
Who am I? I am . . .	_____	_____
Who am I? I am . . .	_____	_____
Who am I? I am . . .	_____	_____
Who am I? I am . . .	_____	_____
Who am I? I am . . .	_____	_____
Who am I? I am . . .	_____	_____

Reflection Probes: Check out your answers with a classmate. Share whatever you want to share and keep private whatever you want to keep private. Take a moment to think of the following questions: Which one identity are you the most proud of? Why? Which one identity are you the least comfortable with? Why? Which one identity, in particular, is shaped by the values of your ethnic-cultural membership? In what ways? If someone wanted to find out more about who you are, how should they approach you? What are the best ways to get to know you? What influences your sharing or self-disclosure process with your classmate throughout this interactive exercise?

Johari Window

One way to understand self-disclosure in more depth is to check out the Johari Window. The label "Johari" takes its name from Joseph Luft and Harry Ingham—the first names of the window's creators. The window can be conceived as having four panels: *open, hidden, blind,* and *unknown* (see Figure 7.1). On a broad level, the *open panel* is defined as information known to self and also information known to generalized others or a specific person. The *hidden panel* is defined as information known to self but unknown to others. The *blind panel* is defined as information not known to self but information that is known to others. Last, the *unknown panel* is defined as information not known to self or to others. One example of this is based on a true story. Two interethnic college friends shared a close friendship, including much sharing about their dating experiences. After graduation, they took a vacation together. While having dinner on the second day of their vacation, the conversation turned deep. One friend, processing all the information and the conversation, came out (admitted she was gay) to the other friend. This surprised them both. The gay friend had no idea until then that she was, in fact, gay. Due to the deep self-disclosure conversation and perceived acceptance, the one friend actually helped the other friend to sort out some of her core identity issues in a very spontaneous yet authentic manner.

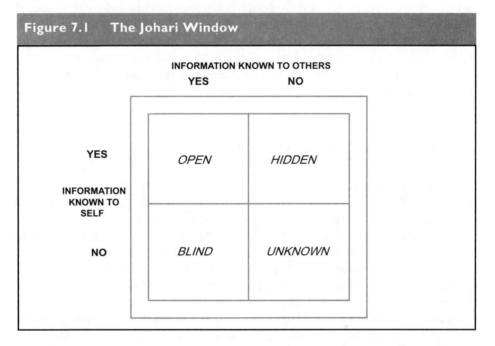

Figure 7.1   The Johari Window

Individuals who have big open panels and small hidden panels are more willing to disclose and share information about themselves compared with individuals with small open panels and big hidden panels. The blind panel can shrink in size by paying attention to feedback and comments from others. The blind area means we are unaware (or in denial) that such attitudes (e.g., sexist, racist, and homophobic attitudes) or behaviors (e.g., gay bashing) exist in us, but our friends actually observe those attitudes or behaviors. Through obtaining feedback from others, information that we are previously unaware of becomes known to us. The mysterious panel, the unknown area, at first glance seems strange. However, we can deduce that the unknown panel exists in all of us because there is always something surprising or new to discover about ourselves and others—through new learning, traveling, life experiences, or meditations about the unconscious self. It is not unusual to discover those "a-ha" moments of unrecognized talents, strengths, resilience, or vulnerabilities. Some of these previously unknown topics can then be moved to the open panel or the hidden panel—depending on whether you want to share them or not.

The relative size of each panel may change from one life stage to anther, from one topic to another, and from one relationship to another. We can analyze our own self-disclosure patterns, for example, about our views on affirmative action, interracial relationships, or gay-lesbian relationships on a general self-disclosure level and on a targeted relationship (e.g., my best friend) level. We can also analyze whether we are in the ethnocentric stage or ethnorelative stage of intercultural learning by being receptive to the feedback and observations from our friends. We can also gain some more self-insights by willingly revealing some of our own honest attitudes and sentiments and exploring why we are the way we are in approaching various interracial or intercultural communication topics.

Intercultural Persuasion Process

Persuasion is the art of influencing someone to do something you want or to accept an idea you believe is important. In intercultural communication, we are constantly engaging in persuasion—for example, an African American student asking her Latino professor to extend a deadline on an assignment; an Asian immigrant asking his European American supervisor to grant him a sick leave to tend to his ailing grandfather; or Disneyland representatives needing to persuade the Chinese to work on developing a China Disney. All of these situations require flexible intercultural persuasion skills and responsive intercultural facework skills. We discuss several persuasion styles in this section.

Before you continue reading, take a couple of minutes to fill out the Know Thyself 7.4 assessment. This brief survey is designed to help you to explore your diverse persuasion styles.

Linear Logic Versus Spiral Logic Persuasion

Low-context communicators tend to practice linear-mode persuasion style, whereas, high-context folks tend to practice spiral-mode persuasion style. The **linear persuasion style** can have one of two forms: the factual-inductive form or the axiomatic-deductive form. The **factual-inductive form** emphasizes the importance of presenting facts, evidence, eyewitness accounts, testimonials, and proofs, and from these specific facts proceeds to draw conclusions or generalizations. The overall U.S. persuasive style has been labeled as following the factual-inductive approach. In comparison, the **axiomatic-deductive form** emphasizes the importance of starting from general principles, or axiom, and then moving forward to fill in specific details. Models, diagrams, and big-picture conceptual frameworks can help to

Know Thyself 7.4 Assessing Your Persuasive Style Preferences

Instructions: Recall how you generally feel and act in various situations. Let your first inclination be your guide and circle the number in the scale that best reflects your overall impression of yourself. The following scale is used for each item:

4 = **YES!** = *strongly agree—IT'S ME!*
3 = yes = *moderately agree—it's kind of like me*
2 = no = *moderately disagree—it's kind of not me*
1 = **NO!** = *strongly disagree—IT'S NOT ME!*

	YES!	yes	no	NO!
1. When I make a request, I like to be as tactful as possible.	4	3	2	1
2. I like to hear a clear "no" if someone does not want to do something.	4	3	2	1
3. I don't like people who brag about their accomplishments.	4	3	2	1
4. I like to be forthcoming and direct when persuading someone to do something.	4	3	2	1
5. I like to offer enough details before making a request.	4	3	2	1
6. I prefer to be clear and concise in my everyday conversations.	4	3	2	1
7. I am sensitive to the other person's feelings when refusing a request.	4	3	2	1
8. I like to get to the point to save time.	4	3	2	1
9. I don't feel comfortable talking about my own achievements at all.	4	3	2	1
10. I believe honesty is the best policy when you try to say "no" to someone.	4	3	2	1

Scoring: Add up the scores on all the odd-numbered items and you will find your high-context persuasive style score. *High-Context Persuasive Style* score: _____.
Add up the scores on all the even-numbered items and you will find your low-context persuasive style score. *Low-Context Persuasive Style* score: _____.

Interpretation: Scores on each persuasive style dimension can range from 5 to 20; the higher the score, the more low context and/or high context you are. If the scores are similar on both persuasive style dimensions, you are a bicontextual communicator.

Reflection Probes: Take a moment to think of the following questions: What do you think of people who converse with you using a different context of communication than you? What do you think are some of the strengths and limitations of your persuasive style? After reading this chapter, do you have any new thoughts and/or feelings about how to deal effectively with a person who uses a different context of communication?

move the negotiation process along from broad to specific points of conclusion.

The overall Russian persuasion style has been identified as following the axiomatic-deductive verbal approach (Glenn, 1981). The Russians will start with an agreement in principle (i.e., the big picture) and then fill in the details. However, one of the major challenges between Russian and U.S. American communication stems from the different ways each approaches verbal diplomacy and compromise. U.S. Americans generally regard compromise as inevitable and desirable. Russian negotiators, on the other hand, consider compromise as a sign of weakness, a retreat from a correct and morally justified position. Russians, therefore, are "great 'sitters,' prepared to wait out their opposite numbers in the expectation that time and Russian patience will produce more concessions. . . . Chess is a Russian national pastime, and Russians negotiate in the same way they play chess, planning several moves ahead" (Richmond, 1996, pp. 150–151).

Alternatively, there are different forms of *spiral persuasion styles*— from the dramatic to the subtle. Members in many Arab cultures, for example, tend to use effusive metaphors, similes, stories, parables, and a wide range of flowery adjectives to reinforce a point. Thus, the dramatic and metaphorical styles of many of the Arabic cultures often tend to emphasize image over digital content and form over function. Members of Italian, Slavic, Jewish, and many African cultures, for example, also have a tendency to use effusive metaphors, parables, or stories to dramatize the emotional impact of their message. Many Asian and Native American cultures, however, may resort to hints, implicit analogies, Zen sayings, and subtle nonverbal gestures to convey an intended meaning. Double Take 7.3 is a Zen story (Pearmain, 1998, p. 119) that illustrates a spiral mode of storytelling.

Double Take 7.3
A Zen Story

Once upon a time, two Buddhist monks were on a journey to a distant monastery when they came to a river. There on the bank sat a young woman. "I beg you," she asked, "could you carry me across? The current is strong today and I'm afraid I might be swept away."

The first monk remembered his vows never to look at or touch a woman, and so, without so much as a nod, he crossed through the heavily flowing currents and soon reached the other side. The other monk showed compassion and bent down so that the woman could climb upon his back to cross the river. Although she was slight, the current was strong and the rocky bottom made it difficult crossing. Reaching the other side, he let the woman down and went on his way.

After some hours journeying down the dusty road in silence, the first monk could no longer contain his anger at the second for breaking ☞

their vows. "How could you look at that woman?" he blurted out. "How could you touch her, let alone carry her across the river? You've put our reputation at stake."

The first monk looked at his companion and smiled. "I put that woman down way back there at the river bank, but I see that you're still carrying her."

What do you think of the above story? Can you rewrite the story to reflect a more linear mode of storytelling? Which persuasive mode do you prefer, the linear mode or the spiral mode? Why? In addition to the linear versus the spiral mode of persuasion, we can also consider the implications of the self-credentialing and self-humbling modes of persuasion.

Self-Credentialing and Self-Humbling Verbal Modes

The **self-credentialing verbal mode** emphasizes the importance of drawing attention to or boasting about one's credentials, outstanding accomplishments, and special abilities. The **self-humbling verbal mode,** on the other hand, emphasizes the importance of lowering oneself via modest talk, verbal restraints, hesitations, and the use of self-deprecation concerning one's effort or performance. For example, let's check out Active Dialogue 7.6, a conversation between Jorge Estrada, who is from Puerto Rico, and Alfred Rohner, who is from Switzerland.

Active Dialogue 7.6

JORGE: Thanks for making the time to see me, Mr. Rohner.

ALFRED: What's on your mind?

JORGE: Well, I heard from Haeme, the production assistant, that there will be open auditions for the new play *But Can He Dance?*

ALFRED: Yes, this is true.

JORGE: Well, I think this is good. It is an excellent play.

ALFRED: Yes?

JORGE: Well, I have been working on designing sets for the past four years, and all have been well received. My work in this theater has never faltered, and I never missed work. [pause] See, I was hoping to get a chance to audition. And since this play is so close to my experience . . .

ALFRED: Oh! You want to audition. I understand. Why do you want this part?

JORGE: Well, as I said, I enjoyed the play. And I always wanted to get my foot into the acting business . . .

☞

> ALFRED: But you are an amazing set designer. Why are you qualified for this role?
>
> JORGE: Actually, the role would give me more money. I have my sister's children who will come to live with me. They need to attend a better high school and college. With more money, I can at least afford to have them both stay in my house.
>
> ALFRED: Jorge, are you serious? You want this role because you have kids coming to live with you? There are many people who have qualifications in acting getting degrees and training. So this does not make any sense to me at all!
>
> JORGE: But Mr. Rohner, I have worked overtime, triple time, covered people who were sick, and never shrugged off any of my duties. I just wanted a chance to audition for this role.
>
> ALFRED: Jorge, who will design the set?!!

Verbal self-humbling or self-effacement is a necessary part of pervasive Puerto Rican American politeness rituals. In Swiss or U.S. culture, we encourage individuals to "sell themselves and boast about their achievements." Otherwise, in a performance review or job interview session, who would notice the accomplishments from a self-effacing individual? However, the notion of merchandising oneself does not sit well with many Puerto Ricans, Mexicans, or Cuban Americans.

Likewise, in many Latin, Native American, and Asian cultures, individuals believe that if their performance is good, their supervisors in situations that have to do with promotion review will notice their behavior. However, from the Western cultural standpoint, if their performance is good, they believe they should document or tell everyone so that their supervisors will be sure to take notice. This difference is probably due to the listener-centric value of the collectivistic, high-context communication pattern, as opposed to the sender-centric value of the Western, low-context communication pattern.

We should note that the pattern of verbal self-humbling cannot be generalized to many Arab or African cultures. In Egypt, for example, a popular saying is "Make your harvest look big, lest your enemies rejoice" (Cohen, 1991, p. 132). Effusive, or highly expressive, verbal style is critical to the enhancement of one's face or honor in some large power distance Arab cultures; expressively complimenting or praising the other person's effort or networking ability is also a common characteristic in these cultures. Additionally, an effusive, other-enhancement persuasion style is also often practiced in many of the Arab cultures. The nature of Arabic as a rather ornate language, in conjunction with larger power distance values, probably contributes to the effect of effusive persuasion style. Furthermore, many Arab hosts feel obligated to engage in effusive other-enhancement talk in communicating with honored guests. The tendency in Arabic to use somewhat exaggerated or dramatic expressions during international negotiation sessions has possibly caused more misunderstandings between the United States and some Arab countries than any other single factor (Cohen, 1987).

Face-Negotiation and Requesting Strategies

How competently we persuade others often relies on how skillful we are at using different facework conversation strategies. **Face** is a claimed sense of social self-worth that a person wants others to have of her or him (Ting-Toomey, 1988). It is tied to the emotional significance that we attach to our own social self-worth and that of the others' social self-worth. It is about maintaining our social poise in conversations and, at the same time, extending our consideration in supporting or threatening the social poise of the other communicator. We can talk about two types of face concerns in conversation: self-face concern and other-face concern. **Self-face concern** means we are much more interested in upholding our identities and favorable self-images in our interaction with others. **Other-face concern,** conversely, means we are much more interested in providing identity respect and support for the other person's interest or need in the face-negotiation process.

Facework refers to the specific verbal and nonverbal behaviors or actions that we engage in to maintain or restore face loss and to uphold and honor face gain. *Face loss* occurs when we are being treated in such a way that our identity claims in a conversation are challenged or ignored. Face loss can be recouped via diverse face-saving strategies. Everyday conversations, such as requests, promises, compliments, criticisms, or conflicts (see Chapter 10), may entail active facework management tactics. For example, in our daily conversations with others, it is inevitable that we make requests for others' help or that others make requests for our help. We may think of *face issues* in terms of how to reject a request or in terms of how to get our own requests granted and not to appear overly imposing. For example, according to research, members of individualistic cultures tend to perceive direct requests as the most effective strategies for accomplishing their interaction goals, but members of collectivistic cultures perceive the requests as the least effective (M.-S. Kim & Wilson, 1994; M.-S. Kim, 2002).

In terms of persuasive strategies between managers and employees, research indicates that U.S. managers prefer to use direct persuasive strategies, such as an *open invitation* (e.g., "Feel free to let me know if you have any ideas to improve this project"), to make *promises* (e.g., "Don't hesitate to offer your creative ideas because this company always rewards innovative input"), or to pay *direct compliments* (e.g., "You are one of the brightest marketing people in this department, and I really value your judgment") in dealing with employees. Japanese managers, however, tend to use altruistic strategies (e.g., "For the future success of our company, please share your suggestions with us") or appeals to duty (e.g., "Remember that it is your duty as a good company employee to model trustworthy behaviors").

To be flexible intercultural conversationalists, we need to develop culture-sensitive persuasion skills. By understanding some of the differences between low-context and high-context communication styles and the different expectations concerning persuasion issues in everyday conversations, we may become more skillful in dealing with culturally diverse others.

Intercultural Toolkit: Recaps and Checkpoints

In this chapter we explored the differences between low-context communication and high-context communication. We examined four low-context verbal styles with ample dialogue examples: direct style, complementary style, informal style, and preference for talkativeness. We also compared these four styles with four high-context verbal styles: indirect style, animated understated style, formal style, and preference for silence. We then moved on to examine an intercultural conversation process more closely through two key concepts: self-disclosure and persuasion. In the self-disclosure section, we introduced the four panels of the Johari Window. In the persuasion section, we introduced several persuasion modes: linear and spiral logic of persuasion, self-credentialing mode and self-humbling mode, and finally, cross-cultural face-negotiation and requesting strategies.

To close the chapter, we present you with the following checkpoints for developing intercultural verbal sensitivity and understanding:

- Understand the fundamental differences between low-context and high-context communication patterns and your potential ethnocentric tendency to negatively evaluate the opposing characteristics.

- Know that individualists tend to engage in direct, low-context verbal communication in expressing thoughts and feelings, and collectivists tend to practice responsive, high-context communication in anticipating the thoughts and feelings of the other person.

- Know that individualists tend to be more self-face oriented in their everyday conversations, and collectivists tend to be more mutual-face and other-face oriented in their everyday relationship development process.

- Remember that individuals who engage in low-context patterns of communication often prefer direct verbal style, matter-of-fact mode, self-credentialing enhancement, and talk-ativeness to pursue effective conversation goals.

• Remember that individuals who engage in high-context patterns of interaction often prefer indirect verbal style, emotionally understated mode, self-humbling talk, and silence to gauge the situation and the cultural stranger.

• To be flexible intercultural communicators, we need the knowledge of both verbal and nonverbal communication to communicate sensitively across cultural and ethnic boundaries.

• Both low-context and high-context communicators need to practice the use of collaborative dialogue in their interactions. Collaborative dialogue is based on a culture-sensitive, respectful inquiry process, in which intercultural parties try to suspend their own assumptions regarding how to conduct a smooth conversation. Rather, they work on inviting the other parties to tell their stories, expectations, and needs. Collaborative dialogue aims to unfold common identity-need issues, such as safety, honor-dignity, boundary, approval, competence, and meaning issues. The more we learn to display a genuine, inquiring attitude in our intercultural conversations, the more we may uncover deep-level common interests and common ground. ✦

Chapter 8

What Are the Different Ways to Communicate Nonverbally Across Cultures?

Chapter Outline

Yoshihiko Kadokawa was a department store executive in Japan. Over time, he noticed that the friendliest clerks were making the biggest sales. In a country that limits overt display of facial emotions, he decided to capitalize on this observation. He quit his job and now charges up to $1,000 to host his "Let's Smile Operation" seminars. For 2 to 3 hours, Japanese executives learn how to smile and be pleasant-looking. The practice of actually widening their mouths to smile is gradually replacing the need for individuals in Japan to "hide" their emotions.

—"Smiley Face."
People Magazine, 1999

As you can see in the example above, nonverbal communication is both a conscious and an unconscious aspect of our everyday life. We can communicate with people without speaking one word. Oftentimes, we don't even realize it! Have you ever walked down the street and a total stranger greeted you with a warm hello or smile or both? Well, if there were a camera nearby, you would find that you were smiling at the stranger without *any awareness of it. We take for granted the importance of our facial expressions, not realizing the impact a smile can make during a conversation, a sales pitch, or an argument.*

Nonverbal messages serve many functions in intercultural situations. If our verbal messages tell us the literal and content meaning of words, then nonverbal messages carry strong identity and relational meaning. For example, nonverbal communication has been called a relationship code because nonverbal cues are often the primary means of signaling a relationship with others. We use nonverbal cues to relate messages that may be too embarrassing or direct to disclose out loud. The use of verbal messages involves human intention, but nonverbal messages can be intentional or unintentional. For example, a popular pair of blue jeans on the market today is a brand called Mavi. Mavi is a company based in France. If you wear these jeans in places that speak Swahili (Tanzania and Kenya), many people may look at you in horror. The name of your jeans in Swahili means "cow dung."

Nonverbal communication occurs with or without verbal messages. Nonverbal messages provide the context for how the accompanying verbal message should be interpreted and understood. They can either create confusion or clarify communication. But more often than not, nonverbal messages can create intercultural friction and miscommunication because (1) the same nonverbal signal can mean different things to different people in different cultures, (2) multiple nonverbal cues are sent, and (3) there are many display rule variations to consider, such as personality, gender, relational distance, socioeconomic status, and situation.

This chapter is organized in four sections. We first discuss the nature of nonverbal communication. We then address different forms of nonverbal communication with many lively intercultural examples. Third, we discuss an important area of nonverbal communication: boundary regulation of space and time. We conclude with a set of recaps and checkpoints to facilitate better understanding of nonverbal intercultural communication.

The Importance of Nonverbal Communication

Nonverbal communication is a powerful form of human expression. It is everywhere. Nonverbal messages are often the primary means of signaling our emotions, our attitudes, and the nature of our relationships with others. Suppose Anup said to Carita, "Oh, I really wanted to come over and say hi, but you looked really busy!" Anup saw that Carita was surrounded by her books, on her cell phone, and talking to another friend. Nonverbal messages can oftentimes express what verbal messages cannot express and are assumed to be more truthful than verbal messages. Many nonverbal experts estimate that in every encounter, about 65 percent is inferred through nonverbal channels. Nonverbal messages signify who we are, based on what we wear, how we speak, and how we present ourselves.

How important are nonverbal cues? One example is the significant changes that have taken place in U.S. airports since September 11, 2001. Airport screeners are now trained by the Federal Bureau of Investigation (FBI) to look for deception clues during routine questioning. For an airport screener to make a quick assessment of whether an individual is lying, she is looking for questionable behavior, which includes darting eyes, hand tremors, and an inconsistent story resulting from rapid questions, suspicious behavior in reactions, and obvious body language. By training airport screeners about nonverbal behaviors, the FBI believes that a suspicious passenger who is lying may be detected.

What Is Nonverbal Communication?

Nonverbal communication is defined as communicating without words through multiple communication channels. **Multiple channels** refer to how the meaning of nonverbal messages can be simultaneously signaled and interpreted through various media, such as facial expressions, body gestures, spatial relationships, and the environment in which people are communicating. In essence, nonverbal communication transcends spoken or written words (Hickson, Stacks, & Moore, 2004). Our culture shapes the display rules of when, where, with whom, and how different emotions should be expressed or suppressed. Nonverbal display rules are learned within a culture. Cultural value tendencies, in conjunction with many relational and situational factors, influence cross-cultural nonverbal behaviors. A former French student, Victoria, said, "When I was younger [and] with my sister, we used to turn off the sound of some soap operas, making up the dialogue ourselves. We always based it on the body language and the facial expressions; it was so funny!"

Nonverbal cues are the markers of our identities. The way we dress, the way we talk, our nonverbal gestures—these tell something about who we are and how we want to be viewed. We rely on nonverbal cues as "name badges" to identify what groups we belong to and what groups we are *not* a part of. All of these cues are interpreted through the mediation of stereotypes. Our accent, posture, and hand gestures further give our group membership away. For example, many Latina who were born in the United States are used to people assuming that they do not speak English fluently, if they speak it at all. Elisa, who worked in a clothing store, remembers a customer who refused to return an item at her cash register because "she would not understand this complex transaction." Elisa remembers her furious anger at this customer's prejudiced attitude and presumption.

It takes a lot of astute observation and deep understanding of a culture to decode nonverbal cues or messages accurately. Think about an interaction you have had recently. Just imagine the difficulty interpreting a five-minute conversation between an Italian friend and a Nigerian friend. Many misunderstandings occur when trying to infer meaning behind nonverbal codes, especially with someone who is from a different culture than yourself. Nonverbal communication is a powerful communication system. It is, in a nutshell, the heartbeat of a culture. Language may be the key to the heart of a culture, but it is nonverbal communication that embodies the rich meaning of a culture.

Actions or Words?

Nonverbal communication is fascinating: We become curious about how some cultures think about and interpret their world. Nonverbal communication includes any cue, such as behaviors, objects, and attributes that communicate a message during an interaction. Most important, nonverbal communication always has some form of social meaning even though no words are spoken.

Nonverbal messages can be used without words, can provide the backdrop to interpret the verbal message, and can create miscommunication. But most of the time, nonverbal messages can create intercultural confusion. There are no set nonverbal rules to follow. There is not one *universal* nonverbal language that we can speak. Instead, nonverbal communication is ambiguous, but at the same time, it is more believable than words.

Many global cities offer dance festivals, featuring modern and traditional dances from across the world. You can watch hula, salsa, and Balinese, to name a few. Each dance group offers us such a unique way of expression, with intricate and complicated moves. Each dance has hand gestures that represent or complement the verbal message. Gestures for love and various types of water and fish are all accompanied by codes. However, all of these codes are communicated without the use of words. If you are not familiar with the code, interpreting the meaning will be almost impossible and will allow plenty of room for inaccurate judgments.

One Code, Many Interpretations

People send a variety of nonverbal cues during each interaction. This creates an interpretive ambiguity. The same nonverbal cue can mean different things to different people in different cultures. One example of a situation in which this may happen is giving the OK sign (i.e., thumb and index finger shaped into an "O" with the other fingers out straight), which means all right or OK in the United States, an insult in Brazil, and money in Japan. Misunderstandings occur because of the intention and variety of such cues (see Snapshot 8.2 for a variety of nonverbal hand gestures).

Many nonverbal communication situations carry a variety of messages and meanings. If a friend gives you a "high five" after you make a basket (as in basketball) in the United States, your friend is congratulating you on your good form. This nonverbal code is purposeful, and the meaning is intended to congratulate you. During an intercultural encounter, conflict and confusion nevertheless occur for two simple reasons. First of all, the same nonverbal signal can mean different things to different people in different cultures (e.g., waving your fingers can mean hello, come here, or I have a question in the United States, the Philippines, and Italy). Second, a variety of hand signals can also carry the same meaning.

Verbal and Nonverbal Similarities

Nonverbal cues can be used independently or together with a verbal message. When used with verbal messages, they relate to verbal messages in five different ways. Nonverbal cues can repeat, contradict, substitute, complement, and accent verbal messages (Knapp & Hall, 1992). We will briefly use some examples to illustrate these concepts.

Nonverbal communication can simply *repeat* the verbal message. If you are going to get your hair cut, oftentimes the barber or stylist will ask you how much hair you want to be cut. You will most likely tell him or her the number of inches followed by a confirmation with your fingers. In this example, a nonverbal gesture repeats the verbal message.

Nonverbal communication can *contradict* the verbal message. You can contradict a message, or you can enhance it. Whenever Vicky tells a lie, she always plays with her hands and avoids eye contact. Unfortunately, her friends are able to see through her immediately. Contradicting a verbal message is a form of leakage or hiding how we really feel. Adults rely more heavily on nonverbal cues for indications of feelings and verbal cues for information about other people's beliefs or intentions.

Nonverbal communication can *substitute* for the verbal message. If you are driving to any border patrol, officers will use hand gestures to tell if you need to stop or continue driving. Smiling at someone at a party signals that you want to start a conversation. The nonverbal message is clear, and no verbal message is needed to clarify the meaning.

Nonverbal communication can *complement* the verbal message. Patting a teammate on the back and saying "What an awesome job" complements the words that are spoken. The look in our teachers' eyes when they tell us they are disappointed in us for doing something inappropriate accompanies the verbal message and underscores their disappointment.

Nonverbal communication may *accent,* or emphasize, parts of a verbal message. If you like to bold some words on a paper or use italics, these are accents. Slamming your hand down on the table during a meeting and saying "Pay attention!" accents the importance of being quiet.

We learn how to use nonverbal communication very early on. Although many similarities in communication function across groups, mindful individuals can learn that different cues are appropriate in different settings and with different groups.

Forms of Nonverbal Communication

To fully understand the significance of nonverbal communication for our communication behavior, we need to examine the variety of nonverbal behaviors used by people in our daily life across cultures. There are seven different forms of nonverbal communication: physical appearance, paralanguage (vocal cues), facial expressions, kinesics (body movement), haptics (touch), oculesics (eye contact), and proxemics (space). We will now illustrate each and note their diverse nonverbal functions.

Artifacts and Clothing

Our physical appearance affects our daily interactions with others. Physical appearance includes body type, height, weight, hair, and skin color. Along with our appearance, we wear clothing, and we also generally display artifacts. **Artifacts** are ornaments or adornments we use to communicate just by wearing the actual item. Both artifacts and clothing serve as markers of our identity. Jewelry, shoes, glasses, gloves, nail polish, tattoos, tongue, facial, and body piercings, and face painting communicate our age, group membership, socieconomic status and class, personality, and gender. We rely on nonverbal cues as a form of comparing ourselves with other groups (Burgoon, Buller, & Woodall, 1996). They can reflect both cultural trends and unique personalities. Famous celebrities, such as Harrison Ford and Ed Bradley (the news commentator on *60 Minutes*), are now spotted wearing earrings on a regular basis.

Nonverbal cues can provide clues for us to determine the specific time in history. You may remember that leg warmers or Van's were trends in the 1980s, but baggy jeans were very fashionable in the 1990s. Tattoos and body piercings (e.g., eyebrows, lip, navel) have been used at various times in history. Traditional Polynesian cultures (e.g., Samoa, Tonga, Maori of New Zealand) have used tattoos and piercings as indicators of class, status, and roles. Trendy now, these traditional tattoos and piercings are common and adopted to express individual difference. These cues serve as identity markers of the individual and also the practices of the larger culture. For example, pop singer Christina Aguilerra has bragged about having 20 different piercings with more to come. At the same time, traditional tattoos (e.g., in Hawaii) have been used to take pride in the rich history that "represents" past ancestors. We (the authors) polled our students informally in two classes (approximately 140 students) and found that the female students had more tattoos than the male students.

Artifacts can also place a person in a particular status or class. Visit any hospital, and you can tell a doctor from a nurse. The doctor typically wears a white uniform; nurses wear scrubs. Uniforms in Japan are worn to differentiate among entertainers, students, workers, and supervisors. A funny thing about artifacts: We make so many judgments about what a person decides to wear. Jessica Ling, for example, a former international student in the United States, was shocked when she went back home to work in Malaysia. She noticed the pressure for more women to keep up with the latest designer trends. Although she lives paycheck to paycheck, she is a consumer of designer labels—a Prada watch, a Tiffany ring, a Chanel bag, Jimmy Choo shoes—to keep up with fashion. The status issue surrounding nonverbal display accessories is common throughout big cities in Asia.

Adornment features, such as clothing, jewelry, cosmetics, and accessories, in different cultures also reflect complex personal identities. Based on our stereotypic knowledge of a particular group, we look for validation of our expectations via nonverbal cues and surface adornment features. Traditional face painting techniques are surface adornment features that are thought to be the foundation of modern cosmetics. In our world today, the cosmetics industry makes a lot of money marketing traditional styles worn in specific cultures. For example, Indian women traditionally henna their hands on special occasions, such as marriage, birth, and death. But recent pop stars, such as Madonna and Demi Moore, use henna as an enhancement to their looks.

One last aspect of artifacts and clothing is impression management. As we become an international community, the need to look global (or, actually, Hollywood *Western*) has some interesting implications. As the winds of globalization sweep through, beauty is not only a trend in the United States. For example, we can find aspects of selling and marketing plastic surgery around the world. According to Schuman (2001), some Korean women have increasingly widened their eyes in a relentless drive to attain the Western image of beauty. More recently, some young Korean women are also getting leg jobs (just as some American women are getting breast implants, false buttocks, face lifts, and Botox injections). The Korean plastic surgeon will operate on part of the calf muscles of the young woman to slim down her legs to look like Western models. In addition, surgeons increasingly perform leg operations in China to elongate the legs of Chinese men and women so that they can compete globally and stand as tall as their Western counterparts.

According to Sciolino (2000), the cool thing to do in Tehran, Iran, is to get a nose job. This may seem shocking in a place where woman are required to cover their hair and conceal the shape of their bodies. But some Iranian women are not content with their noses. This was demonstrated on the cover of *Zahran* (August 2003), a feminist magazine in Iran that showed a woman with a new nose superimposed on her face. The monthly magazine devoted eight pages to the subject of "Young Women and Men and the Hot Market in Nose Jobs." Body alterations definitely serve the nonverbal function of intentional identity management. If used successfully, they can enhance an individual's self-esteem and appearance. However, if used haphazardly or if the operation fails, they can also strip away an individual's remaining self-confidence or distinctive personality. One would do well to proceed with caution when thinking of body alteration techniques or operations to enhance one's face or body image. At the same time, if a safe operation can help someone's self-image, others may learn to accept that person's choice or decision and give any needed support.

Paralanguage

Beyond artifacts, another form of nonverbal communication that gives away our cultural, ethnic, and gender identity is paralanguage. **Paralanguage** is the sounds and tones we use in conversation and the speech behavior that accompanies the message. Simply put, it is *how* something is said, not *what* is said. The nonword sounds and characteristics of speech are called paralinguistic features. Aspects of paralinguistic features include a variety of voice qualities, such as the following:

- *Accent:* how your words are pronounced together

- *Pitch range:* your range from high to low

- *Pitch intensity:* how high or low your voice carries

- *Volume:* how loudly or softly you speak

- *Articulation:* if your mouth, tongue, and teeth coordinate to speak precisely or to slur your words

- *Pace:* the rate of how quickly or slowly you speak

Each of these characteristics may be represented on a continuum. For example, U.S. Americans often interpret and mimic the sounds of Chinese speakers as "whiny" and "loud and screaming," typically associating their sounds with old kung fu movies. In contrast, Arabs oftentimes evaluate the speaking style in the United States as nonexpressive, cold, distant, and harsh. Whatever the perspective, members of different cultures use their own cultural nonverbal standards as guidelines for proper or improper ways of speaking and evaluating others.

Through the use of paralanguage, we encode a sense of self via different nonverbal features and behaviors. People who perceive others tend to use their own standards to judge others through nonverbal markers. Some of these markers can be intentionally sent, but others can be unintentional. For example, if you raise your voice, the interpretation is that you are angry. However, some ethnic or cultural groups raise their voices because it indicates sincerity or authenticity. For example, some African Americans tend to have emotionally expressive voices and are passionate about their conversation points. This is commonly mistaken for anger. This is also true in other cultural groups. Manal, a college sophomore, recalls that the Arabic norm is to speak in a loud voice, repeat points, and pound on the table for emphasis. In her house, both the men and the women speak in a loud voice that might be misinterpreted as a display of anger. If someone who does not understand Arabic (or Farsi) observes a conversation between two Middle Easterners, he might think that the two people talking sincerely about something are actually mad at each other. Manal says, "My stepfather is constantly thinking that my mother and grandmother are arguing about something, but they are actually carrying on a normal conversation."

Paralanguage can change the meaning of a sentence simply by accenting different words. These three statements have different meanings depending on the way you say them:

Are you for real?

Are *you* for real?

Are you for *real*?

Or, try the statement "Oh, really!" by varying the sounds with a classmate. In hearing or conversing in a foreign language, we often cannot pick up subtle vocal changes that may help us understand that either playfulness or sarcasm is intended by the speaker. If you don't pick up the nuances of playfulness or humor in the voice, for example, misunderstandings will affect your relationship with the speaker. You can unintentionally offend, frustrate, or hurt someone without realizing how powerful your voice sounds. Additionally, your vocal message may be misunderstood and inappropriately judged.

Facial Expressions

We assume the feelings and attitudes of strangers from the nonverbal messages we receive during an interaction. One important form of nonverbal communication that conveys feelings and attitudes is kinesics. **Kinesics** is the study of posture, body movement, gestures, and facial expressions (see Snapshot 8.1). Kinesics comes from the Greek word *kinesis*, meaning "movement." The face is capable of producing about 250,000 expressions. Nonverbal researchers generally agree that there is relative universality in the decoding of basic facial expressions. It appears that there is consistency across cultures in our ability to recognize at least seven emotions in an individual's facial expressions. We can refer to these recognizable facial emotions by the acronym **SADFISH: S**adness, **A**nger, **D**isgust, **F**ear, **I**nterest, **S**urprise, and **H**appiness (Richmond & McCrosky, 2000). People are able to recognize not only the emotion but also the intensity of emotion and often the secondary emotion being experienced. Take a look at the following photos.

Snapshot 8.1

Can you identify the emotions represented by each facial expression?

On a general level, different cultural groups have interpreted these various facial expressions with a high degree of accuracy. However, the ability to recognize specific emotions on the SADFISH list may vary from one specific culture to the next. For example, studies indicate that students in the United States are better at identifying anger, disgust, fear, and sadness than are Japanese students (Matsumoto & Juang, 2003). The reason is that Japanese students learn at a very young age to suppress their emotions because this display can be threatening to others and also create disharmony in their everyday relationships. As you can see, identifying facial expressions through a photograph is actually quite difficult. What is more interesting is that children, when asked, have a harder time expressing these emotions randomly. The special difficulty in interpreting the two facial emotions of disgust and anger only fuels the problem of having the "correct" answer of what the expression looks like. Part of this problem has to do with cultural display rules.

Moreover, there are cultural differences in the display rules we use for expressing emotions. **Cultural display rules** are the procedures we learn for managing the way we express our emotions (Ekman & Friesen, 1975). The rules tell us when it is or is not acceptable to express our emotions. For example, in individualistic cultures, it is acceptable to express anger or disgust alone or in the presence of others. In collectivistic cultures, anger and disgust are not expressed in public, especially in front of individuals with higher status. For example, in Indonesia, people will be quiet and hide their feelings if they are angry with their boss, but those in Australia (individualistic) will openly express their anger toward their boss.

Cultural display rules have progressed through the invention of the Internet. As we progress with our advanced technology, sending messages via e-mail or text has resulted in a more efficient way to communicate, affecting how we express emotions. If you have been to South Korea or Japan, you will know that cell phones are used as a keyboard. Many people are no longer talking on the cell phone but instead are typing in text messages. The use of icons during IM (instant messaging) and in text messages became popular because of the great need to replace long sentences, words, and expressions of our feelings with a quick keyboard symbol. Universal icon expressions have become a significant way to converse without face-to-face interaction. These give senders everywhere the ability to talk with others without having to explain in detail the weight of their feelings. For example, do you recognize any of these emoticons: :-o, 8-O, :-l, :-/, :-ll, :-* ? Take a guess and check out Jeopardy Box 8.1. Witmer and Katzman (1997) found that women are more likely to use icons in their e-mail messages than men. And what is the most popular icon? The smile: :)!

Despite the popularity, frequency, and success of icons, there are some clear disadvantages to text messaging and icons in general. First, many people who use icons and text messages on a daily basis can talk about an exact time and place in which they were misunderstood or their words were taken the wrong way after an IM session or an e-mail. Reading an emoticon in a message cannot replace the depth of feelings

Jeopardy Box 8.1 Commonly Used Worldwide Emoticons		
-) = Happy	:-/ = Skeptical	;-) = Happy with wink
:'-) = Happy with tears	:-@ = Scream	:-| = Indifferent
:-o = Surprised	:-O = Very surprised	8-O = Shocked
:-(= Sad	:-C = Very sad	: = Snobby
:-[= Angry	:-|| = Very angry	`:-) = Raised eyebrow
:-D = Laughing	:-* = Kiss	8-) = Glasses
|-O = Yawn	%-) = Confused	[:] = Robot

a person has to convey or the difficulty expressing how she or he truly feels. Second, joking around and sarcasm are difficult to interpret. Many people complain that they spend much time putting out the flame of a potential conflict because a sentence was misrepresented. This conversation takes us back to paralanguage and misunderstandings due to sarcasm, joking, or tone of voice.

Snapshot 8.2

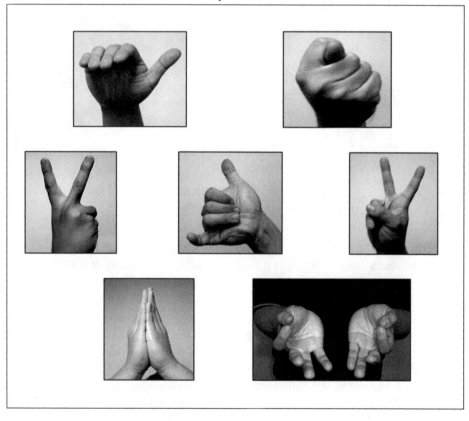

How many intercultural gestures can you decode?

Gestures

Gestures are culturally specific and significant forms of nonverbal communication (see Snapshot 8.2). In fact, they are much more elaborate and more frequently used in Italian culture than in U.S. culture. The four basic categories of hand gestures and body movements (Ekman & Friesen, 1975) have been categorized as *emblems, illustrators, regulators,* and *adaptors*.

Emblems are gestures that substitute for words and phrases. The nonverbal gesture replaces the need to speak. For example, when you shrug your shoulders to say "I don't know," this is an emblem. An emblem for Filipinos is using the lips to point to an object, a direction, or a person. Emblems are usually gestures or movements that are displayed with clear intent and are recognized by members of your ingroup. Greeting rituals, gestures to call someone over, peace or insult gestures, and head movements indicating "yes" or "no" are emblems. Every culture has a large variety of emblems with

Snapshot 8.3

A Chinese "shame on you" nonverbal gesture.

Snapshot 8.4

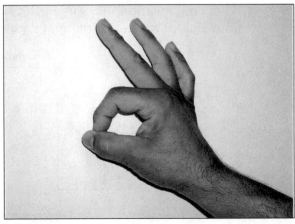

This United States "OK" gesture can mean "money" to the Japanese, a sexual insult in Brazil and Greece, a vulgar gesture in Russia, or "zero" in France.

specific meanings and rules of their displays (see Snapshot 8.3). However, emblems can contribute to intercultural misunderstandings or conflicts. For example, emblems may hold contradictory meanings in different cultures. A "fist" among African Americans signified "Black Power" in the 1970s. But a fist can also trigger a fighting stance. Putting your thumb and index finger together and making a circle with your other three fingers straight can mean "okay." But in some cultures, this means the number zero (see Snapshot 8.4).

Joe Whitecotten, an anthropologist, tells a colorful nonverbal story that highlights potential misunderstandings. Check out Double Take

---

Double Take 8.1

I spent a lot of time in Italy. As a huge football fan, I can only imagine the confusion that would happen if the Italians were watching U.S. college football between the University of Oklahoma (OU) and University of Texas at Austin.

The OU fans always hold up their index finger (which means "We are Number 1!"), and the Texas fans respond with a sign holding up the index finger and the little finger simultaneously (which means "Hook 'em, Horns," referring to their mascot, the Longhorn).

To the Italian, these gestures would have very different meanings. The index finger means "Up yours," like the middle finger in American culture, and the simultaneous index finger and little finger signify "You are a cuckold." This is one of the worst insults you can give to an Italian male, because it means that his wife (or girlfriend) has cheated on him because he is sexually inadequate.

—Joe, *College Instructor*

8.1. This fun story is an example of emblems that are culture specific and the basis for potential misunderstanding (see also Snapshot 8.5).

Illustrators are nonverbal hand gestures that we use along with the spoken message—they literally illustrate the verbal message. When you are describing a shape, such as a triangle, you are likely to make angles with your fingers. If you talk with your hands and use mostly hand gestures, then you are a person who enjoys expressive illustrators. Egyptians and Italians generally use broad, full arm gestures to illustrate points when they are speaking, more so than the reserved British and Asians. We are so used to making these movements that it is very difficult to reverse them or make inappropriate gestures. Many people wonder why Asian groups don't use more illustrators. The answer is that Asians prefer to focus more on the interaction process and consider the use of too many hand gestures to be distracting, rude, and even undisciplined.

Regulators are nonverbal behaviors we use in conversation to control, maintain, or "regulate" the pace and flow of the conversation. When we are listening to someone, we acknowledge the speaker by nodding our head and adjusting or maintaining eye contact, and we make paralinguistic sounds (e.g., "mm-hmm," "really," "no kidding!"). Next to emblems, regulators are considered to be culturally

Snapshot 8.5

This United States "thumbs-up" gesture can be interpreted as a very offensive gesture throughout the Arab world.

specific nonverbal behaviors. These are also the most rule-governed kinesic behaviors. Regulators act as the nonverbal traffic signal to control the dynamics of a conversation. For example, in the United States, when we interrupt a speaker with "Really?" we are in agreement, we are assisting them with their story, or we are showing them that we are paying attention to their story. If we are in Japan, saying "Really?" while a person is talking is considered to be rude and inappropriate.

We learn regulators at a very young age. We use them at lower levels of consciousness. Depending on what region you are visiting, vocal segregates, such as "Sure, you're right" in the U.S. South and *"Nay nay"* among Korean elders, can be classified as nonverbal regulators. These words mean "I am hearing you," but the literal translation in English of the latter is "no" to those who do not speak Korean.

Adaptors are habits or gestures that fulfill some kind of psychological or physical need. Some adaptors are learned within a culture (e.g., covering the mouth when we sneeze, or covering the mouth when we laugh aloud). Others are more automatic (e.g., scratching an itch on your head, picking your nose until you are satisfied). Most adaptors are not intended to communicate a message. However, some of these habits can be considered rude in the context of another culture. For example, in a meeting, when you are listening with your arms folded across your chest, some people may assume that you do not want to talk with others, but you may actually feel cold. In the library, you may notice that while studying, some people consistently play with a pen or pencil with their fingers. You may think they are nervous, but they are merely concentrating.

Haptics

The nonverbal function of **haptics** examines the perceptions and meanings of touch behavior. Different cultures encode and construe touch behavior to be either appropriate or inappropriate. Past research indicates that touch behavior is used to fulfill five communicative functions: as a greeting ritual, to express affection, to be playful, to have controlling behavior, and to have task-related functions (Andersen, 1999).

Different cultures have different rules about touch. For example, same-sex touch and handholding in Malaysia, China, Sudan, Japan, Nepal, and Saudi Arabia is considered to be acceptable and part of daily life. However, contact among the opposite sex is considered to be taboo. This is better known as "PDA" or the public display of affection. In the United States, same-sex handholding pertains to the gay/lesbian/ bisexual community. However, opposite-sex handholding is an appropriate PDA in the United States. Latino/as from Latin American cultural regions tend to engage in more frequent touch behaviors than do U.S. Americans and Canadians. But it is important to remember that the touch behaviors in both the Arab and the Latin American cultures are usually confined to same-sex touching, not opposite-sex touch.

There are also differences among a high-, moderate-, and low-contact cultures (Ting-Toomey, 1999). French, Russians, Latin Americans, and Italians are members of high-contact cultures. **High-contact cultures** often look each other in the eye directly, face each other, touch and/or kiss each other, and speak in rather loud voices. East Asians and Asian Americans, such as Chinese, Japanese, and Indians, are members of low-contact cultures. **Low-contact cultures** often engage in little if any touching, preferring indirect eye gazes and speaking in a lower tone. The United States, Canada, and Australia are **moderate-contact cultures,** which is a blend of both. Research (Remland, 2000; Remland, Jones, & Brinkman, 1995) also reveals that southern Europeans touch more than northern Europeans. After observing a thousand couples at many train stations in different countries, nonverbal researchers found that the highest frequency of touching—from the most frequent to the least frequent touch cultures—occurs in descending order as follows: Greece, Spain, Italy, Hungary, Germany, Belgium, England, Austria, and the Netherlands. The researchers also pointed out that much of the intercultural haptics or touch research depends heavily on gender, age, context, duration of the relationship, and personality factors.

In addition, in real life, high-contact cultures can also bother a low-contact culture to a great extent. Let's check out Melissa's story and her semester abroad in Double Take 8.2.

Double Take 8.2

When I lived in Spain, I had to get used to [the people's] constant PDA. They would do this continuously, especially on the metro. In Spain, you cannot bring home friends, boyfriends, etc. Usually, only family is allowed [at home]. Maybe that is why many Spaniards take advantage of their alone time in public and make out. But this is where "psychological space" comes into play. I definitely did a lot of that [psychological space] in Spain. I would just pretend it [the making out] wasn't happening, even though it would be right in front of my face. But one thing I noticed in Spain, which was weird, I didn't observe the parents being very high contact with their children.

—M. Diaz, *College Student*

Let's also briefly examine nonverbal situational appropriateness. The "buttock pat" is an excellent example of a situational touch cue. This is used in the United States, frequently in male sports. The pat is a sign of encouragement, team bonding, and congratulations for a job well done and has spread to European sports. But in Germany, Austria, Eastern Europe, and the Middle East, the buttock slap is given as a sign of an insult (Morris, 1994). Outside the sports context, the fear of touch among U.S. males is high. Therefore, knowing the appropriate context, individual likes and dislikes, and appropriate relationship is vital in intercultural nonverbal communication.

Boundary Regulations

How do you deal with space? For example, when you enter a classroom for the very first time, is there a "place" that is your target space? Do you park yourself on the seat, put your bag down, and remember where you sit from that time on? When the class meets again, do you sit in the identical seat? How do you feel if someone else is sitting in your seat?

Space and time are boundary regulation issues. As human beings, we are territorial animals (see Snapshot 8.6). We claim and mark our territory. When someone or something invades our territory, we become much more sensitive to the invasion. It is a feeling of vulnerability and a threatening experience. Marking our territory has more to do with psychological ownership than physical ownership. This is the feeling we have of owning a particular spot. If our territory becomes a precious commodity, we react without taking a moment to think about our behavior and our actions, because we feel violated. Friends and colleagues in San Francisco will complain when someone "parks in their spot." Although parking is free, finding a space is sometimes impossible, so the violation feels even stronger if one's psychologically owned spot is invaded.

Snapshot 8.6

Different doorways or gates regulate inner and outer space.

Everyday, ordinary behavior includes some aspect of marking our space. If you hang out in coffee shops, you will probably put your stuff down at the table to "claim" the seat. If someone sits in your seat when you go to get your coffee, a conflict may occur. This is a violation, breaking the unspoken rules of territory. In an interesting article about a famous restaurant called Elaine's in New York, this very famous bar was described as having a seating chart and tables associated with Elaine's favorite people. The assigned spots were not to be changed under any circumstances . . . unless by Elaine herself. In the next section, we discuss four broad themes of space issues: interpersonal boundaries, environmental boundaries, psychological boundaries, and temporal regulation.

Regulating Interpersonal Boundaries

Before you begin this section, take Quick Poll 8.1 to determine your interpersonal space orientation.

Quick Poll 8.1
On the following continuums, place a check mark where you would place yourself spatially when communicating with
Strangers: _____
Acquaintances: _____
Teachers: _____
Classmates: _____
Parents: _____
Siblings: _____
Same-Sex Friends: _____
Opposite-Sex Friends: _____
Romantic Partners: _____

Edward T. Hall was one of the first anthropologists to write extensively about how we "mark" and define our territory. This is the study of proxemics. **Proxemics** is the study of space between persons, physical contact, and the inner anxiety we have when people violate our space. In the United States, according to Hall, we have four spatial zones: intimate, personal, social, and public (Hall, 1959, 1966). The *intimate* zone is 0 to 18 inches. This space is reserved for those who are closest to us, such as family, an emotional situation, and our close friends. The *personal* zone is from 18 to 48 inches, reserved for closer friends, some acquaintances, and colleagues. *Social* zones occur in a larger event, such as a party, at 48 inches to 12 feet. Finally, the *public* zone is any distance that is 12 feet or more. Any violation of these zones can result in feelings of anxiety.

What constitutes appropriate personal distance for one cultural group can be perceived as crowding by another group. The average conversational distance of personal space for European Americans is approximately 20 inches. The average personal space of many Latin American and Caribbean cultures is 14 to 15 inches. In Saudi Arabia, the ideal conversational distance is only 9 to 10 inches. Personal space serves as a hidden dimension of intercultural misunderstanding and discomfort.

Personal space is a unconscious protective territory that we carry around with us and deem sacred, nonviolable, and nonnegotiable. Although members of all cultures engage in the claiming of space for themselves, the experience of space and violation varies across cultures and gender groups. Many of our U.S. students agree: In a movie theater with plenty of open seats, most male friends will leave an empty seat between them. But females will watch the movie together, sitting right next to each other. Let's check out a fun, nonverbal space story in Double Take 8.3.

Double Take 8.3

When I was in the airport in Tel Aviv, Israel, there was no such thing as an orderly line or an open space in the shuttles. People were practically enmeshed in one another, [and] you would be staring at the back of someone's head or armpit. This was actually quite humorous for me. As soon as I learned how people squeezed themselves in front of a counter, I did the same.

It was interesting for me to watch my stepfather's transformation. In the beginning of our trip, he was incredibly disturbed by the lack of space between strangers. But by the end of our trip, he was the one rushing up to the counters, and he would not even flinch when an Israeli man would practically have his nose inside my stepfather's back (he is very tall). If my stepfather had kept to Hall's regulations for space depending on the relationship, he would not have lasted as long as he did in a country that redefines those regulations.

—Laleh, *College Student*

Boundary regulations in different cultures are large in variety, and they may also vary within a family. Melissa, a Mexican American, describes her experience growing up in a traditional Mexican family in Double Take 8.4.

Double Take 8.4

I have always been very close with all of my aunts, cousins, grandmas, parents, and siblings. We have always shared our great affection for one another with plenty of kisses and hugs. But with my parents, I am definitely more intimate with my mother. I have noticed that in a lot of Mexican families, the father is the guardian, the role model, and the authority figure. [The parents] usually keep a little distance between themselves and their children (daughters in particular). My dad is a lot less affectionate than my mom. But my mother and my two sisters and I are very affectionate with one another—we touch, hug, and kiss all the time.

—Melissa, *College Student*

Environmental Boundaries

In addition to our interpersonal space, we also have boundaries related to our environment. Environmental boundaries are defined as the claimed sense of space and emotional attachment we share with others in our community. Concepts of territory and identity are interconnected because we usually invest time, effort, emotion, and self-worth in places that we claim as our primary territories. Our home territory or immediate environment asserts a strong influence on our everyday lives.

Lewin (1936) addressed the significance of how the environment influences our behavior with the following formula: B = f(P, E) in which B = *behavior*, P = *person*, and E = *environment*. This means that our *behavior* is defined by the *persons* interacting as well as the *environment* in which the communication takes place. For example, middle-class neighborhoods in Canada and the United States are very different from the middle-class neighborhoods in many Latin American and Asian cultures, and these environments influence how people in those cultures behave.

In the United States, a home in a typical middle-class neighborhood is physically separated from the community by a fence, a gate, a yard, a lawn, or some combination of these. Homes often symbolize an individual identity related closely with the owner. Environmental boundaries within the home are exercised through the use of separate bedrooms, private bathrooms, and many locks. In contrast, the middle-class neighborhood in Mexico is designed so that houses are integrated with a central plaza, possibly containing a community center and a church. Homes do not have many locks and many family members share bedrooms and bathrooms. U.S. middle-class homes appear to reflect individualistic qualities, and Mexican middle-class homes appear to promote collectivism and group-based interaction.

Cultural groups have different expectations concerning the specific functions of different rooms in the house. For example, in cultures such as China, Korea, and Japan, the proper way to entertain guests is in a formal restaurant, because the home is "not worthy" of entertaining guests. In contrast, many Arabs, like U.S. Americans and Canadians, do not mind entertaining guests in their homes. Many Arab homes reserve a specific formal room to entertain guests, and the guests may not see any other part of the house until trust is established in the relationship. Many U.S. American hosts showcase the house with a grand tour. This informal tour happens within the first minutes of arrival, before settling in. In many Arab homes, separate quarters are also reserved for male and female activities. This is also true in many traditional Korean homes.

In other related room functions, traditional Japanese and Korean homes do not make clear distinctions among the living room, dining room, and bedroom. Thus, when close friends are invited over, it is critical for them to remove their shoes before entering the multipurpose space, the floor of which is covered with straw mats used for sitting and sleeping. This practice is also common among homes in Hawaii. Removing your shoes and slippers before entering an apartment, condo, or home is a norm. Countries such as Japan and Indonesia have clear distinctions between the bathroom and the toilet. The bathroom is used strictly for bathing. From this cultural perspective, to mix up bathing (a cleaning function) and toileting (a dirtying function) is against their code of civility and personal hygiene (see Snapshot 8.7).

Many individualistic cultures encourage a home environment that is unique to the owner, but many collectivistic cultures encourage communal-type home settings. These cultural norms have been gained from early childhood, where we learned instinctively how to deal with space and boundary issues through social roles, furniture setting, and proper interaction rules to be performed in each room. We turn now to psychological space and privacy regulation issues.

Snapshot 8.7

A Japanese bathroom: The Japanese prefer to separate clearly the bathing funtion from the toileting function.

Psychological Boundaries

If you have ever lived or visited densely populated countries, you have probably dealt with psychological space or intrapersonal space. Crowded conditions make it almost impossible for people in many Asian countries (e.g., China, India, Indonesia, and Japan) to experience privacy as it is known in the United States (i.e., being alone in a room). *Intrapersonal space* refers to the need for information privacy or psychological silence between the self and others. Let's do Quick Poll 8.2 and explore your need for privacy.

Even though privacy regulation is a major concern in many Western social environments, the issue may not be perceived as critical in collectivistic-oriented cultures. In fact, even the concept of privacy is construed as offensive in many collectivistic cultures (see Snapshot 8.8). For example, the Chinese words that closely correspond to the concept of privacy are those for *secretive* and *selfishness*. These words imply that many Chinese feel that relational interdependence comes before the need for personal privacy in everyday interactions.

Quick Poll 8.2		
Use your gut-level reaction and circle "yes" or "no" to the following privacy violation scenes. Do you usually get irritated or stressed out when someone . . .		
Enters your room without knocking:	YES	NO
Parks in your favorite spot:	YES	NO
Stands close to you in an elevator:	YES	NO
Sits too close to you in a movie:	YES	NO
Sits in your favorite spot in the classroom:	YES	NO
Walks on your lawn:	YES	NO
Peeps at your e-mails:	YES	NO
Interrupts you:	YES	NO
Stands too close to you:	YES	NO
Touches your arm in conversations:	YES	NO

Another aspect of psychological space is creating the mood or atmosphere of a room. Many people will invest money on the practice and art of feng shui. **Feng shui** literally means "air" and "water" in Chinese. Used for thousands of years, feng shui is the philosophy of combining elements to attain good energy within a room, a building, or an area. For example, many feng shui experts believe that if your bed directly faces a door, all of your good energy and luck will flow out of the room. This basic example is one of many used to design harmony within a house or room. Currently, there are feng shui designers, architects, and counselors in the United States and worldwide. Creating this form of psychological space promotes a more harmonious living condition. There are even feng shui magazines online, for example, *http://www.wofs.com/*. The practice offers advice, such as "Do not overdecorate your toilets (e.g., with flowers, paintings, antiques, golden taps and showerheads) because you may inadvertently activate the bad energies there."

If cultural groups do not emphasize categories for "privacy" and "solitude" to guide everyday interactions, then such categories may not be a critical part of the everyday social reality. Language, in conjunction with multiple nonverbal cues, directs our perceptions and attitudes toward the functions of space and time. Psychological and physi-

Snapshot 8.8

A Korean office space.

cal boundaries protect our levels of comfort and safety. Space is a powerful way to mark and define our ingroup and outgroup boundaries in this regard.

Regulating Time

Let's do the Know Thyself 8.1 assessment on time orientation. Are you a monochronic-time person, a polychronic-time person, or a bichronemic-time individual? Please read on.

Know Thyself 8.1 Assessing Your Monochronic Time and Polychronic Time Tendencies

Instructions: Recall how you generally feel and act in various situations. Let your first inclination be your guide and circle the number in the scale that best reflects your overall impression of yourself. The following scale is used for each item:

4 = YES! = *strongly agree—IT'S ME!*
3 = yes = *moderately agree—it's kind of like me*
2 = no = *moderately disagree—it's kind of not me*
1 = NO! = *strongly disagree—IT'S NOT ME!*

	YES!	yes	no	NO!
1. Time is not necessarily under our control.	4	3	2	1
2. It's very important for me to stick to a schedule.	4	3	2	1
3. I'm very relaxed about time.	4	3	2	1
4. Meeting deadlines is very important to me.	4	3	2	1
5. Unexpected things happen all the time— just flow with it.	4	3	2	1
6. I get irritated when people are not on time.	4	3	2	1
7. It's OK to be late when you're having a wonderful conversation with someone.	4	3	2	1
8. I like to be very punctual for all my appointments.	4	3	2	1
9. I'm more concerned with the relationship in front of me than clock time.	4	3	2	1
10. I keep an appointment book with me all the time.	4	3	2	1

Scoring: Add up the scores on all the even-numbered items and you will find your monochronic-time preference score. *Monochronic-Time Preference* score: _____.
Add up the scores on all the odd-numbered items and you will find your polychronic-time preference score. *Polychronic-Time Preference* score: _____.

Interpretation: Scores on each time dimension can range from 5 to 20; the higher the score, the more monochronic and/or polychronic time tendencies you ☞

👉

> **Know Thyself 8.1 Assessing Your Monochronic Time and Polychronic Time Tendencies (*continued*)**
>
> have. If the scores are similar on both time dimensions, you are a bichronemic-time communicator.
>
> **Reflection Probes:** Take a moment to think of the following questions: Do you like your monochronic and/or polychronic time tendencies? Why or why not? Where do you learn your sense of time or clock rhythms? How do you think you can deal effectively with people who have a very different time preference from you?

Temporal regulation is defined as the attitudes we have about time. The study of time is known as the study of chronemics. **Chronemics** concerns how people in different cultures structure, interpret, and understand the time dimension.

We are in a constant struggle with time. The faster we go, the faster we want to go. The faster we go, the more impatient we become. Modern appliances take advantage of our need for time by producing faster results. Do you have no time to make dinner? Modern appliances can speed-chill a bottle of wine and roast a whole chicken in four minutes. E-mails are faster than sending letters. The efficiency of receiving e-mails results in an urgency to reply. Our life stages (birth, development, aging) are closely tied in with the sense of time. Our religious or spiritual beliefs, in terms of where the universe begins and ends and where life begins and ends, are two time-related worldview considerations.

Cultural patterns of time designate when and how we should start the day; when we should eat, take a break, work, play, sleep, and die; and if and how we will reincarnate.

We are all affected by the norms and values of time from our own culture. More often than not, we don't realize this until a norm or value has been violated in some way. Nevertheless, we are unconsciously aware of cultural values and norms. For example, if you are doing business in Spain and you are not familiar with the working hours there, you will be completely thrown off by the pattern of the day. In Barcelona, people often start work at 10:00 a.m., have lunch at 3:00 p.m., get back to work at 5:00 p.m., and then work until 8:00 p.m.

In 2000, French workers averaged fewer hours per week than workers in most developed nations (C. Smith, 2003). Many workers in France complain that the country's 35-hour workweek, adopted in January 2000, makes it too hard to work. What other countries do you think work the shortest hours per week and the longest hours per week? Take a guess and check out Jeopardy Box 8.2.

As you can see, workers in South Korea average a 47-hour workweek. But in the future, the workweek will be cut to 40 hours. This

Jeopardy Box 8.2 Per-Week Work Hours for Ten Countries

Country	Work Hours per Week
1. South Korea	55.1
2. Turkey	54.1
3. Argentina	53.5
4. Taiwan	53.4
5. Vietnam	53.3
6. U.S. and China	42.4
7. Canada	42.2
8. Britain	41.9
9. Italy	40.5
10. France	40.3

Source: Baker, M. (2001).

includes employees of government corporations, banks, and all large corporations. By July 2006, the reduced-hour regulations will make their way to all small firms.

Hall (1983) distinguished between two patterns of time that govern different cultures: the *monochronic-time schedule (MT)* and the *polychronic-time schedule (PT)*. (See Table 8.1). According to Hall and Hall (1987), MT and PT are polar opposites. People in MT cultures pay close attention to clock time and do one thing at a time. In MT cultures, people use time in a linear way, employing segments to break up time into scheduled and divided allotments so a person can concentrate on one thing at a time. The schedule is given top priority. The United States, Germany, and Switzerland are classic examples of MT-time cultures. Students attending college or a university belong to an MT culture as well. For example, Shawna is monochronic: "I live by a very strict schedule and hate to deviate from it. This is only because I am most productive if I have a schedule."

People in PT cultures pay attention to relational time (involvement with people) and place more emphasis on completing human transactions than on holding to schedules. For example, two polychronic Gua-

Table 8.1 Characteristics of Monochronic and Polychronic Time

Monochronic Time	Polychronic Time
Clock Time	Situational Time
Appointment Time	Flextime
Segmented Activities	Simultaneous Activities
Task-Oriented	Relationship-Oriented
Future-Focused	Past/Present-Focused
Tangible Outcome Perspective	Historical Perspective

temalans conversing on a street corner would likely opt to be late for their next appointment rather than abruptly terminate the conversation before it came to a natural conclusion. For Hall and Hall (1987), Arab, African, Latin American, Asian, and Mediterranean cultures are representative of PT patterns. One example of a place with PT cultural patterns is Africa. Pennington (1990) said that for many Africans, time creates group harmony and participation among the members. Group connectedness can be seen in the dances and drumming. Time for traditional Africans is viewed as organic rather than mechanical.

When PT and MT people interact, disagreements and misunderstandings often occur, for example, in planning a vacation. An MT traveling companion will feel comfortable if the tickets were purchased, if a hotel or hostel room was confirmed, if a daily schedule was planned, and so on. The PT person will respond by waiting to do these things just prior to departure. As Shawna says, "This drives me crazy. I hate waiting until the last minute to do things, and he hates to do too many things in advance. We plan trips around the e-fares, so that means sometimes we don't even know where we are going until a few days before we leave."

To be flexible, we must work toward living with both types of time orientation. This adds a lot of spontaneity to life. Gray, a Pottery Barn employee, offers his take on time in Double Take 8.5.

Double Take 8.5

If my friends or family ever needed anything, I would set aside my schedule and be there for them. Since I am so monochronic, when I do get off schedule I can get back on schedule. I am monochronic only when it has to do with things that need to be done, but when it comes to my friends and relationships, I am much more polychronic.

I think that relationships are the most important part of my life, and I don't let time constraints get in the way, unless it has to do with school. It is hard to live a polychronic life when you are in school because there are so many deadlines and things that need to get done. When you are in the "real world," I think that it may be more important to act [in ways that are] both monochronic and polychronic—there's a schedule to stick to and there's a need for flexibility. I think that it would be best if you were able to live somewhere in between the extremes of MT and PT. Then you would have the best of both worlds.

—Gray, *College Student*

Studies indicate that members of individualistic cultures tend to follow the MT pattern, whereas members of collectivistic cultures tend to follow the PT pattern (Hall, 1983). Members of individualistic cultures tend to view time as something that can be controlled and arranged. Members of collectivistic cultures tend to view time as experientially based (i.e., living and experiencing time fully rather than mechanically monitoring clock time).

Now let's do Quick Poll 8.3.

Quick Poll 8.3
Your MT friend is waiting for you at a restaurant. What will you say if you are

5–10 minutes late?	_____
10–15 minutes late?	_____
15–30 minutes late?	_____
30–45 minutes late?	_____
45–60 minutes late?	_____

According to most people's answers, Hall (1959) made distinctions for arriving late in the U.S. in accordance with chunks of time within 5 minutes. Therefore, in the above question, if you are 5 to 10 minutes late, you are in the "mumble something" time, and you offer a small statement. "Slight apology" time is 10 to 15 minutes late, and therefore you are required to apologize. "Mildly insulting or serious apology" time is 15 to 30 minutes late, so you are expected to offer a persuasive reason for your tardiness. The last two, "rude" time (30 to 45 minutes) and "downright insulting" time (45 to 60 minutes), are both unacceptable. Time is omnipresent. Chronemic cues allow us to manage our intercultural interactions and facilitate clearer understandings regarding this form of nonverbal communication. Studying chronemics gives us a better understanding of the rhythmic dance of time.

In sum, it is so easy to draw conclusions about people without even understanding their culture. When someone from a different culture does not look you in the eye, it is easy to jump to the conclusion that he or she disrespects you, is shy, or is not interested. However, some cultural groups believe that looking someone in the eye is disrespectful. Before drawing any conclusions from watching people's actions, engage in a conversation and find meaning behind the gestures. Nonverbal cues communicate status, power, ingroup and outgroup differences, and unique identities. In attempting to understand within-culture and across-culture nonverbal variations, look to interpersonal sensitivity, respect, and open-minded attitudes as good first steps in gaining nonverbal entrance to a culture.

Intercultural Toolkit: Recaps and Checkpoints

In this chapter, we have discussed the importance of many forms of nonverbal communication across cultures. More specifically, we have explored artifacts and clothing, paralanguage, facial expressions, various nonverbal hand gestures, haptics or touch, and cross-cultural regulation of space and time (see the answers to Snapshot 8.1 and 8.2 in Snaphots 8.9 and 8.10). Each form of nonverbal communication reflects our larger cultural values and also expresses our unique personalities and identities. More important, the situation in which the nonverbal behavior takes place is quite critical in adding meaning to our accurate interpretation.

To be a flexible nonverbal communicator across cultures, you should be mindful of your own nonverbal behaviors and signals. You also need to be cautious in interpreting the unfamiliar gestures and nonverbal signals in a new culture. We present you with a set of nonverbal checkpoints to consider in communicating across cultures:

- Be flexible when you observe and identify nonverbal display rules. Your observation and initial reaction may not match the rules across cultural groups. Flexibility allows you to be patient when you observe and match identities, status, distance, expectations, and appropriate nonverbal behaviors in various situations.

- Go deep: different meanings and expectations of nonverbal norms and rules are more than what one sees; there is typically a deeper-than-surface explanation. This may help you move toward an alternative explanation and move toward a clearer picture.

- Remember that what someone says is not as important as how he says it. It is important to be aware of one's actions when expressing feelings in words. Sometimes a person can portray a more serious and unaccepting physical presence than the intended meaning. If you do not feel comfortable adapting nonverbally to the intercultural stranger, check yourself and your environment. Realize that the functions and interpretations of any nonverbal cues are tied closely to identity, emotional expression, conversational management, impression formation, and boundary regulation issues.

- As a flexible nonverbal communicator, express emotions and attitudes that correspond to your comfort level but, at the same time, be adaptive and sensitive to the appropriate nonverbal display rules in a particular culture.

- Because nonverbal behavior is oftentimes so ambiguous and situation-dependent, learn to be less judgmental and more tentative in interpreting others' unfamiliar nonverbal signals.

Snapshot 8.9

Did you correctly identify the emotions represented by each facial expression?

Snapshot 8.10

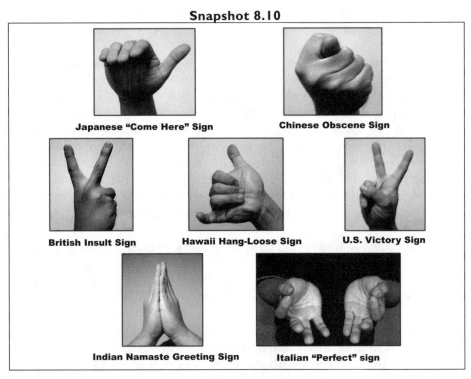

How many intercultural gestures could you decode? ✦

Chapter 9

What Causes Us to Hold Biases Against Outgroups?

Chapter Outline

Scenario 1:

Although the paperwork for my identity change process (i.e., from an international student to a United States resident) went quickly, the affective metamorphosis process was incremental. Unlike Iowa City, the U. W. University District, in the late '70s, did have a mix of White students, Asian students, and some Black students. The interesting thing was that despite this diversity, I encountered more racist remarks and episodes (especially directed at me or to my husband, such as saying, "I heard you are married to a Chink"—along with making a "slant eye" gesture) than in all my four years in Iowa City.

I guess the concepts of majority and minority can be formed and intergroup consciousness can be developed only when a critical mass of people creates a rigid ingroup/outgroup boundary. Having a consciousness such as this, people begin to perceive scarce resources and intergroup competitions. During this stage, I was very conscious of my being "different"—with a burden.

—Stella, *College Instructor*

Scenario 2:

I was born in Korea, but a European-American family in Oklahoma adopted me. I never paid much attention to the color of my skin or felt I was different in any way; I always thought of myself as a White American. However, when I was in junior high school, we had an assignment to bring one baby picture to class. As each person's picture was taped up on the board, students had difficulty guessing the identity of each child. Finally, when it was my turn, the whole class shouted in unison, "That's Jarod!" I was shocked. How did they all know? And that is when I realized I was different.

—Jarod, *Engineer*

These real-life examples are but two of millions available. Ask members of a majority or minority group if they have ever been mistreated, or stereotyped, by others, and the answer would be a resounding "Yes!" However, if we ask the same persons if they are prejudiced or carry prejudicial feelings, we may get a resounding "No!" These examples illustrate two very important points about interactions with people from cultural groups other than our own. First, we usually experience interaction anxiety because we do not have enough information—or the information we have is outdated. When we communicate with people outside of our own group, our usual script may or may not work. This lack of knowledge can lead to misunderstanding, or ineffective communication, or both. If we feel vulnerable or don't have enough information, we may experience cultural or ethnic-racial identity distinctiveness.

Second, if we have only partial norms and rules to direct us through the communication interaction, we may fall back into using stereotypes. Although some of the stereotypes may have an aspect of truth, many group-based stereotypes are inaccurate. This scenario is the classic recipe for intergroup misunderstandings and prejudice. Communicating with strangers from other cultural groups involves the interplay between ingroup and outgroup membership boundaries.

This chapter is organized into four main sections. First, important concepts such as perception, ethnocentrism, and stereotypes will be discussed. Next, we will discuss the effects of interactions with those who are different from ourselves. Third, recommendations are given to filter out stereotypes, minimize prejudice, and find a sense of peace in our chaotic world. Last, we look at practical checkpoints to deal with ethnocentrism and prejudice issues.

Through Our Lenses: Communication Filters

As discussed previously, culture shapes the way we see our world. Our vision of the world and information we absorb occurs through a complex filtering process. Both cognitive and affective (i.e., having to do with emotions) filters serve as eyeglasses we wear to interpret and evaluate behaviors of intercultural strangers. These eyeglasses allow us to see the world around us, make sense of the world, and interpret behaviors around us. But eyeglasses may also limit our vision to see what is directly in front of us.

Perception and Communication

Human **perception** is the process of selecting cues from the environment, organizing them into a clear pattern, and interpreting that pattern. Perception is typically a three-step process of *selection, organization,* and *interpretation.* Each of these steps is heavily affected by cultural socialization. In the **selection process**, we pick out cues from our cultural landscapes. We learn to pay closer attention to the cues that are valuable in our culture. Because it is mentally impossible to pick up every detail and stimulus we receive, we selectively choose incoming data. What kind of data stands out for us? Any stimulus that is distinct or gets our attention quickly. If you are walking around a shopping mall, a person who has full-body tattoos, rainbow-dyed hair, or loud clothes may get you to do a double take. As another example, if a teacher speaks with a heavy accent, you will pay less attention to the lecture material but concentrate more on the sound of the teacher's voice, pitch, or tone. You may ask yourself, "Where is this accent from?" Another characteristic of the selection process is observing any change in the environment or with other people around. For example, suppose you walk into a movie theater where everyone is chatting. Suddenly, it turns quiet. You will probably be a little more observant of your behavior with those around you to assess why people have stopped talking. Culture plays a big part in what we selectively choose to pay attention to.

The second step in the perception process is **organization.** Our culture and the language we speak guide us to aspects of our environment that we consider important. We have learned from our cultural/ethnic socialization to organize our perceptions by grouping similar objects or things together and labeling them with a symbol or name. For example, ordinary folks name and catalog colors, such as gray, blue, green, red, orange, and so forth. However, if you are a fabric buyer for the Gap, you can probably use more distinctive labels to identify the different shades of gray and assign gender to them. For instance, you might assign chambray heather for men but heather gray for women. You might choose different shades of blue for women, such as blue lotus, Miami sky, and dream. We also tend to fill in missing information in what we perceive to provide a more comprehensive and complete whole.

Suppose you are at the grocery store and you see a woman pushing a child in a baby stroller. You will "fill in" your inference that the woman is a mother and the child is hers. This "filling-in-the blank" tendency is derived from the meanings that we form in our everyday enculturation process. Due to cultural and personal experience differences, every individual has his or her own unique perceptual processes. What you choose to focus on depends on how you feel; what you see, hear, taste, smell, and touch; and the context.

The last step is **interpretation.** Interpretation allows us to attach meaning to the data we receive, which is also known as expectations. Expectations involve what we anticipate and predict about how others will communicate with us during an interaction. Our expectations influence the way we perceive and interpret cultural strangers' behaviors, and likewise their reactions to us are based on their expectations and preconceptions. Expectations are the filters of our perceptions of others. We have an image of how we expect people to act in a given situation. If a person violates our expectations, we will become surprised and emotionally aroused and pay more attention to this person's strange behavior (Burgoon, 2000).

More important, cultural differences in our perceptions are quite dramatic and reveal much about a culture. For example, food is an expression of the values and identities associated with a particular group. One of the most culturally specific meals is breakfast (Kapnick, 1999). What one cultural group finds pleasure in eating—fish and rice stew, tamales with red chilies, or miso soup—another group may find repulsive or disgusting. Peering in to see what other cultural groups eat for breakfast allows us to examine our individual filtering process:

- *Sudan:* Sudanese people wake up and drink coffee and tea. They start eating a "breakfast meal" at about 10 a.m. This meal typically is a bowl of *foul* (fava beans) mixed with onions, tomatoes, and feta cheese served with bread.

- *Northern China, Taiwan, and Hong Kong:* People eat warm or cold soybean milk, sweet or salty, served with a variety of condiments, including dried pork or shrimp, preserved cabbage, scallions, soy sauce, and vinegar topped with deep-fried breadsticks.

- *Vietnam:* A typical breakfast is *pho* (a beef-based broth soup), rice noodles, and meat with onions, herbs, jalapenos, bean sprouts, and hot plum sauce served on the side.

- *Japan:* Japanese people eat a bowl of miso soup, a bowl of rice, and a side dish of tofu, grilled fish, or vegetables for breakfast.

- *India:* Rice with *sambar* (lentils, spice, and vegetables), fish and rice stew, a yogurt salad, and tropical fruit.

- *Mexico:* Chilies with eggs, beans, or chorizo sausages, sweet bread, and rolls.

- *France:* Coffee with crisp bread, which is topped with butter and jam.

- *Russia:* *Tvorog*, farmer cheese mixed with jam and buttermilk.

- *Germany:* Soft-boiled eggs, cereal, cheese, spreadable liver sausage, ham or other cold cuts, rolls, and mixed bread.

- **South China, South Korea, and Japan:** Rice *congee* (boiled leftover rice with water) is served with a variety of side dishes, including spicy peanuts, preserved and salted duck egg, and *kim-chee* (spicy preserved cabbage) topped with green onions.

- *United Kingdom:* Coffee or tea, bacon, sausage, and eggs or a bowl of porridge, and sometimes toast with *marmite* (a concentrated, black yeast paste).

- *United States:* Eggs and toast are served with bacon, sausage, or ham. In the South, add grits, biscuits, and gravy but omit the toast. In the North, add hash brown potatoes. And in Hawaii, add two scoops of rice, spam, and gravy.

Interpretation, then, is all within an individual. How we perceive breakfasts has a lot to do with our own meanings of a "good breakfast." Interestingly enough, Sharon Kapnick (1999) believes that the U.S. breakfast is showing signs of globalization because "the U.S. breakfast is spreading with U.S. influence in the world—and the expansion of McDonalds and other fast-food eateries" (p. 106). In fact, Finbar, a man from Wales, agrees. The traditional Finnish breakfast (i.e., fried eggs, fried bread, fried tomatoes, ham, fried potatoes, and toast) has now been replaced with coffee or tea and toast. Because time has become a precious commodity, we need to conduct business, eat, and play in a timely manner. Simple fast food, regretfully, does replace the extended morning ritual of culture-based, deliciously prepared breakfast.

These three perceptual filters act as major barriers to effective intercultural communication. Ineffective communication between cultural groups often occurs because we assume that we perceive and interpret other people's behavior in an objective, unbiased manner. The reality, however, is that our perceptions of others are highly subjective, selective, and biased. However, by being more mindful of the biased mindset we carry inside our mental map, perhaps we can "catch our-selves" more often and counter our preconceived expectations with flexible adjustments. In practicing flexible communication, we are ready to try on different styles and shades of eyeglasses—and to learn to see things from different lenses. We turn now to a discussion of three main filters that affect communication with intercultural strangers.

Ethnocentrism and Communication

In the United States of America, there are three major team cham-pionship games. Teams compete to win the title and be declared National Football League Superbowl World Champions, National Bas-ketball Association World Champions, and Major League Baseball World Series Champions. What these three examples illustrate is the ethnocentric tendency of U.S. sports. Are U.S. football, basketball, and baseball games played globally, internationally, and across borders? No. But the winners are declared the best in the world.

Before continuing your reading, fill out the brief Know Thyself 9.1 survey. The assessment is designed to help you determine the degree of your ethnocentrism tendencies.

Know Thyself 9.1 Probing Your Ethnocentrism Tendencies

Instructions: The following items describe how people generally think about themselves and their cultural groups. Let your first inclination be your guide and circle the number in the scale that best reflects your overall agreement with the statement. The following scale is used for each item:

4 = SA =	*Strongly Agree*	
3 = MA =	*Moderately Agree*	
2 = MD =	*Moderately Disagree*	
1 = SD =	*Strongly Disagree*	

	SA	MA	MD	SD
Generally speaking . . .				
1. I believe my culture has the best lifestyles compared with other cultures.	4	3	2	1
2. I like routines and a stable environment.	4	3	2	1
3. My culture is very advanced in comparison with other cultures.	4	3	2	1
4. I don't like ambiguous or uncertain situations.	4	3	2	1

☞

☞

Know Thyself 9.1	Probing Your Ethnocentrism Tendencies (continued)				
5.	My culture provides the best opportunity for its members to achieve their goals.	4	3	2	1
6.	I get very stressed in unfamiliar settings.	4	3	2	1
7.	My cultural group has the most colorful language and vocabulary.	4	3	2	1
8.	I don't like to approach strangers for anything.	4	3	2	1
9.	My culture has a very rich history and traditions.	4	3	2	1
10.	I get quite intimidated thinking of living in another country for more than a year.	4	3	2	1

Scoring: Add up the scores on all the odd-numbered items and you will find your ethnocentrism score. *Ethnocentrism* score: _____. Add up the scores on all the even-numbered items and you will find your tolerance of ambiguity score. *Tolerance of Ambiguity* score: _____.

Interpretation: Scores on each attitude dimension can range from 5 to 20; the higher the score, the more ethnocentric and/or intolerant of ambiguity you are. If the scores are similar on both attitude dimensions, you are high on cultural ethnocentrism and high on your fear of ambiguous situations.

Reflection Probes: Take a moment to compare your scores with a classmate's. Think of the following questions: Where did you learn your attitudes about your own culture and its value compared with other cultures? What fears do you have in approaching new or unfamiliar situations? Why? How do you think you can prepare yourself more effectively in dealing with new cultural situations and cultural strangers?

Ethnocentrism comes from two Greek words and can be broken down into its components. *Ethno* refers to "one's own ethnic or cultural group," and *centrism* means that "one's own group should be looked upon as the center of the world." *Ethnocentrism* means that we consider the views and standards of our own ingroup as much more important than any outgroups. Outgroups are often at a disadvantage because we constantly make judgments about outgroups based on our own group's standards and values. Examples of standards include beliefs that one's own group practices the correct religion, knows how to treat people with respect, employs the best ways of educating their children, and votes for the most qualified political candidates (Brislin, 2003). Visually, ethnocentrism is the core (i.e., our valued ingroup is in the center), and all outgroups are placed at the periphery, the outside (see Double Take 9.1).

These comments are more common outside of the United States. Ethnocentrism has a way of allowing us to focus specifically on events that matter more on our soil than 10,000 miles away. This relates back to our discussion of proxemics: Whatever is closer to us has a little

> ## Double Take 9.1
>
> My husband, Don, was at a self-serve gas station a few years ago and, while in line, a white middle-aged customer became angry when the Korean cahsiers communicated to each other in Korean. He yelled, "Speak English. This is America!" Then he turned to my (also white and middle-aged) husband and angrily stated that these foreigners ought to go back to where they came from. My husband realized that the angry man just assumed he'd agree with the comments be- cause they looked alike, and my husband wanted to let everyone within earshot know that he completely disagreed with the angry man. So, he responded by loudly saying, "Oh, no. I don't agree. I like them. I want more of them to come to our country." This silenced the impatient man, and my husband hoped it indicated, to everyone else who heard, that not all white middle-aged men were the same.
>
> —Alex, *College Instructor*

more value. There are many examples of ethnocentric tendencies. The above example with sports events assumes that U.S. teams are the best, even though they are playing teams only within U.S. borders. The two Chinese characters for *China* translate as the "Middle Kingdom." The characters or pictographs for *China*, first written more than 4,000 years ago during the Hsia dynasty, are translated as "the center of the universe." Take a look at a nation's world atlas; it is not surprising that every nation depicts its own country in a central position on the map, with neighboring states shown as peripheral on the outside.

Ethnocentrism is a defense mechanism used to view our culture as superior to other cultures, and thus we perceive our way of life as the most reasonable and proper. As a result, we expect that all other groups should follow our way of living and behaving. Where does ethnocentrism come from? Like our perceptions, ethnocentrism is reinforced and learned through a cultural socialization process. It can consist of both implicit and explicit attitudes toward outgroup members' customs or behaviors.

As human beings, we display ethnocentric tendencies for three reasons: (1) we tend to define what goes on in our own culture as *natural* and *correct* and what goes on in other cultures as *unnatural* and *incorrect;* (2) we tend to perceive ingroup values, customs, norms, and roles as universally applicable; and (3) we tend to experience distance from the outgroup, especially when our group identity is threatened or under attack (Triandis, 1990). Let's take a look at the following example.

In 1998, U.S. actress Claire Danes and her movies were banned by the City Council of Manila, the Philippines. The actress made comments about her experience in Manila while filming scenes for *Brokedown Palace.* She said that the city "just . . . smelled of cockroaches. . . . There's no sewage system in Manila, and people have nothing there. People with, like, no arms, no legs, no eyes, no teeth. Rats were everywhere" (Spines, 1998, p. 66). After hearing the reaction from the Philippines, Danes apologized by releasing this statement: "Because of the subject matter of our film, *Brokedown Palace*, the cast was exposed to the darker and more impoverished places of Manila. My comments . . . only reflect those locations, not my attitude towards the Filipino people" (1998, September 30).

Claire Danes provides a sad but rich example of how we communicate ethnocentrism and racism. In fact, ethnocentrism comes in different gradations. Lukens (1978) used the communicative distances of indifference, avoidance, and disparagement to discuss the degrees of ethnocentrism. The **distance of indifference** (i.e., low ethnocentrism) reflects the lack of sensitivity in our verbal and nonverbal interactions in dealing with dissimilar others. From the use of insensitive questioning approaches to the use of "foreigner talk" (i.e., exaggeratedly slow speech or a dramatically loud tone of voice, as if all foreigners were deaf), the speech pattern serves as a reminder that these strangers are somehow exotic and quaintly different. The **distance of avoidance** (i.e., moderate ethnocentrism) reflects attempted linguistic or dialect switching in the presence of outgroup members, as well as displayed nonverbal inattention (e.g., members of the dominant group maintain eye contact only with members of their group) to accentuate ingroup connection and avoidance of outgroup members. Finally, the **distance of disparagement** (i.e., high ethnocentrism) refers to the use of racist jokes or hate-filled speech to downgrade outgroup members. For example, if you ask persons living in Manila or the Philippines or beyond, most of them would likely interpret Danes' comments as racist. The remarks were particularly offensive and drew international attention, because by insulting the country, Danes insulted the entire population of 84,525,639 Filipino people in the Philippines plus the Filipinos beyond the national border.

Stereotypes and Communication

Stereotypes are exaggerated pictures we make about a group of people on the basis of our inflexible beliefs and expectations about the characteristics or behaviors of the group (Lippman, 1936; Stephan & Stephan, 1992; 1996). Before we discuss the concept of stereotypes further, let's check out the following story in Double Take 9.2.

Group membership (e.g., "Hawaiians," "Asians," "Latino/as," "lawyers," "janitors," and "New Yorkers") conjures certain stereotypic images in our mental map. A *stereotype* is an overgeneralization toward a group of people without any attempt to perceive individual variations. Stereotypes contain the content of our social categories. A stereotype can refer to a subconsciously held belief about a membership

---

Double Take 9.2

I remember one incident, in particular, in which my graduate advisor's support was critical in encouraging me to move on. The incident was an exchange between myself and a professor when he explained why I did not receive a full-year teaching assistantship like the rest of the TA's. The exchange went something like this: "Stella, it's not that you're not good. It's just that life is like a horse race. Some horses get the first prize, and others are runners-up. . . . *With your accent, it's just very difficult for you to make it to first place. . . . What I'm trying to say is . . .*"

My heart sank upon hearing those words. At that moment, I genuinely had serious doubts about whether I belonged to this very Americanized "speech" communication discipline. It was my advisor's comforting words and academic faith in me that held me together in those days. It was also what my husband said to me that echoes still: "Stella, you should go back and tell your professor, what happens in a real horse race is that most people bet on the wrong horse—they have chosen poorly."

—Stella, *College Instructor*

---

group. The content of stereotypes can convey both positive and negative information (e.g., "Mexicans have large families and many children," "All Asians are martial artists," or "French people are arrogant"). Thus, we use preconceived images in stereotyping a large group of individuals without tending to individual variations. When we stereotype French people as rude or believe that Mexicans have large families, we may be basing our stereotypes on past observations, media images, or what we have heard from others. The stereotype may stem from two to three communication incidents with just a handful of French people. Nevertheless, we devise categories that frame the expectation and meaning we attach to people's behavior or actions in general.

For example, when we learn that someone is *transgendered,* we tend to be instantaneously guided by the language category of transgendered. Frequently, an explanation of describing such a person will start with "imagine that you wake up one morning and find yourself in the body of the other gender." A transgendered male or female is unhappy as a member of the sex (or gender) to which he or she was assigned by the anatomical structure of the body, particularly the genitals. The person is physically normal but feels that he or she *belongs* to the other sex, or wants to *be* and *function* as do members of the opposite sex. We start assuming that this individual's every word and movement come from his or her sexual orientation. Unfortunately, we may be so captivated by the distinctive features of this label or naming process that we often forget to pay close attention to other unique and social qualities of this multifaceted person. Let's look at another example.

In 1998, someone blew up the Murrah building in Oklahoma City. Within the hour, "wanted" images of Arab Americans were highlighted across every national and international news channel. Arab Americans living in Oklahoma City, Norman, and other larger cities received constant phone threats and verbal assaults. Stereotypes of "terrorist" activity were focused only on Arab Americans, without considering other sources or alternative possibilities. The reality, in the end, was that two White Americans, Timothy McVeigh and Terry Nichols, were the "terrorists" who did the atrocious act.

Many factors shape our mindscape. One reason people stereotype is because of language usage. Paired words in the English language, for example, often encourage polarized thinking: straight or gay, us and them, females and males, Blacks and Whites, to name a few. Although polarized language usage allows us to manage our social environment more efficiently, polarized perception often leads us to interpret the social world as either good *or* evil, fair *or* unfair, and right *or* wrong. Beyond language and selective personal experience, the contemporary media play a critical role in shaping our stereotypes about our own group and those of others.

Stereotypes and Media

Media images shape the way we view dissimilar others from different cultural/ethnic groups. As a result, we associate different stereotypes as "character types," or as specific ethnic groups who represent the associated images. For example, Elizabeth Bird (1999) observed that American Indian males seen in films and on television are often cast as "doomed warriors" who are strong and attractive. However, they are also often cast as either sidekicks to European American male actors or loved by strong, independent-spirited White women (e.g., *The Last of the Mohicans*). Another stereotype is the wise elder, who has the knowledge and is the source of ancient wisdom. Female American Indians are seen as maidens or princesses (e.g., Pocahontas), who are symbols of ancient wisdom and harmony with nature, more so in graphic art than on television and in movies (Bird, 1999). African Americans and Latino/as do not have it any easier. According to Orbe and Harris (2001), African American males are typically relegated to comedic roles, such as Sambo (lazy and content), Uncle Tom (quiet and respectful), and Buck (athletic and sexually powerful). African American women, however, are either sexually enticing or asexual and nurturing mammies. Latino/a Americans are limited to stereotypical roles associated with lower-status occupations.

It is inevitable that all individuals stereotype. The key to dealing with the issue is to learn to distinguish between inflexible stereotyping and flexible stereotyping. *Inflexible stereotyping* holds on to preconceived and negative stereotypes by operating on automatic pilot. We dismiss information and evidence that is more favorable to the outgroup, and we presume one member's behavior represents all members' behaviors and norms. In comparison with inflexible stereotypes, we need to address the characteristics of *flexible stereotyping* (see Table 9.1).

Table 9.1 Inflexible Versus Flexible Stereotyping	
Inflexible Stereotyping	**Flexible Stereotyping**
Automatic-Pilot Reaction	Mindful of Categorization
Rigid Categories	Open-Ended Categories
Premature Closure	First Best Guesses
Polarized Evaluations	Loose Interpretations
Information Distortion	Information Openness
Unwilling to Change Categories	Willingness to Change Categories

Essentially, to be more mentally flexible means to become aware that we can and will stereotype members of an entire group. However, refraining from typecasting an entire group on the basis of slim evidence, or no evidence, is a good first step. Using loose, descriptive categories rather than evaluative categories is another way to mindfully *flex* our stereotypes. Using a qualifying statement or a contextual statement to frame our interpretations allows an outgroup member to be an individual and *not* a representative of an entire group. This is a critical destereotyping step. Finally, being open to new information and evidence gives us an opportunity to get to know, in-depth, the most important membership identities of the individuals within the group.

Flexible stereotyping allows us to be more open-minded, but inflexible stereotyping makes us shortsighted. Flexible stereotyping reflects a willingness on our part to change our loosely held images based on diversified, direct face-to-face encounters. Interacting with individuals who are different from us can be uncomfortable at times. We may even feel nervous or anxious because of their strange behaviors or unfamiliar accents. By being aware of our own zone of discomfort and admitting that we are anxious or confused in terms of how to approach the cultural stranger, we may also be taking a solid step forward, moving from inflexible stereotyping to flexible relating and connecting. *Perceptions, ethnocentrism,* and *stereotypes* provide the contents of our filtering process. We now move on to the outcome, our response to intercultural outgroup members.

Nearsighted Focus: Ingroup/Outgroup Membership Boundaries

Us Versus Them

Social identity theory is the study of ingroup and outgroup membership. It is part of the formation of our personal identity. Recall from our earlier discussions in Chapters 2 and 5 that ingroup members are people with whom you feel close and have some kind of emotional connection, such as family members, close friends, and church members. Outgroup members are individuals to whom you do not feel emotionally close; you feel a sense of detachment and perhaps distrust. Being with ingroup members gives you a sense of security and belonging, and being with outgroups gives you a foundation for comparing group values, norms, and behaviors (Brewer & Miller, 1996).

From this perspective, members of particular social groups often prefer to perceive their ingroup more positively than negatively, especially if the comparison is with another group (e.g., gang members). We oftentimes tend to avoid interacting with outgroups as much as possible due to emotional vulnerability and interaction uncomfortableness. One aspect of ingroup membership is loyalty. *Loyalty* is defined as "adherence to ingroup norms and trustworthiness in dealings with fellow ingroup members" (Brewer & Miller, 1996, p. 24). Social groups in the United States pledge their loyalty in many ways: wearing fraternity and sorority T-shirts and emblems, wearing colors or tattoos associated with gang membership, wearing team colors, or dressing up like the mascot during sporting events. This ethnocentric loyalty to and preference for our own group increases both our self-esteem and our esteem of our group, resulting in stronger ingroup ties. For example, Wisconsin's Green Bay Packers football fans are known as "cheeseheads." Cheeseheads wear silly cheese hats and feel great camaraderie with other cheeseheads, even though outgroup members think this is very weird.

As ingroups and outgroups communicate with each other, intergroup communication occurs. **Intergroup communication** happens "whenever individuals belonging to one group interact, collectively or individually, with another group or its members in terms of their group identification . . ." (Sherif, 1966, p. 12). Group loyalty and attachment are prominent. The **ingroup favoritism principle** states that there is positive attachment to and predisposition for norms and behaviors that are related to one's group. Ingroup favoritism ultimately enhances our desired ingroup and personal identities. *Personal identity* refers to the individual attributes that we use to conceptualize our sense of *unique self* (e.g., individual motivation, intelligence, attractiveness) in comparison with other individuals. The ingroup favoritism principle can also translate to our understanding of why people behave ethnocentrically in different cultures (see the "Ethnocentrism and Communication" section). When we behave ethnocentrically, we are basically protecting our group membership boundaries and, more fundamentally, our habitual ways of thinking, feeling, and responding. Countless research studies across cultures (see Devine, Hamilton, & Ostrom, 1994; Leyens, Yzerbyt, & Schadron, 1994) indicate that people in all cultures tend to behave with ingroup favoritism and outgroup prejudice.

Where Do I Fit In?

Membership in an ingroup is a matter of degree and variation. If norms, values, and social relationships within an ingroup influence the communication patterns of group members, the influence should depend on the extent to which one shares the norms (Kim, 1988). Admission to the ingroup and acceptance by the ingroup, on the basis of shared norms and values, are interrelated: The more an individual associates with the ingroup, the greater the conformity that is expected and reinforced. At the same time, if the ingroup does not approve of an individual's behavior, it can reject the ingroup member. Because of this variation in conformity among ingroup members, the boundary lines of ingroup and outgroup are sometimes blurred.

Although our ingroups offer us a sense of belonging and security, they also have the power to reject us. Chung (1998) interviewed Korean Americans and Vietnamese Americans in Oklahoma to understand why and when individuals felt like outgroup members within their own group. She found two explanations. First, some individuals perceived themselves as ethnically attached to their own ethnic groups. However, during ingroup interactions, they were perceived by their ingroup members as Americans—not as members of their own ethnic groups. They shared statements such as the following: "I think I am very Vietnamese and American at the same time, but each of the two groups perceives me as not totally one or the other"; "Koreans think I am too American, but at the same time I am really a true Korean." In one sense, both groups believed this person was not a clear "fit" in accordance with their stereotypic group images. This implies a sense of marginality because to associate with two groups, an individual tries to claim ties with both cultures.

The second explanation has to do with the context and status of the individual with whom one interacts. For example, a 29-year-old graduate student of Vietnamese ethnic descent but who was born in the United States said,

> "Definitely!! [Most ethnic] people (especially the elders) are very traditional and conservative. If everything is not done in a traditional manner . . . they think I am too 'American' even though [similar ethnic] people of my age think the same way I do. [Many] people do not see you for who you are, they only see that you are different, therefore you must be bad." (Chung, 1998, p. 62)

The context can embody a strong set of ethnic traditions and values that are associated with status, age, and deference. Traditional Asian values emphasize the importance of reserve and formality in interpersonal relations, for example, and these values reflect the biggest communication problems among different generations of Korean Americans and Vietnamese Americans. The struggle often implies reconciling the conflict between the need to retain ethnic values and the need to pursue the prevalent American cultural values—individualism and equality of respect.

In sum, many persons engage in an ingroup/outgroup boundary-regulation mentality to satisfy their need for security and inclusion. Having an overly strong ingroup loyalty, however, may result in unfair stereotyping, intergroup prejudice, and discrimination.

Intergroup Attributions

One of the outcomes of interacting among outgroup members is intergroup attributions. The intergroup attribution process helps us to make sense of our encounters by allowing us to interpret and evaluate outgroup members' behavior. Every day, we try to figure out why people behave the way they do. If expectations refer to our anticipations of what will happen in a given interaction, **attributions** are the explanation—the meaning of why people behave as they do. We use assumptions and built-in social categories to explain behaviors or events occurring around us. (See Figure 9.1).

There are three biases that typically occur during intergroup encounters. The first is known as the *fundamental attribution error*. A Chicano student, Fernando, gave an example:

> If a competitor or someone I dislike would go to an interview and not get the job, I would say something like "it's because he's lazy and stupid, that's why he didn't get the job." Now if I went to a job interview and did not get the job, I would say something like "it's because of the economic recession, budget cuts, or those foreigners coming in to grab my job."

In Fernando's example, with competitors or strangers, we tend to engage in negative dispositional attributions by *overestimating negative personality factors* in explaining a stranger's negative event and *underestimating situational factors*. However, if we encounter a negative event, we want to protect our self-image by using situational attributional factors to explain away the negative episode.

The second attribution bias is called the *principle of negativity*. We typically place more emphasis on negative information concerning our competitors or outgroup members. That is, negative news catches our eye more than the positive news, and we often fall back on negative stereotypes when interacting with outgroup members. For example, if Tyrone holds a negative bias against Sydney, an outgroup member, when his friend asks him what he thinks of her, Tyrone will pick out the one or two negative incidents he has observed and ignore all of her positive qualities. Furthermore, Tyrone might subscribe to the *illusory correlation principle* and typecast the entire outgroup (in this case, all women) as incompetent or tardy on the basis of a negative overgeneralization of the entire group.

The third attribution, the *favorable self-bias principle,* arises from positive events concerning our own behavior versus a stranger's behavior. For example, if we get a job promotion (a positive event), we will tend to attribute it to hard work and personal perseverance (positive dispositional attributions). However, if a cultural stranger gets a job, we would more likely attribute the promotion to luck or situational pressure (e.g., quota system, affirmative action). If we do not get the promotion (a negative event), we might well attribute our own misfortune to the bad economy or budget cuts (situational attributions). However, if a stranger does not get the promotion, we would tend to use negative dispositional attributions, such as incompetence or lack of leadership qualities.

There are many comparisons between how we view situational versus personality traits when comparing individualistic and collectivistic cultures. When comparing how U.S. and Japanese students attribute success, or failure, in recalling details of slides of scenes in foreign countries, U.S. students tend to remember more successful incidents and they explain their success in terms of their positive personal qualities and abilities. Japanese students, in contrast, remember more failed incidents and tend to attribute their failures to lack of ability, which reflects what some term the *self-effacement bias* (Kashima & Triandis, 1986; P. Smith & Bond, 1993).

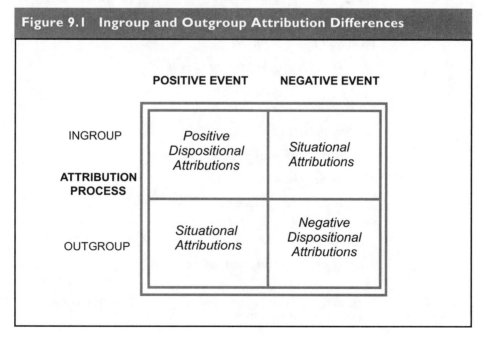

Figure 9.1 Ingroup and Outgroup Attribution Differences

ATTRIBUTION PROCESS	POSITIVE EVENT	NEGATIVE EVENT
INGROUP	Positive Dispositional Attributions	Situational Attributions
OUTGROUP	Situational Attributions	Negative Dispositional Attributions

To sum up, using the beginning example of getting the job, if one of our ingroup members were to get a promotion, we would tend to attribute it to positive personality traits, such as being a hard worker and motivated. However, if an outgroup member got the job, we would attribute this event to any of the following possibilities: (1) luck or a special advantage; (2) manipulating and networking the right people; or (3) the person being an exception to the group (Pettigrew, 1978). In reverse, if one of our ingroup members did not get the job, we might be upset and believe it was an instance of unfair treatment or the bad economy. However, if an outgroup member did not get the job, we would likely use negative personality attributions to explain this (e.g., She wasn't going to get it anyway because she was a really lazy, irresponsible person).

Shattered Lens: Prejudice, Discrimination, and Racism

Before we discuss issues of prejudice, let's check out the poem in Picture This 9.1: "looking at the world from my key hole," by Feven Afewerki.

Picture This 9.1

looking at the world from my key hole
by feven afewerki, Born in Eritrea (Northeast Africa)
Graduate Student at California State University, Long Beach

i am racist and prejudice
looking at the world from my key hole

i am afraid to use my key
to open the door
and meet the morning sun of openness
the wind of change
the storm of the unexpected

when will i face the sun, the wind, and the storm
looking at the world from my key hole

Feven Afewerki, "looking at the world from my key hole." Copyright © Feven Afewerki. Used by permission of the author.

A young child picks up behavioral cues from family members, the educational system, the peer group, mass media, and the general socialization process. These cues signal who belongs to the ingroup and who belongs to the outgroup. The term **prejudice** generally describes an individual's feelings and predispositions toward outgroup members in a perjorative or negative direction. However, prejudice can actually refer to either negative or positive predispositions and feelings about outgroup members—you can be indiscriminately for or against members of a particular group.

In the intercultural context, prejudice is a sense of antagonistic hostility toward a group as a whole or toward an individual because she or he is a member of that group. Such feelings are based on a "faulty and inflexible generalization. It may be felt or expressed" (Allport, 1954, p. 7). This hostility toward outgroup members stems from biased judgments made with little evidence to support the overgeneralization. Most people who hold prejudices do not interact with members of other groups because they believe it is a waste of their time.

Prejudiced Remarks . . . or Innocent Jokes?

Prejudicial behaviors take many forms. One aspect includes comments and remarks. Let's think about this question for a moment: Do "innocent" remarks or biased jokes directed at an individual or ethnic group make them tolerable or acceptable? For example, in 2002, Los Angeles Lakers guard Shaquille O'Neal (Shaq) was interviewed on Fox television's *Best Damn Sports Show Period*. When the subject Yao Ming, a new basketball star, was mentioned, Shaq spoke with a mock Chinese accent and made mock kung fu moves. He told a reporter, "Tell Yao Ming, 'ching-chong-yang-wah-ah-soh . . .' I look forward to breaking down that mother f-----'s body. . . . He [Yao Ming] said my name three times, two in Chinese and one in American. You don't ever call me out. I'm from LSU" (Brown, 2003, p. D7). Shaq's comment was, in fact, problematic, according to Tang (2003), and many people knew about it from listening to Fox Sports Radio's *Tony Bruno Morning Extravaganza*, which played a recording several times.

Bruno, the radio host, said that Shaq's comment was "not racist" (Tang, 2003) and then invited listeners and radio commentators to call in jokes making racist fun of Chinese. For hours, people cracked jokes, such as offering free bike parking to increase Chinese attendance at basketball games, and so on. In the uproar following the broadcast, Shaq apologized to the public, calling his comments a joke. Yao accepted the explanation but added that many Asian people would not call this a joke. The question remains: Where do we draw the line? When is an ethnic joke just a joke, a form of prejudice, or a racist remark (see Snapshot 9.1)? Reflect on some of your favorite jokes or recent jokes you have received online or via friends. How many are based on stereotypes or other forms of prejudice?

So, where do we draw the line? This question is difficult to answer. The main problem has a lot to do with our boundaries and the intention of the person who made the comment. We can argue that this form of ignorance has no malice or intent to offend. We can understand

Snapshot 9.1

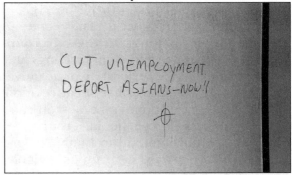

Mindless graffiti, or intentional racist statement?

that in the unconscious incompetence stage, individuals do not realize that they are making comments that are hurtful, offensive, and intolerant. Shaq issued an apology. Many would argue that we should move on and forget about this little joke; Shaq meant no harm. However, communication is not only about intent; it is also about consequence or impact. When in doubt, we need to be mindful of our words and deeds—many times, words can actually inflict more emotional scars and pain than any physical damage. Furthermore, perpetually making such comments with intent to offend, hurt, and attack is the opposite side of the spectrum; opening a radio forum to invite more such comments is not mindful but a consciously incompetent, terrible act. Promoting such an event as Bruno did is disrespectful on many levels. Inciting groups to make ethnic or racist jokes against each other and pitting one against the other are hurtful, pernicious acts in very bad taste.

Individuals can hold prejudice against people on the basis of skin color, accent, and cultural or religious practices, for example. One illustration is the gay community. A popular South Korean star concealed his homosexuality for years. Hong Suk Chun admitted his sexual orientation during an interview with a magazine. Henry Chu (2003) reported that "fellow actors shunned him, teenage boys hurled abuse at him in the street, his parents suggested that the [entire] family should commit suicide for the shameful disclosure, and the job offers vanished, leaving Hong to ponder the wreckage of a once successful life" (p. A3). In a country that values traditional Confucian principles, rigid norms about sex-role differentiation make it virtually impossible to be "accepted" if one behaves in a different way. These societal norms and conventional expectations sow the seeds of prejudiced behaviors.

Prejudice: Explanations and Functions

To understand how the development of prejudice occurs, Schaefer (1990) outlined four explanations:

1. *Exploitation theory* views power as a scarce resource: To maintain higher status and power, one restrains those of lower status to improve one's own group position and security. Many people believe that the "glass ceiling"—meaning no minority has an equal opportunity at high-ranking positions—is an example of exploitation theory.

2. *Scapegoating theory* suggests prejudiced individuals believe that they are the victims of society. If something is not going well in their life, they will blame a minority group instead of accepting the basic responsibility for some other type of failure (e.g., bad economy, lack of skills).

3. *An authoritarian personality approach* emphasizes personality features, including a rigid observance of [or adherence to] conventional norms, complete acceptance of authority, and a high concern for those in power.

4. *A structural approach* to prejudice stresses the climate in one's society whereby institutions promote a "pecking order" among group members. For example, under Japanese law, anyone who was born abroad or whose parents or grandparents were born abroad is considered a foreigner, and foreigners have no voting rights.

Schaefer's set of explanations allows us to understand the development of prejudice by connecting concepts such as power, class, and position. These concepts serve as deep-seated barriers that are usually unpredictable and difficult to overcome.

Prejudice also serves communication functions as well. First, a prejudiced mindset acts as an *ego-defense mechanism*, acting as a shield to protect our fragile egos. For example, individuals can blame outgroup members for a failed event and, thus, protect their long-held values, beliefs, and standard ways of operation. Second, in our chaotic world, we have a need for *regularity*. To maintain this regularity, individuals view their own cultural values, norms, and practices as the proper and civilized ways of thinking and behaving. Some people are disgusted by the idea that Mexican Americans actually eat *menudo* (tripe soup). A comment such as "Why can't the Mexican Americans eat normal soup like us" reflects this function of prejudice.

Another reason why people engage in prejudiced remarks is that they *lack accurate cultural knowledge*. Knowledge takes time and energy to acquire. It is faster to defend the areas of knowledge we have already and ignore the unfamiliar. For example, if our ingroup is proficient in computer programming, we may see outgroup members who have not learned to master computer programming as incompetent and backward. Finally, individuals engage in prejudiced communication to collect ingroup *rewards* and *approval*. Individuals can collect intangible rewards (e.g., approval, laughs) from the ingroup by acting out consensual beliefs.

The examples of these functions of prejudice allow us to understand the nature of the hostile and biased attitudes toward outgroup members. Some persons hold more prejudice than others, and prejudice also operates in conjunction with the context. We typically swing back and forth when dealing with our feelings of prejudice. Some individuals may display favorable attitudes toward one minority group but demonstrate strong racist attitudes against another. Some individuals may harbor no deep resentments against outgroups until their identity status is seriously threatened or challenged by the arrival of other groups.

Discrimination and Practice

A prejudiced attitude, in any form, is difficult to censure and avoid. Prejudice is a biased mindset. Discrimination, however, refers to the verbal and nonverbal actions that carry out prejudiced attitudes. According to Feagin (1989), four basic types of discriminatory practices exist in a society: (1) isolate discrimination; (2) small-group discrimination; (3) direct institutional discrimination; and (4) indirect institutional discrimination.

When an ingroup member engages in *isolate discrimination*, harmful verbal and nonverbal action is intentionally targeted toward an outgroup member. This discriminatory behavior occurs on an individual basis. It ranges from the use of racist slurs to violent physical action. Read the story about Lee Ann Kim, telling about her first job in Missouri (see Double Take 9.3). What would you have done in her shoes?

Double Take 9.3

A true story—Lee Ann Kim,
Anchor, *Channel 10 News*,
San Diego

In 1995, I got a job offer as the weekend anchor from the NBC station in Springfield, Missouri. At the time, I was working as the main news anchor in Tuscaloosa, Alabama, which was a very small news market located an hour outside of Birmingham. While most Asian Americans cringe at the thought of living in the South, frankly, my experience in Alabama was a positive one. There were no burning crosses or men in ☞

☞ white sheets. The region had already gone through so many lessons of the Civil Rights Era, and since there were many African Americans who lived in the South, people of color weren't as big of a deal.

Little did I know that my employment there would make broadcast history. I was described in Springfield's local newspaper as "the first person of color to ever anchor the news in Springfield." Located an hour north of the Arkansas border, Springfield—or the Ozarks, as it is commonly referred to—[is] nearly 99 percent white, and anyone who was an ethnic minority seemed to be [among] the few immigrant Chinese who ran the drive-through Chinese restaurants.

Race was never made an issue with my coworkers, who welcomed me with open arms. However, out in the community, I was constantly reminded of how I was different. Almost daily, people would ask me, "How did you learn how to speak English so well?" Or "Where do you come from?" "How come your eyebrows are so high above your eyes?" Although these questions may seem ignorant and sometimes offensive, they were asked with genuine curiosity. Simply, this community was not familiar with diversity.

On the second weekend on the job, I was driving into work when I noticed our station's huge, white satellite dishes [had been] vandalized. Overnight, someone had spray painted them with swastikas and the words "F*** you N*****" and "N***** go home." "That's funny," I thought, "there aren't any African Americans around here." As I entered our newsroom, I was surprised to see my news director and general manager there since it was a Saturday. They were huddled with other coworkers, and the way they looked at me made it instantly clear that the racist graffiti outside had something to do with me. "Are you okay?" they asked me. "Yeah, I'm fine," I answered. There was a pause. Then the epiphany came.

"Wait. That graffiti outside, that's about me, isn't it?" I exclaimed. My bosses and coworkers stood there, uncomfortably silent, then nodded their heads. It was later explained to me that our proximity to Arkansas and lack of diversity in Springfield made it an active region for the KKK, who considered anyone that was not white and Protestant as the "N" word. Frankly, I wasn't the least bit threatened by the whole incident. "At least we know they're watching," I said to everyone jovially, which managed to break the tension. My colleagues seemed much more offended by the vandalism than I was.

The way I see it, people respond to change in different ways. In this case, someone wanted to scare me because of their own insecurities and ignorance. Instead of scaring me, it gave me motivation to be the best journalist I could be, proving to that community that someone who looks like me can speak perfect English and cover the news as well as any white journalist. And hey, maybe people will eventually see beyond my eyes and think of me as an American. I stayed in Springfield for exactly a year before taking my current job in San Diego. But during that year, I became the unofficial corporate hog farm reporter. It was an experience I will always embrace.

—Lee Ann Kim—*1st person story and real name used with permission*

When a band of individuals from an ingroup engages in hostile and abusive actions against outgroup members, this is known as **small-**

group discrimination. These actions do not have the normative support of the larger organizational or community network. Activities on
the Internet are filled with such examples. A Website created for the
World Church of the Creator invited anyone to join racist conversations. This group is dedicated to the "survival, expansion, and advancement of the white race" (Williamson & Pierson, 2003). This "us versus
them" mentality is one of the pernicious outcomes of small-group discrimination.

If there is a community-prescribed endorsement of discrimination,
we can call this **direct institutional discrimination.** Such practices
are not isolated incidents but are carried out routinely by a large number of individuals protected by the laws of a large-scale community.
For example, blatant institutional discriminatory practices against
Japanese Americans were carried out in World War II. Though we were
at war with the Italians, Germans, and Japanese, the Japanese Americans were the only group in the United States to be interned. Over
110,000 Japanese Americans were forced to live in shabby internment
camps in California and Oregon.

Let me share a story with you. On May 6, 1882, Congress passed a
bill prohibiting Chinese laborers from entering the United States. This
was the first major restriction on any immigrant group entering the
United States. In 1902, the Chinese Exclusion Act was made permanent. To this day, no other immigrant group has ever been banned from
the United States. When the act was lifted in 1943, older and younger
Chinese women were finally able to join their families after years of
separation. This particular act hits close to home with me (Chung). If
this act had not been lifted, my grandmother would never have seen
her husband and her son again. The seventeen years my grandmother
waited to rejoin and reunite with her husband and son were extremely
long, heartbreaking, and painful.

Indirect institutional discrimination is a broad practice that
indirectly affects group members without intending to. For example,
the Standard Aptitude Test (SAT) serves as an indirect discriminatory
tool. The tests use a "homogenized" standard—a strong White, middle-
class orientation that assesses the mathematical and verbal fluency
level of *all* high school seniors—and is, thus, an example of indirect
institutional discrimination. Along with high school grades, the SAT is
supposed to predict academic performance of first-year college students. Critics have long attacked the SAT as unfair because it tends to
favor students who have wealthier families, attend better schools, or
have access to test-preparation courses and tutors. From personal
experience, we agree.

In my inner-city public school (Chung), we did not have the tools
and equipment to prepare seniors to take the test. There was no budget, preparatory class, or strong honors program. The majority of parents were from the lower rungs of the socioeconomic ladder and did

not have the money or means to pay for test preparation. The unfair advantage and use of such "standardized" instruments in diverse populations in the United States have led to an exclusion of group members seeking better educational and, hence, brighter economic opportunities for their future. Without intending to, an institution has discriminated against these group members on a nonlevel playing field.

Different Types of Racism

More specifically, the direct effect of discrimination and its very practice is racism. **Racism** can be summarized by the three following principles:

- feelings of superiority based on biological or racial differences, or both,

- strong ingroup preferences and solidarity; rejection of any outgroup that diverges from the customs and beliefs of the ingroup, and

- a doctrine that conveys a special advantage to those in power (Jones, 1997, p. 373).

People have racist attitudes and engage in racist practices because of many factors. One such factor is internal fear. Fear gives rise to our emotional fragility and vulnerability. When individuals worry that their cultural or social habits are being threatened, they want either to pounce or flee. Racism includes not only verbal insults but also what is *unspoken*. There are three basic examples we will discuss: racial profiling, perpetuating stereotypes, and hate crimes.

Racial Profiling. Ever since 9/11, complaints about racial profiling have escalated across the globe. For example, Mark Arner of the *San Diego Union Tribune* (2003) reported that for the second time in two years, more African American and Latino drivers in San Diego were pulled over compared with Asian and European American drivers. In San Diego, African Americans make up 7 percent of the population but were stopped by the police 10.4 percent of the time. Hispanics make up 23 percent of the population in San Diego. They were pulled over 27.7 percent of the time. Look at the statistics in Table 9.2.

Table 9.2	Drivers and Traffic Stops in San Diego	
Ethnic Group	**Percentage of Drivers**	**Percentage of Traffic Stops**
African American	7	10.4
Asian/Pacific Islander	15	11.7
Hispanic	23	27.7
White	55	50.2

Source: Arner, M. (2003, January 14). Study: Blacks, Latino drivers stopped more. *San Diego Union Tribune*, pp. B1, B5.

In another example, in December 2002, the U.S. Immigration Service recommended that all Arab Americans register at the office of immigration. More than 400 people were arrested or detained under suspicion of visa violations but *not* under suspicion of terrorism. Racial profiling is a bias that intentionally or unintentionally promotes unfair treatment. It also hides behind an invisible shield of serving and protecting the community. Until such biased practices are known, discriminatory actions are more difficult to pinpoint.

In another example, Lydia Polgreen (2002) talked about the first U.S. tour of Samyuktha Verma, a huge Bollywood Indian star who is comparable to Julia Roberts. When flying into New York City with her father, mother, and sister, popular singer Biju Narayanan, and comedian Jairaj Kattanellur, another passenger on board became suspicious. The authorities called in two fighter jets to escort the plane to La Guardia Airport. After 17 hours of questioning, the group was released. They had been asked what they were doing in America, whether they had been to Pakistan or Afghanistan, and what religion they practiced. They are all Hindus. Samyuthka Verma claimed she had no hard feelings about being singled out. "At first I thought I would never want to come to America again, I was so scared," she said. "But the police were very nice to us. They made sure we were comfortable and they treated us well." Although Ms. Verma did not feel personally threatened or offended, the actions of these officials are simply unacceptable.

Perpetuating Stereotypic Images. Racism is displayed as a "top-down phenomenon" (Jones, 1997). This occurs when members of the majority group present their group in a positive light and the minority in a negative light. The whole process is couched in terms of "protecting the majority group's image of fairness and objectivity, while making disparaging or condescending remarks about those other groups" (Jones, 1997, p. 385).

Let us examine the controversial clothing Abercrombie and Fitch promoted in 2002. In one of the three ads, Abercrombie and Fitch (A and F) pitched a campaign using stereotypical images of Chinese immigrants on their new shirts. Featured are two "Wong" men with slanty eyes, rice caps, and Chinese jackets. They own a laundry service. There is a "Rick Shaw," who sells good meat and quick feet hoagies by foot, and a man who operates a "wok and bowl"—a place to bowl and eat Chinese food (Abercrombie & Fitch, Summer Catalogue, 2000). The caricatures were chosen with historical antecedents in mind. The misleading message is that portraying Asian Americans as coolies, laundrymen, and rickshaw drivers is harmless fun. The Asian Americans, of course, did not find the caricatures amusing—the pictures reminded them of years of historical racism, institutional racism, and personal injury. Because of active protests by diverse Asian American groups, the shirts were pulled—and a formal apology stated that A and F did not intend to offend any Asian groups. Its intention was to design a line of clothing with a twist of humor and levity added to the new fashion line. Even though A and F's intentions may not have been rooted in racism, its decision to construct these ads was not made mindfully and resulted in the perpetuation of harmful racist images.

Hate Crimes. A hate crime is typically motivated by hostility to the victim as a member of a group (e.g., on the basis of ethnicity/race, disability, age, religion, gender, or sexual orientation). These crimes may include such acts as physical assault, assault with a weapon, harassment, vandalism, robbery, rape, verbal harassment, an attack on people's homes or places of worship, various forms of vandalism, and murder. They can occur anywhere: in schools, in the workplace, on the Internet, in public places, and in the home. Unfortunately, proving a hate crime can be difficult because the authorities must show that a victim was purposely selected for the hateful behavior because she or he is a member of a group. Since 9/11, there have been three times the number of cases involving Arab-looking victims (Serrano, 2002). In Dallas, Mark Stroman "killed a clerk from Pakistan and another from India, and he partially blinded a third from Bangladesh" (Serrano, 2002, p. A8) because of their cultural origins and the way they looked.

In addition to racially motivated hate crimes, the threat to one's sexuality and sex role identity can lead to hate crimes, and even death. The Gender Public Advocacy Coalition (GPAC) Website reported that two-thirds of the transgendered population said they had been physically or sexually assaulted. The most famous transgendered hate crime is the case of Brandon Teena. In 1993, two men, who found out that *he* was really a *she*, assaulted Brandon Teena. Despite threats of retaliation, Brandon filed charges. The police department and the Richardson County Sheriff did nothing. Three days later, the same young men killed Brandon. In 2002, Eddie "Gwen" Araujo, a young man from Vallejo, California, was beaten to death by three of his friends when they found out that Gwen was really a man. What is more disturbing is that it took two weeks for people who knew details of the crime to come forward. Hate crimes range from small incidents, to racially motivated incidents, to violent death.

Emotional insecurity or fear in the psyche of the perpetrator is one of the major causes of hate crimes. When individuals fear losing power or control, they may lash out aggressively. They may also fear outgroup members, who may bring alternative values, lifestyles, and norms that challenge the comfort zone of the ingroup. For example, a Chicana student told the class,

> In my household, it is seen as wrong to be attracted to someone from the same sex. We have a very traditional Mexican home. I think this has a lot to do with how people respond. Our parents are very religious and see homosexuality as a sin because in their homes it was never talked about. They were never educated about

the issue. I also believe that in the Mexican household, image is everything. Even if a girl were to get pregnant or the son would marry at a young age, the first words [from their family] would be "what are other people going to say?" There are a lot of things that are to be considered, from how people respond and react to how safe the individuals feel when they decide to disclose their truth and their choice.

This primal fear triggers a host of other powerful emotions such as confusion, frustration, hostility, anger, anxiety, and hate. Although some of these feelings may be legitimate and need mindful redirection, others have absolutely no merit.

Reducing Prejudice and Discrimination

Reducing our own prejudice and discriminatory practice does not have to be difficult. Just by gaining accurate knowledge and being open-minded, we have started walking along an elastic path. Changing the way we feel or confronting our own vulnerable spots has a lot to do with the intentional reframing of how we view ourselves and others. Here are four practical guidelines to observe:

1. Start by being honest with yourself. Question everything you have learned and gained from your socialization process. Do retain the good ideas from your cultural or family socialization process but also confront unchecked biases and ethnocentric attitudes. Ask yourself, Why do I feel this way? Where or from whom did I learn this? Am I totally sure that this is an accurate fact and not a subjective interpretation about an outgroup member's behavior?

2. Check yourself before you evaluate the behavior of an outgroup member. Ask yourself, Am I engaging in overgeneralization? Am I using a well-balanced attribution process? A bias will be created by judging someone too quickly so that the interaction goes in a predictable manner. To engage in effective intercultural communication, taking the time to really know someone—without relying on preconceived stereotypes—can save long-term heartaches and headaches.

3. Remember that negative images concerning outgroup members will distort your perceptions. If you harbor any form of prejudice against outgroup members, you have just bought into the principle of ingroup favoritism and outgroup negativism.

4. Communicate your feelings by addressing them in the most comfortable forum. If you observe, read, or hear something

that is remotely unfair, then raise your voice assertively. For example, *Vanity Fair* magazine (February 2003) made an attempt at a humorous answer to a letter, but it backfired. The letter asked "Dame Edna" which language would be the most beneficial to learn. She responded by telling the person to forget about learning Spanish and, on top of that, made other offensive comments directed at Spanish-speaking people. One thousand responses flooded the publisher's e-mail box. As a result, *Vanity Fair* issued an apology for having made tasteless comments and prejudiced remarks.

In essence, we need to continue to dialogue about these culturally sensitive issues. Many times, such discussions can be painful, or even hurtful. But the fact that we are willing and able to express indignation at the pain, humiliation, anguish, frustration, and despair shows that we care. In our partnership dialogue, we need to be sensitive to those who suffer but not be overwhelmed by our emotions to the point of paralysis or inaction. *There is no right way to say the wrong thing.* Listening with an open mind, an open heart, and emotional alertness may help both ingroups and outgroups to connect on a deeper level.

Intercultural Toolkit: Recaps and Checkpoints

To be more *flexible communicators* during intergroup encounters, we have to understand the basic concepts that form mindset filters, such as ethnocentrism, stereotypes, and prejudice. In this chapter, we talked about key factors that cause us to hold biases against outgroups. These key factors are selective perception, ethnocentrism, and inflexible stereotypes. In addition, we also discussed intergroup attribution biases with many vivid, yet painful, examples. We also explained the underlying reasons why people engage in prejudiced thinking and discriminatory acts. To round off our discussion, we suggested several effective ways to reduce prejudice and racism in an assertive manner. In becoming more flexible intergroup communicators, remember to check the following:

- *Start with a clean slate.* Be flexible with your first best guesses. Look below the surface of the iceberg and remember that appearances or looks more often than not do not represent an individual's multifaceted self. The more you remind yourself with a "clean slate" mentality, the less clutter in terms of flexible communication with dissimilar others.

- *Use your most precious gift: your brain.* You have the ability to think carefully about how you are thinking and how others are thinking and behaving. By being open to multiple perspectives, you can meta-talk with yourself and conclude, "I don't behave that way. But I will not make any judgment until I understand how this behavior meets the expectations or norms of the other person's culture."

- *Continue learning, reading, and gaining knowledge about those who are around you.* We all come from different paths. Taking this intercultural class is a very good start. Let your teacher and other classmates help you—stay humble in your learning, but do form your own flexible judgments as you cumulate your learning in this class. Be informed and check out the original sources of some of the ideas that have been exchanged in class and stories that you have heard through secondhand sources. Take some quiet time to reflect on your intercultural learning journey.

- *Remember, all of us are works in progress.* Analyzing your ethnocentric tendencies in an honest manner forces you to consider your deep-rooted beliefs, values, and habitual ways of thinking. This type of self-exploration brings to the forefront all of the issues you did not think existed with "you." "Do I have prejudices? Make judgments about others? Speak and behave insensitively? Never!" That is what you used to say. Be committed and be aware of your ethnocentric biases.

- *Monitor inflexible stereotyping of outgroup members.* Know that you cannot *not* stereotype in social interaction. However, in stereotyping outgroup members, you are categorizing the behavior of a large group of individuals under generalized labels or categories. Because stereotyping is an inevitable process, you must monitor your typecasting process of outgroup members and your ingroups. Thus, you have to engage in flexibly "minding" your own social categorization process. ✦

Chapter 10

What Are the Best Ways to Manage Intercultural Conflict?

Chapter Outline

During the second baseball game of the 2000 U.S. World Series, Roger Clemens, the pitcher for the New York Yankees, was playing against Mike Piazza, the batter for the New York Mets. While Piazza was jogging down from the first-base line on a foul ball, Clemens had seemingly lost his mind on the mound. Clemens, catching part of Piazza's broken baseball bat, threw the broken bat hard at Piazza. The broken bat whipped past Piazza in a near miss.

Amazingly, Mike Piazza of the New York Mets did absolutely nothing. In a polite society, some may view Mike Piazza's non-reactive behavior as keeping his cool. However, in the context of sports culture, Piazza appeared like a wimp. Challenged by the media and fans, Mike Piazza looked like the accused rather than the victim.

U.S. media analysts believed that Mike Piazza had seriously embarrassed himself and actually lost face by not reacting to or challenging Roger Clemens. Although Piazza was the one who seems to have handled the situation with a mature attitude, he was looked down upon even by his teammates. Mike Piazza commented: "It's a no-win situation. If I go after him, I'm being selfish to the team [because I could be suspended]. If I don't, I'm gutless." The question remains: Did Piazza lose face or did he gain face?

—C. Jenkins
San Diego Union Tribune,
October 24, 2000

The question can be rephrased as follows: From which cultural perspective should we be answering the above question? From an individualistic cultural perspective, Piazza has indeed lost face by not "standing up like a man" and confronting this insulting episode immediately. However, from a collectivistic cultural lens, Piazza may have gained tremendous face by his mature, self-disciplined stance for not striking back at Clemens, his attacker. It is interesting to note that in some Japanese baseball games, the players actually try to win only by a slim margin so that the losing team is not totally humiliated in front of the public. At times, the two sports teams may even aim for a tie so that neither team "loses face." As discussed in Chapter 9, individuals coming from two different cultural communities bring with them different filtered lenses with which to look at their intercultural encounters.

Intercultural conflict often starts with different expectations concerning appropriate or inappropriate conflict behavior in an interaction scene. Different cultural members often have contrasting images of how conflict should be properly handled. In this chapter, we first explore some cultural background factors that influence the escalation of an intercultural conflict episode. Next, we take a close look at important conflict process factors, such as cross-cultural conflict styles and facework behaviors. Third, we introduce some steps and skills in managing intercultural conflict competently. Finally, we identify specific checkpoints to help you in approaching different intercultural conflicts mindfully.

Conflict occurs whenever we are fighting over some incompatible goals or unmet emotional needs. We define **intercultural conflict** as the implicit or explicit emotional struggle or frustration between persons of different cultures over perceived incompatible values, norms, face orientations, goals, scarce resources, processes, and/or outcomes in a communication situation (Ting-Toomey & Oetzel, 2001). Intercultural conflict in and of itself is not necessarily bad. Instead, it is how we approach the conflict and how we manage the conflict that often determine the outcome. If the different cultural members continue to engage in rigid or ineffective conflict styles, the miscommunication can easily spiral into a polarized conflict situation.

Intercultural Conflict: Cultural Background Factors

Let us look at the following communication episode between Darrien (an African American student) and Celina (a Latina student). Darrien and Celina are in the library discussing their team project due the next day (see Active Dialogue 10.1).

Active Dialogue 10.1

DARRIEN (irritated): Where is the rest of our group? You know, we have been waiting 15 minutes already. I think you should call them again.

CELINA (trying to appease Darrien): Yeah, but I left messages already. They know we are supposed to meet at the library. Perhaps they got stuck in traffic. A and B both have to take the freeway, and it's rush hour.

DARRIEN (still irritated): Whatever the case may be, we have a deadline. You know A and B better than I do . . . you've had two classes with them, right? Are they always like this? I did all my work already. I have limited time today.

CELINA (in a soothing tone): A and B are cool. They're really creative and pull their own weight. If we want an "A," we definitely need the research data that they have for the presentation to go smoothly . . . it'll rock!

DARRIEN (impatient): All right. You wait here for a sec. I am just going to the computer room to surf the net.

(10 minutes later)

DARRIEN (really agitated now): No way! They are not here yet? Did they call?

CELINA (in an apologetic tone): No . . . but I think they are on their way. They won't flake on us!

DARRIEN (really fed up now): This is so crazy and disrespectful of my time! I have way too many things going on to keep waiting for them to show up. Considering that I did all my work already. . . . It's so irritating! It's this kind of thing that ABSOLUTELY DRIVES ME NUTS working with groups!

CELINA (in a conciliatory tone): Look. Why don't you just give me your write-up? I can incorporate your ideas with A's and B's. I'm sure they'll show up any time soon. I don't mind waiting for another 15 minutes. We'll just meet before class tomorrow.

In the above dialogue example, Darrien and Celina tend to make different attributions concerning what's going on with their classmates A and B. An intercultural conflict episode often involves complex, multilayered factors. These factors include different cultural conflict lenses, different conflict perceptions, different conflict goals, and different viewpoints on scarce resources. Let's examine two different conflict lenses that result from individualistic and collectivistic cultural patterns.

Culture-Based Conflict Lenses

Recall that Chapter 3 looked at the value patterns of individualism and collectivism. Cultural value patterns such as individualism and collectivism often color our conflict attitudes, expectations, and behaviors when we are involved in emotionally frustrating episodes. Different cultural lenses and assumptions serve as the first set of factors that contributes to initial intercultural irritations.

Before you continue your reading, fill out the Know Thyself 10.1 conflict lens assessment and get a sense of what your conflict lens, or worldview, looks like.

Know Thyself 10.1	**Assessing Your Individualistic and Collectivistic Conflict Lenses**

Instructions: The following items describe how people think about themselves and communicate in various conflict situations. Let your first inclination be your guide, and circle the number in the scale that best reflects your overall value. The following scale is used for each item:

4 = SA =	*Strongly Agree*
3 = MA =	*Moderately Agree*
2 = MD =	*Moderately Disagree*
1 = SD =	*Strongly Disagree*

In most conflict situations, I try to . . .	SA	MA	MD	SD
1. Consider the interests and needs of the other person.	4	3	2	1
2. Win and feel good about myself.	4	3	2	1
3. Focus on the conflict process.	4	3	2	1
4. Focus on the concrete conflict outcome.	4	3	2	1
5. Listen carefully to what the other person is telling me.	4	3	2	1
6. Be assertive to get my viewpoint across.	4	3	2	1
7. Work toward some compromise.	4	3	2	1
8. Be decisive in terms of how the conflict should work out.	4	3	2	1
9. Be sensitive to mutual face-saving issues.	4	3	2	1
10. Be certain to protect my own self-image.	4	3	2	1

Scoring: Add up the scores on all the even-numbered items and you will find your individualistic conflict lens score. *Individualistic Conflict Lens* score: _____. Add up the scores on all the odd-numbered items and you will find your collectivistic conflict lens score. *Collectivistic Conflict Lens* score: _____.

Interpretation: Scores on each conflict lens dimension can range from 5 to 20; the higher the score, the more individualistic and/or collectivistic you are. If all the scores are similar on both conflict lens dimensions, you are a bifocal conflict lens person.

Reflection Probes: Compare your scores with a classmate's. Take a moment to ☞

Know Thyself 10.1 Assessing Your Individualistic and Collectivistic Conflict Lenses (*continued*)

☞ think of the following questions: What factors shape your conflict lens? Do you come from a conflict-approach or a conflict-avoidance family? Do you know that individualists tend to approach conflict and collectivists tend to avoid conflict? What do you think are the pros and cons of either approaching a conflict directly or dealing with a conflict indirectly? How can you deal with conflicts constructively when you and your conflict partner have very different conflict lenses?

Let's start with the value patterns of individualism and collectivism. For example, for individualists or independent-self personality types, intercultural conflict resolution often follows an outcome-oriented model. Using an **independent-self conflict lens,** a person often views conflict from (1) a content conflict goal lens, which emphasizes tangible conflict issues above and beyond relationship issues; (2) a clear win-lose conflict approach, in which one person comes out as a winner and the other person comes out as a loser; (3) a "doing" angle, in which something tangible in the conflict is broken and needs fixing; and (4) an outcome-driven mode, in which a clear action plan or resolution is needed. Have you ever noticed that during team presentations in class, a team member may say, "In my part of the project, this is what I did." This person makes every effort to bring attention to his or her individual accomplishments. From this individualistic conflict lens, the person wants to stand out and be noticed for all of his or her task accomplishments.

Comparatively, for collectivists or interdependent-self personality types, intercultural conflict management often follows a "process-oriented" model. Using an **interdependent-self conflict lens,** a person often views conflict from (1) a relational process lens, which emphasizes relationship and feeling issues; (2) a win-win relational approach, in which feelings and "faces" can both be saved; (3) a "being" angle, in which relational trust needs to be repaired and loyalty needs to be amended to preserve relational harmony; and (4) a long-term compromising negotiation mode that has no clear winner or loser in the ongoing conflict. For example, team projects are often difficult for collectivists because they are always the ones who will stay up all night working on the last-minute presentation details—especially when one or two members have failed to carry the workload that was distributed. In their team presentations, collectivists will also often use phrases such as "we as a team" and "we really pulled through together" to save the team face and put the best group face forward.

Overall, independent-self types are concerned with conflict outcome closure, whereas interdependent-self types are concerned with interpersonal and ingroup face-saving and face-honoring process issues. These implicit conflict lenses or assumptions taint many intercultural perceptions and orientations concerning antagonistic conflict episodes (see Table 10.1).

Table 10.1 Individualistic and Collectivistic Conflict Lenses	
Individualistic Conflict Lens	**Collectivistic Conflict Lens**
Outcome-Focused	Process-Focused
Content Goal-Oriented	Relational Goal-Oriented
Doing-Centered	Being-Centered
Use Personal Equity Norms	Use Communal Norms
Self-Face Concern	Other-Face Concern
Low-Context Conflict Styles	High-Context Conflict Styles
Competitive/Dominating Behaviors	Avoiding/Obliging Behaviors
Conflict Effectiveness	Conflict Appropriateness

Intercultural Conflict Perceptions

The second set of background factors involves conflict perceptions and orientations. Conflict involves both perception and interaction. Conflict is an aggravating disagreement process between two interdependent parties over incompatible goals and the interference each perceives from the other in her or his effort to achieve those goals (Wilmot & Hocker, 2001).

The primary perception features of intercultural conflict are the following: (1) conflict involves intercultural perceptions—perceptions are filtered through our lenses of ethnocentrism and stereotypes; (2) ethnocentric perceptions add biases and prejudice to our conflict attribution process; and (3) our attribution process is further complicated by dealing with different culture-based verbal and nonverbal conflict styles. Recall that ethnocentrism is defined as the tendency to view our cultural practices as the *correct* ones and to rate all other cultural practices with reference to our standards. Similarly, when members of a culture believe that their own approach is the only *correct* or *natural* way to handle conflict, they tend to see the conflict behaviors of other cultures as *deviant* from that standard. A rigidly held ethnocentric attitude promotes a climate of distrust in any intercultural conflict. In real-life conflict scenarios, individuals often practice ethnocentric behaviors and biased attributions without a high degree of awareness.

For example, the following Active Dialogue 10.2 between Ms. Copeland (a Jewish American supervisor) and Mr. Miguel Molina (a recent South American immigrant) in a United States-South American joint venture firm illustrates the different conflict styles and attribution processes:

Active Dialogue 10.2

MS. COPELAND (in the main office): Miguel, where is your project report? You said you'd get it done soon. I need your part of the report so that I can finish my final report by the end of this week. When do you think you can get it done? [Attribution: Miguel Molina is such a slacker. I should never have trusted him with this time-sensitive document. I thought I was giving him a break by putting him in charge of this report.]

MR. MOLINA (hesitantly): Well . . . Ms. Copeland . . . , I didn't realize the deadline was so soon. . . . I will try my best to get it done as soon as possible. It's just that there are lots of details I need to cross-check and sources I need to verify, and I am waiting for Mr. Nam to get back with me. . . . [Attribution: Ms. Copeland is sure a tough lady. Anyway, she is the supervisor. Why didn't she tell me the exact deadline early on? Just last week, she told me to take my time on the report. She knows that verifying sources takes a lot of time! I'm really confused. In Venezuela, the supervisor always tells the workers what to do.]

MS. COPELAND (frustrated): Miguel, how soon is soon? I really need to hear about your strategic plan of action. You cannot be so vague in answering my questions all the time. I believe I've given you plenty of time to work on this report already. [Attribution: Miguel Molina is trying to be sneaky. He does not answer my questions directly at all. I wonder if all Venezuelans are that sneaky? Or maybe he is not comfortable working for a Jewish American? Or a female? Anyway, I have to press him to be more efficient and responsible. He is in America. He has to learn the American way.]

MR. MOLINA (after a long pause): Well . . . I'm really not sure, Ms. Copeland. I really don't want to do a bad job on the report or disappoint you. I'll try my best to finish it as soon as possible. Maybe I can finish the report next week. [Attribution: Ms. Copeland is a real pushy boss. She doesn't seem to like me, and she is causing me to lose face in front of all my peers. Her voice sounds so harsh and loud. I have heard that American people are hard to work with, but she is really something—rude and overbearing. I'd better start looking for a new job tomorrow.]

In Active Dialogue 10.2, Ms. Copeland uses an assertive, emotionally expressive verbal style in dealing with the conflict. Mr. Molina, on the other hand, uses a hesitant, indirect verbal style in answering her questions. Ms. Copeland uses a *straight talk* low-context approach in dealing with the work problem, whereas Mr. Molina uses a *face talk* high-context approach in dealing with the issue. If both had a chance to understand concepts such as low-context and high-context communication styles, they might arrive at a better understanding of each other's behavior.

Ms. Copeland is using her low-context style to evaluate Mr. Molina's behavior (e.g., "Miguel Molina is trying to be sneaky") and Mr. Molina is using his high-context script as a baseline to evaluate Ms.

Copeland's "rude and overbearing" behavior. For more satisfying outcomes, Ms. Copeland might learn to talk privately to Mr. Molina rather than engage in such direct face-threat behavior in public. Mr. Molina, on the other hand, might learn to be more direct and forthcoming in answering his supervisor's questions and use fewer pauses and hedges in his conflict interaction style.

Intercultural Conflict Goal Issues

The third set of cultural background factors involves conflict goal issues. The perceived or actual differences in an intercultural conflict often rotate around the following goal issues: content, relational, and identity (Wilmot & Hocker, 2001). By **content goals** we mean the practical issues that are external to the individuals involved. For example, an interfaith couple might argue about whether they should raise their children to be Buddhists or Catholics or whether they should raise them as bilinguals or monolinguals. Intercultural business partners might argue about whether they should hold their business meetings in Toronto, Berlin, or Miami. Content conflict goals also affect the perceptions of relational and identity goals.

The phrase **relational conflict goals** here refers to how individuals define the particular relationship (e.g., intimate vs. nonintimate, informal vs. formal, cooperative vs. competitive) or would like to define it in that interactive situation. For example, individualists generally crave more privacy and collectivists generally desire more connectedness in an intimate relationship. The struggle to define *independence* and *interdependence* can cause chronic relationship problems in many intercultural couples.

In the business setting, if one business partner (from Melbourne) opts to scribble a note and fax it to another international partner from Jakarta, the latter might view this gesture as a signal of disrespect for proper professional distance. The Jakartan partner perceives the informal gesture of a scribbled note as a violation of formal business exchange. However, the Melbourne business partner may not realize that he or she has committed a *faux pas* by sending this casual message. The informal note was actually intended to indicate "pleasant friendliness" and "closer distance" for the sake of establishing a relaxed working atmosphere.

Research shows that across many cultures, females tend to be more comfortable addressing relational conflict goal issues than males (Ting-Toomey, 1991; Wood, 1997). Males, in comparison, tend to prefer addressing content conflict goal issues with more ease than pursuing relational conflict topics. In addition, from the collectivistic cultural standpoint, relational conflict goals usually take precedence over content goals. The rationale from the collectivistic point of view is that if the relationship is in jeopardy, it is useless to spend time talking about practical or content issues. Identity goals, however, are paramount to both individualists and collectivists as well as to males and females across a wide range of conflict situations.

The phrase **identity-based goals** in this text means face-saving and face-honoring issues in a conflict episode. They are basically about self-respect and other-consideration issues in a conflict situation. Recall from Chapter 4 that identity-based goals can involve respect or disrespectful attitudes concerning three identity issues in conflict: cultural, social, and personal. *Cultural identity* can mean how an individual identifies himself or herself culturally or ethnically, and linguistically or religiously. *Social identity* can imply matters of profession, age, and social class to gender identity issues. *Personal identity* can mean personal self-esteem and personal self-respect issues. For example, while an interfaith couple is arguing about which religious faith they should instill in their children, they are also asserting the *worthiness* of their religious beliefs and identities. To the extent that the couple can engage in a constructive dialogue about this important issue, the conflict can act as a catalyst for their relationship growth. However, many intercultural or interfaith couples may not possess the necessary conflict skills to deal with important identity issues constructively.

At a minimum, in any conflict scene, conflict parties should realize that they are interdependent in the relationship or within the workplace system. If not, they can walk away from the conflict scene without the necessity of fighting over incompatible goals. For example, in Active Dialogue 10.2, Ms. Copeland is dependent on Mr. Molina to finish his report before she can put her final report together. Ms. Copeland's final report to the senior management can mean a promotion or more name recognition for her in the firm. However, Mr. Molina is dependent on Ms. Copeland to give him a good performance review for the year-end bonus. Thus, both have personal and mutual interests in resolving the conflict. Unfortunately, oftentimes culture-based conflict styles and behaviors lead to intercultural collisions in the negotiation process. With their views of the situation distorted by ethnocentric lenses and mindless stereotypes, both parties in the conflict may be stuck in their polarized positions and perceptual views. They need to learn new conflict management skills to get "unstuck" and free themselves from their negative conflict loops.

Perceived Scarce Resources

The fourth set of background factors is perceived scarce resources. *Conflict resources* are tangible or intangible rewards that people strive for in the dispute. The rewards or commodities may be scarce or perceived as scarce by individuals in the conflict. Perceived scarce resources may spark the initial flame behind conflict.

Tangible resources include how much money to spend on a new car, a sound system, or choice of location for a vacation. Some tangible commodities are indeed scarce or limited (e.g., only one promotion for three finalists). Other tangible resources are only *perceived* to be scarce (e.g., not enough parking spaces for everyone when abundant spaces are reserved for administration) rather than involve actual scarcity. **Intangible resources,** however, may include deeply felt desires or emotional needs, such as emotional security, inclusion, connection, respect, control, and meaning issues. Recurring conflict between disputants often involves unmet (or frustrated) intangible needs rather than conflicting tangible wants. Scarce intangible resources can be real or perceived as real (e.g., two children fighting for the perceived lack of attention from their parent) by individuals in the conflict episode. Both tangible and intangible resources can be managed constructively or destructively, depending on whether the disputants are willing to spend the time and energy in probing the underlying concerns and needs of the other conflict party.

Intercultural conflict expert Rothman (1997) recommended the following three techniques in negotiating scarce resources in a conflict situation: differentiation, expansion, and compensation. **Differentiation** means taking an active stance to acknowledge the different cultural perspectives and lenses in a conflict situation. At the same time, the conflict parties display good faith in addressing the conflict case by dividing up the large puzzle into different pieces or slices. They also strive to maintain constructive momentum to keep on moving forward to reach a shared goal or vision. For example, twin brothers are fighting over an orange. One actually wants the orange juice, and the other actually wants the orange peel. By articulating their basic needs in a collaborative dialogue format, the brothers can share the orange productively without the need to compromise or make unnecessary concessions.

Expansion means an active search for alternative paths or creative solutions to enlarge the amount, type, or use of available resources (e.g., using existing resources in imaginative ways or cultivating new resources) for mutual gains. For example, the twins may want to plant the orange seeds and cultivate more orange trees. They can also learn to work together to mix resources (e.g., water and fertile soil) for mutual gains for the future of the orange tree orchards. By engaging in frequent cost-cutting activities guided by a shared goal or dream, we can reduce rigid stereotypes of the other side and get closer to each other's humanity.

Last, **compensation** means conflict parties can offer exchanges, compensations, or concessions for conflict issues they value differently. For example, one twin brother desperately needs the orange juice to quench his thirst, but the other twin is not in a hurry to use the orange seeds to plant a tree. The thirsty twin can offer his brother some money (e.g., monetary compensation that is worth more than the price of the original orange) to compensate for his time to go and buy another orange—thus reflecting the compensation technique via seeking out other pragmatic alternatives. As Rothman (1997) noted, "Pieces of peace, that one side may offer the other in exchange for something else, can be powerful in fostering confidence and advancing the constructive cycle of cooperation" (p. 64). Culture-sensitive collaborative dialogue helps the disputants come to recognize their positive interdependence in a mindful manner.

Through flexible conflict communication skills, the conflict parties may invent creative alternatives or paths to generate additional resources for mutual gain. We have discussed four cultural background factors—culture-based conflict lenses, intercultural conflict perceptions, conflict goals, and perceived scarce resources—that influence an actual intercultural conflict negotiation process. We now turn to a discussion of important conflict process factors.

Intercultural Conflict Process Factors

The following section draws from the conceptual explanations of Ting-Toomey's (1988, 2004) face-negotiation theory and presents some interesting research findings concerning conflict styles and facework behaviors in diverse cultural and ethnic groups. *Face* is really about socially approved self-image and other-image consideration issues. *Facework* is about the verbal and nonverbal strategies that we use to maintain, defend, or upgrade our own social self-image and attack or defend (or "save") the social images of others. For example, when others confront us with face-threatening conflict messages, we are likely either to engage in defensive facework strategies or to flee the scene altogether to recoup our face loss. The following section discusses three approaches to the study of conflict style and defines each conflict style. It then describes some cross-cultural and cross-ethnic conflict styles and facework behaviors.

Defining Conflict Styles

Know Thyself 10.2 contains a short questionnaire designed to assess broad conflict styles. Take a couple of minutes to complete it now. The higher the score on the left-hand column, the more direct or low context you are in your conflict style. The higher the score on the right-hand column, the more indirect or high context you are in your conflict style. Overall, **conflict communication style** refers to patterned verbal and nonverbal responses to conflict in a variety of frustrating conflict situations (Ting-Toomey & Oetzel, 2001). There are three approaches to studying conflict styles: the dispositional approach, the situational approach, and the systems approach.

Know Thyself 10.2 General Conflict Style Assessment

Instructions: Consider several conflict situations in which you find your goals or wishes differing from those of another person. How do you *usually* respond to those conflict situations?

Following are some pairs of statements describing possible behavioral responses. For each pair, circle the "A" or "B" statement that is **most characteristic of your own conflict behavior in most conflict situations.**

Overall, in most of the conflict situations . . .

1. A. I attempt to stand firm in my conflict requests.
   B. I do my best to soothe the other person's feelings and tend to the relationship.

2. A. I tend to take time to understand the background context of the conflict story.
   B. I tend to separate conflict task issues from conflict relationship issues.

3. A. I try to verbally defend my position to the best of my ability.
   B. There are often times that I shy away from facing the conflict person or problem.

4. A. I try to downplay the importance of the conflict disagreement.
   B. I tend to be direct in expressing my conflict feelings.

5. A. I try to show him or her the logic and reasons of my position.
   B. I emphasize that our relationship is much more important to me than the conflict itself.

6. A. I'm usually firm in pursuing my conflict goals.
   B. I'm usually sensitive to the fact that other people might hear our conflict arguments in public.

7. A. I can usually figure out whether the other person is angry by tuning in to her or his feelings.
   B. I like to get potential conflicts out on the table as soon as I am aware of the problem.

8. A. I usually try to persuade the other person that my way is the best way.
   B. I try not to discuss the problem in front of others.

9. A. I usually apologize just to soothe feelings and soften the conflict situation.
   B. I believe in dealing with conflict in an up-front, honest manner.

10. A. I usually articulate and assert my conflict goals clearly.
    B. If it makes the other person happy, I sometimes flow along with his or her wishes.

11. A. I try to do what is necessary to avoid useless tensions.
    B. I am usually firm in pursuing my conflict intentions.

12. A. I try to postpone facing the issue until I have had time to think it over.
    B. In most conflict situations, I press to get my conflict points made.

☞

Know Thyself 10.2 General Conflict Style Assessment (continued)

☞ **Scoring:** Circle the letters below that you previously circled on each previous item of the questionnaire.

1.	A	B
2.	B	A
3.	A	B
4.	B	A
5.	A	B
6.	A	B
7.	B	A
8.	A	B
9.	B	A
10.	A	B
11.	B	A
12.	B	A

Total number of items circled in each column:

Left Column: _____   Right Column: _____
          [LCC]   [HCC]

Scoring: Add up the circled items on the left-hand column and you will find your low-context conflict style score. Low-context conflict style score:_____. Add up the circled items on the right-hand column and you will find your high-context conflict style score. High-context conflict style score:_____.

Interpretation: Scores on each general conflict communication dimension can range from 0 to 12; the higher the score, the more low-context and/or high-context you are in your general conflict behaviors. If the scores on both columns are similar, you tend to use both direct/low-context, and indirect/high-context conflict approaches.

Reflection Probes: Take a moment to think of the following questions: Is your family a "low-context" conflict engagement family or a "high-context" conflict avoidance family? Do you have a consistent approach in dealing with conflicts or do you switch conflict styles often? Are you happy with your own conflict approach? Do your cultural or ethnic groups value a low-context or a high-context approach in dealing with various conflict situations? Why?

Share some of your conflict perspectives and stories with a classmate.

A **dispositional approach** emphasizes that individuals do have predominant conflict style tendencies in handling a wide variety of conflict situations in different cultures. Conflict style is learned within the primary socialization process of one's cultural or ethnic group. It also depends highly on one's dispositional or personality traits. For example, an extrovert will tend to use a more dominating or expressive conflict style, but an introvert will tend to use a more avoiding or obliging conflict style. A **situational approach,** on the other hand, stresses the importance of the conflict topic and the conflict situation in shaping what conflict styles will be used in what types of relationships and in what contexts, or both of these. Situational factors such as the conflict intensity, topic, situation, time pressure, and whether the conflict occurs in a public or private setting can have a strong influence on whether we will engage in the conflict or avoid the conflict altogether.

A **systems approach** integrates both dispositional and situational approaches. It recognizes that most individuals have predominant conflict style profiles because of strong cultural and family socialization conflict scripts. However, individuals also modify their styles on the basis of the particular conflict situation and on their partners' responses and reactions to their conflict behaviors. Among other conflict styles factors are intergroup conflict histories, ethnocentric filters, prejudiced mindset, mood, and conflict competence skills. We take a systems approach in understanding most cross-cultural conflict style issues.

Without realizing it, over the years you probably have developed some patterned conflict styles to deal with various conflict issues. You may be the individual who flees from any conflict scene or gives in easily to keep the peace. Or you may be the diametrically opposite type— one who gets stimulated by a conflict-challenging environment. Many researchers conceptualize conflict styles along two dimensions. For example, Rahim (1992) based his classification of conflict styles on the two conceptual dimensions of concern for self and concern for others.

The first dimension illustrates the degree (high or low) to which a person seeks to satisfy her or his own conflict interest or face need. The second dimension represents the degree (high or low) to which a person desires to incorporate the other's conflict interest. The two dimensions are combined resulting in five styles of handling interpersonal conflict: dominating, avoiding, obliging, compromising, and integrating.

Before you continue reading, take the fun test in Know Thyself 10.3 and obtain your specific conflict style scores.

The five-style conflict grid represents one way of conceptualizing these different conflict style tendencies (see Figure 10.1).

The **dominating** (or **competitive/controlling**) **style** emphasizes conflict tactics that push for one's own position above and beyond the other person's conflict interest. The dominating style includes aggressive, defensive, and controlling to intimidating conflict tactics. The **avoiding style** involves dodging the conflict topic, the conflict party, or the conflict situation altogether. This style includes behavior ranging from glossing over the topic and denying that conflict exists, to exiting the conflict scene. The **obliging** (or **accommodating**) **style** is characterized by a high concern for the other person's conflict interest above and beyond one's own conflict position. Individuals tend to use the

Know Thyself 10.3 Assessing Your Specific Five Conflict Styles

Instructions: Recall how you generally communicate in various conflict situations with acquaintances. Let your first inclination be your guide and circle the number in the scale that best reflects your conflict style tendency. The following scale is used for each item:

4 = YES! = *strongly agree—IT'S ME!*
3 = yes = *moderately agree—it's kind of like me*
2 = no = *moderately disagree—it's kind of not me*
1 = NO! = *strongly disagree—IT'S NOT ME!*

	YES!	yes	no	NO!
1. I often "grin and bear it" when the other person does something I don't like.	4	3	2	1
2. I "give and take" so that a compromise can be reached.	4	3	2	1
3. I use my influence to get my ideas accepted in resolving the problem.	4	3	2	1
4. I am open to the other person's suggestions in resolving the problem.	4	3	2	1
5. I generally give in to the wishes of the other person in a conflict.	4	3	2	1
6. I usually avoid open discussion of the conflict with the person.	4	3	2	1
7. I try to find a middle course to break an impasse.	4	3	2	1
8. I argue the case with the other person to show the merits of my position.	4	3	2	1
9. I integrate my viewpoints with the other person to achieve a joint resolution.	4	3	2	1
10. I generally try to satisfy the expectations of the other person.	4	3	2	1
11. I try not to bump into the other person whenever possible.	4	3	2	1
12. I try to play down our differences to reach a compromise.	4	3	2	1
13. I'm generally firm in pursuing my side of the issue.	4	3	2	1
14. I encourage the other person to try to see things from a creative angle.	4	3	2	1
15. I often go along with the suggestions of the other person.	4	3	2	1
16. I usually bear my resentment in silence.	4	3	2	1
17. I usually propose a middle ground for breaking deadlocks.	4	3	2	1

Know Thyself 10.3 Assessing Your Specific Five Conflict Styles (*continued*)				
18. I am emotionally expressive in the conflict situation.	4	3	2	1
19. I dialogue with the other person with close attention to her or his needs.	4	3	2	1
20. I do my best to accommodate the wishes of the other person in a conflict.	4	3	2	1

Scoring: Add up the scores on items 1, 6, 11, 16 and you will find your avoidance conflict style score. *Avoidance Style* score: _____. Add up the scores on items 2, 7, 12, 17 and you will find your compromising conflict style score. *Compromising Style* score: _____. Add up the scores on items 3, 8, 13, 18 and you will find your dominating/competing conflict style score. *Dominating Style* score: _____. Add up the scores on items 4, 9, 14, 19 and you will find your integrating/collaborating conflict style score. *Integrating Style* score: _____. Add up the scores on items 5, 10, 15, 20 and you will find your obliging conflict style score. *Obliging Style* score: _____.

Interpretation: Scores on each conflict style dimension can range from 4 to 16; the higher the score, the more you engage in that particular conflict style. If some of the scores are similar on some of the conflict style dimensions, you tend to use a mixed pattern of different conflict styles.

Reflection Probes: Compare your conflict style scores with a classmate's. Take a moment to think of the following questions: Where did you learn your conflict style tendencies? What do you think are the pros and cons of each specific conflict style? When you are having a conflict with someone from a different culture, how would you address the different conflict style issues? What skills do you need to practice more to be a culturally sensitive conflict negotiator?

Source: Scale adapted from Ting-Toomey et al. (2000).

obliging style when they value their relationship more than their personal conflict goal. They tend to either smooth over the conflict or give in to the wishes of their conflict partners. The **compromising style,** however, involves a give-and-take concession approach to reach a midpoint agreement concerning the conflict issue. In using the compromising style, individuals tend to use fairness appeals, trade-off suggestions, or other quick, short-term solutions. It is an intermediate style resulting in some gains and some losses for each party. Finally, the **integrating** (or **collaborative**) **style** reflects a commitment to find a mutual-interest solution and involves a high concern for self-interest and also a high concern for the other person's interest in the conflict situation. In using an integrative style, individuals tend to use nonevaluative descriptive messages, qualifying statements, and mutual-interest clarifying questions to seek common-ground solutions. This is the most time-consuming style of the five conflict styles.

Johnson (1986) equated the five different styles to the following animals: shark = *dominating style*, turtle = *avoiding*, teddy bear = *obliging*, fox = *compromising*, and owl = *integrating*.

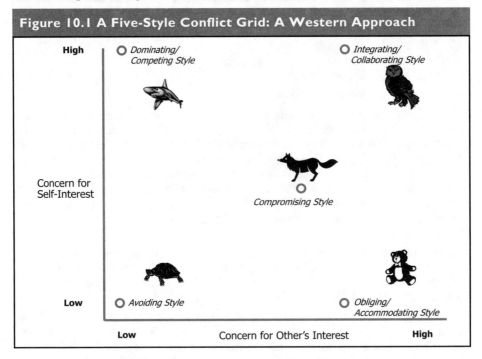

Figure 10.1 A Five-Style Conflict Grid: A Western Approach

It should be noted here that in the U.S. conflict research literature, obliging and avoiding conflict styles are often described as being negatively disengaged (i.e., *indifferent* or *fleeing* from the conflict scene). However, collectivists do not necessarily perceive obliging and avoiding conflict styles as negative. For example, collectivists often use these two conflict styles to maintain mutual-face interests and ingroup harmony (Ting-Toomey, 1988). From the collectivistic cultural lens, obliging and avoiding styles can be viewed as two very constructive, face-sensitive conflict styles.

Cross-Cultural Conflict Styles

Face-negotiation theory helps to explain how individualism-collectivism value patterns influence the use of diverse conflict styles in different cultural situations (Ting-Toomey & Kurogi, 1998). The premise of the theory is that members who subscribe to individualistic values tend to be more self-face-oriented and members who subscribe to group-oriented values tend to be more other- or mutual-face-oriented in conflict negotiation. The face-orientations, shaped by the various cultural, personality, and situational factors, frame our different motivations to use different conflict styles. Individuals who are more self-face-oriented tend to use a direct, low-context conflict style to assert their rights in a conflict situation. Individuals who are more other-face- or mutual-face-oriented tend to use an indirect, high-context conflict style to maintain other or mutual face and to preserve relational harmony. The more independent or individualistic you are, the more likely you use a linear logic, low-context approach in managing your conflict. The more interdependent or collectivistic you are, the more likely you use a spiral logic, high-context approach in dealing with your conflict.

Research across cultures (e.g., in China, Hong Kong, Japan, Korea, Taiwan, Mexico, and the United States) clearly indicates that individualists tend to use more self-defensive dominating and competitive conflict styles in managing disputes than do collectivists. In comparison, collectivists tend to use more integrative and compromising styles in dealing with conflict than do individualists. It is important to point out that in the individualistic research literature, the compromising style often connotes task-based compromises—you have to give something tangible in order to get something back and reach a midpoint compromising solution. However, for collectivists, the term "compromise" often means relational give-and-take concessions from a long-term reciprocity perspective. Finally, research also indicates that collectivists tend to use more obliging and avoiding conflict styles in a wider variety of conflict situations than do individualists (Oetzel, Ting-Toomey, & Matsumoto, et al., 2001; Ting-Toomey et al., 1991, 2000).

It is interesting to note that whether conflict is with a member of the ingroup or a member of an outgroup also clearly affects how collectivists manage conflict. Chinese, for example, are more likely to pursue a conflict with an outgroup member and less likely to pursue a conflict with an ingroup member than U.S. Americans (Leung, 1988). Likewise, Japanese tend to use a competitive/dominating conflict style with outgroup members and an obliging style with ingroup members more than do U.S. Americans. U.S. Americans actually do not differentiate too much whether they are having a conflict with an outgroup member or an ingroup member (Ting-Toomey & Oetzel, 2001). On the personal attributes level, independent-self individuals tend to use more competitive/dominating conflict styles than do interdependent-self individuals, and interdependent-self individuals tend to use more avoiding, obliging, integrating, and compromising styles than do independent-self individuals (Oetzel, 1998, 1999). Thus, to gain an in-depth understanding of an individual's conflict styles, we have to understand his or her cultural conditioning process, personality attributes, and ingroup/outgroup conflict situations (Oetzel & Ting-Toomey, 2003).

Cross-Ethnic Conflict Styles and Facework

In terms of different ethnic conflict styles and facework behaviors, most conflict research has focused on European American conflict styles in both interpersonal and organizational conflict domains. Overall, European Americans tend to prefer solution-based conflict strategies and tend to compartmentalize socioemotional conflict issues away from task-based conflict issues more than do African Americans (Ting-Toomey, 1985, 1986). European Americans also tend to use more dominating/controlling conflict strategies in dealing with romantic relationships than do Asian Americans (Kim & Kitani, 1998).

Distinctive conflict styles and facework strategies exist within different ethnic groups in the United States. The following section first addresses the African American conflict styles and then the Asian American, Latino/a American, and Native American conflict style orientations.

African American Conflict Styles. African American conflict styles are influenced simultaneously by both individualistic and collectivistic values. At the same time that traditional African values are collectivistic (e.g., community, interdependence, being at one with nature, and church/religious participation) and large power distance-based (e.g., respecting grandparents and pastors), they are also in constant struggle against the power dominance of Whites in the White-privileged U.S. society (Asante & Asante, 1990).

The White-privileged social position refers to a primarily favored state of Whites holding power over other minority groups in all key decision-making avenues (McIntosh, 1995). There is also a tendency for European Americans or Whites to view racism episodes as individual acts rather than as part of a problematic, power-imbalance institutional package. Thus, assertive conflict styles and emotionally expressive facework behaviors may be one method for African Americans to uphold self- and ingroup-membership dignity.

Research also reveals that African Americans tend to be more emotionally engaged in their conflict approach, whereas European Americans tend to be more emotionally restrained in their conflict discussion (Ting-Toomey, 1986). The *Black mode* of conflict is high-keyed (e.g., energetic, nonverbally animated, and emotionally expressive), whereas the *White mode* of conflict is relatively low-keyed (e.g., dispassionate, nonverbally disciplined, and emotionally restrained) (Kochman, 1981, p. 18). Let's check out Active Dialogue 10.3. Ron, a European American, is the movie director of a small company, and Kelvin, an African American, is the cameraman. Tamara, a European American, is the assistant producer.

Overall, in a conflict situation, African Americans tend to prefer an emotionally engaged, assertive mode of conflict discussion, but some European Americans tend to prefer an analytical, neutral-tone mode in

---

Active Dialogue 10.3

RON: So Kelvin, what is your opinion about our film? What is the best action plan?

KELVIN (enthusiastically): I think we need to go back and reshoot the conclusion. The ending is useless and we have had more complaints, and we need closure.

RON (analytically): Tamara, what do you think?

TAMARA (analytically): Ron, I think the ending is doable. It just needs to be tweaked with a better soundtrack.

KELVIN (with an animated voice): ARE YOU KIDDING ME??? We did this last time and the movie bombed! Using music to cover up the basic flaws does not support this movie and just doesn't work!

RON (takes a deep breath): Are you finished, Kelvin? Good—then here is the plan. Given the time constraint, think about tweaking the ending with music. Tamara, contact Kristi in the production department and see how much it'll cost to bring in some hard rock music. Also, set up a prescreening test for . . .

KELVIN (interrupts Ron): . . . Ron, it's NOT GONNA WORK! Remember last time . . .

RON (losing his cool): OK, KELVIN! I heard you the first time already . . . Now . . .

KELVIN (raising his voice and trying hard to be heard): I am serious, Ron. We are aiming to lose money . . .

RON (in a take-charge voice): ALL RIGHT, enough is enough, KELVIN! I don't know what YOU THINK I can do. You seem to be ALWAYS challenging my decisions . . .

---

controlling their conflict emotions. It is also interesting that, according to cross-ethnic conflict research (Ting-Toomey et al., 2000), African Americans who identify strongly with the larger U.S. culture tend to use a more give-and-take compromising style in conflict than African Americans who identify weakly with the larger U.S. culture. As a complex and diverse group, many African Americans have an integrative system of individualistic and collectivistic values. Their affectively laden conflict pattern is strongly influenced by ethnic/cultural values, social class, and reactions to racial oppression factors.

Asian American Conflict Styles. In terms of Asian American conflict orientations, research shows that the philosophy of Confucianism strongly influences proper facework and conflict enactment. Confucius was a Chinese philosopher of practical ethics who lived from 551 to 479 B.C. His practical code of conduct emphasizes hierarchical societal structure and appropriate family role performance. Confucianism remains the fundamental philosophy that underlies many Asian cultures (e.g., China, Taiwan, Singapore, Korea, and Japan). Some core Confucian values are a dynamic long-term orientation, perseverance, ordering relationships by status, having a sense of shame, and emphasizing collective face saving (L. Chen, 1997; G. M. Chen, 2001; Gao & Ting-Toomey, 1998). A collective or interdependent sense of shame includes the constant awareness of other people's expectations of one's own performance and the concern for face-losing behaviors.

Asian Americans who adhere to traditional Asian values tend to use avoiding or obliging conflict styles to deal with a conflict at hand. They sometimes also use "silence" as a powerful, high-context conflict style. Moreover, they may resort to third-party help—especially from trusted family members or networks—to mediate the conflict situation. Asian Americans who identify strongly with the larger U.S. culture tend to use an integrative conflict style to find content solutions to the conflict more than do Asian Americans who tend to identify weakly with the larger U.S. culture (Ting-Toomey et al., 2000).

Given the diversity of the Asian American population, we should also pay close attention to the country of origin, immigration experiences, acculturation, generation, language, family socialization, and levels of ethnic and cultural identity importance that create tremendous distinctions among and within these multiple groups.

Latino/a American Conflict Styles. In the context of traditional Latino/a Americans' conflict practices, *tactfulness* and *consideration of others' feelings* are considered to be important facework norms. Tactfulness is conveyed through the use of other-oriented facework rituals, such as the use of accommodation (i.e., "smoothing over") and avoidance conflict behaviors (Garcia, 1996).

For example, in Mexican American culture, the word *respeto* connotes the honor, respect, and *face* that we accord to listeners in accordance with their roles and hierarchical statuses. In Mexican American culture, facework is closely related to family loyalty, honor, name, respect, and extended family approval. Thus, well-mannered and diplomatic facework behaviors are preferred in managing conflicts in the Mexican American ethnic community. Avoidance conflict style is sometime preferred over a head-on confrontative style in dealing with minor or midrange conflict issues. Collectivism and large power distance values are the underlying value patterns that frame the Latino/a American conflict expectations and attitudes. In dealing with annoying conflict situations, however, it has also been found that Latino/a Americans who identify strongly with their traditional ethnic values tend to use more emotionally expressive conflict styles than Latino/a Americans who do not strongly identify with their traditional ethnic values (Ting-Toomey et al., 2000).

With the tremendous diversity that exists under the "Latino/a American" label, we would do well to increase the complexity of our understanding of the values and distinctive conflict patterns of each group (e.g., Puerto Rican group, Cuban group, Mexican group).

Native American Conflict Styles. In comparison, Native Americans prefer the use of verbal restraint and self-discipline in emotional expressions during conflict. Some of the value patterns of Native Americans that have been identified by researchers are the following: (1) sharing—honor and respect are gained by sharing and giving; (2) cooperation—the family and tribe take precedence over the individual; (3) noninterference—one is taught to observe and not to react impulsively, especially in meddling in other people's affairs; (4) time orientation—individuals tend to be more present-oriented than future-oriented and believe that life is to be lived fully in the present; (5) extended family orientations—there is a strong respect for elders and their wisdom and generational knowledge; and (6) harmony with nature—the tendency is to flow with nature and not want to control or master one's outer environment (Sue & Sue, 1999).

Given these value patterns, we can infer that in terms of emotional expression, Native Americans tend to be more other- and mutual-face-sensitive in dealing with disputes in their everyday lives. Out of consideration for the other person's face, they use more emotionally understated expressions in trying to resolve their conflict peacefully. They are also likely to go to a third-party elder to solicit wisdom in resolving the conflict issue and, thus, help each other to maintain face. They also tend to use more deliberate silence in conveying their displeasure. Communal and large power distance values frame many Native Americans' nuanced emotional expression styles.

However, given the fact that there are over 500 Native groups, any generalizations should serve only as preliminary cultural knowledge (rather than rigid stereotyping) that help us to be more mindful and flexible in generating alternative viewpoints in interpreting an entangled conflict situation. We should realize that, for example, Native Americans who live on or near reservations are more likely to subscribe to traditional values, while other Native Americans may adhere to predominant, mainstream values or a set of bicultural values (Ting-Toomey & Oetzel, 2001).

Competent Intercultural Conflict Skills

Competent intercultural conflict management depends on many factors. One of the key factors is the ability to apply adaptive and flexible conflict communication skills. This section identifies four skills that are critical to competent intercultural conflict management: facework management, mindful listening, cultural empathy, and mindful reframing (see Snapshot 10.1).

Facework Management

Facework skills address the core issues of protecting our own communication identity during a conflict episode and, at the same time, allowing us to deal with the communication identity of the other conflict party. All human beings value the feeling of *being respected and being accepted*—especially during vulnerable conflict situations. How diverse individuals protect and maintain self-face needs and, at the same time, how they learn to honor the face needs of the other conflict party very likely differs from one culture to the next, and differs from one particular conflict scene to the next.

Snapshot 10.1

The U.S. classroom is becoming more diverse every day—we should learn to honor all the diverse minds and creative hearts.

On a general level, both individualists and collectivists need to learn to *save face* strategically and *give face* appropriately to each other during a conflict episode. **Self-oriented face-saving behaviors** are attempts to regain or defend one's image after threats to face or face loss. **Other-oriented face-giving behaviors** are attempts to support others' face claims and work with them to prevent further face loss or help them to restore face constructively. *Giving face* means not humiliating others, especially one's conflict opponents, in public.

For *individualists having conflicts with collectivists, giving face* means acknowledging collectivists' ingroup conflict concerns and obligations. Further, it means learning to mindfully listen and hold a mutual-orientation perspective in the conflict process, learning to apologize when you are part of the conflict problem, and giving credit to the teamwork or family members that frame the collectivists' action or accomplishment. For *collectivists having conflicts with individualists, giving face* means honoring others by sharing your voice (or opinions) actively with other conflict parties in a candid manner, engaging in explicit verbal acknowledgment and feedback during a conflict negotiation process, recognizing the person's abilities and complimenting his or her unique contributions, and understanding the differences between acting assertively and passive aggressively.

Mindful Listening

Mindful listening is a face-validation and power-sharing skill. In a conflict episode, the disputants have to try hard to listen with focused attentiveness to the cultural and personal assumptions that are being expressed in the conflict interaction (see Table 10.2). They have to learn to listen responsively or *ting* (the Chinese word for listening means "attending mindfully with our ears, eyes, and a focused heart") to the sounds, tones, gestures, movements, nonverbal nuances, pauses, and silence in a given conflict situation. In mindful listening, facework negotiators tend to practice dialogic listening, one-pointed attentiveness, mindful silence, and responsive words and posture.

By listening mindfully, conflict disputants can learn to create new categories in interpreting the unfolding conflict sequences. *Creating new categories* means learning to apply culture-sensitive concepts to make sense of conflict variation behaviors. We can also practice mindful listening by engaging in paraphrasing and perception-checking skills. **Paraphrasing skills** involve two characteristics: (1) verbally summarizing the content meaning of the other's message in your own words, and (2) nonverbally echoing your interpretation of the emotional meaning of the other's message. The verbal summary, or restatement, should reflect your tentative understanding of the conflict party's content meaning, such as "It sounds to me that . . ." and "In other words, you're saying that . . ." You can also try to paraphrase the emotional meaning of the disputant's message by echoing your understanding of the emotional tone that underlies her or his message. In dealing with high-context members, your paraphrasing statements should consist of deferential, qualifying phrases, such as "I may be wrong, but what I'm hearing is that . . ." or "Please correct me if I misinterpret what you've said. It sounded to me that . . ." In interacting with low-context members, your paraphrasing statements can be more direct and to the point than with high-context members.

Table 10.2 Mindless Versus Mindful Listening Characterstics

Mindless Listening	Mindful Listening
Ethnocentric Lens	Ethnorelative Lens
Reactive Approach	Proactive/Choice Approach
Selective Hearing	Attentive Listening
Defensive Posture	Supportive Posture
"Struggle Against"	"Struggle With"
Judgmental Attitude	Mindful Reframing
Emotional Outbursts	Vulnerability Shared
Coercive Power	Shared Power
Positional Differences	Common Interests
Fixed Objectives	Creative Options
Win-Lose/Lose-Lose Outcome	Win-Win Synergy

Moving beyond paraphrasing, **perception-checking skills** are designed to help ensure that we are interpreting the speaker's nonverbal and verbal behavior accurately during an escalating conflict cycle. Culture-sensitive perception-checking statements involve both direct (for low-context individuals) and indirect (for high-context individuals) perceptual eyewitness statements and perceptual verification questions. They usually end with questions. For example, a high-context perceptual statement can be "You look puzzled. Let me clarify in case I was not clear. When I mentioned to you that I needed the report by early next week, I meant at the latest by Tuesday at 5:00 p.m. Do you have any questions about the deadline? Or is there something else [pause]?" Perception checking is part of mindful observation and mindful listening skills, to be used cautiously in accordance with the particular topic, relationship, timing, and situational context.

Mindful listening involves a fundamental shift of our conflict perspective. It means taking into account not only how things look from one's own conflict perspective but also how they look and feel from the other conflict partner's perspective. Over time, mindful listening can lead to the development of cultural empathy.

Cultural Empathy

Cultural empathy has two layers: cultural empathetic understanding and cultural empathetic responsiveness (Ridley & Udipi, 2002). **Cultural empathy** is the learned ability of the participants to understand accurately the self-experiences of others from diverse cultures and, concurrently, the ability to convey their understanding responsively and effectively to reach the "cultural ears" of the culturally different others in the conflict situation.

Some suggested cultural empathy techniques (Ridley & Udipi, 2002; Ting-Toomey, 1999) include the following: (1) check yourself for possible cultural biases and hidden prejudices in the conflict episode, (2) suspend your rigidly held intergroup stereotypes, (3) do not pretend to understand—ask for clarification, (4) use reflective time and appropriate silence to gauge your own understanding of the other's conflict perspective, and (5) capture the core conflict emotion, metaphor, meaning, and facework theme of the other conflict party, and echo the theme back to the conflict party in your own words—with carefully phrased responsive words and gestures.

Mindful Reframing

Mindful *reframing* is a highly creative, mutual-face-honoring skill. It means creating alternative contexts to frame your understanding of the conflict behavior. Just as in changing a frame to appreciate an old painting, creating a new context to understand the conflict behavior may redefine your interpretation of the behavior or conflict event. **Reframing** is the mindful process of using language to change the way each person or party defines or thinks about experiences and views the conflict situation.

This skill uses language strategically for the purpose of changing the emotional setting of the conflict from a defensive climate to a collaborative one. Through the use of neutrally toned (to positively-toned) language, reframing can help to soften defensiveness, reduce tension, and increase understanding. The following are some specific suggestions for mindful reframing: (1) try to restate conflict positions in common interest terms, (2) try to change complaints to requests, (3) try to move tensed interactions from blaming statements to mutual-focused, problem-solving statements, (4) try to help conflict parties recognize the benefits of a win-win synergistic approach, and (5) try to help conflict parties see the "bigger picture" that is involved in the conflict situation.

Reframing is a critical conflict management skill because how you *frame* the conflict event may change how you respond to it. In sum, competent intercultural conflict management requires us to communicate flexibly in different intercultural situations, which necessitates adaptation. Constructive conflict management requires us to be knowledgeable and respectful of different worldviews and multiple approaches to dealing with a conflict situation. It requires us to be sensitive to the differences and similarities between individualistic and collectivistic cultures. It also demands that we be aware of our own ethnocentric biases and cultural-based attributions when making snapshot evaluations of other people's conflict management approaches.

Intercultural Toolkit: Recaps and Checkpoints

To summarize, this chapter discussed the many complex factors that shape an intercultural conflict episode. In addition to the different culture-based conflict lenses, individuals use very different conflict styles and facework behaviors to approach a conflict situation. The latest research on cross-national and cross-ethnic conflict styles illustrated the struggles in an intercultural conflict negotiation process. Four specific communication skills—*facework management, mindful listening, cultural empathy,* and *mindful reframing*—were recommended as starters to practice competent conflict management.

Some specific recommendations can also be made based on differences in individualistic and collectivistic styles of conflict management. These suggestions, however, are not listed in any order of importance. To deal with conflict constructively in the collectivistic culture, *individualists need to do the following:*

- Be mindful of the mutual face-saving premises in a collectivistic culture, especially the use of specific facework skills in managing the delicate balance of humiliation and pride, respect and disrespect, and shame and honor issues.

- Practice patient, mindful observation: Be mindful of past events that bear relevance to the present conflict situation, and also limit the number of verbal *why* questions—because collectivists typically focus on the nonverbal *how* process.

- Practice mindful listening skills: Attend to the sound, movement, and emotional experience of the other person. This indicates that one person is attending to the other person's identity and relational expectation issues; remember that the word *listen* can become *silent* by rearranging the letters.

Some specific recommendations also can be made for collectivists in handling conflict with individualists. When encountering a conflict situation in an individualistic culture, *collectivists need to do the following:*

- Engage in an assertive style of conflict behavior that emphasizes the right of both parties to speak up in the conflict situation and respects the right to defend one's position; learn to open a conflict dialogue with a clear thesis statement and then systematically develop key points.

- Assume individual accountability for the conflict decision-making process: Use "I" statements when expressing opinions, sharing feelings, and voicing thought processes; assume a sender-responsible approach to constructively manage the conflict; learn to ask more *why* questions and probe for clear explanations and details.

- Engage in active listening skills: Engage in active verbal paraphrasing and perception-checking skills to ensure that the other person thoroughly understands each point; learn to occasionally disclose emotions, attitudes, and experiences within the conflict process itself; do not rely solely on nonverbal signals or count on other people to *gauge* personal reactions.

To manage intercultural conflict competently, we must be prepared to take alternative cultural perspectives into consideration. If another party is an interdependent-self collectivist, we may want to pay attention to his or her "process-oriented" assumptions during our conflict negotiation. If others are independent-self individualists, we may want to be sensitive to their "outcome-oriented" assumptions during the conflict negotiation. Competent intercultural conflict management means using culture-sensitive communication skills to manage the process and outcome of conflict adaptively and flexibly. ✦

What Are the Challenges in Developing an Intercultural-Intimate Relationship?

Chapter Outline

At 22, I am a fiercely independent, nontraditional Jain Indian woman living in the United States with my parents. For a number of reasons, I decided to pursue an arranged marriage. When I came back with my husband from India, my parents were the envy of all their friends because not only am I the oldest daughter, but I actually chose to have a traditional arranged marriage. After one month, however, I realized that this was the biggest mistake of my life!

My husband is not the man he claimed to be, and I am now totally miserable and want a divorce. My parents are adamantly against my even thinking of the "d" word. If I get a divorce, I will be the outcast of the entire community, my parents will be shamed, my relatives will be embarrassed, and I will be perceived as a tainted woman.

I must grin and bear it—for now.

—Mona

To many Asian Indian women and men who have decided to pursue arranged marriages or are being pressured to follow the traditional path, Mona's relational situation is not an exceptional one. However, from the lens of our own cultural worldview, we may read the situation with amazement or astonishment. Why would any independent woman choose to go to India and marry an individual whom she has never dated or barely even knows? What is the role of love in this arranged marriage? What is the role of passion in this relationship pairing? Why should Mona "grin and bear" a miserable marriage? After all, Mona is a grown-up, 22-year-old woman. Don't her parents care enough about her to let her decide her own future?

If we probe deeper into how different cultures handle intimate relationship issues, we may learn more about the challenges, decisions, and creative solutions that occur as they deal with different relationships. Their decisions may open our eyes to diverse ways of communicating in an intimate relationship. According to Webster's New Collegiate Dictionary, intimacy means "a relationship that is very personal or private in nature, marked by warmth and familiarity." Intimate relationships can include deep friendships, romantic relationships, and close family relationships.

This chapter examines the challenges individuals face in forming voluntary intercultural-intimate relationships. The discussion first addresses the relationship challenges that individuals face when they come from diverse cultural value systems. Next, it identifies the facilitating factors that prompt relational partners to be attracted to each other. Third, the chapter addresses particular obstacles that some couples face when they desire to move the relationship to marital bonding stages. Fourth, it explores issues of raising secure, bicultural children. Finally, there are guidelines for developing a healthy intercultural-intimate relationship. Understanding the challenges, facilitating factors, obstacles, and rewards of an intercultural-intimate relationship can help us to be more mindful in dealing with our own diverse intimate relationships.

Developing Intercultural-Intimate Relationships: Invisible Challenges

Before looking at why individuals are attracted to one another across cultural or ethnic lines, we need to look deeper into the iceberg and understand the hidden values that come into play in any relationship. Let's first revisit some familiar terms, such as individualism and collectivism, and draw out their implications for culture-based relationship expectations. Then everyone can explore some communication decoding issues that may cause relationship misunderstandings.

Different Cultural-Ethnic Membership Values

Cultural values, such as *individualism* and *collectivism,* shape our interpretations of concepts such as *autonomy* and *connection* in a close relationship. In a capsule description, the core building block of individualism-collectivism lies in its relative emphasis on the importance of the "I" identity and the "we" identity (see Chapter 4). "I" identity cultural members (e.g., the Swiss and Australians) tend to emphasize personal privacy issues and relationship privacy issues. In contrast, "we" identity cultural members (e.g., Malaysians and Guatemalans) tend to emphasize family and ingroup network connection issues (see Table 11.1). From the collectivistic cultural standpoint, relationship development is closely intertwined with the fate of others within the ingroup network. In our opening scenario, for example, Mona wanted the approval and acceptance of her family and extended family network in the very beginning. She opted for the traditional path of an arranged marriage. Even though she is suffering from her miserable marriage, she does not want to cause her family or family network to *lose face* or to be embarrassed on her behalf. This explains her "grin and bear it" marital attitude.

Table 11.1 Individualistic and Collectivistic Relationship Orientations	
Individualistic Orientation	**Collectivistic Orientation**
I-Identity Relationship Expectations	Ingroup Relationship Pressures
Couple's Privacy and Autonomy Needs	Ingroup's Connection and Concerns
Voluntary Personal Commitment	Family and Social Reactions
Low-Context Emotional Expressions	High-Context Emotional Expressions
Unique Relational Culture	Conventional Relational Culture

Despite some individualistic and collectivistic cultural differences, it is also important to know that in nearly all of 37 cultural samples studied (D. Buss et al., 1990), both females and males also endorsed *mutual attraction-love, dependability, emotional stability, kindness-understanding,* and *intelligence* as top-ranked mate-selection criteria. Overall, the greatest cultural variation is found in the attitude toward *premarital chastity*. Respondents in China, India, Nigeria, Iran, and Zambia (i.e., reflective of collectivistic values) differ from those of the continental United States and western Europe (reflective of individualistic values) in placing a premium value on premarital chastity.

Different Expectations of Love

Although passionate love is treasured where kinship ties are weak (e.g., as in the larger U.S. culture), passionate love is diluted where kinship ties are strong (e.g., in Korea and India). Romantic passionate love has been found to be a critical component in the "falling in love" stage of many individualists (Gao, 1991). This is one of the reasons why individualists believe that getting married without love appears to be a disastrous action. However, research indicates that many collectivists value companionate love (i.e., companion comfort and support) more than passionate love in romantic relationships (Gao, 1991).

In individualistic cultures, most individuals typically "fall in love" first (which sometimes involves intensive dating procedures) and then either get married or move on to another dating partner. One study, for example, showed that German and U.S. respondents scored higher in their attitudes of valuing romantic love than did Japanese respondents in their dating relationships (C. Simmons, Wehner, & Kay, 1989). However, many traditional collectivists (e.g., in India, Iran, and northern Nigeria, in which arranged marriages are still the norm) get married and then take their time to "fall in love."

In reviewing cultural perspectives on romantic love, intercultural love experts (Dion & Dion, 1996) concluded that the high divorce rate that characterizes "U.S. society is due in good part to the culture's exaggerated sense of individualism" (p. 286). They observe that in the United States, subscribers of "expressive individualism" face the following dilemmas in romantic relationships:

> First, one can "lose" one's self and the feeling of personal autonomy in a love relationship, feeling used and exploited as a result. Second, satisfying the autonomous needs of two "separate" individuals in a love relationship obviously becomes a difficult balancing act. Third, the spirit of American individualism makes it difficult for either partner in a relationship to justify sacrificing or giving to the other more than one is receiving. Finally, and inevitably, Americans confront a fundamental conflict trying to reconcile personal freedom and individuality, on the one hand, with obligations and role requirements of marital partner and parent, on the other. (p. 286)

In the United States, romantic love often poses major relational paradoxes. Although intimate partners desire to "lose" themselves in a romantic love-fused relationship, many of them also struggle with their desires for independence and personal freedom. Comparatively, for many traditional collectivists, the meaning of being *in love* takes long-term commitment and time to develop. Thus, they can continue to learn to "fall in love" after their marriages. Alternatively, as they learn to "grin and bear" it, they may also have a change of heart and learn to accept the flaws and virtues of their lifetime partners (see Jeopardy Box 11.1).

Jeopardy Box 11.1 Top-10 Wedding Songs in the United States	
Song	**Artist**
1. "From This Moment On"	Shania Twain/Bryan White
2. "At Last"	Etta James
3. "Power of Love"	Celine Dion
4. "I Cross My Heart"	George Strait
5. "Unchained Melody"	Righteous Brothers
6. "Amazed"	Lonestar
7. "Wonderful Tonight"	Eric Clapton
8. "I Finally Found Someone ..."	Barbra Streisand/Bryan Adams
9. "Always & Forever"	Heatwave
10. "After All"	Cher/Peter Cetera

Source: http://www.weddingzone.net/p-top50t.htm
(Retrieved February 1, 2004).

Different Expectations of Autonomy-Connection Issues

In addition, in developing a relational culture between individuals from two contrastive cultures, friends or romantic partners often face the choice of how to manage autonomy and connection issues competently (see Snapshot 11.1). Here *autonomy* means the need for privacy and personal space in a relationship. *Connection*, however, means the need for relatedness and fluid merging of personal space. But independent-self intimate partners often view the autonomy-connection theme as a delicate high-wire act, balancing "me-we" dialectical forces (Baxter & Montgomery, 1996). In contrast, interdependent-self indi-

Snapshot 11.1

Managing intercultural-intimate relationship conflict takes hard work and commitment.

The end result of a good intercultural-intimate relationship is very rewarding.

viduals often view autonomy and connection as a quadrangular contest, a "me-we-they-they" juggling act between the two partners and both family networks. Meanwhile, collectivists find that the two partners are never truly free from the grip of their family obligations, duties, and extended family reactions.

Further, in terms of relational commitment issues, individualists would tend to expect voluntary personal commitment from their partners in approaching their intimate relationships. However, for collectivists, structural commitment in an intimate relationship may be more important (or at least on an equal footing) than personal commitment in a long-term romantic relationship. Here **personal commitment** means the individuals' desire or intent to continue the relationship based on their subjective emotional feelings and experiences; **structural commitment,** on the other hand, means the individuals take into consideration various external social and family reactions in deciding to either continue or terminate a relationship (M. Johnson, 1991). As in the previous scenario, Mona has opted for the importance of structural commitment over personal sentiments or satisfaction and, therefore, stays in her arranged marriage (see Jeopardy Boxes 11.2 and 11.3).

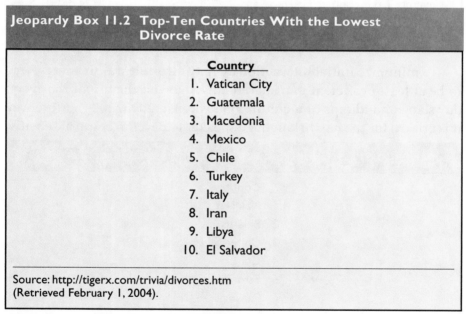

Jeopardy Box 11.2 Top-Ten Countries With the Lowest Divorce Rate

	Country
1.	Vatican City
2.	Guatemala
3.	Macedonia
4.	Mexico
5.	Chile
6.	Turkey
7.	Italy
8.	Iran
9.	Libya
10.	El Salvador

Source: http://tigerx.com/trivia/divorces.htm
(Retrieved February 1, 2004).

Communication Decoding Issues

Many interesting things can happen in an intercultural relationship development journey. For example, let us consider the following incident in Double Take 11.1. Kalene and Jose are classmates in the basic intercultural communication class at the University of Hawaii. Kalene is an ethnic mix of Hawaiian and African American, and Jose is from Peru.

Double Take 11.1

After three weeks of small talk and group work, Kalene was thinking of asking Jose out. One evening, right after the intercultural class, Kalene got up the courage to talk with Jose. She stopped him and said, "Jose, I would really like to hang out with you sometime this weekend. Will you have time?" Jose was dazed and confused.

As a newly arrived Peruvian international student on campus, Jose had pretty decent English proficiency. But he did not understand the word *hang out* as meaning either "to relax and get together informally" or "to relax at a place to watch *futbol*." He was quite confused by the meaning of the words *hang out* in this context. Had he even understood it, this request—from Jose's collectivistic, masculine view-point—might well have come too early in their initial acquaintance.

Jose felt embarrassed and hesitant in his response. Meanwhile, Kalene felt that she had made a fool of herself. Both Jose and Kalene experienced emotional embarrassment in this interaction episode. Jose, looking at the expression of Kalene, realized that he somehow had offended or insulted her. Kalene, on the other hand, did not realize that Jose was having verbal decoding problems with the word *hang out*. Nor did she realize the different gender-role expectations concerning initiating a dating request from the Peruvian viewpoint. She just felt awkward and embarrassed. Both parties experienced emotional anxiety and information uncertainty.

To minimize initial interaction anxiety, two cultural strangers need to be at least proficient in a shared language and the use of the everyday slang and idioms of a culture (Gudykunst, 2003, 2004). Moreover, it is critical for the native language speaker to develop cultural sensitiv-

Jeopardy Box 11.3 Countries With the Highest Divorce Rate

Country

1. Maldives
2. Belarus
3. United States
4. Cuba
5. Estonia
6. Panama
7. Puerto Rico
8. Ukraine
9. Russia
10. Antigua and Barbuda

Source: http://www.aneki.com/divorce.html
(Retrieved February 1, 2004).

ity for a relational partner who is not a native language speaker. That is, even if Jose had understood the idiomatic phrase "hanging out with you" (or the word *date*, as in "dating" and not a fruit on the tree), Kalene's dating request might still have hit a brick wall because of the masculine gender role expectations in Peru. Thus, beyond a shared language and an open-minded attitude, in-depth knowledge of the other's cultural values, expectations, idioms, nonverbal moves, and dating rituals would have greatly helped Kalene to accomplish her "hanging out" goal.

Although individualists often use a low-context, direct verbal approach in initiating, maintaining, and ending a close relationship, collectivists often use a high-context, indirect approach in dealing with relationship formation and development issues. Take, for example, the movie *Crouching Tiger, Hidden Dragon*. The main male character is never explicit about his deep emotional feelings for the woman he goes on loving for years—until the very end when he is dying. Actually, even to the very end, his emotional exchange with his relational partner is very subtle and nuanced. In the United States, we often scoff at such emotional understatement as shyness. In an individualistic culture, it is instead expected that relational partners would engage in active verbal self-disclosure with phrases such as "I love you" and "I miss you."

Take another example: In the popular U.S. television series *Friends*, Rachel flies all the way to London to tell her ex-boyfriend that she loves him—at his own wedding. Rachael does not care if he does not feel the same. She is motivated to risk humiliation and the possibility of breaking up a wedding to reveal to the ex-boyfriend her passion for him. However, from the collectivistic cultural lens, if you love someone, you reveal it through your attentiveness and sincere caring actions. For collectivists, love is in the details of paying attention to the other person's needs, desires, and wishes and the fact that you are also ready to sacrifice yourself on your relational partner's behalf. If both individuals are from the high-context communication zone, they will be able to understand each other's caring implicit gestures. However, in an intercultural-intimate relationship in which relational partners come from different communication zones, they may carry diametrically opposite relationship expectations and experience major communication decoding problems. To address such problems, relational partners need to make a strong commitment to communicate in a culture-sensitive manner and to decode both the content and relational meanings of the communication exchange process. This means learning to truly understand her or his relational partner's beliefs, values, needs, and interaction styles, as well as how she or he interprets core identity and relationship issues.

Intercultural-Intimate Relationship Attraction: Facilitating Factors

Though intercultural relationship development has some clear cultural-based influences, these are also subject to a multitude of factors that affect a couple's initial attraction, just like for any other couples in interpersonal relationship attraction stages. People who research intercultural interpersonal relationships have identified the following factors that facilitate dyadic relationship attraction: perceived physical attractiveness, perceived similarity, self-disclosure, and ethnic identity and self-concept. Each concept is considered in this section.

Perceived Physical Attractiveness

Recent research evidence indicates that physical attractiveness is critical to initial attraction, but so are cultural differences of attribution. For example, attractive persons are perceived to be high in potency in the United States (i.e., high energy and enthusiasm); however, Koreans perceive attractive persons to be high in integrity and concern for others (Wheeler & Kim, 1997). In initial relationship encounter stages, individuals are often concerned with creating a favorable impression in the presence of others so that others can either be attracted to them or at least find them credible. Thus, an individual may interact in a way that seems attractive to him or her, but this person is still not perceived as attractive to an individual from another culture.

Impression formation and *interpersonal attraction* are two interdependent concepts. Attractive physical appearance is closely associated with overall perceived attractiveness. Overall perceived attractiveness, in turn, is related to desirable personality attributes, such as appearing more sensitive, kind, sociable, pleasant, likable, and interesting. Attractive people are also evaluated as more competent and intelligent in the United States (Ross & Ferris, 1981).

In comparing U.S. and Japanese perceptions of facial attractiveness, U.S. college students have consistently rated smiling faces (both American and Japanese faces) as more attractive, intelligent, and sociable than the neutral faces. The Japanese students, on the other hand, have rated the smiling faces as more sociable but not necessarily more attractive or intelligent. They actually perceive neutral faces as more intelligent than the smiling faces. They also do not perceive smiling faces as more attractive than the neutral faces (Matsumoto & Kudoh, 1993). In terms of the perceived credibility aspect, facial composure and body posture appear to influence our judgments of whether individuals appear to be credible (i.e., high social influence power) or not credible (i.e., low social influence power). In some Asian cultures (e.g., South Korea and Japan), for example, influential people tend to use restrained facial expressions and practice postural rigidity. In the U.S. culture, however, animated facial expressions and postural relaxation are associated with credibility and positive impression formation (Burgoon et al., 1996). Overall, it can be concluded that perceived attractiveness or credibility is in the eye of the beholder. The meaning of such concepts reflects social agreements that are created and sustained through cultural nonverbal practices (check out the different facial expressions of the bridegroom and the bride in Snapshot 11.2).

Perceived Similarity

Perceived simlarity refers to the degree to which people think others are similar or dissimilar to themselves. It implies perceived shared views in beliefs, values, attitudes, communication, interests, and/or hobbies. The similarity-attraction perspective (Byrne, 1971) has received intense attention in intergroup-interpersonal attraction research for the last three decades. The argument behind this perspective (with a distinct individualistic-based focus) posits that individuals are motivated to maintain or increase their positive self-evaluation by choosing to associate with others who reinforce dimensions relevant to the self.

Snapshot 11.2

A Japanese-style wedding.

The similarity-attraction hypothesis supports this assumption: a positive relationship exists between perceived similarity and interpersonal attraction (Berscheid & Reis, 1998). There are three possible explanations to account for this hypotheis: (1) we experience cognitive consistency if we hold the same attitude and outlook in our relationship; (2) cognitive consistency reinforces our ego and provides identity rewards and affirmation; and (3) with similar others, we tend to invest less time and energy in managing relational vulnerable feelings, which gives a boost to interpersonal attraction.

In the context of intergroup-interpersonal attraction, perceived similarity takes on a variety of aspects, such as perceived cultural-racial similarity. For low-prejudiced individuals, race is a nonissue, but perceived physical attractiveness is the decisive factor in intergroup attraction (Byrne, 1971). In contrast, for high-prejudiced individuals, racial dissimilarity is viewed as creating insurmountable barriers to intergroup attraction. Additionally, a recent study indicated that the more the relational partners in initial interethnic encounters hold similar viewpoints concerning communication orientations (e.g., ways to support each other's self-concepts, ways to comfort each other), the more they are attracted to each other (Lee & Gudykunst, 2001).

In sum, people may be attracted to dissimilar strangers if they have repeated chances to interact with them under favorable contact conditions and with a positive mindset. Proximity, together with perceived similarity, definitely influences initial intercultural attraction. We can communicate only with people we meet via face-to-face situations or in cyberspace. Proxemic nearness to others creates more interaction opportunities. With repeated interaction opportunities, individuals may uncover important attitudinal and communication similarity issues (e.g., relationship philosophy, family outlook, similar communication styles, and common interests) and thus increase their confidence in relating to each other.

Self-Disclosure

Self-disclosure involves the process of revealing exclusive information about ourselves to others that the other individuals do not know. We can disclose information concerning the different parts of the public self (e.g., interests, hobbies, political opinions, career aspirations) and the private self (e.g., family secret issues, self-image and self-esteem issues). The study of self-disclosure is related to social penetration theory (Altman & Taylor, 1973). The topic of verbal self-disclosure has also been discussed in Chapter 7.

In its most general form, social penetration theory posits that interpersonal exchange usually progresses from superficial, nonintimate self-disclosure to more deep-layered, intimate self-disclosure. This developmental process also involves the **breadth** (i.e., number of topics we are comfortable and willing to disclose to reveal our dynamic self) and **depth** (i.e., intimate layers that reveal our emotionally vulnerable self) of self-disclosure. Deep-layered self-disclosure, as a hallmark of intimacy, is defined as an individual's willingness to reveal exclusive private information to a significant other.

Self-disclosure and intimacy are interdependent: Appropriate self-disclosure can increase intimacy, and increased intimacy prompts more self-disclosure. Self-disclosure develops interpersonal trust, emotional support, and mutual identity validation. However, self-disclosure can also open up the vulnerable self to hurt, disappointment, and information betrayal. However, without the risk of self-disclosure, intimate partners cannot move the relationship to a deeper level of sharing and identity resonance. Thus, self-disclosure often involves a dilemma of trust and risk taking: To trust, one has to learn to take risks, and to take risks, one must learn to trust. This dilemma applies to many close relationships within and across cultures.

Overall, individualists have been found to engage in more active self-disclosure than collectivists (Barnlund, 1975, 1989) across topics and different "targets," or receivers (e.g., parents vs. friends). When comparing the Japanese and U.S. groups, both agreed on their disclosure *target* preferences in the following order: same-sex friend, opposite-sex friend, mother, father, stranger, and untrusted acquaintance. U.S. college students consistently score themselves higher in the overall amount of self-disclosure than the Japanese and Chinese college students. Female college students also report a significantly higher amount of self-disclosure than male college students, regardless of culture (Ting-Toomey, 1991).

In the area of ethnic self-disclosure, European Americans tend to self-disclose more with people they do not know than do African Americans. However, in close friendship situations, African Americans tend to self-disclose more and at a deeper level than do European Americans (Hecht & Ribeau, 1984). In addition, African Americans repeatedly emphasize the importance of *acceptance, problem-solving,* and *lifetime support* in close friendships; in comparison, European Americans emphasize *confiding in each other* and being *free to be myself;* Mexican American interviewees emphasize terms such as *mutual sharing* and *mutual understanding* in explaining close friendships (Collier, 1991).

In sum, self-disclosure helps us to gain insights into our partners' feelings, thoughts, and beliefs. It also helps us to clarify our own emotions, ideas and values via the intimate sharing process. Appropriate self-disclosure helps to increase relational rapport and expand common interests. It also helps to alleviate some of the challenges and burdens that the relational partners face with their families and extended family reactions concerning their relationship situations.

Ethnic Identity and Self-Concept

According to interethnic attraction research, the strength of individuals' ethnic identities is related to intergroup attraction and dating (Chung & Ting-Toomey, 1999). Individuals with assimilated, bicultural, or marginal identities have a greater tendency to date and/or marry out of their own groups than those who view their ethnic identities and traditions as very important aspects of their self-concept. There are also times during which individuals are attracted to culturally dissimilar others because they perceive these partners as typical or atypical of their own culture. This means that people do activate their stereotyping process in initial intercultural attraction stages—be they positive or negative stereotypes. In addition, there is also a **"Romeo and Juliet" effect** at work in an intercultural-intimate relationship: The more the respective families are against this intimate relationship, the more the couples want to rebel against their parents and "do their own thing" and, therefore, they find each other more attractive.

Generation is also an important predictor of interethnic dating and marriages. The later the generation in the United States, the more likely the individuals tend to date outgroup members. Additionally, the less prejudice they perceive in the intergroup relations, the more likely they are open to date members from that group. For example, third-generation Asian Americans are five times more likely to marry outside their ethnic groups than first-generation Asian Americans (Kitano et al., 1998).

In discussing interracial intimate relationship development, experts (Foeman & Nance, 1999) conclude that interracial couples move through the following stages of "racial" awareness and awakening: racial awareness, coping, identity emergence, and relationship maintenance. The first stage, **racial awareness,** refers to the gradual awakening stage when the partners in the interracial relationship become conscious of each other's views and societal views on intimate racial relationship matters. The second stage, **coping,** refers to the struggles the couple has to face in gaining approvals from their families and friends and the strategies they come up with in dealing with such external pressures. In the third stage, **identity emergence,** both partners gain a new sense of security and bravely announce their intimate relationship to their families and ingroups. The fourth stage, **relationship maintenance,** refers to the continuous hard work the couple has to face in dealing with new challenges such as having children, moving to new neighborhoods, and meeting new social circles.

Intercultural-Intimate Conflict: Major Obstacles

Intercultural dating or marriage is fertile ground for culture clash and shock. At the same time, it is a hopeful arena for honoring and reconciling cultural differences. According to a recent census report, there are more than 1.3 million racially mixed marriages in the United States. This tally does not include interethnic marriages (e.g., Bolivians and Peruvians) within the same race. The highest rate of intermarriage occurs between European American males and Asian American females, and the lowest rate is that between European American males and African American females (Wehrly, Kenney, & Kenney, 1999).

There are many sources of intercultural-intimate conflict. **Intercultural-intimate conflict** is defined as any antagonistic friction or disagreement between two romantic partners due, in part, to cultural or ethnic group membership differences. Some of the prominent conflict sources are cultural-ethnic value clashes (see first section), prejudice and racism issues, and raising bicultural and biracial children. This section examines prejudice and racism reactions in the everyday environment of the romantic couple. It also explores the different coping strategies that couples use to counter racist attitudes and includes a discussion of identity issues in raising a bicultural or biracial child.

Encountering Prejudice and Racism

Of all the contrasts that interracial couples bring to their relationship, the most visible and inescapable is that of their ethnicity. Interethnic (or interfaith) couples of the same ethnicity can choose how and when they will reveal their differences to outsiders, but interracial couples display obvious visible differences. An African American and German couple is visually different because of their outward appearance: markers of skin color and facial features. Interracial couples must find different ways to cope with various family and social reactions as well as with each other's reactions toward the role of their ethnic group membership in their relationship.

Although the emotional reactions from an outgroup member can range from complete acceptance to utter ostracism, the couple's reactions in considering race as a factor in their relationship can also range from deep understanding to total dismissal. Conflict often arises when intercultural and interracial couples have to deal with the dilemma of whether or not to talk about matters of race or racism in their surrounding environment and within their own relationship context.

Prejudice is about biased, inflexible prejudgments and antagonistic feelings about outgroup members. However, racism is about a personal/institutional belief in the cultural superiority of one race and the inferiority of other races (Jones, 1997). Racism also refers to the practice of power dominance of a "superior" racial group over other "inferior" races. Couples often encounter initial conflict when they speak to their respective parents about plans for marriage. Their respective families' reactions can range from responses of support, acceptance, rejection, or fear, to outright hostility. For example, let us look at Gina's family's response from the following interview excerpt (Gina is a White woman planning to marry a Black man):

> Well, when I told my parents, they both looked kind of shocked, and then my father sort of blew up. He was yelling and screaming and told me that I had just thrown my life away and was I happy about that. But the whole time, I didn't hear my mother say anything against us. Later, after my father went to bed, she came up to me and told me that while she couldn't go against my father's wishes, she just wanted to make sure that I was happy. (McNamara, Tempenis, & Walton, 1999, p. 76)

Consider James' family response (James is an African American man planning to marry a White woman):

> My father was absolutely against my marrying a White woman. He said I was a traitor to my race and that I was not giving Black women a chance at a wonderful life. He would not talk to Donna, would not see her under any circumstances, and we did not talk to each other for over five years. (McNamara et al., 1999, p. 84)

For many White families, fear is the basic reason for the opposition to an interracial marriage. Their reasons can include societal or community disapproval, fear for the general physical and emotional well-being of the couple, fear of ostracism, and self-esteem issues concerning their biracial grandchildren (Frankenberg, 1993). As one White woman commented:

> I am sitting in a small restaurant with my daughter, my husband, my grandson, and my son-in-law. I look at my two-year-old grandson. I have a warm feeling and think to myself, "This is my first grandchild." Then my pleasure dissolves into anxiety as I realize that everyone in the restaurant is looking at us. My grandson is brown. My son-in-law is black. And my daughter is no longer mine. (Crohn, 1995, p. 90)

In terms of societal reactions, one of the most common problems experienced by interracial couples is the blatant, open stares from strangers. In addition to the stares, prejudicial treatment by some restaurant servers and real estate agents and racism within their own workplace may deeply disturb the couple's relationship. For example, listen to Russell's (an African American husband) comments:

> We go into a restaurant, together, with our children. We will order the meal and when we are done, the waitress hands us separate checks. Like she is saying "There is no way you two could be together." And here we are sitting with our children, who are obviously fair-skinned: whom does she think they belong to? ((McNamara et al., 1999, p. 96)

Finally, simply because the partners are in an intimate relationship, there is no guarantee that they are free of racism or matters of race in their own evolving relationship. In times of anger and conflict, couples may have expressed racial epithets or racial attitudes to vent their frustrated feelings, and these expressions can seriously hurt each other. Although some of the words may have been exchanged in a joking/teasing or sarcastic way during an intimate conflict, those words or phrases can be taken as hurtful, racist comments.

Sometimes a White partner's indifference to or ignorance of a racial issue may actually perpetuate a racist worldview. Gloria (an African American woman married to a White man) said in an interview excerpt:

> I told him someone yelled, "nigger." I was on the corner down there; I was with the baby, just driving by. And his first reaction is, "Well, what did you do to provoke that?" . . . And I thought, "That's the difference between being Black and White. Why would I have to do anything to provoke it?" (Rosenblatt, Karis, Powell, 1995, p. 240)

The White partner's insulated stance toward racism issues reflects his lifelong privilege of being a White male in a dominant, White society (see McIntosh, 1995). The concept of White privilege refers to the invisible systems that confer dominance or power resources on Whites. Thus, White males can walk down the street at night or drive their cars routinely without the need for awareness of potential racist remarks directed at them without cause, nor do they need to be particularly concerned with racial profiling issues by the police on the highways.

Fortunately, not all European American males have such a chilling, indifferent reaction to racism issues faced by their intimate partners. As Adam (a White male married to an African American female) commented:

> It takes being open to your own racism. It's all well and good to be sensitive to others in how they react to you, but you ought to be a little bit sensitive when you can and recognize your own mistakes, try to learn why what you've just said or done offended your partner . . . for example, there's an experience where Wanda would say, "Yeah, I understand that," and I say, "I don't understand it. What was happening? Help me out here." (Rosenblatt et al., 1995, p. 243)

When two intimate partners bring to their relationship strong identities as members of two different minority groups, they are hypersensitive to identity conflict issues. The following heated debate between Alan (with a strong sense of African American identity) and Sara (with a strong sense of Jewish identity) illustrates this point:

> *ALAN:* How can you know what it means to be discriminated against? You grew up in a comfortable, safe neighborhood. You got to choose whether or not you revealed to others that you were Jewish. My ancestors were brought here as slaves.

> *SARA:* I can't believe you're saying this stuff. You know that I lost great-aunts and great-uncles in the Holocaust. You don't have any monopoly on suffering. What right does the past give you to say how we lead our lives? (Crohn, 1995, p. 171)

Alan and Sara's identity conflict issues—cultural, racial, and religious identities—obviously tapped into very intense, core emotions in their own identity construction. They will need time to really get to know the identity of each other and to find meaningful ways to connect to each other's cultures as well as their own.

Countering Racism and Prejudice: Coping Strategies

In dealing with prejudice and racism outside their relationship, some couples may talk about racism issues as a lifetime project, whereas others dismiss them as inconsequential. Some reinforce the idea that to deal with prejudice issues, they have to learn to be honest about prejudices that they carry within themselves. Other couples try to keep matters of race a small part of their relationship and focus their attention more on love, grocery shopping, raising children, doing the laundry, washing the dishes, planning vacations, and handling all the details of a shared life (Rosenblatt et al., 1995). In addition to race issues, emotional issues (e.g., work stress, money, sex, housework, and a new baby) are the most common topics of marital squabbles (Gottman & Silver, 1999). These are the frequent "emotional tasks" that couples have to deal with in their everyday lives and that often reveal their very different cultural and personal perspectives on how to approach such issues.

Most interracial couples, however, have developed specific coping strategies to deal with recurring prejudice and race situations. These coping strategies include *ignoring/dismissing* (especially for minor offenses, such as staring or nasty comments), *normalizing* (thinking of themselves and appealing to others to treat them as "normal" couples with marital ups and downs), and *withdrawing* (avoiding places and groups of people who are hostile to interracial couples). In addition, they use *educating* (outreach efforts to help others to accept interracial couples), *confrontation* (addressing directly the people who insult or embarrass them), *prayer* (relying on faith to solve problems), and *humor* (adding levity in distressing situations) to ease or ward off the pains of racism (McNamara et al., 1999). Partners usually use ignoring/dismissal coping strategies to deal with minor threats but use more direct strategies—such as educating and confronting—when countering major racist comments or slurs.

Because the discussion of any racial or religious identity issue is so complex and emotionally charged, most couples actually avoid the topic altogether in their own relating process. However, refraining from dealing with identity issues (especially from the beholder's viewpoint) is like "buying peace for your relationship on a credit card. You may enjoy the temporary freedom from anxiety you 'purchased' by avoiding the difficult topics, but when the bill finally comes due, the 'interest' that's accumulated in the form of resentment and regret may be devastating" (Crohn, 1995, pp. 183–184). Partners in an intercultural-intimate relationship often wonder whether their conflicts are a result of genuine differences of opinion, personality clashes, cultural value differences, or the prejudiced attitude of one of the partners. To achieve a genuine understanding of these intertwined issues, couples have to learn to listen, to probe for accuracy, and to listen some more. As a final example, let us listen to the following comments by an African American male who is married to a White female:

> If I had to pick the perfect wife that I could have, she is very close to it. . . . She knows me better than anyone else . . . [and] she helps me a lot too. I like to talk to her and trust her and the fact that we both trust each other was there from the start. I know that she is really sensitive to issues of race and that is because we have experienced so much together. But I also know how difficult that has been for her. So I always try to keep her feelings in the front of my mind. I can't do anything about my race, but I can do something about how it affects her, at least sometimes I can. She does the same for me, which means that we are always thinking of each other. That's one of the reasons why I think we have lasted for so long—we are a lot stronger because we are really sensitive to the problem. (McNamara et al., 1999, p. 150)

A fundamental acceptance of the cultural-racial and religious aspects of a partner's identity and a mutual willingness to explore cultural codes, as well as a mutual openness in discussing racism issues, can facilitate greater relational satisfaction. Whether we are in an intimate intracultural or intercultural relationship, we will do well to regard each interpersonal relationship as if it is an intercultural one.

Raising Secure Bicultural Children

The common refrain from many intercultural marital couples is, "We were doing fine until the kids came along . . ." Most intercultural parents easily slip back into their own childhood memories to use their own family models to discipline, to guide, and to raise their children. In the context of bicultural family socialization, some of these parents may hold conflicting values and attitudes in teaching their children "good" from "bad" behaviors, or "proper" from "improper" ways of communicating with their grandparents, parents, siblings, or extended family members. There are two themes in this section: raising bicultural-biracial children and helping children to develop a secure identity.

Raising Bicultural-Biracial Children

In any intercultural-intimate relationship, the topic of raising children is a major stress point. Both parents and children have multiple options to choose from and to follow. Some of the factors that influence their choice are these: Does one parent have a greater intensity of identification with her or his cultural or racial group (or religious faith) than the other? What degree of involvement do members of the immediate and extended families play in the child's life? What is the cultural and religious composition of neighborhoods and schools? Do parents reach a mutually satisfactory consensus about an identity path for the family and in raising the child? Take a minute, and read the poem "What Is the Color of Love?" in Picture This 11.1. Discuss your reactions and feelings with your classmates.

Picture This 11.1

WHAT IS THE COLOR OF LOVE?
by Nobuko Miyamoto
(for my son, Kamau)

he came to me
he saw through me
and he gave me his heart
we found harmony
so much in common
though we were from worlds apart

when I saw him
I loved him and he loved me
what could be simpler to see
but clouds of fear hovering near
coloring the truth
afraid to let it be . . . let it be

we had a son
and being half black
he asked some hard questions

☞

☞

at six, while building sand
castles at the beach
he said, "mommy I wonder
what people think
seeing a Black kid with a
Japanese lady?"

at seven, he watched a white
neighbor scream at me
"you should be ashamed for
having a Black child!"
and my son said
"mommy is there something
wrong with that lady?"

at eight years old he came home
from school one day and said
"why do some people hate
Black folks so much?"
I didn't know how to answer
But I hope he never runs out of questions

love so strong
like a simple song
it made two worlds into one
but I'm still left with a child's question
what is the color of love?
what is the color of love?

The children of intercultural or interracial marriages often face different cultural-racial identity issues at different stages of their life cycle development. There are basically four forms of identity with which these children or adolescents can choose to identify, or they can also create their own unique combinations. The four identity forms in which many bicultural or biracial children find themselves are (1)

majority-group identifiers—children identify with the parent from the dominant culture or religion, and they may or may not publicly acknowledge the identity of their other parent (in this case a minority-group background); (2) **minority-group identifiers**—children identify with the parent who is a minority, and they may either acknowledge that their other parent is from a different background or they may deny (or minimize) their dual heritage background; (3) **synthesizers**—children acknowledge the influence of both aspects of their parents' cultural backgrounds and synchronize and synthesize the diverse aspects of their parents' values into a coherent identity; and (4) **disaffiliates** (i.e., "none of the above" identifiers)—children distance themselves or claim not to be influenced by their parents' cultural backgrounds, and they often create their own identity labels and rebel against any existing label that is imposed on them as part of a particular racial or cultural group (Crohn, 1995).

Children or teenagers at different developmental stages may experience different identity emotions. They may opt for different identity forms—depending on their peer group attitudes, their parents' socialization efforts, their own self-identity explorations, and the larger society's support or rejection of such an identity search process.

Helping Children to Develop a Secure Identity

To facilitate a stronger dialogue between parents and children regarding cultural and religious identity issues, here are some practical guidelines. First, take time and make a commitment to work out a family identity plan as early in your relationship as possible; understand the salient aspects of your own and your partner's cultural-racial and religious identity. Second, learn to listen to your children's identity stories and experiences; their ambivalence is oftentimes part of a normal, developmental process. Learn not to judge or be hurt by their truthful revelations. Third, try to provide your children with plenty of cultural enrichment opportunities that celebrate the diversity of both of your cultures; offer them positive experiences to appreciate and synthesize the differences (Crohn, 1995). Fourth, be truthful in dealing with prejudice and racism issues; nurture a secure sense of personal self-esteem and self-worth in your children regardless of how they wish to identify themselves. Parents should model constructive, assertive behaviors in confronting prejudice and racism issues. Finally, recognize that your children will grow up and choose their own path; keep the dialogue open and let your children or teenagers know that you will always be there for them. A secure home environment, listening to their stories with patience and interest, giving them room or space to grow, and finding meaningful ways to relate to who they are and are becoming are some very basic means that parents can use to signal their heartfelt caring and mindful presence in their children's lives.

To conclude this chapter, we should recognize that in any intercultural-intimate conflict, it is difficult to pursue all "my needs" or all "your needs" and come up with a neat conflict resolution package. In most intimate conflicts, couples who engage in constructive conflict tend to cultivate multiple paths in arriving at a mutually satisfying destination. These couples learn to listen to their partners' viewpoint with patience, and they are open to reconsidering their own position. They are committed to understanding their partners' cultural intimacy lenses and expectations. They are also willing to actively share and self-disclose their vulnerabilities, dreams, and hopes. Finally, they are able to inject humor and to laugh with each other in times of stress. They are also able to be mindfully there for their children and adolescents— in their quest for cultural identity meanings.

Intercultural Toolkit: Recaps and Checkpoints

This chapter focused on the challenges in developing an intercultural-intimate relationship. It explored different culture-based relationship expectations concerning love, privacy and connection, and communication issues. The sections discussed the facilitating factors—*perceived physical attractiveness, perceived similarity, self-disclosure, ethnic identity,* and *self-concept*—that shape the direction of an intercultural-intimate relationship. The pressures that an intercultural couple faces in dealing with various racism issues and also the increasingly important topic of raising bicultural-biracial children were presented. These and other obstacles are best handled by culture-sensitive dialogue, genuine relational commitment, and extra attention to cultural, ethnic, and relational identity development issues.

The following guidelines are drawn from the preceding discussion of various challenges and obstacles that face an intercultural-intimate couple. They may help you in managing diverse intimate relationship issues:

- Pay close attention to culture-based challenges in developing an intercultural-intimate relationship.

- Be mindful that individualists and collectivists hold different expectations concerning communication issues, such as dating requests or self-disclosure.

- Be sensitive to your relational partner's family reaction issues. Learn to deal with the individualistic and collectivistic value gaps adaptively.

- Be committed in developing a deep friendship with your intimate partner as a cushion to deal with both internal and external stressors down the road.

- Be unconditionally accepting of your partner's core personality. You must make your partner feel that you try hard to understand the cultural context that she or he is coming from.

- Be flexible in learning the communication styles of your intimate partner and learn to code-switch from direct to indirect styles or from verbal to nonverbal attending behaviors.

- Be responsive to the "emotional tasks" awaiting you in your intimate relationship and learn to share them responsibly and with enjoyment.

- Be diligent in depositing emotionally supportive messages in your relationship. Research (Gottman & Silver, 1999) indicates the validity of the "5-to-1 ratio"—you need to deposit five positive messages in your intimate relationship to counteract one negative message.

- Be positive in your relationship memories. Research (Gottman & Silver, 1999) indicates that the more you engage in positive relationship memory reflections, the more you think positively about the current state of your intimate relationship. ✦

Chapter 12

What Are the Communication Issues Facing a Global Identity?

Chapter Outline

In India, yoga is a 5000-year-old spiritual practice. Through different breathing techniques, chanting, and exercise, one attempts physical purification to reach a state the Hindis called *ananda*. Outside of India, yoga is becoming a booming fashion and fitness craze worldwide. This spiritual regimen has gone mainstream and is a big business, with accessories such as mattresses, designer handbags and clothes, and a full-scale expo all available for those who "do" yoga. Is it still considered yoga if you just do the poses, but do not meditate or chant? Can you be called a yoga teacher if you are certified after a weekend crash course? Most spiritually inclined gurus and yogi masters will say no; but certified trainers beg to differ.

—Paul Tullis, *Los Angeles Times*,
September 21, 2003

In this global age, "new" cultural communities are emerging with a highly techno-savvy population, changing the outlook and composition of personal identity. Global role models are not limited to the confines of the United States. Our sport icons, Tiger Woods and Michelle Kwan, for example, are just as popular overseas as they are here. We also have international celebrity icons (e.g., Iman, model and makeup designer; Gloria Estefan, Cuban singer; and David Beckham, soccer player). As global *citizens, we are moving at an incredible rate of speed. We need to take a moment to sit down and reflect on how modern technology has influenced the development of our changing identity and communication styles.*

The concern of this chapter is twofold: First, how do technology and popular culture shape contemporary identities on a global level? Second, what is the impact of this global self on intercultural communication? Let's begin with a definition of the background of a contemporary identity through a new concept we the authors have coined, the e.net'er identity. Next, we explore some of the important issues that individuals face as active technology users and communicators at the global level. Third, the effect of popular culture on the development of a contemporary identity is explained. Finally, the chapter concludes with some checkpoints for daily intercultural practice.

The E.net Self: Local Versus Global Outlook

Past studies have assumed, although incorrectly, that the ethnicity of an individual (via ancestral ties) automatically guarantees group membership. However, we learned in Chapter 5 that ethnicity is not a static phenomenon. Rather, it is a subjective experience that involves the active management of ingroup/outgroup boundaries. In this twenty-first century, both individualists and collectivists, regardless of their cultures, are at the crossroads of redefining, exploring, and reinventing their contemporary identities.

Local Versus Global Identity

Let's examine the following story: 19-year-old Thi Nguyen was a contestant for Miss Vietnam 2003, Southern California. Throughout the pageant, she was challenged by others (and also by her own opinion) concerning whether she was "Vietnamese enough" in this larger U.S. cultural world. "It's hard," she mused, "because most of us were born here in the U.S., and we're very Americanized. However, we're all in that same boat of not being American enough for the Americans and not being Vietnamese enough for the Vietnamese. It is hard to find that balance" (Nguyen, 2003, p. A4). Another contestant with red highlights in her hair, Kelly Ly, remarked, "My parents tell me all the time that I don't fit into the traditional [image of a] Vietnamese girl. . . . I figure I should try to stand out by being myself" (Nguyen, 2003, p. A4).

Recall our earlier discussion in which identity differentiation and identity inclusion appear to be the repeated themes that run through the old and new generations of the twenty-first century. What these two young women are describing is a constant shift between wanting to be an "individual" and wanting to remain a part of the group as well. However, there is a sense that they are separated from the group for not being ethnic enough. These two Vietnamese American women want to feel a sense of group belonging and connection *and,* at the same time, assert their unique personalities.

On a global scale, new generations of individuals are attempting to create a third identity—a fusion of individualism and collectivism. At the same time that they embrace the function of individual privacy and expression, they also long for global belonging and connection that transcends traditional ethnic-cultural boundaries. The Internet, somehow, provides the ideal link to bridge these diametrically opposite values and desires.

Defining the Background of E.net'ers

The Internet is a central hub—the channel that offers us a wide-open space to communicate globally and to connect with individuals from diverse walks of life. More important, this hub pulses with speed and efficiency. The Internet gives us a common language—English—with which to communicate and bond with fellow global citizens (Swerdlow, 1999). The English language, in operation with virtual reality, hooks people together on an instantaneous global level. This global connection is so appealing, so "hip," and so very persuasive that it constantly shapes and recontours our sense of composite self.

The Internet allows users to develop relationships across the barriers of time, space, geography, and cultural-ethnic boundaries. Of course, we realize that this global space is also a very privileged space—accessible only to members and cultural groups who have the access and means to afford such technological resources. It also privileges individuals who can use English comfortably as a medium of Internet communication. It has been estimated that approximately 605 million people use the Internet on a daily basis, and they e-mail each other across diverse age-groups and across diverse cultural boundaries—from Mongolia to Argentina, and from Iceland to New Zealand (http://www.nua.ie/surveys/how_many_online/). For example, one out of every four children in U.S. kindergartens now uses the Internet to play and do homework (Feller, 2003). When discussing important issues in intercultural communication, we can no longer afford to ignore the powerful influence of modern technology.

Think back for a moment to the discussion of value orientations in Chapter 3. Our values allow us to attach meanings and explanations concerning people and events that are happening around us. Both cultural and personal values give us a sense of direction in terms of what is good or bad, right or wrong, fair or unfair. Cultural and personal values also change over time. They are not static entities. The role of the Internet connection adds another layer of complexity to our understanding of changing values in the twenty-first century. The following sections explain the authors' newly coined term, the *e-net'er identity*.

E.net'ers: Who Are They?

The **e.net'er identity** stands for a new generation of individuals, from any age group, wired to the Internet via intersecting space. E.net'ers have both a local self and a global self. Some may call this a "hybrid" identity because it is a blend of many aspects of the local and global environment that is shared by all. Some may call this "globalization" because we are now all residents of a big global village. Though it is a hybrid global phenomenon, the e.net identity is also an outcome of power and popular culture.

The aspect of power comes from the fact that access to the Internet and new technologies is limited. Not everyone can afford to be hooked up to the global superhighway. Behind the medium of identity reconstructions and image shaping are teams of corporations, businesses, marketers, and public relations specialists who intend to spread the latest technological gadgets. One of the primary purposes of image reshaping is for profit making and profit recycling. To be connected and to be "in," affluent individuals on a global level are willing to pay money to purchase the latest and hottest gadgets and discard outdated models. In essence, being technologically updated allows e.net individuals to *distinguish* themselves as being the "first-wave users" while simultaneously belonging to a fast-track, disposable culture.

The e.net identity is also linked to pop culture. Pop culture is not only *mass* culture, the culture of the imagined community, it is also a system of beliefs and habits consumed in various ways, by different people (Zelizer, 2001). In addition, popular culture fosters a climate in which "globally ethnic" is actually appealing to diverse groups on a global level. For example, actor Vin Diesel refuses to discuss his ethnicity (still unknown), and singer Mariah Carey (European American and Venezuelan) did so only under significant media pressure. The new ambivalent-looking, *global-ethnic* celebrity has mass appeal in any ethnic market. She or he can connect with the masses on various levels and can also appeal to those who do not define themselves clearly within a particular ethnic group. The celebrity icon has at once no clear ethnic-cultural identity and so reflects a distinctive global-ethnic identity because of her or his fusion look and hybrid taste.

Think for a moment about your own identity: How do you think technology has shaped your identity? How do you think pop culture has influenced your sense of self? What would happen if you woke up tomorrow morning and your computer, your mobile phone, your pager, and your television had all disappeared from your house? Could you survive for one week without all these electronic gadgets?

We can view an e.net'er identity, or the short-form term, **e.net identity,** as a composite identity that is shaped by technology, by popular culture, and by mass consumption. An e.net self can have both internal and external facets. Internally, one can hold hybrid components of ethnic-cultural values (e.g., collectivism and individualism) and contemporary aspects of being-in-doing value orientations (recall the Chapter 3 discussion about "Value Orientation Patterns"). In addition, the e.net individual can swing flexibly between the high-context and low-context communication systems. An individual with an e.net identity has a sense of communal belonging on a global level. She or he is hooked up with diverse yet like-minded individuals who actively carve out a distinctive "adopted community" (e.g., by hobbies, by game types) and communicate fervently via chat rooms or e-discussion groups.

Let's examine some of these *e-characteristics* and how they relate to communication:

Electronic: The e.net self is linked to the age of electronics. Gadgets and devices (e.g., cell phones, Palm Pilots, e-mail) allow e.net'ers to communicate at any time or place, making this the central hub of communication.

Exclusive: the e.net self is an exclusive group of individuals who are in between groups. They may be members of specific ethnic or racial groups, but they are also loyal to the Internet community. For e.net'ers, the Internet serves as the main connection to the world.

Ethnic Identity: The e.net self includes individuals who may have ethnic loyalties to their traditional groups. However, they often tend to display more solidarity with their techno-global networks. Their social group identities are multifaceted and network-based. They also feel flexible in "borrowing" ethnic identities from other groups in terms of outward appearances and use of ethnic artifacts.

Exploring: As a consumer-based identity, the e.net self appeals to individuals who are in search of the *next* big thing, whether it is fashion, music, trends, or Websites. The Net serves as a way of creating a space and a community in which they can belong.

Emoticon: The e.net'ers communicate with emoticons. Emoticons (see Chapter 8) are conveyed through text messaging, instant messaging, and e-mail. A simple emoticon is worth three sentences and gives the sender a chance for anonymity. Who has time to go in depth?!

Entertainment: Kurt Cobain, the former lead singer for Nirvana, sang, "here we are now, entertain us!" The entertainment industry in the United States is a 480-billion-dollar industry (Wolf, 1999). Most e.net'ers have an insatiable appetite for entertainment. With movies, DVDs, games, and downloadable accessories, why leave the house? And this appetite is not limited to the United States. According to McClure (2002), Japanese young adults under age 25 spent more money on cell phones and videogames than young adults in any other countries.

Economy: The e.net self is tied to the booming Internet economy. Trendy fashion statements are discovered and purchased online, or through specific online magazines, or via chat room conversations. E.net'ers are willing to spend large amounts of money to keep up-to-date. Wehrfritz (2000) reported that millions of wired shoppers in Japan surf the net for products, and one in four in South Korea browses the Web to shop, play games, or day-trade. Across the globe, e.net'ers can access eBay.com and bid on auctioned items for a reasonable price. Why wait for the newest or retro Chicago Cubs baseball cap when you can click onto eBay.com?

These are only a few of many characteristics of an e.net identity, a self that reflects a new generation of techno-savvy individuals. Can you come up with your own e.net-ism?

The E.net Identity: Dialectical Challenges

The e.net identity is a cornerstone of contemporary identity development. This section highlights some of the important issues that concern the interplay between technology and global identity development. Perhaps one of the most striking challenges of the e.net interaction is the aspect of dialectics. **Dialectical tensions** are conflicts that come from two opposing forces that exist at the same time (Baxter & Montgomery, 1996). For example, tensions can exist when sometimes you want to spend lots of time with your relational partner, and other times you feel your relational partner is cramping your style or making you feel stifled by not leaving you alone. These tensions create challenges for an individual and for the dyadic relationship. However, such dialectical tensions can also spark interpersonal collaboration and creativity—if the dialectics are managed flexibly and adaptively. The following pages discuss three of the major dialectical pulls: space, time, and identity (see Table 12.1).

Before launching into this discussion, please check your reactions on Quick Poll 12.1.

Table 12.1 Global Identity: Dialectical Challenges	
SPACE:	Private - Communal
TIME:	Monotrack- Multitrack Tempos
IDENTITY:	Identity Alienation- - - - - - - - - - - - - - - - - - Identity Inclusion

Quick Poll 12.1

Please check the words or phrases that best describe your overall attitude toward the use of the Internet and compare your results with a classmate's:

Alone Time	_____	Communal Time	_____
Quietness	_____	Bustling Noises	_____
Focused	_____	Excitement	_____
Work	_____	Playful	_____
Effort	_____	Action	_____
Fiction	_____	Reality	_____

Spatial Zone Dialectics

For an e.net'er, the Internet provides privacy and anonymity in the safe environment of one's free space. The e.net culture transforms space in such a way that individuals can experience both the *privacy pole* and the *communal pole* in instant space and time zones. If you have checked words on both the left-hand and right-hand columns of Quick Poll 12.1, you're not going crazy. You're just one of the many individuals who interpret the use of the Internet from both dialectical poles. Within the privacy pole, the Palm Pilot, personal computer, and mobile phone are accessed in private, personal space. We are not confined to a computer lab or room to access the Internet. We can travel through the visual world in a sports stadium, at the movies, sitting in the park or a lecture hall, or while traveling on an airplane. Oftentimes, we do not have to wait more than 20 seconds to have a communication exchange with another human being. We can enjoy a simple text message, instant message, or even .jpg pictures.

Simultaneously, the Internet provides a sense of shared communal space. Chat rooms, online journals, message boards, and fan-based Websites offer an individual a sense of communal connection and belonging to a particular group. Sharing this *public* space in the Web community allows individuals to engage, explore, and interact with each other across cultural boundaries without actual face-to-face contact. E.net'ers see the Internet as providing wonderful opportunities to reconnect with long-lost friends and high school sweethearts, create new relationships, enhance global team creativity, and empower people through human rights and international support groups. College students can collaborate across cultures via online discussion boards or e-mails. Faculty and researchers who have never met each other face-to-face can engage in online collaboration and research projects across national borders.

At the same time, however, at the click of a button, all these sounds, images, sights, and actions can instantaneously vanish. The individual can reclaim his or her quiet space or privacy in seconds. This peculiar sense of reality versus fiction exists as a blurry line in the virtual reality world.

Temporal Zone Dialectics

The Internet has also drastically reoriented our sense of time. It has contracted and, at the same time, expanded space and time via its multichannel, multiclicking, and instantaneous door-to-door delivery format. It offers individuals simultaneous opportunities to move quickly back and forth between monochronic amd polychronic time schedules (recall the Chapter 8 "Regulating Time" section). Externally, individuals may experience tensions by constantly shifting between **monotrack focus** (i.e., working on one project at a time) and **multitrack focus** (i.e., tending to multiple e.net tasks or activities) on the Internet. Communicationwise, individuals with monotrack focus can also often bump into misunderstandings with individuals who enjoy multitrack focus because of their multitasking habits on the Internet.

More specifically, the *monotrack e.net communicators* can concentrate on only one task at a time. While they are working on a task project on the computer, they would find it difficult to be simultaneously talking to their friends on a cell phone, switching to answering e-mail relational messages, and talking to someone right next to them. However, *multitrack e.net communicators* can be quite adept at multitracking—working on multiple projects, such as surfing the Net and at the same time chatting with friends on their cell phones. The e.net multitrack individuals also adhere to a being-in-doing value philosophy. While on the net, they can chat with friends across the globe, access daily newspapers in several languages, and download new song releases. The **being-in-doing e.net philosophy** means that e.net multitrack individuals can fuse the "being mode" value dimension with the "doing mode" value dimension—they can be fully enjoying the here-and-now moment, spending *being* time with their multiple friends in the chat room and also *doing* other task activities. There is no doubt that the e.net generation is a changed generation in terms of traditional cultural values and norms held by their parents' or grandparents' generation.

In sum, while the e-net monotrack folks can focus only on one thing at a time and tend to compartmentalize task projects and relational *fun* chats on the net, the multitrack folks can move in and out smoothly between task activities and relational activities in a split second. It is obvious that both monotrack individuals and multitask individuals have to make a greater effort to apply all the skills that we have discussed in this book to manage their e.net cultural habits adaptively and flexibly. With intercultural sensitivity, monotrack individuals have to understand that multitask individuals perceive multitracking as part of their virtual and existential reality. Likewise, multitrack individuals have to learn to give more time and space to the monotrack individuals to wrap up one task and then get their full attention on another task or project.

Identity Zone Dialectics

An individual's sense of alienation from the actual cultural world also often pushes him or her to search for something more communal in terms of social ties. The Internet alleviates *identity alienation* and satisfies the group-based *identity inclusion* need. However, it also reinforces the individual's isolation from others in the real world. The more that individuals claim the e.net world as their newfound cultural world, the more they will experience alienation or loneliness in the real world, and vice versa. However, dialectically speaking, the same individuals may also slowly shed their alienation through learning to reach out in the Internet world. They can transpose some of the social skills developed via online chats and apply them adaptively with folks in real-life social settings. Many individuals around the globe link to the Internet as a way to escape from the traditional confines of their respective cultural worlds. In a sense, they give birth to a "second self" through their sustained immersion in the Internet womb.

Many elderly individuals also claim that the Internet world reconnects them with people from different age-groups in different cultures. Senior citizens living in assisted living or nursing homes definitely appreciate the Internet as offering a chance to break away from monotonous living conditions and meet newfound intercultural friends in faraway cultures. For people with disabilities, the Internet operates on a level playing field. Through the Internet, they develop relationships or learn online—without ever needing to self-disclose their disabilities if they so choose. Likewise, minority group members report that the Internet affords them a forum to be "themselves" without ever being judged prematurely because of the color of their skin. But, paradoxically, the Internet also acts as a global outlet to evoke fear and hate— many hate sites advocate violence toward immigrants, gays, Jews, Arabs, and others. Of course, this gives law officials and global peace activists a chance to fight back and track down these hate-filled Websites and the hatemongers who are behind them.

As cultures on a global level become more interconnected and matrix-based, the e.net identity reflects the dynamic interplay between privacy and community, monotrack and multitrack tempo, and identity alienation and inclusion. To further understand the effects of the e.net self, four specific areas will be discussed: television, music, fashion statements, and video games.

Global Identities in Action

The term *globalization* has both positive and negative implications in the contemporary social world. Broadly speaking, it means the cultural interdependence and realignment processes due to the global economy, e-commerce, mass media, and the flux of immigration patterns. Individuals who support globalization see the world as becoming more interdependent and inevitably so. The global economy and global mass media, in particular, bring us all to develop global citizenships of a worldwide "global village"—thus breaking down national and cultural boundaries.

From a different analytical standpoint, opponents view globalization as negative because it destroys cultural boundaries and Westernizes many indigenous cultures. For example, it has exported images of U.S. wealth, consumerism, and other U.S. mass media images throughout the world and created many "consuming" colonies with a strong U.S.-dominant flavor. According to its opponents, globalization dilutes or destroys cultures, languages, cultural etiquettes, values, and traditions. See, for example, the top-ten all-time worldwide box office grossing movies (Jeopardy Box 12.1) and check out the global influence of Hollywood. To further explore this topic of globalization, let's first look at television trends on the global level.

The Lens of Television: Identity Imitation

Just how does a person's identity develop? If you think back to prior chapters, the influence of our parents, socialization, and peers is especially relevant. Growing up, did you ever watch *Sesame Street*? *Pokemon*? *Power Rangers*? *Yu Gi Oh*? As you watched the show, did you ever ask yourself, "Gee, I wonder if kids in India are watching the same show?" Don't worry if you never thought about this. Major U.S. television shows are easily accessible in the international market.

One of the ways in which an e.net person learns about his or her identity or another person's identity is through television. Television shapes the way we see our world. It is a compelling aspect of marketing culture, lifestyle, trends, and news. It also influences how we form our

Jeopardy Box 12.1	All-Time Box Office Worldwide Gross

Rank	Title
1.	*Titanic* (1997)
2.	*Lord of the Rings: The Return of the King* (2003)
3.	*Harry Potter/Sorcerer's Stone* (2001)
4.	*Star Wars: Episode I: The Phantom Menace* (1999)
5.	*Lord of the Rings: The Two Towers* (2002)
6.	*Jurassic Park* (1993)
7.	*Harry Potter and the Chamber of Secrets* (2002)
8.	*Lord of the Rings: The Fellowship of the Ring* (2001)
9.	*Finding Nemo* (2003)
10.	*Independence Day* (1996)

Source: http://www.imdb.com/Charts/worldtopmovies
(Retrieved March 1, 2004).

stereotypes of people in different cultures and ethnic groups. Two types of television shows are consistently in demand in the global market: action shows and dramas. Action shows are enticing to watch because of their combination of action, violence, and sex. Viewers do not need to really listen to the show's words when they have vivid images and a lot of visual action. Drama shows have also done very well in the international market, and they are also usually dubbed into the local language. For example, in Israel, Argentine *telenovelas* (soap operas) with Hebrew subtitles are a "blissfully frivolous obsession!" (Rotella, 2003).

Watching TV drama shows gives the international viewer an opportunity to check out trends, styles, and fashion statements. For example, when Jennifer Aniston made her debut on *Friends*, a popular TV sitcom, her layered hairstyle went global. Many women in various parts of the globe requested the "Aniston" cut. When the Japanese TV cartoon show *Pokemon* debuted in the United States, every kid had to buy Pokemon trading cards. This brings up a question: Exactly how global are we?

In the United States, entertainment is the second-largest export (Zelizer, 2001). U.S. television is everywhere. Different countries have different tastes and many are captivated by U.S.-exported television shows. The success of exported television shows runs the gamut from older series to newer series. For example, in Germany, the most popular television shows are the newer shows, *Buffy the Vampire Slayer* and *Charmed*, but in Italy, an older series, *Walker, Texas Ranger*, has the largest audience. France and Spain prefer the action series *Alias*. Syndicated shows are equally popular. Zelizer (2001) reports that Iranians enjoy old *Laurel & Hardy* shorts, Egyptians enjoy *Friends* and *ER*, but

Hercules: The Legendary Journeys, The Cosbys, and soap operas, including *Dynasty*, are equally popular. In Pakistan, with a large English-speaking population, *Frasier, M*A*S*H*, and *Baywatch* are popular. As more countries produce their own television shows, the variety increases with availability and funding.

U.S. networks are purchasing international and homegrown productions, a reverse flow of globalization. International TV gives us a comparison of culture-specific and culture-universal display rules (e.g., nonverbal cues). Individuals in the United States are allowed to take a snapshot of the similarities and differences in communication. The result? In the United States, we are hooked on reality TV—something for which we can thank Japan (*Iron Chef*), the United Kingdom (*Trading Spaces*), Sweden (*Survivor*), and the Netherlands (*Big Brother*)!

For example, *Iron Chef* was a phenomenal hit series in Japan. In this one-hour program, three iron chefs (Japanese, Chinese, and French cooking styles) had to work with one "surprise" ingredient and create the most innovative dishes with that theme ingredient. However, an outside chef, who worked across from the iron chef, challenged one of them. The show concluded with a taste test and the announcement of the winner. The series was so engaging and popular that in 1999, FoodTV, a cable station in the United States, bought the rights for the show. It became an instant hit with fans across the United States, who began watching and hitting Web pages devoted to the show. *Iron Chef* attracted such a large audience that the three iron chefs were invited to the United States in a special epsiode, called *Battle of the Iron Chefs: New York Battle*. This was the last show taped for the series. FoodTV, however, continues to air repeats of old battles due to popular demand.

Reality TV comes in many forms, but the most common focus of these shows is the development of interpersonal relationships. *Real World* debuted on MTV in 1992. From the start, this show was new, exciting, and unfamiliar. Seven roommates were chosen to live with each other for three months. Although targeting a young demographic, the show generated viewers across age-groups interested in the dramatic lives of these seven individuals living in the same house. *Real World* is now in its ninth season, spawning three reality knockoff shows: *Road Rules* (filming seven individuals living on the road), *Battle of the Sexes* (former *Road Rules* and *Real World* cast members), and *Road Rules Versus Real World*. As a side note, one couple has actually married after meeting on the series.

The desire to watch real-life people on camera has extended to various contexts and situations. The result? More shows have been developed to tap into the reality universe. A brief summary lists past and present shows that promote "reality checks":

- *Big Brother* (originated in the Netherlands): roommates compete for one million dollars;

- *The Bachelor/Bachelorette* (2000–present): individuals narrow down 50 dates to one marriage proposal;

- *American Idol* (2001–present): singers compete for a record contract;

- *Fear Factor* (2001–present): contestants compete for money, overcoming many of their "fears" in the process;

- *Joe Millionnaire* (2003–present): women compete for "Joe," who they erroneously believe is a wealthy man.

In their everyday lives, lonely consumers can create community with the lives and relationships formed on television. Reality TV gives the e.net individual the opportunity to live vicariously through the lives of others and to make connections. These shows are directly linked to the Internet, forming fan-based Websites devoted to sharing opinions, even complaining about the characters as if they were our friends. This is a direct result of the e.net virtual reality culture. Reality television promotes a form of virtual bond between the reality characters and the audience. Sometimes, televised events are real enough to generate actual fear, challenges, or rewards for the viewers. For example, the *Real World* series actually educated viewers with public service announcements based on "real" events that occurred on the show, such as teen pregnancy, alcohol abuse, discrimination, and homophobia.

In sum, television is a form of entertainment watched globally. This global connection, a visual aid to match the cultural or universal narrative, is one of the most powerful aspects of the e.net identity. Unlike in radio and print, e.net'ers are afforded a visual tour to actually check out the culturally specific tastes, sounds, reactions, and local people in the scene. These sounds and images may exist on a very superficial level; however, they may also serve as a first enticement to e.net'ers to fly to that country and do more in-depth exploration.

Rap and Hip-Hop Music: Identity Expression

Through music, some e.net'ers find a common identity expression and connection with others—especially because music expresses exactly what they may be feeling. Music inspires trends, fashion, and alternative ways of expression and makes a statement. Music may also bring controversy, conflict, and resistance. In the past, radio was the most common medium used to listen to popular tunes and catch live shows. Presently, radio is on the brink of extinction. One major reason is the e.net group. E.net'ers download music titles off the Internet, burn them directly to a CD, and watch the newest and latest music videos (i.e., radio alone does not fully capture the music, mood, and attitude behind the group and its singers). As a result, music creates identity and sparks a communal sense of space and time. These e.net individuals aspire to "be like" a singer, a group, or a band. Nothing has influenced global e.net identity as much as hip-hop music. Hip-hop music, when combined with music videos, has cross-pollinated popular media and changed the dynamics of identity formation across the globe. This visual aid has influenced more youth across the globe than any other trend in history.

Hip-hop music (or rap, as it was once called and is still referred to by some) sprang from the inner-city ghettos of the United States in the mid-1970s. Rap music has been associated with graffiti (or tagging), dance trends (breakdancing), scratching (a deejay simultaneously mixing two or more vinyl records), and artifacts (gold and platinum jewelry, or "bling-bling"). Rap and hip-hop music came from African American youth who were discouraged by racial oppression and the inequality of life. Rapping was an art, a way of expressing the problems they faced living on the outer edges of society. As the music increased in popularity and progressed from the inner city to the suburbs, rap music and hip-hop became big business when White teenagers started to listen and buy the music (Zwingle & McNally 1999). At that point, hip-hop exploded. In the past three years, hip-hop has continued to generate the highest music sales in the United States and international markets. Do you know what were the top-ten Billboard Singles in Fall 2003? (Check out Jeopardy Box 12.2.) For the first time in music history, on October 3, 2003, Billboard reported that the top-ten singles in the United States were by rappers (with the exception of the number

Jeopardy Box 12.2	Top-Ten Billboard Music Singles in the United States, October 3, 2003
1. "Baby Boy"	Beyonce, Featuring Sean Paul
2. "Shake Ya Tailfeather"	Nelly, P. Diddy & Murphy Lee
3. "Get Low"	Lil Jon & The East Side Boyz Featuring Ying Yang Twins
4. "Right Thurr"	Chingy
5. "Frontin'"	Pharrell, Featuring Jay-Z
6. "Damn!"	YoungBloodZ, Featuring Lil Jon
7. "P.I.M.P."	50 Cent
8. "Into You"	Fabolous, Featuring Tamia Or Ashanti
9. "Stand Up"	Ludacris, Featuring Shawnna
10. "Where Is the Love?"	Black Eyed Peas

http://www.billboard.com/bb/charts/hot100.jsp
(Retrieved October 3, 2003).

one song, Beyonce's "Baby Boy," which features Sean Paul from Jamaica). It is easy to see the worldwide influence of this genre of music that is cast across diverse cultural borders. Let's check out the following story in Double Take 12.1.

Double Take 12.1

While hiking through beautiful, pristine "Heidi Country" in Switzerland, I was glancing around at all the amazing scenery—the cows with big bells that were echoing over the fields, the wildflowers, the small farmhouses, the vast rolling fields that touched the base of the towering Alps. And then I saw it: 2Pac's picture tagged on the gate of a fence.

—Katie, *College Student*

This example reflects the global impact of hip-hop music. Tupac Shukar, or "2Pac," was a very popular rap artist in the United States. He was famous for his ability to relate to both young and older audiences. He was a mixture of a gangsta "thug" and somone with a genuine, "real" persona. In 1996, Tupac was shot and killed in Las Vegas. Tupac's music continues to live on, in CD sales, posthumously. Tupac's sustaining success as an icon has a lot to do with the type of person he represents: smart, aware of his surroundings, deep in his observations of the world around him, and taking pride in his community. This sense of belonging and representing his community is an identity value many e.net'ers can relate to.

Though many e.net'ers take pride in asserting their individual voice and rights and in protecting their personal privacy, they also value loyalty to the community and protection of the "turf" and neighborhood. In fact, it is not surprising that many contemporary global citizens practice a new form of individualism and collectivism that integrates the selective aspects of "I-identity" and "we-identity" value orientations. We can call these hybrid value orientations a creative synthesis of *collaborative individualism.*

Outside the United States, the rise of the hip-hop identity can be linked with MTV, which is seen in 79 million U.S. households and 384 million households across the world (Viacom, 2003). MTV has become so popular in countries such as India that East Asian youth are known as the new pan-Asian youth culture (McClure, 2002, December 28). Young elites in Bombay are also falling for the MTV style hip-hop (Takahashi, 2003). With the help of MTV, South Korea has exploded into the music industry, changing the identity and look of South Koreans. The South Korean music is called K-Pop or *gayo.* K-pop singers are known for their unique and hip style of music but are heavily influenced by U.S. styles. Taking rap and hip-hop trends (e.g., break-dancing) and adding unique dance twists and styles have resulted in a global fusion identity.

The music combines elements of U.S. music (reggae and rap), fashion (surf wear, blonde hair, and baggy clothes), and Korean styles to make a new form of music. Dyed hair, baggy jeans, and designer labels are all features of K-pop singers. Asian cities are falling for the identity, attitude, and values of hip-hop, but U.S. rappers are looking to the Asian culture for unique and unusual beats. Rappers and hip-hop artists in the United States have also borrowed heavily from the East (Wu Tang Clan, Jay-Z, Missy Elliott, R. Kelly, Ja Rule, and Busta Rhymes). Some actually use Asian instruments (Missy Elliott, Ja Rule, R. Kelly) and produce major hits across the globe (e.g., "Get ur freak On," "Between Me and You").

Outside the genre of hip-hop, music as an identity expression in social interaction is popular. For example, many e.net individuals have been exposed to karaoke from Japan. The rise of karaoke in Japan has been successfully marketed in countries such as Australia, New Zealand, Southeast Asia, North America, and Europe (Kelly, 2000). Karaoke is a cross-cultural phenomenon—crossing age, gender, ethnic, and status lines. What does singing karaoke give to us? According to Kelly (1998), karaoke satisfies the desire for personal identity expression on a vocal level. We can emulate and copy our favorite singers, relieve stress, and enjoy soul-satisfying communication. Indeed, it is really a form of a fantasy fulfillment. The TV contest show *American Idol*, for example, is a huge success in the United States in both its first and second seasons. The show allows individuals with little, some, and plenty of talent to sing in front of a mass audience. This is, in reality, an integrative function of the need for personal identity expression and personal identity attention, and at the same time, it creates a shared experience of audience participation and communal solidarity.

Finally, MTV Europe also has extensive showcases for rappers. In 1999, MTV Europe launched three 24-hour digital programming services in the United Kingdom. For example, MTV Base in England, the first music channel dedicated exclusively to R&B and dance music, reflects hybrid global hip-hop music trends. The success of rap and hip-hop covers MTV Latin America, MTV Australia, and MTV Asia. As cultural boundaries blur via MTV music generations, music is no longer ethnic-specific or genre-specific. Instead, music has crafted a communal space or global sound stage for e.net'ers to relate to one another, to vent, and to be heard at the soulful level. What is fashionable and soulful in Asian, Latin American, and European regions is also fashionable in the United States or New Zealand. This created, e.net-shared music space appears to transcend ethnicity, culture, and gender groups.

Fashion and Gadgets: Identity Construction

A consumer's sense of alienation from the actual cultural world often pushes her or him to search for something more communal in terms of social ties. One way to connect is to keep up-to-date on the latest fashion. In recent years, you might have noticed young girls in Japan known as *ganguro* or *yamanba*. *Ganguro* ("black faces") visit tanning salons regularly to maintain a dark-brown tan or apply a dark-brown foundation. They dye their hair brown or gold and wear blue contact lenses. The result is a combination of the California beach girl and disco era looks. The centerpiece of their look is the six-inch, or higher, platform shoes or sandals. Despite the hazards of wearing platforms, these shoes have been in fashion for some time now. Though the trend is fading, it is part of an ongoing identity evolution of Japan's female teenagers and part of the constructed e.net identity.

In an article about this fashion statement, Murakami Mutsuko (2000, February 11) claimed that not only is this look uniquely Japanese, but "it is a magnet for young women armed with wads of yen and looking for ideas to spend them on" (p. 1). To understand this fashion statement in Japan, we must probe a little deeper. The image of Japanese *ganguro* girls exists because they perceive themselves as not fitting into the "norms" of any groups. These outgroup members (or *ganguro* girls) seek out clubs that advocate difference, and in these clubs, they find a sense of community acceptance. The Japanese traditional values of conformity and collectivism appear to be too confining to them. They intentionally "darken" their skin colors to imitate African American women in the United States—as part of a disenfranchised or marginal group. Of course, the African American women might find this fashion odd or even "distasteful." In carving out their borrowed identities, the *ganguro* girls are making a clear statement of rebellion against the traditional idea of White/pale skin as the standard of beauty and are advocating their own imitational brand of identity uniqueness.

Another fashion statement is *athletic wear*. Some sporting events are equivalent to a fashion show: Teams who compete wear uniforms symbolizing their team logo and showcasing their identity in front of a national or international audience. In the 2002 Winter Olympics, for example, many U.S. individuals clicked onto the Net to purchase the Root's brand Canadian hat and jackets worn by the players. The look was "chic" and different. Capitalizing on such interest in sportswear, big firms such as Nike, Addidas, and Reebok "donate" money to individual teams to represent their products. As a result, these brands are all household names. Nike is a worldwide corporation, with factories in Indonesia, China, Taiwan, and Vietnam. Michael Jordan, a former Chicago Bulls basketball star, was the highest paid representative for

Nike. Michael Jordan's global success is unprecedented. He is the most popular man in China, although he has never set foot there!

E.net'ers are also often quick to pick up on the latest electronic gadgets online. For example, the diffusion of the *mobile phone* came primarily from Japan. Mobile phones quickly became a popular way to communicate in a very densely populated city. In places such as Africa and Pakistan, mobile phones were quickly embraced due to the efficiency and low cost of the call. In the United States, the growth of the mobile phone has been a bit slower. Only 50 percent of the U.S. population own mobile phones, compared with the 85 percent who own a mobile phone in Asia and Europe. It is inevitable that in several years mobile telephones will replace the use of fixed-line phones on a global level.

The mobile phone becomes part of an e.net identity when an individual makes distinctive, personal choices to mark his or her unique e.net self. For example, the sale of downloading personal ringing tones has been lucrative for cell phone companies. Personal text messaging is another popular component to the cell phone. However, Asian users rely more frequently on reading text messages and drawing icons than on talking on the phone. Finally, cell phones can mark our identities through the use of personalized items. For example, one can order a very intricate cell phone: It flashes while it rings, has a downloaded dragon on the faceplate, and has little bells attached to the antenna.

As a form of communication, the mobile phone distracts the user from face-to-face conversation. In the past, face-to-face conversations could last for hours. Now, during a conversation, as college graduate Dan claims, "I can't go ten minutes without my friend answering the phone. My father owns a construction company in Oakland, California. In 1999, he purchased phones for all his employees and managers. These 100 phones were to be used strictly for business purposes. Now, it is a social tool. The mobile phone is a main channel of everyone being hooked up to everyone else. Phones are part of the everyday workplace. People are constantly talking on the phone in the field. My father is really furious about how the cell phone has gone from a work tool to a social tool for all of his contractors" (Personal interview with Dan Sullivan, 2003).

Fashion accessories and *electronic gadgets* are large markets for many e.net consumers. Being hip and up-to-date is a reflection of differentiating themselves from their traditional parents and from a traditional society. Being fashionable also means social belonging and upgraded social status. This e.net consumerism culture may also reflect the transitional stages and changes between the local culture and the global culture.

Video: Identity Transformation

New to media studies, the video revolution has changed the way we see our world today. There were once very quiet towns and cities without satellite dishes or VCRs. In 1985, Pico Iyer traveled to Asia and captured the *hybrid* cultures of East and West. He was one of the first to describe how, through video, U.S. culture has transformed the people of Asia:

> Suddenly, then, America could be found uncensored in even the world's most closed societies, intact, in even its most distant corners. Peasants in China or the [former] Soviet Union could now enjoy images of swimming pools, shopping malls, and other star spangled pleasures of the Affluent Society inside their own living rooms; remote villagers in Burma could now applaud Rambo's larger-than-life heroics only days after they hit the screens of Wisconsin; and the *Little House on the Prairie* was now part of the neighborhood in 108 countries around the world. (1989, p. 6)

Beyond video, video games have also significantly changed the face of the media industry. Brian Graden, MTV's Executive Vice President of Music and Talent Programming, commented, "When it comes to pacing, action, and capturing youth culture right now, it's all coming from video games" (as cited in Jensen, 2002).

New technology has definitely changed the face of video games. Japanese companies started making game machines for the home that were bigger, stronger, and faster. No longer did you need coins or change for the arcade; video games were more complex. Over 60 percent of U.S. Americans play video games (over 145 million people, with an average age of 28) (Jensen, 2002). With the advanced technology and greater talent of graphic artists, even hip-hop stars are crossing over to video games to appear as characters in games. Jeff Jensen (2002) proclaimed that video games have become "the medium, capable of creating icons (e.g., Mario, Sonic, Lara Croft), crazes (e.g., *Pokemon* and *Dance Dance Revolution* are sweeping arcades and PlayStations worldwide), and larger cultural ripples (e.g., from transforming TV sports presentations to changing the way stories are told in films)" (p. 23).

In a sense, video games allow us the same pleasure as watching reality television: living through the eyes of another and trying to find out who we are through interacting with those who are living outside of our world. We cannot talk about the influence of video games without mentioning anime. *Anime*, or animation, has become an important aspect of mainstream U.S. culture. Its popularity is not limited to the United States. Animation extends its boundaries to East Asian countries as well as Europe. Anime is a form of mainstream popular culture and an intellectually challenging art form (Napier, 2001). On television, *anime*-based shows are very popular, such as *Yuh Gi Oh* and *Pokemon*. Movies such as *Spirited Away* and *Princess Mononoke* have also done extremely well at the box office in the United States and internationally.

Through the explosion of technology, the intersection of our identities is at the edge, standing at the crossroads. Individuals dance to their own beat; they are not bound by tradition but express their identity through various Internet sources and gadgets. The four technology examples presented earlier—television, music, fashion and gadgets, and video—are all very symbolic, but they share the same pulse. For example, the Internet provides an escape from tradition-based cultural values. It also forges a sense of global communal belonging when individuals do not relate to their particular cultural or ethnic group. While searching for a sense of belonging to a group, individuals end up finding each other in cyberspace. The future of the twenty-first century depends heavily on how individuals on a global level can use new technology and popular culture productively—to engage in increased creativity, collaboration, and dialogue between the local culture level and the global consumerism level. Flexible intercultural communication skills may be one answer to start our dialogue with respect and also with genuine concern for the changes that are taking place in many local cultures.

Intercultural Toolkit: Recaps and Checkpoints

This chapter explored shifting value patterns and the development of an e.net global identity. The authors believe that the e.net culture has started a new communication revolution that drastically transforms individuals' sense of space, time, and identity issues on a global level. More important, through the dialectical lens, three dialectical challenges face e.neters in their contemporary communication process: privacy versus community, monotrack versus multitrack orientation, and identity alienation and inclusion. This section named numerous pop culture examples to illustrate global identities in action. In particular, import-export television shows, hip-hop music, fashion accessories and electronic gadgets, and video games as well as their influence on the local community and at the global level were discussed. New generations of individuals are attempting to create a distinctive e.net global identity based on a collaborative fusion of individualism and collectivism, thus, engaging in *collaborative individualism*. We need to develop e.net communication flexibility by reflecting on some of the following checkpoints:

- Our identity is vulnerable and changing. Try to develop a deeper understanding with those who share our physical space and virtual space. We are now, in some select aspects, more similar than we have been because of virtual reality influences. There is a sense of shared common-ground community with others who live across the globe.

- Flexibility allows one not to become so Internet-centric nor contact-centric. Those individuals who are not digitally savvy need to understand how the Internet can help them communicate on a different playing field. Internet-centric individuals must learn from contact-centric individuals that their behaviors may appear rude. Try to understand that an open-minded attitude can help both Internet-centric individuals (i.e., those who rely heavily on e.net exchanges) and contact-centric individuals (i.e., those who rely heavily on face-to-face contacts) to gain better insights into the other group. Remember—we learn most from people who are different from us. Creativity also blossoms because of diverse mindsets and diverse work habits.

- Be aware of the impact and export of U.S. culture. Modern technology has blurred distinctive cultural lines. Be open to those who think they share aspects of U.S. culture (at least the tip of the iceberg of U.S. culture) and who form impressions and stereotypes about U.S. culture based on this exported culture.

- Ask questions in a culture-sensitive manner! Do not be afraid to seek additional information when you are not sure about the e.net identity of another. Learn to be patient with nontechnological cultural types and vice versa.

- Because of the influence of different electronic gadgets, we are going to communicate more and more with individuals who have diverse learning styles (e.g., visual, auditory, tactile/kinesthetic); we need to be mindful of our own learning styles and also respectful of and adaptive to others' learning styles and preferences. ✦

Chapter 13

How Can We Become Ethical Intercultural Communicators?

Chapter Outline

In recent years, Ireland has experienced a massive rise in the number of children born to foreign nationals, specifically, women from sub-Saharan Africa and a majority of them from Nigeria. Ireland is the only European Union (EU) country that grants automatic citizenship to babies born within its borders. In 2002, 3,000 non-EU immigrants were granted Irish residency because they were parents of babies born in Ireland. However, in 2003, the Irish Supreme Court ruled that parents of such children would not automatically qualify for Irish citizenship anymore.

Amazingly, a number of these women continued to travel while actually in painful labor. There was usually little time for medical pre-screening and prenatal care. Many of the Nigerian women put their own health and lives in jeopardy, in the hope that their babies would gain Irish citizenship and, hence, have better lives in their newly adopted homelands.

—BBC News,
October 16, 2003

In many intercultural situations, we have to make choices about how to solve problems, how to make decisions, and how to arrive at ethical judgments of what constitutes right or wrong behavior. In reading the above news story, what is your reaction? Is it fear for the mother, fear for the baby, concern for the overcrowded Irish hospitals, or concern that non-EU immigrants are taking advantage of the Irish citizenship program? In making an ethical decision, there are many things to think about, such as the intent, the action, the consequence, the situation, and the cultural context of the case.

In any intercultural decision-making situation, we have to make hard choices between upholding our own cultural values and considering the values of the other culture. We also have to consider our own personal values and the values and motives of the persons in the ethical dilemma situation. Many of these choices have to do with whether or not we should emphasize our own cultural/personal standards or the others' cultural/personal standpoints and motivations. In addition, we should probably be pondering the means versus the end goals.

When we behave mindlessly in an intercultural situation, we tend to judge reactively the other person's behavior based on our own cultural standards and personal preference. However, when we choose to behave mindfully, we realize that making a wise, well-balanced judgment concerning any cultural issue is a complex, multifaceted process. Much of the complexity derives from the tension between whether ethics is a culture-bound concept, or whether ethics should be understood apart from the culture.

This chapter begins by defining different ethical positions and then examining the advantages and disadvantages of these different positions. Next, it offers some core procedures, concepts, and guidelines in the development of a meta-ethical philosophy. Third, the intercultural path model, which captures the overall themes in this textbook, is presented. The chapter concludes by identifying a set of final passport checkpoints for the continuous development of intercultural communication flexibility.

Comparing Different Ethical Positions

What is ethics? *Ethics* is a set of principles of conduct that governs the behavior of individuals and groups. Ethics has been defined as a community's perspective on "what is good and bad in human conduct and it leads to norms (prescriptive and concrete rules) that regulate actions. Ethics regulates what ought to be and helps set standards for human behavior" (Paige & Martin, 1996, p. 36). Thus, ethics is a set of standards that upholds the community's expectations concerning "right" and "wrong" conduct. There are four positions in the discussion of ethics and culture. These four positions are *ethical absolutism, ethical relativism, ethical universalism*, and *meta-ethics*. Each approach has both positive and negative implications.

Ethical Absolutism Position

Before you read this section, take a couple of minutes to fill out the ethical orientation assessment (Know Thyself 13.1). Once you have determined whether you lean toward ethical absolutism or ethical relativism, read on.

Know Thyself 13.1	Discovering Your Own Ethical Position: Ethical Relativism or Ethical Absolutism?

Instructions: The following items describe how people think about themselves and communicate in various conflict situations. Let your first inclination be your guide and circle the number in the scale that best reflects your overall value. The following scale is used for each item:

4 = SA = *Strongly Agree*
3 = MA = *Moderately Agree*
2 = MD = *Moderately Disagree*
1 = SD = *Strongly Disagree*

In making cultural judgments . . .

	SA	MA	MD	SD
1. To treat each person consistently across cultures means fairness.	4	3	2	1
2. We should take cultural circumstances into account in making any judgments.	4	3	2	1
3. There should be one clear standard that all people in all cultures go by.	4	3	2	1
4. There are always exceptions to the rule— we should pay more attention to cultural insiders' viewpoints.	4	3	2	1
5. What is right is always right in all cultures.	4	3	2	1
6. What is wrong in one cultural situation may be deemed as right in another culture.	4	3	2	1
7. We should never be too flexible in applying clear, ethical principles.	4	3	2	1
8. We should understand the cultural contexts and customs before making any judgments.	4	3	2	1
9. Even if cultural circumstances change, rules are rules.	4	3	2	1
10. Without understanding the cultural traditions and values, we cannot judge fairly.	4	3	2	1

Scoring: Add up the scores on all the even-numbered items and you will find your ethical relativism score. *Ethical Relativism* score: _____. Add up the scores on all the odd-numbered items and you will find your ethical absolutism score. *Ethical Absolutism* score: _____.

Interpretation: Scores on each ethical position dimension can range from 5 to 20; the higher the score, the more ethically relative and/or ethically universal you are. If all the scores are similar on both ethical position dimensions, you hold a biethical value system.

Know Thyself 13.1   **Discovering Your Own Ethical Position: Ethical Relativism or Ethical Absolutism? (*continued*)**

☞ **Reflection Probes:** Compare your scores with a classmate's. Take a moment to think of the following questions: Where did you learn your ethics? What do you think are the pros and cons of holding an ethical relativist position? What do you think are the pros and cons of holding an ethical absolutist position? As a reminder, the ethical absolutist position can be an "imposed ethical universal" position put forward by many industrialized Western cultures to the rest of the world. Can you think of any current events that support or refute this last statement?

Ethical absolutism emphasizes the principles of right and wrong in accordance with a set of *universally* fixed standards regardless of cultural differences. Under the ethical absolutism position, the importance of cultural context is minimized. Thus, the idea of *universality* means that one set of consistent standards would guide human behavior on a global, universal level.

Ethical absolutists believe that the same fixed standards should be applied to all cultures in evaluating *good* and *bad* behavior. Unfortunately, the dominant or mainstream culture typically defines and dominates the criteria by which ethical behavior is evaluated. Cultural or ethnic differences between membership groups are often minimized (Pedersen, 1997). For example, a dominant culture may view Western medicine as the best "civilized" way of treating a patient and thus impose this view on all groups. If a Hmong woman, for example, gives birth to a new baby and requests the nurse or doctor to give her the placenta, a Western doctor may find this request to be odd, strange, or bizarre and will likely refuse such an "uncivilized" request. However, within the Hmong culture, the act of burying the placenta has extremely important cultural significance and is related directly to the migration of one's soul and also to matters of life after death (Fadiman, 1997).

The positive aspect of ethical absolutism is that one set of fixed standards is being applied to evaluate a range of practices, thus preserving cross-situational consistency. The negative aspect is that ethical absolutism is a "culturally imposed" perspective that reflects the criteria set forth by members in the dominant cultures or groups (e.g., First World nations vs. Third World nations). The ethical-absolutism approach often results in marginalizing or muting the voices of nondominant individuals and groups in both domestic and international arenas. It pushes a colonial ethnocentric worldview.

Colonial ethnocentrism is defined as the rights and privileges of groups who are in a dominant power position in a society (whether it is at a political, economic, social class, or societal level), and these groups can impose their ethical standards on other nondominant groups or powerless individuals. For example, one of the biggest debates in recent years in the United States is the legalization of gay marriages. As of May 2004, only one state (Massachusetts) legally recognizes same-sex marriages. Randy Thomasson, Executive Director of Campaign for California Families, argues vehemently that same-sex couples "disobey the clear orders of the people" and that they have "trashed the vote of the people and perverted the sacred institution of marriage" (Marech, 2003, April). The tone of the message is that heterosexual marriages are *sacred* and gay marriages are *deviant* from the standardized norms as upheld by the mainstream groups in U.S. society. However, gay couples believe that their rights and desires for marriage should be treated with respect equal to those of heterosexual couples. Same-sex couples believe that their love and long-term commitment to their partners are as sacred as the same characteristics in opposite-sex couples.

Ethical Relativism Position

Ethical relativism emphasizes the importance of understanding the cultural context in which the problematic conduct is being judged. Under the ethical-relativism position, the critical role of cultural context is maximized. It is important to elicit the interpretations and to understand problematic cases from the cultural insiders' viewpoint. The notion of relativism values understanding and evaluating behavior in accordance with the underlying traditions, beliefs, and values of the particular culture; these factors determine the evaluation of that behavior as appropriate or inappropriate.

Ethical relativists try to understand each cultural group on its own terms. They advocate the importance of respecting the values of another culture and using those value systems as standards for ethical judgments. They emphasize that *ethical* and *unethical* practices should be understood from a cultural insider lens (Barnlund, 1980). The positive implication of this approach is that it takes the role of culture seriously in its ethical decision-making process. It takes into account the importance of ethnorelativism rather than ethnocentrism.

However, the danger is that this view encourages too much cultural flexibility and ignores ethical principles that are developed beyond each cultural context. Thus, evaluative standards of ethical behavior are related closely to the conventional customs in each cultural context. These standards can then vary from place to place, group to group, and culture to culture.

Furthermore, ethical relativism can continue to perpetuate intolerable cultural practices (e.g., female genital mutilation in Somalia and Sudan). Dominant groups in a society are often the ones that preserve cruel or intolerable cultural practices for their own gratification. They also perpetuate those practices that reinforce the status quo, which maintains its one-upmanship and keeps nondominant groups in sub-servient, powerless roles.

Ethical Universalism Position

A third approach, a derived **ethical-universalism** position, empha-sizes the importance of deriving universal ethical guidelines by placing ethical judgments within the proper cultural context. Evaluations about "good" or "bad" behaviors require knowledge about the underly-ing similarities across cultures and about the unique features of a cul-ture (Pedersen, 1997). A derived ethical universalism approach high-lights an integrative culture-universal and culture-specific interpretive framework. Unfortunately, this is easier said than done.

Although a derived universalistic stance is an ideal goal to strive toward, it demands collaborative dialogue, attitudinal openness, and hard work from members of all gender, ethnic, and cultural groups. It demands that all voices be heard and affirmed. It also demands equal power distributions among all groups that represent a diverse range of cultures. Furthermore, under authentic trusting conditions, represen-tatives of diverse groups should also be able to speak up with no fear of sanctions. Most of the current "ethical universalism" approaches, unfortunately, are "imposed ethics" that rely heavily on Eurocentric moral philosophies to the exclusion of many minority group voices. Ethical universalism is an ideal goal to strive for—especially when multinational inclusive efforts have been made to include representa-tive members from all disenfranchised groups to share their visions, dreams, and hopes.

Meta-Ethics Contextualism Position

A more analytical perspective for guiding our actions in contempo-rary society may be that of the meta-ethics contextualism position. This approach emphasizes the importance of understanding the prob-lematic practice from a layered, contextual stance. A **layered contex-tual perspective** means that the application of ethics can be under-stood only through peeling away the different layers of the ethical dilemma—using in-depth case-by-case understanding, layer-by-layer 360-degree analysis, person-by-person consideration, situation-by-sit-uation probes, intention-and-consequence comparative viewpoints, and integrative inclusion of ethnorelative and humanistic concerns.

From this meta-ethics or layered contextual perspective, subscrib-ers tend to treat each ethical dilemma as a unique case with unique conditions, and each context as a unique ethical context that deserves the full attention, effort, and time commitment of in-depth analysis. Ethical contextualists emphasize the importance of systematic data collection from a wide range of sources plus the important consideration of taking the total situation and the total cultural system into account. They also encourage the importance of cultivating creative options and seeking globally inclusive solutions to address these ethically wrangling situations. They try hard to move beyond polarized either-or thinking and advocate the importance of using human imagination and a creative mindset to come to some constructive resolution.

The strength of this approach is that it emphasizes in-depth fact-finding and layer-by-layer interpretations. It also takes into serious consideration the importance of culture, context, persons, intentions, means, consequences, and global humanism. The problem is that the layered contextual perspective is a time-consuming approach that involves lots of human power, hard work, fact-finding, and collaborative back-and-forth negotiation from diverse cultural groups. The plus side is that, in the long run, the time invested to understand the problematic practice from multiple contextual angles may ultimately help to save time and prevent further human suffering.

With clarity of understanding of the context that frames the behavior in question (on multiple sociohistorical, sociocultural, sociopolitical, socioeconomic, and situational levels), intercultural learners can make mindful choices concerning their own degree of commitment in approaching ethical situations. The concept of meta-ethics contextualism is really a broader philosophical outlook on how an ethical dilemma should be conceptualized and approached. It implies the importance of understanding the richly layered contexts that give rise to the right or wrong behavior. To engage in a contextually sensitive layered analysis, the next section suggests some practical guidelines to help you in framing your ethical stance.

Meta-Ethics: Procedures and Guidelines

The term **meta-ethics** basically refers to the cultivation of an ethical way of thinking in our everyday lives that transcends any particular ideological position. To prepare ourselves to develop an everyday meta-ethics mindset, we may use the recommendations from ethical experts (e.g., Moorthy et al., 1998) who outline the following preliminary procedures in analyzing problematic international business cases:

1. Collecting factual data (i.e., before rushing to premature conclusions, check out the details and facts of the case from multiple, interpretive angles).

2. Considering the total situation and the cultural context (i.e., suspend ethnocentric judgment and be willing to see things from the other cultural frame of reference).

3. Identifying the intentions and motives of others from three viewpoints: the intention independent of the action, the action independent of the intention, and both the intention and the action taken as a whole.

4. Analyzing the weighted positive and negative consequences that follow from the intention and action taken together.

Good intentions are necessary for good action; however, you usually cannot know the true intentions of others. You can only observe their actions and infer backward. However, you do know and should systematically train yourself to know transparently what your own intentions or motives are for why you behave the way you behave in a particular situation. Thus, you can assume full responsibility for your own decision-making choices and, hence, strive to act ethically in both intentions and actions.

Though you may encounter many ambiguities in your own developmental decision-making stage, do recognize that ambiguities are part of a maturing inquiry process. You can learn to live with ambiguous feelings while searching for the kernel of truth in a case. Additionally, you can motivate yourself to move forward, to think proactively of the multiple consequences of each of your choices in assessing an ethical dilemma.

Identifying Key Meta-Ethics Concepts

Ethical scholars recommend serious consideration of some of the following meta-ethics concepts—*rights, duties, traditions and stories, fairness and justice, consequences, virtues,* and *ideals*—in analyzing a particular ethical dilemma (Moorthy et al., 1998).

Rights are what you are entitled to as a human being or as a citizen of a country. We can think of human rights—the right to an abuse-free life—and everything is secondary to that tenet. The right to clean air, clean water, basic food and shelter, and freedom of movement and thoughts are, of course, also very critical. We can also think of civic rights—the rights of a citizen or permanent resident in accordance with the laws of a country. For example, the *habeas corpus* law in the United States means you cannot detain or jail individuals without letting them know what the charges are that are being brought against them.

When confronting an ethical dilemma, you can ask these key questions: Whose rights are being violated in the problematic case and with what consequences? Who or which group perpetuates this violation? Who or which group is suffering? The events of September 11, 2001, in the United States, for example, have dramatically affected many Arab communities across the nation. A colleague, whose last name is Mohamed, is frequently detained at the airport for lengthy periods of time. In one instance, even after showing his California driver's license, he was asked if he could show his passport in order to fly on a domestic flight. Mohamed was born and raised as a U.S. citizen in the middle of America—Iowa City, Iowa. His parents were also born and raised as U.S. citizens. Unfortunately, because of his name and physical features, he may never enjoy the full benefits and rights of a full-fledged U.S. citizen.

To counterbalance rights or entitlements, we also have to consider the concept of duties. The word **duties** implies obligations and responsibilities. Recall our opening scenario about the Nigerian women who were crossing the sea to Ireland to give birth to their babies in order to earn Irish citizenship status for them. Many of these women, no doubt, were thinking of their obligations and responsibilities as mothers to offer the best opportunities for their children to grow up in an affluent society.

The simple word *duties* has both culture-specific and culture-general aspects. The culture-*specific* aspect refers to the standardized norms and expectations of a culture in conjunction with the role performance of the individuals. From the Nigerian women's viewpoint, giving birth to babies in Ireland would guarantee their sons and daughters a brighter tomorrow. Their traditional motherhood roles reinforce their sense of obligation and duty to their children. The culture-*general* aspect, on the other hand, refers to the pan-human aspects of duty and responsibility to our fellow human beings. On this general level, every individual in a society can assume an ethical leadership role in his or her terrain. You can be an active leader in exercising your voice to speak up against injustice and human rights violation issues. You can be a "just" individual by paying fair attention to multiple sides of cultural perspectives. You can also be a positive role model by displaying mindful ethical conduct in your classroom, workplace, family, neighborhood, intimate relationships, and other facets of your everyday life.

Traditions and stories call for reflections in viewing the problematic case as part of the larger history or storyline in the cultural milieu. In any society, there are some good and some bad traditions. Good traditions or policies should be continued, and bad traditions call for social change and revolution. For example, the story in Double Take 13.1 is quite interesting and revealing.

Fairness and *justice* are twin concepts that have both personal and cultural implications. **Fairness** means equitable treatment on a personal level or on a community-interest level. For example, if you studied long hours for an exam and you noticed several classmates were cheating during the exam period, would you tell the teacher? You may decide it is none of your business, or you may feel very indignant and report the cheating incident immediately to your teacher. If the teacher does nothing, you may even report the incident to the dean because you feel it is unfair that you did all the hard work studying while the

---

Double Take 13.1
Indian Dowry: Tradition Versus Change

Through a matrimonial advertisement in an Indian newspaper, the parents arranged their daughter's, Nisha Sharman's, marriage. However, on her wedding day, Ms. Nisha Sharman unwittingly became a national heroine in India after calling off her wedding.

Ms. Sharman actually sent her groom packing to jail on their wedding day. Because, in addition to her regular dowry, the groom at the last minute demanded a car, a flat, and nearly £16,000 in cash. In India, calling off a wedding can be a lifelong stigma. Some women have been tortured or even killed by in-laws' families for inadequate dowry. Dowry tortue or death has been legally banned since 1986.

On this day, Ms. Nisha Sharman became a national heroine because of her finally saying "enough is enough" on behalf of many Indian women!

Source: Laws pertaining to dowry, http://www.ananova.com/news/story (Retrieved October 19, 2003).

---

other classmates cheated. **Justice** implies impartial treatment of cases by using a consistent set of standards in dealing with similar cases. However, words like *fair* or *unfair, just* or *unjust* often reflect the meanings and value standards of the larger cultural community. Again, it is critical to understand the different cultural viewpoints in terms of how they view the problematic situation as fair or unfair, and just or unjust.

Consequences refers to taking into consideration the ramifications that affect all parties who are directly or indirectly involved in the problematic case. For example, in the case of the Nigerian women in trying to give birth in Ireland, we should consider multiple intentions and consequences of the case by asking the following: What are the authentic intentions of the Nigerian women in giving birth to their babies in Ireland? What are the consequences of such action—to the women, to the babies, to Irish society, and so on? Why are they doing what they are doing? Do the ends justify the means? Do the means in the process bring potential risks and/or rewards to the parties who are involved directly or indirectly? What are the short-term and long-term harms and gains? Are there any alternative paths or constructive solutions to such cases? Overall, if more positive outcomes than negative consequences result from the behavior for all interested parties concerned, then the means or behavior may be justified. Simultaneously, the means or the behavior of achieving the consequence has to be humanistically virtuous.

Virtues exemplify the commendable qualities of an individual. On a universal level, the qualities of human courtesy, respect, courage, honor, dignity, and integrity may be some pan-human virtues. You may also want to add your own set of virtues at different developmental stages of your life. When in doubt, you may also want to think of how a role model (i.e., someone you admire or respect) with virtuous qualities would decide in similar circumstances. Finally, the concept of **ideals** regards actions that are not required but that you still take because it is the right thing to do. Additionally, your decisions have extrinsic and intrinsic merits to the community in which you are serving (Moorthy et al., 1998).

A *meta-ethical decision* is a discovery process, digging deeper into our own value system to find inconsistencies, resonating points, and creative problem-solving commitments. It also prompts us to gather multiple-level information to understand the reasons that give rise to these problematic practices. After understanding the reasons behind an objectionable practice, we can then decide to accept or condemn such problematic "customs." Although some questionable behaviors across cultures can be deemed to be mildly offensive (and we may be using our ethnocentric lenses to evaluate such behaviors), other practices are completely intolerable on a humanistic scale. For example, the genocide in Rwanda and the conflict in Bosnia-Herzegovina between 1992 and 1995 were atrocious acts condemned by the international community at large.

You may also think of the following two questions in making a final meta-ethical decision: (1) Can you think of creative solutions other than the ones investigated? and (2) Is there any way to prevent similar ethical dilemmas from arising in the future in this culture? Grassroots movements and the commitment to change at the local culture level are two ways to eliminate traditional problematic practices. Let us examine the following ethical case in Double Take 13.2 and discuss what you believe are the main issues from this case study.

Double Take 13.2
ABC Inc.: To Bribe or Not to Bribe?

ABC Inc. was faced with the issue of needing to pay bribes in a certain country, with full knowledge that they should not do so ethically. The only clear solution seemed to be to forgo business there. But ABC Inc. used its business savvy. Somehow, ABC Inc. learned that the bribes were not pocketed by individuals but put into a communal fund for work needed by the local community. Learning of the community's needs, ABC Inc. offered to help local officials to set up a school and a hospital for the townspeople.

Contributions were made openly and were considered part of the company's mission and social responsibility. Subsequently, the company was enthusiastically received by the local community. Interestingly enough, there was also no longer a question of being asked to pay bribes in doing business with this particular cultural community.

Adapted from Moorthy et al. (1998), p. 32.

At first glance, ABC Inc. looks like the clear winner in this case, cultivating its image as a benefactor—changing from the possible bribery approach to channeling its funds along alternative routes. When we look at this case from a meta-ethics analytical standpoint, however, the contextual reasons have to be placed against the cultural background in which the questionable practice occurs. We should also question the intention-action-consequence dynamics in the case.

So we can ask, Is it ethical that ABC Inc. continues to give money to the cultural community in the name of "charity" now? What is their authentic intention? What is their action? What are the positive versus negative consequences for the local cultural community? What are the positive versus negative consequences for ABC Inc.? Did they engage in virtuous, just, and fair practices in taking the interest of the local community into serious consideration? Are they continuing to exploit the local people, or are they actually doing something positive that would benefit the local community in the short or long term?

In each problematic ethical case, we have to mindfully place the ethical dilemma against our own personal standards and cultural judgments. We may not personally condone business bribery, but at the minimum we have to understand the societal conditions that contribute to such a practice. We can then reason that "bribery, within this cultural context, is a common practice because of the following reasons . . ." or "unfair child labor practice originated in this cultural context because . . ." Once we thoroughly understand the sociohistorical, cultural, economic, situational, and realistic reasons for a particular practice, we can then employ imaginative solutions that can benefit the local people. The following meta-ethical guidelines will further help you to clarify questions you have about making meta-ethical choices and decisions.

Meta-Ethical Decisions: Further Guidelines

Let us turn mindfully to our own ethical decision-making process on a personal level. In reading Double Take 13.3, imagine that you are reading a story about your friend Roland, who lives in Germany.

What do you think of this ethical dilemma? Should Roland steal the drug? If he asks you to go along with him to help out, will you? Why or why not? If Roland does not love his wife, should he still steal the drug for her? Why or why not? Suppose the case involves a pet animal he loves. Should Roland steal to save the pet animal? If the case involved your own mom or dad, sister or brother, close friend or life partner, would you go ahead and steal or would you see your loved one wasting away?

In everyday life, we make choices that have multiple consequences for our own lives and the lives of others. In the intercultural decision-making arena, we need to mindfully ask ourselves the following ques-

Double-Take 13.3
Roland: To Steal or Not to Steal?

Roland's wife is near death with a special kind of cancer. The only drug that the doctors think might save her is a form of radium. The drug is expensive to make. A local druggist, Hans, has the special drug but is charging 20 times what the drug cost him to make—from $200 to $4,000. Your friend Roland goes to everyone he knows to borrow the money, including asking you, but he can only get together $3,000.

Roland tells Hans, the druggist, that his wife is in agonizing pain and is dying a painful death. She really needs the new drug or she will die in the next six weeks. Roland begs Hans to sell the drug cheaper or let him pay later. But Hans responds harshly: "No! It took me years of testing to discover the drug! During this time, my own wife left me for another man and my own daughter also abandoned me! No, I am planning to make some money out of this drug!" Your friend Roland gets desperate and seriously considers breaking into the drug store and stealing the drug for his dying wife.

Adapted from Cortese (1990), p. 159.

tions when we encounter culture-based tug-and-pull ethical situations (Ting-Toomey, 1999):

1. Who or which group perpetuates this practice within this culture and with what reasons?

2. Who or which group resists this practice and with what reasons? Who is benefiting? Who is suffering—voluntarily or involuntarily?

3. Does the practice cause unjustifiable suffering to an individual or a selected group of individuals at the pleasure of another group?

4. What is my role and what is my "voice" in this ethical dilemma?

5. Should I condemn/reject this practice publicly and withdraw from the cultural scene?

6. Should I go along and find a solution that reconciles cultural differences?

7. Can I visualize alternative solutions or creative outcomes that can serve to honor the cultural traditions and at the same time get rid of the intolerable cultural practice?

8. At what level can I implement this particular creative solution? Who are my allies? Who are my enemies?

9. Should I act as a change agent in the local cultural scene via grassroots movement efforts?

10. What systematic changes in the culture are needed for the creative solution to sustain itself and filter through the system?

Many problematic cultural practices perpetuate themselves because of long-standing cultural habits or ignorance of alternative ways of doing things. Education or a desire for change from within the people in a local culture is usually how a questionable practice is ended. From a meta-ethics contextualism framework, making a sound ethical judgment demands both breadth and depth of culture-sensitive knowledge, context-specific knowledge, and genuine humanistic concern. A meta-ethics contextual philosophy can lead us to develop an inclusive mindset and pave the way to a derived set of genuine, universal ethics.

An Intercultural Discovery Path Model

Snapshot 13.1

Intercultural discovery path: Path A.

To conclude this book, let's return to the theme of flexible intercultural communication (see Snapshot 13.1). First, check out the following story in Double Take 13.4.

To be flexible intercultural communicators, we need to communicate with adaptability and creativity. We also need to learn to communicate appropriately, effectively, and ethically in a variety of intercultural situations. To engage in flexible intercultural communication, we need to take some risks and try out some new behaviors. We also need to be mindful of our own thought patterns, emotions, language usage, and nonverbal rhythms in relating to others (see Snapshot 13.2).

At the same time, we should also make a strong commitment to consider the perspectives and experiences of our intercultural partners. We also need to be willing to experiment with different styles of thinking, sensing, experiencing, valuing, behaving, and learning. In the process of changing our own approach to dealing with everyday intercultural communication, we can develop a more inclusive way of relating to individuals right next to us—in our classroom, workplace, and neighborhood. This means we need to intentionally shift our mindset from an ethnocentric state to a global, ethnorelative state.

Double Take 13.4

I was age 11 when I fled Vietnam. At the time, I had no idea that I would be leaving my parents behind for 10 years. I just remember going to a meeting place with my aunt, two sisters, and my 6-year-old nephew to board a fishing boat. The sea was incredibly rough and devastating. Out of the 96 people, 6 died. I was so deathly ill my sisters did not think I would make it. For close to 10 days we were drifting on the South China Sea. On day five, we encountered a big storm. On day six, our boat began to leak. We were slowly sinking. We saw many big ships going by, but no one wanted to help us. On day eight, two big ships came by. They saw our miserable condition but declined to help. Out of desperation, our boat captain and a few men jumped off our boat and swam to the big ships to force them to rescue us. They finally took pity on us and took us in. We survived. We ended up in Thailand.

The first seven years in the U.S. were traumatic. I could not speak English, we were poor, and I was extremely shy. I was virtually raised by my aunt, sisters, and brothers—crammed in a two-bedroom apartment. We all had to go to English school and work at various odd jobs. I had no friends. I was really lonely. The turning point came when I hit 20. I decided to go to China to study for a semester. For the first time in my life, I experienced real freedom and independence. But more important, I found friends, a group of close friends I bonded with. They accepted me for who I am. I blos-

somed and came out of my shell. I am so grateful for my China trip and my metamorphosis.

I have been in the hotel business now for 14 years. I am now a regional director of sales for an ultra-luxury hotel chain. Never did I imagine I would end up in sales: part of the job is networking and reaching out to new international clients. I have to make sure that I understand the needs and wishes of all these diverse clients and special celebrities. I guess I've slowly overcome my shyness! The job demands both personableness and confidence. At times, I'm still overwhelmed and intimidated by all these reaching out efforts and talking to international clients around the world through phone, fax, e-mails, or face to face . . . but I just keep going.

Guess I must be pretty good at it now because I have won many company awards as the top sales manager. I attribute a lot of my success to the strong support of my family and close friends. Timing in life is everything. Knowing when to open the door when the opportunity knocks is also very important. Being able to roll with the punches and being flexible and adaptable are also critical. When you encounter roadblocks or failures, don't give up easily. There is always another day. These are the lessons I've practiced in my adopted culture. It's really all about survival, *and*, yes, to *really live!*

TTB, *a Vietnamese Immigrant/Sales Director*

As his Holiness the Dalai Lama mentioned in a recent interview

Snapshot 13.2

Intercultural discovery path: Path B.

I believe that to meet the challenge of our times, human beings will have to develop a greater sense of universal responsibility. Each of us must learn to work not just for his or her own self, family or nation but also for the benefit of all humankind. Universal responsibility is the real key to human survival. It is the best foundation for world peace, the equitable use of natural resources, and through concern for future generations, the proper care of the environment . . . without knowing it, we have neglected to foster the most basic human needs of love, kindness, cooperation and caring. (*Shambhala Sun*, 2003, September, p. 63)

From Ethnocentrism to Ethnorelativism

As a vision of what we, the authors, hope you have gained by reading this textbook, we would like you to check out the *path model* (see Figure 13.1), which evolves from ethnocentrism to ethnorelativism. The model conceptualizes ethnocentrism as having two stages: defensive ethnocentrism and ambivalent ethnocentrism. **Defensive ethnocentrism** refers to having a rigidly held mindset and a tendency to create a superior-inferior gap with outgroup members. This defensive attitude leads to the use of racist jokes, hate-filled speech, aggressive acts, and even physical violence, to marginalize or obliterate outgroup members. **Ambivalent ethnocentrism,** on the other hand, refers to the confused feelings you may have about outgroup members. Cognitively, you start realizing that you have certain blind spots in yourself that you need to confront more honestly. But among outgroup members, you still act indifferent or avoidant in your behavior. Confusion or ambivalence, however, is part of an intercultural discovery journey. Confusion and bewilderment can turn into "a-ha!" insight and clarity.

Do you recall the individual falling backward along the unconscious incompetence staircase model in Chapter 1? Likewise, stumbling back and forth on the intercultural communication competence staircase takes courage, determination, and open-mindedness. We are all not perfect communicators, but we can constantly remind ourselves that we are works in progress. Thus, do not be discouraged—even the best intercultural communication specialists slip into intercultural accidents or puddles! (See Double Take 13.5, about the rabbit and the turtle race.) The key is to be mindful of each step you take along the path and try to refocus your energy and commitment and continue on your ethically guided intercultural journey (see Snapshot 13.3).

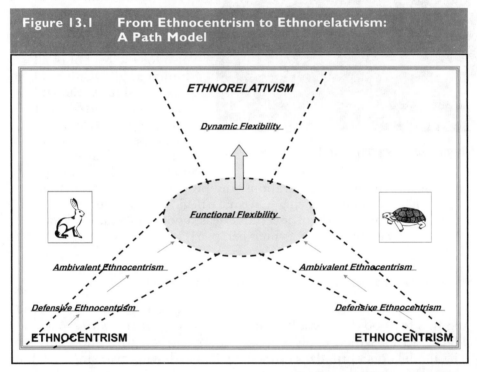

Figure 13.1   From Ethnocentrism to Ethnorelativism: A Path Model

With each incremental step, hop, or jump, you may reach the functional flexibility stage. The **functional flexibility stage** means you can function adaptively in using appropriate verbal and nonverbal styles in communicating with dissimilar others. Cognitively and affectively, however, you may continue to retain your cultural/ethnic value patterns or beliefs. It takes time to change deep-seated cultural values. You may also intentionally choose not to change the cognitive or affective layers of your identity. Finally, you may arrive at the **dynamic flexibility stage** in which you can integrate the

Snapshot 13.3

Revisiting the staircase model: As you finish reading this book, at what stage do you now think you are on the staircase model of intercultural communication competence?

Double Take 13.5
The Rabbit and the Turtle

A Rabbit one day ridiculed the short feet and slow pace of the Turtle. The Turtle, lightheartedly, replied: "Though you can be swift as the wind, I will beat you in a race." The Rabbit, believing the Turtle's assertion to be simply impossible, agreed to the proposal. They agreed that the Fox should choose the course and fix the goal.

On the day appointed for the race, the two started together. The Turtle never for a moment stopped, but went on with a slow but steady pace straight to the end of the course. The Rabbit, thinking that she had plenty of time, took a nap by the wayside, and soon fell fast asleep.

At last waking up, and moving as fast as she could, the Rabbit saw the Turtle had reached the end of the race course. Under the shade, the Turtle waited comfortably for the out-of-breath Rabbit.

Indeed, slow but steady wins the race.

Adapted from *Aesop's Fables*

best of your ethical, cognitive, affective, and behavioral layers of your identity and dance adaptively with your intercultural partner.

A dynamic, flexible intercultural communicator tries to integrate knowledge, an open-minded attitude, and culture-sensitive skills and communicates ethically with culturally dissimilar others. The following quotation sums up the spirit of *dynamic flexibility:*

> The globally literate mind is a flexible mind. It remains agile and nimble as we learn to travel across boundaries and borders. Comfortable with chaos and change, it is able to contain conflicting and often opposing forces while creating cohesion and harmony from disparate parts. It's a mind that tolerates ambiguity and difference as it builds bridges across language, politics, and religions. And it's a mind that thinks and acts at the same time, all with a sense of tolerance and balance. By combining linear, logical reasoning with circular, systematic thinking, the global mind prepares us for the twenty-first century world. (Rosen, Digh, Singer, & Phillips, 2000, p. 174)

The dynamic, flexible communicator can swing comfortably from low-context mode to a high-context mode and vice versa, code-switch from individualistic thinking to collectivistic thinking, hold both value sets simultaneously, and see the merits and filters in both value patterns. In essence, the dynamic, flexible communicator is mindful of the complex layers of self-identity and other-identity issues and is attuned to the situational context and the symbolic exchange process that flows between the two intercultural communicators (see Snapshot 13.4).

Becoming a Dynamic Global Leader

After surveying 75 CEOs in 28 countries in a landmark four-year study, Rosen and colleagues (2000) contend that the following four global literacies are critical in the making of an effective global leader:

1. *Personal literacy:* Understanding and valuing yourself

2. *Social literacy:* Engaging and challenging others

3. *Business literacy:* Focusing and mobilizing your organization

4. *Cultural literacy:* Valuing and leveraging cultural differences

Accurate, culture-based communication knowledge, an open-minded ethical posture, and flexible communication skills are three key dimensions that we believe enhance the profile of a global-minded, dynamic leader. When asked to identify the most important personal qualities for leadership, business executives (in Rosen et al.'s study, 2000, p. 67) identified the following qualities as most important:

Snapshot 13.4

Intercultural discovery path: Path C.

- Leading by example: 56 percent

- Facing change and uncertainty with confidence: 45 percent

- Being motivated by strongly held principles and beliefs: 38 percent

- Knowing one's own strengths and shortcomings: 31 percent

- Being committed to continuous learning: 30 percent

Furthermore, drawing from decades of analysis within world-class organizations, researchers indicate that *resonant leaders*—whether CEOs or managers—excel not just through personality or skill but also by connecting with others using emotional intelligence (EI) competencies (Goleman, Boyatzis, & McKee, 2002). These same researchers have identified four main domains of EI: *self-awareness, self-management, social awareness,* and *relationship management.* Drawing from EI research work (Bennett-Goleman, 2001; Goleman et al., 2002), we as authors believe that in developing a global-minded approach to ethical communication, one needs to develop a strong sense of emotional self-awareness and accurate assessment of his or her own ethnocentric states.

We also need to develop a sense of nimbleness to adapt to the changing intercultural situations on a day-to-day basis. We should therefore take time to develop both analytical and emotional empathy to experience things from the other person's cultural frame of reference. For example, to be an ethical global leader, you can assume active responsibility at your campus or workplace to foster an inclusive climate and to cultivate a respectful vision for members from diverse walks of life. You can thus serve as a positive change catalyst to inspire others to learn about intercultural and domestic diversity issues in your very own backyard.

Finally, ethical intercultural communicators practice the following passport guidelines:

- Flexible intercultural communication is adaptive.

- Flexible intercultural communication is creative.

- Flexible intercultural communication is experimental.

- Flexible intercultural communication is making detours and having the courage to try again.

- Flexible intercultural communication is knowing thyself on a continuous basis.

- Flexible intercultural communication is other-centered.

- Flexible intercultural communication is about identity respect issues.

- Flexible intercultural communication is the intentional development of mindfulness.

- Flexible intercultural communication is making hard, ethical choices.

- Flexible intercultural communication is a developmental, lifelong learning journey.

In Conclusion . . .

This book highlights some of the knowledge and skills that all of us can practice in approaching everyday intercultural situations. To engage in dynamic flexibility, we have to be simultaneously adaptive and creative in synchronizing our words, movements, and breath with the words, movements, and breath of the culturally dissimilar other. Dynamic flexibility also calls forth our adventurous spirit and risk-taking abilities in reaching out to communicate with culturally dissimilar others.

An intercultural life is a creative life that demands both playfulness and mindfulness in transforming one's intercultural journey into a discovery process. Your journey may be filled with trials and tribulations and meandering paths. However, with the knowledge and skills presented in this book and with committed practice, you will surely uncover many hidden trails and unexpected delights. May you have the courage to experiment and to explore new terrain in your everyday intercultural walk, strolling and experiencing the diverse richness of the human spirit. ✦

References

Abercrombie and Fitch. (2002). *Summer 2000* [Catalogue]. 6301 Fitch Path. New Albany, OH 43054.

Adelman, M. (1988). Cross-cultural adjustment. *International Journal of Intercultural Relations, 12*, 183–204.

Adler, N. (1997). *International dimensions of organizational behavior* (3rd ed.). Cincinnati, OH: South-Western College Publishing.

Afewerki, F. "looking at the world from my key hole." 1995-2003 EdChange.org and Paul C. Gorski.

Agar, M. (1994). *Language shock: Understanding the culture of conversation.* New York: Morrow.

Alba, R. (1990). *Ethnic identity: Transformation of White America.* New Haven, CT: Yale University Press.

Allport, G. (1954). *The nature of prejudice.* Cambridge, MA: Addison-Wesley.

Altman, I., & Taylor, D. (1973). *Social penetration.* New York: Holt, Rinehart & Winston.

Andersen, P. (1999). *Nonverbal communication: Forms and functions.* Mountain View, CA: Mayfield.

Andersen, P., Hecht, M., Hoobler, G., & Smallwood, M. (2003). Nonverbal communication across cultures. In W. Gudykunst (Ed.), *Cross-cultural and intercultural communication.* Thousand Oaks, CA: Sage.

Anderson, L. (1994). A new look at an old construct: Cross-cultural adaptation. *International Journal of Intercultural Relations, 18*, 293–328.

Archer, C. (1991). *Living with strangers in the U.S.A.: Communicating beyond culture.* Englewood Cliffs, NJ: Prentice Hall.

Arner, M. (2003, January 14). Study: Black, Latino drivers stopped more. *San Diego Union Tribune*, pp. B1, B5.

Asante, M., & Asante, K. (Eds.). (1990). *African culture: The rhythms of unity.* Trenton, NJ: African World Press.

Ash, R. (2002). *The Top 10 of everything 2003.* London: Dorling Kindersley Publishing.

Ash, R. (2003). *The Top 10 of everything 2004.* London: Dorling Kindersley Publishing.

Atkins, J., Mays, R., & Lorenzo, I. (2001). Between me and you [Ja Rule featuring Christina Milian]. On *Rule 3:36* [CD]. New York: Murder, Inc./ Def Jam.

355

Baker, M. (2001, August 21). In the land of longest hours, workers get a break, http://www.csmonitor.com/2001/0821/p1s3-woap.html (Retrieved on March 15, 2004).

Balint, K. (2002, January 17). Time-saving technology doesn't always help get us ahead. *San Diego Union Tribune*, pp. C1, C7.

Barker, O. (2001, March 21). The Asianization of America: But Eastern influences does not mean Asian Americans are insiders. *USA Today*, pp. A1, A2.

Barnlund, D. (1962). Toward a meaning-centered philosophy of communication. *Journal of Communication, 2*, 197–211.

———. (1975). *Public and private self in Japan and the United States*. Tokyo: Simul Press.

———. (1980). The cross-cultural arena: An ethical void. In N. Asuncion-Lande (Ed.), *Ethical perspectives and critical issues in intercultural communication*. Falls Church, VA: Speech Communication Association.

———. (1989). *Communicative styles of Japanese and Americans: Images and realities*. Belmont, CA: Wadsworth.

Bass, C. D. (2000, December 16). Hiring bias has sound of its own. *San Diego Union Tribune*, p. D2.

Basso, K. (1970). To give up on words: Silence in Western Apache culture. *Southern Journal of Anthropology, 26*, 213–230.

Baxter, L. A., & Montgomery, B. M. (1996). *Relating: Dialogues and dialectics*. New York: Guilford Press.

Benjamin, H. (1999). *The transsexual phenomenon* [Electronic version]. Düsseldorf, Germany: Symposion Publishing.

Bennett, J., & Bennett, M. (2004). Developing intercultural sensibility: An integrative approach to global and domestic diversity. In D. Landis, J. Bennett, & M. Bennett (Eds.), *Handbook of intercultural training* (3rd ed.). Thousand Oaks, CA: Sage.

Bennett-Goleman, T. (2001). *Emotional alchemy: How the mind can heal the heart*. New York: Three Rivers Press.

Bernstein, B. (1971). *Class, codes, and control* (Vol. 1). London: Routledge and Kegan Paul.

Berry, J. (1994). Acculturation and psychological adaptation. In A. Bouvy, F. van de Vijver, P. Boski, & P. Schmitz (Eds.), *Journeys into cross-cultural psychology*. Lisse, The Netherlands: Swets & Zeitlinger.

Berry, J. (2004). Fundamental psychological processes in intercultural relations. In D. Landis, J. Bennett, & M. Bennett (Eds.), *Handbook of intercultural training* (3rd ed.). Thousand Oaks, CA: Sage.

Berry, J., Kim, U., & Boski, P. (1987). Psychological acculturation of immigrants. In Y. Y. Kim & W. Gudykunst (Eds.), *Cross-cultural adaptation: Current approaches*. Newbury Park, CA: Sage.

Berscheid, E., & Reis, H. (1998). Attraction and close relationships. In D. Gilbert, S. Fiske, & G. Lindzey (Eds.), *The handbook of social psychology* (4th ed.). Boston: McGraw-Hill.

Bharati, A. (1985). The self in Hindu thought and action. In A. Marsella, G. DeVos, & F. Hsu (Eds.), *Culture and self: Asian and Western perspectives*. New York: Tavistock.

Bianchi, A., & Sama, G. (2003, May 7). Brands enter lexicon in Latin America. *Wall Street Journal*, p. B6.

Bird, E. (1999). Images of the American Indian in popular media. *Journal of Communication, 49*(3), 61–83.

Black, J., Gregersen, H., Mendenhall, M., & Stroh, L. (1999). *Globalizing people through international assignments*. New York: Addison-Wesley Longman.

Blake, D., & Griffin, G. (2002). Addictive [Truth Hurts]. On *Truthfully speaking* [CD]. Aftermath/Interscope Records.

Blank, R., & Slipp, S., with Ford, V. (2000). *From the outside in: Seven strategies for success when you're not a member of the dominant group in your workplace*. New York: Amacom.

Bochner, S. (1986). Coping with unfamiliar culture: Adjustment or culture learning? *Australian Journal of Psychology, 38*, 347–358.

Bragg, R. (2002, June 30). A few hang on to sinking Louisiana island. *Honolulu Star Bulletin*, p. A5.

Brett, J. (2001). *Negotiating globally: How to negotiate deals, resolve disputes, and make decisions across cultural boundaries*. San Francisco: Jossey-Bass.

Brewer, M. (1991). The social self: On being same and different at the same time. *Personality and Social Psychology Bulletin, 17*, 475–482.

Brewer, M., & Miller, N. (1996). *Intergroup relations*. Pacific Grove, CA: Brooks/Cole.

Brislin, R. (1993). *Understanding culture's influence on behavior*. Fort Worth, TX: Harcourt Brace Jovanovich.

———. (2003, January 19). Culture clash: Understanding other cultures means moving beyond ethnocentrism and prejudice. *Star Bulletin*. http://www.starbulletin.com/columnist/column.php?%20id=2282&col_id=19

Brooks, D. (2003, November 8). Love, Internet syle. *New York Times*. http://www.nytimes.com/2003/11/8/opinion/08BROO.html?th

Brown, D. (2003, January 11). O'Neal issues apology. *Los Angeles Times*, pp. D1, D7.

Burgoon, J. (2000). Cross-cultural and intercultural application of expectancy violation theory. In R. Wiseman (Ed.), *Intercultural communication theory*. Thousand Oaks, CA: Sage.

Burgoon, J., Buller, D., & Woodall, W. G. (1996). *Nonverbal communication: The unspoken dialogue* (2nd ed.). New York: McGraw-Hill.

Burns, J. (2003, September 21). Cherokee tribe aims to revive language. *San Diego Union Tribune*, A4, A16.

Buss, A. (2001). *Psychological dimensions of the self*. Thousand Oaks, CA: Sage.

Buss, D. et al. (1990). International preferences in selecting mates: A study of 37 cultures. *Journal of Cross-Cultural Psychology, 21*, 5–47.

Byrne, D. (1971). *The attraction paradigm*. New York: Academic Press.

Cai, D., & Fink, E. (2002). Conflict style differences between individualists and collectivists. *Communication Monographs, 69*, 67–87.

Carbaugh, D. (1996). *Situating selves: The communication of social identities in American scenes*. Albany: State University of New York Press.

Carroll, R. (1987). *Cultural misunderstandings: The French-American experience.* Chicago: University of Chicago Press.

Carter, S., Mosley, T., Joshua, K., Butler, C., & Freeman, B. (1999). Big Pimpin (with UKG). On *Volume 3: The life and time of Shawn Carter* [CD]. New York: Roc-a-fella/Def Jam Records.

Chaika, E. (1989). *Language: The social mirror* (2nd ed.). New York: Newbury House.

Chang, W.C., Chua, W. L., & Toh, Y. (1997). The concept of psychological control in the Asian context. In K. Leung, U. Kim, S. Yamaguchi, & Y. Kashima (Eds.), *Progress in Asian social psychology* (Vol. 1). New York: John Wiley.

Charon, J. (2004). *Ten questions: A sociological perspective* (5th ed.). Belmont, CA: Wadsworth.

Chen, G.-M. (2001). Toward transcultural understanding: A harmony theory of Chinese Americans. In V. Milhouse, M. Asante, & P. Nwosu (Eds.), *Transcultural realities: Interdisciplinary perspectives on cross-cultural relations.* Thousand Oaks, CA: Sage.

Chen, L. (1997). Verbal adaptive strategies in U.S. American dyads with U.S. Americans or East Asian partners. *Communication Monographs, 64,* 302–323.

Chu, H. (2003, February 8). A South Korean star came out of the closet and fell into disrepute. *Los Angeles Times,* p. A3.

Chung, L. (1998). *Ethnic identity and intergroup communication among Korean Americans and Vietnamese Americans in Oklahoma.* Unpublished doctoral dissertation, University of Oklahoma.

Chung, L. C., & Ting-Toomey, S. (1994, July). *Ethnic identity and relational expectations among Asian Americans.* Paper presented at the annual conference of the International Communication Association, Sydney, Australia.

——. (1999). Ethnic identity and relational expectations among Asian Americans. *Communication Research Reports, 16,* 157–166.

Church, A. (1982). Sojourner adjustment. *Psychological Bulletin, 91,* 540–572.

Cohen, R. (1987). Problems of intercultural communication in Egyptian-American diplomatic relations. *International Journal of Intercultural Relations, 11,* 29–47.

——. (1991). *Negotiating across cultures: Communication obstacles in international diplomacy.* Washington, DC: U.S. Institute of Peace.

Cole, M. (1990, November). Relational distances and personality influences on conflict communication. Paper presented at the annual conference of the Speech Communication Association, Chicago, IL.

Collier, M. J. (1991). Conflict competence within African, Mexican, and Anglo American friendships. In S. Ting-Toomey & F. Korzenny (Eds.), *Cross-cultural interpersonal communication.* Newbury Park, CA: Sage.

——. (Ed.). (2001). *Constituting cultural difference through discourse.* Thousand Oaks, CA: Sage.

Cortese, A. (1990). *Ethnic ethics: The restructuring of moral theory.* Albany, NY: State University of New York Press-Albany.

Crohn, J. (1995). *Mixed matches: How to create successful interracial, interethnic, and interfaith marriages.* New York: Ballantine/Fawcett.

Cross, W., Jr. (1971). The Negro-to-Black conversion experience: Toward a psychology of black liberation. *Black World, 20,* 13–27.

——. (1978). The Thomas and Cross models on psychological Nigrescence: A literature review. *Journal of Black Psychology, 4,* 13–31.

——. (1991). *Shades of Black: Diversity in African-American identity.* Philadelphia: Temple University Press.

——. (1995). The psychology of Nigrescence: Revising the Cross model. In J. Ponterotto, J. Casas, L. Suzuki, & C. Alexander (Eds.), *Handbook of multicultural counseling.* Thousand Oaks, CA: Sage.

Cross, W., Jr., Smith, L., & Payne, E. (2002). Black identity: A repertoire of daily enactments. In P. Pedersen, J. Draguns, W. Lonner, & J. Trimble (Eds.), *Counseling across cultures* (5th ed.). Thousand Oaks, CA: Sage.

Csikszentmihalyi, M. (1996). *Creativity: Flow and the psychology of discovery and invention.* New York: HarperCollins.

Cupach, W., & Canary, D. (Eds.). (1997). *Competence in interpersonal conflict.* New York: McGraw-Hill.

Cushner, K., & Brislin, R. (1996). *Intercultural interactions: A practical guide* (2nd ed.). Thousand Oaks, CA: Sage.

Dalai Lama. (2003, September). Developing the mind of great capacity. *Shambhala Sun,* pp. 53–63.

Davis, W. (1999, August). Vanishing cultures. *National Geographic, 196*(2), 62–90.

"Death Toll of September 11," http://www.cnn.com/2003/US/09/11/sept11.vigils/index.html (Retrieved January 25, 2004).

DellaPergola, S. (2003, January). World Jewish population. In D. Singer, & L. Grossman, L. (Eds.), *American Jewish Yearbook 2002.* New York: American Jewish Committee.

Devine, P., Hamilton, D., & Ostrom, T. (1994). *Social cognition: Impact on social psychology.* New York: Academic Press.

Dion, K. K., & Dion, K. L. (1996). Cultural perspectives on romantic love. *Personal Relationships, 3,* 5–17.

Earley, P. C., & Ang, S. (2003). *Cultural intelligence: Individual interactions across cultures.* Stanford, CA: Stanford University Press.

Edna, D. (2003, February). Ask dame Edna. *Vanity Fair, 510,* 116.

Edwards, J. (1994). *Multilingualism.* London: Routledge.

Ekman, P. (1972). Universals and cultural differences in facial expressions of emotion. In J. Cole (Ed.), *Nebraska Symposium on Motivations, 1971.* Lincoln, NE: University of Nebraska Press.

Ekman, P. (2003). *Emotions revealed: Recognizing faces and feelings to improve communication and emotional life.* New York: Times Books.

Ekman, P., & Friesen, W. (1969). The repertoire of nonverbal behavior: Categories, origins, usage, and coding. *Semiotica, 1,* 49–98.

Ekman, P., & Friesen, W. (1975). *Unmasking the face.* Englewood Cliffs, NJ: Prentice-Hall.

Elliott, M., & Mosley, T. (2001). Get Ur Freak On [Missy Elliott]. On *So Addictive* [CD]. New York: Electra/Asylum.

Espiritu, Y. (1992). *Asian American panethnicity.* Philadelphia: Temple University Press.

Fadiman, A. (1997). *The Spirit catches you and you fall down.* New York: Farrar, Straus, & Giroux.

Farb, P. (1973). *Word play: What happens when people talk?* New York: Bantam Books.

Feagin, J. (1989). *Racial and ethnic relations* (3rd ed.). Englewood Cliffs, NJ: Prentice-Hall.

Feller, B. (2003, November 24). Students rule net population. *Marketing News, 37(24),* 5

Fishburn, D., & Green, S. (Eds.). (2003, January). 2002: The year in review. *The Economist* [Special issue]. London, UK.

Foeman, A. K., & Nance, T. (1999). From miscegenation to multiculturalism: Perceptions and stages of interracial relationship development. *Journal of Black Studies, 29(4),* 540–557.

Fong, C., & Yung, J. (1995/1996). In search of the right spouse: Interracial marriage among Chinese and Japanese Americans. *Amerasia Journal, 21*(3), 77–98.

Fowler, G. (2003). Labels find east-west duets boost sales. *Wall Street Journal,* pp. B1, B4.

Frankenberg, R. (1993). *White women, race matters: The social construction of whiteness.* Minneapolis, MN: University of Minnesota Press.

Freilich, M. (1989). Introduction: Is culture still relevant? In M. Frielich (Ed.), *The relevance of culture.* New York: Morgan & Garvey.

Furnham, A. (1988). The adjustment of sojourners. In Y. Y. Kim & W. Gudykunst (Eds.), *Cross-cultural adaptation.* Newbury Park, CA: Sage.

Furnham, A., & Bochner, S. (1982). Social difficulty in a foreign culture. In S. Bochner (Ed.), *Cultures in contact.* Elmsford, NY: Pergamon.

Gannon, M. (2004). *Understanding global cultures: Metaphorical journeys through 28 nations, clusters of nations, and continents* (3rd. ed.). Thousand Oaks, CA: Sage.

Gao, G. (1991). Stability in romantic relationships in China and the United States. In S. Ting-Toomey & F. Korzenny (Eds.), *Cross-cultural interpersonal communication.* Newbury Park, CA: Sage.

Gao, G., & Ting-Toomey, S. (1998). *Communicating effectively with the Chinese.* Thousand Oaks, CA: Sage.

Garcia, W. R. (1996). Respeto: A Mexican base for interpersonal relationships. In W. Gudykunst, S. Ting-Toomey, & T. Nishida (Eds.), *Communication in personal relationships across cultures.* Thousand Oaks, CA: Sage.

Gardenschwartz, L., & Rowe, A. (1998). *Managing diversity in health care.* San Francisco: Jossey-Boss.

Gender Public Advocacy Coalition. (GPAC). Retrieved from http://www.gpac.org/

Gitanjali. (1994). Second generation; Once removed. In C. Camper (Ed.), *Miscegenation blues: Voices of mixed race women.* Toronto, Canada: Sister Voices. [Interview excerpt: p. 133]

Glenn, F. (1981). *Man and mankind.* Norwood, NJ: Ablex.

Goleman, D., Boyatzis, R., & McKee, A. (2002). *Primal leadership: Realizing the power of emotional intelligence.* Boston: Harvard Business School Press.

Gonzalez, A., Houston, M., & Chen, V. (Eds.). (2004). *Our voices: Essays in culture, ethnicity, and communication* (4th ed.). Los Angeles: Roxbury.

Gottman, J., & Silver, N. (1999). *The seven principles for making marriage work.* New York: Crown.

Granovetter, M. (1973). The strength of weak ties. *American Journal of Sociology, 78,* 1360–1380.

Griffen, G. (2003, September 9). As roles for Latinos increase, many actors hiring coaches to turn accent on or off. *San Diego Union Tribune,* p. E.1.

Gudykunst, W. (2003). Intercultural communication theories. In W. Gudykunst (Ed.), *Cross-cultural and intercultural communication.* Thousand Oaks, CA: Sage.

——. (2004). *Bridging differences: Effective intergroup communication* (4th ed.). Thousand Oaks, CA: Sage.

Gudykunst, W., & Lee, C. (2003). Cross-cultural communication theories. In W. Gudykunst (Ed.), *Cross-cultural and intercultural communication.* Thousand Oaks, CA: Sage.

Gudykunst, W., Matsumoto, Y., Ting-Toomey, S., Nishida, T., Kim, K. S., & Heyman, S. (1996). The influence of cultural individualism-collectivism, self construals, and individual values on communication styles across cultures. *Human Communication Research, 22,* 510–543.

Gudykunst, W., & Ting-Toomey, S., with Chua, E. (1988). *Culture and interpersonal communication.* Newbury Park, CA: Sage.

Guerrero, L., Andersen, P. A., & Afifi, W. (2001). *Close encounters: Communicating in relationships.* Mountain View, CA: Mayfield.

Gullahorn, J. T., & Gullahorn, J. E. (1963). An extension of the U-curve hypothesis. *Journal of Social Issues, 19,* 33–47.

Hague, M. (1985). *Aesop's fables.* New York: Henry Holt.

Hall, E. T. (1959). *The silent language.* New York: Doubleday.

——. (1966). *The hidden dimension* (2nd ed.). Garden City, NY: Anchor/Doubleday.

——. (1976). *Beyond culture.* New York: Doubleday.

——. (1983). *The dance of life.* New York: Doubleday.

Hall, E. T., & Hall, M. (1987). *Hidden differences: Doing business with the Japanese.* Garden City, NY: Anchor Press/Doubleday.

Halvorson, G. (2003, August 8). Diversity done well, is a clear winner. *CEO Journal online.* www.insidekp.kp.org/insidekp/communicate/CEOhome/ceojournal/2003_journal/ceojournal_08

Hamon, R., & Ingoldsby, B. (Eds.). (2003). *Mate selection across cultures.* Thousand Oaks, CA: Sage.

Haslett, B. (1989). Communication and language acquisition within a cultural context. In S. Ting-Toomey & F. Korzenny (Eds.), *Language, communication, and culture.* Newbury Park, CA: Sage.

Healy, J. (2003). *Race, ethnicity, gender, and class: The sociology of group conflict and change* (3rd ed.). Thousand Oaks, CA: Pine Forge Press.

Heath, C. (2002, November 14). The next Christina Aguilera. *Rolling Stone Magazine, 909,* 50–55.

Hecht, M., Collier, M. J., & Ribeau, S. (1993). *African American communication: Ethnic identity and cultural interpretation.* Newbury Park, CA: Sage.

Hecht, M., & Ribeau, S. (1984). Sociocultural roots of ethnic identity. *Journal of Black Studies, 21,* 501–513.

Hecht, M., Ribeau, S., & Sedano, M. (1990). A Mexican American perspective on interethnic communication. *International Journal of Intercultural Relations, 14,* 31–55.

Helms, J. (Ed.). (1993). *Black and White racial identity: Theory, research, and practice.* Westport, CT: Praeger.

Hickman, J. (2002, July 8). America's 50 best companies for minorities. *Fortune Magazine, 146*(1), 110–120.

Hickson, M., III, Stacks, D., & Moore, N.-J. (2004). *Nonverbal communication: Studies and application* (4th ed.). Los Angeles: Roxbury.

Ho, M. K. (1987). *Family therapy with ethnic minorities.* Newbury Park, CA: Sage.

Hofstede, G. (1991). *Cultures and organizations: Software of the mind.* London: McGraw-Hill.

——. (1998). *Masculinity and femininity: The taboo dimension of national culture.* Thousand Oaks, CA: Sage.

——. (2001). *Culture's consequences: Comparing values, behaviors, institutions, and organizations across nations* (2nd ed.). Thousand Oaks, CA: Sage.

Hotz, R. L. (2000, January 25). The struggle to save dying languages. *Los Angeles Times,* pp. A1, A14–A16.

Howell, W. (1982). *The empathic communicator.* Belmont, CA: Wadsworth.

Hum, T. (2002). Asian and Latino immigration and the revitalization of Sunset Park, Brooklyn. In L.T. Vo & R. Bonus (Eds.), *Contemporary Asian American Communities.* Philadelphia: Temple University Press.

Hymes, D. (1972). Models of the interaction of language and social life. In J. Gumperz & D. Hymes (Eds.), *Directions in sociolinguistics: The ethnography of communication.* New York: Holt, Rinehart & Winston.

http://news.bbc.co.uk/1/hi/world/europe/3199024.stm.

"Irish baby laws attract Africans." (2003, October 16). *BBC News.*

Iyer, P. (1989). *Video night in Kathmandu and other reports from the not-so-Far-East.* New York: Vintage Departures.

Jackson, R. (1999). *The negotiation of cultural identity.* Westport, CT: Praeger.

Jenkins, C. (2000, October 24). Piazza takes heat for keeping his cool. *San Diego Union Tribune,* pp. D1, D6.

Jensen, J. (2002, December 6). Video game nation: How games are changing the face of pop culture. *Entertainment Weekly, 685,* 20–43.

Johnson, D. W. (1986). *Reaching out: Interpersonal effectiveness and self-actualization* (3rd ed.). Englewood Cliffs, NJ: Prentice Hall.

Johnson, M. (1991). Commitment to personal relationships. In W. Jones & D. Perlman (Eds.), *Advances in personal relationship* (3). London: Kingsley.

Jones, J. (1997). *Prejudice and racism* (2nd ed.). New York: McGraw-Hill.

Judy, R., & D'Amico, C. (1997). *Work force 2020: Work and workers in the 21st century.* Indianapolis, IN: Hudson Institute.

Kapnick, S. (1999, January). What's for breakfast? *Hemispheres: United Airlines Inflight Magazine, 100–106.*

Kashima, Y., & Triandis, T. (1986). The self-serving bias in attributions as a coping strategy: A cross-cultural study. *Journal of Cross-Cultural Psychology, 17, 83–97.*

Kelly, R. (2000). Feelin in your Booty. On *TP-2.com* [CD]. New York: Jive.

Kim, E. (1996). Personal story in Apendix. In E. Kim & E. Ying-Yu (Eds.), *East to America: Korean American life stories.* New York: New Press.

Kim, M.-S. (2002). *Non-western perspectives on human communication: Implications for theory and practice.* Thousand Oaks, CA: Sage.

Kim, M.-S., & Kitani, K. (1998). Conflict management of Asian- and Caucasian-Americans in romantic relationships. *Journal of Asian Pacific Communication, 8, 51–68.*

Kim, M.-S., & Wilson, S. (1994). A cross-cultural comparison of implicit theories of requesting. *Communication Monographs, 61, 210–235.*

Kim, Y. Y. (1988). *Communication and cross-cultural adaptation: An integrative theory.* Clevedon, UK: Multilingual Matters.

———. (2001). *Becoming intercultural: An integrative theory of communication and cross-cultural adaptation.* Thousand Oaks, CA: Sage.

———. (2003). Adapting to an unfamiliar culture: An interdisciplinary overview. In W. Gudykunst (Ed.), *Cross-cultural and intercultural communication.* Thousand Oaks, CA: Sage.

———. (2004). Long-term cross-cultural adaptation: Training implications of an integrative theory. In D. Landis, J. Bennett, & M. Bennett (Eds.), *Handbook of intercultural training* (3rd ed.). Thousand Oaks, CA: Sage.

Kitano, H., Fujino, D., & Sato, J. (1998). Interracial marriages. In L. Lee & N. Zane (Eds.), *Handbook of Asian American psychology.* Thousand Oaks, CA: Sage.

Kluckhohn, E., & Strodtbeck, E. (1961). *Variations in value orientations.* New York: Row, Peterson.

Knapp, M., & Hall, J. (1992). *Nonverbal communication in human interaction* (3rd ed.). New York: Harcourt Brace.

Kochman, T. (1981). *Black and white styles in conflict.* Chicago: University of Chicago Press.

———. (1990). Force fields in Black and White communication. In D. Carbaugh (Ed.), *Cultural communication and intercultural contact.* Hillsdale, NJ: Erlbaum.

Kraus, E. (1991). *The contradictory immigrant problem: A socio-psychological analysis.* New York: Lang.

Krishnan, A., & Berry, J. (1992). Acculturative stress and acculturative attitudes among Indian immigrants to the United States. *Psychology and Developing Societies, 4, 187–212.*

Kroeber, A., & Kluckhohn, C. (1952). Culture: A critical review of concepts and definitions (*Papers of the Peabody Museum*, Vol. 47). Cambridge, MA: Peabody Museum.

Langer, E. (1989). *Mindfulness.* Reading, MA: Addison-Wesley.

———. (1997). *The power of mindful learning.* Reading, MA: Addison-Wesley.

Larimer, T. (2000, September 27). Failure is not just an individual matter. *Time Asia* Website. www.time.com/asia/features/2000/09/27/int.jap.urushibara. html

Laws pertaining to dowry, http://www.ananova.com/news/story/sm_ 782099.htm (Retrieved on October 19, 2003).

LeBaron, M. (2003). *Bridging cultural conflicts: A new approach for a changing world.* San Francisco: Jossey-Bass.

Lee, C., & Gudykunst, W. (2001). Attraction in initial interethnic encounters. *International Journal of Intercultural Relations, 25,* 373–387.

Lee, S., & Fernandez, M. (1998). Trends in Asian American racial/ethnic intermarriage: A comparison of 1980 and 1990 census data. *Sociological Perspectives, 41*(2), 323–343.

Lennon, J. (1971). "Imagine<@148 [John Lennon]. On *Imagine* [CD]. New York: Capital Records.

Leung, K. (1988). Some determinants of conflict avoidance. *Journal of Cross-Cultural Psychology, 19,* 125–136.

Lewin, K. (1936). *Principles of typological psychology.* New York: McGraw-Hill.

Leyens, J.-P., Yzerbyt, V., & Schadron, G. (1994). *Stereotypes and social cognition.* London: Sage.

Lippman, W. (1936). *Public opinion.* New York: Macmillan.

Littlejohn, S., & Domenici, K. (2001). *Engaging communication in conflict.* Thousand Oaks, CA: Sage.

Locke, D. (1992). *Increasing multicultural understanding: A comprehensive model.* Newbury Park, CA: Sage.

Lukens, J. (1978). Ethnocentric speech. *Ethnic Groups, 2,* 35–53.

Lysgaard, S. (1955). Adjustment in a foreign society. *International Social Science Bulletin, 7,* 45–51.

MacGregor, H. (2002, August 4). Adopt, then adapt. *Los Angeles Times,* pp. E1, E3.

Madonna & Orbit, W. (1998). Shanti/Ashtangi [Madonna]. On *Ray of light* [CD]. New York: Warner Brothers.

Maltz, D., & Borker, R. (1982). A cultural approach to male-female communication. In J. Gumperz (Ed.), *Language and social identity.* Cambridge, UK: Cambridge University Press.

Marech, R. (2004, April). The battle over same-sex marriage. *San Francisco Chronicle,* A1.

Markus, H., & Kitayama, S. (1991). Culture and the self: Implications for cognition, emotion, and motivation. *Psychological Review, 2,* 224–253.

———. (1994). A collective fear of the collective: Implications for selves and theories of selves. *Personality and Social Psychology Bulletin, 20,* 568–579.

Marshall, G. (1994). *The concise Oxford dictionary of sociology.* Oxford: Oxford University Press.

Martin, J., & Harrell, T. (1996). Reentry training for intercultural sojourners. In D. Landis & R. Bhagat (Eds.), *Handbook of intercultural training* (2nd ed.). Thousand Oaks, CA: Sage.

——. (2004). Intercultural reentry of students and professionals: Theory and practice. In D. Landis, J. Bennett, & M. Bennett (Eds.), *Handbook of intercultural training* (3rd ed.). Thousand Oaks, CA: Sage.

Matsumoto, D. (1991). Cultural influences on facial expressions of emotion. *Southern Communication Journal, 56,* 128–137.

Matsumoto, D., & Juang, L. (2003). *Culture and psychology* (3rd ed.). Belmont, CA: Wadsworth.

Matsumoto, D., & Kudoh, T. (1993). American-Japanese cultural differences in attributions based on smiles. *Journal of Nonverbal Behavior, 17,* 231–243.

McClure, S. (2002, December 28). Year in Asia. *Billboard Magazine, 114*(52/1), pYE-24.

McIntosh, P. (1995). White privilege: Unpacking the invisible backpack. In A. Kasselman, L. D. McNair, & N. Scheidewind (Eds.), *Women, images, and realities: A multicultural anthology.* Mountain View, CA: Mayfield.

McLeod, P. L., Lobel, S. A., & Cox, T. H. (1996). Ethnic diversity and creativity in small groups. *Small Group Research, 27,* 248–264.

McNamara, R. P., Tempenis, M., & Walton, B. (1999). *Crossing the line: Interracial couples in the South.* Westport, CT: Praeger.

Milhouse, V., Asante, M., & Nwosu, P. (Eds.). (2001). *Transcultural realities: Interdisciplinary perspectives on cross-cultural communication.* Thousand Oaks, CA: Sage.

Miyamoto, N. (1999). What is the color of love? In A. Ling (Ed.), *Yellow light: The flowering of Asian American arts.* Philadelphia: Temple University Press.

Moorthy, R., DeGeorge, R., Donaldson, T., Ellos, W., Solomon, R., & Textor, R. (1998). *Uncompromising integrity: Motorola's global challenge.* Schaumberg, IL: Motorola University Press.

Mora, P. (2000). "Elena." In *My own true name: New and selected poems for young adults.* Houston,TX: Arte Publico Press.

Morris, D. (1994). *Bodytalk: The meaning of human gestures.* New York: Crown.

Musuko, M. (2000, February 11). Selling with Style. In Asiaweek.com http://www.asiaweek.com/asiaweek/magazine/2000/0211/biz.japan.html.

NAFSA: Association of International Education Fact Sheet, 2003. Top-Ten Countries of Origin of International Students to the United States, 2002/2003, http://opendoors.iienetwork.org (Retrieved on September 1, 2003).

Nash, D. (1991). The cause of sojourner adaptation: A new test of the U-curve hypothesis. *Human Organization, 50,* 283–286.

Nash, M. (1989). *The cauldron of ethnicity in the modern world.* Chicago: University of Chicago Press.

National Geographic (2003). *Concise atlas of the world.* Oxford: Oxford University Press.

Ngyuen, K. (2003, January 31). Walking a runway—and a thin line. *Los Angeles Times*, pp. A1, A4.

Oberg, K. (1960). Culture shock and the problems of adjustment to new cultural environments. *Practical Anthropology, 7*, 170–179.

Oetzel, J. G. (1998). Culturally homogeneous and heterogeneous groups: Explaining communication processes through individualism-collectivism and self-construal. *International Journal of Intercultural Relations, 22*(2), 135–161.

———. (1999). The influence of situational features on perceived conflict styles and self-construals in small groups. *International Journal of Intercultural Relations, 23*(4), 679–695.

Oetzel, J. G., & Ting-Toomey, S. (2003). Face concerns in interpersonal conflict: A cross-cultural empirical test of the face-negotiation theory. *Communication Research, 30*(6), 599–624.

Oetzel, J., Ting-Toomey, S., Masumoto, T., Yokochi, Y., Pan, X, Takai, J., & Wilcox, R. (2001). Face behaviors in interpersonal conflicts: A cross-cultural comparison of Germany, Japan, China, and the United States. *Communication Monographs, 68*, 235–258.

Okabe, R. (1983). Cultural assumptions of East and West: Japan and the United States. In W. Gudykunst (Ed.), *Intercultural communication theory: Current perspectives.* Beverly Hills, CA: Sage.

Ong, S.-J. (2000). *The construction and validation of a social support scale for sojourners: The Index of Sojourner Social Support (ISSS).* Unpublished master's thesis, National University of Singapore.

Orbe, M. (1998). *Constructing co-culture-theory: An explication of cultures, power, and communication.* Thousand Oaks, CA: Sage.

Orbe, M., & Harris, T. (2001). *Interracial communication.* Belmont, CA: Wadsworth.

Osland, J. (1995). *The adventure of working abroad: Hero tales from the global frontier.* San Francisco: Jossey-Bass.

Pack-Brown, S., & Williams, C. (2003). *Ethics in multicultural contexts.* Thousand Oaks, CA: Sage.

Paige, M., & Martin, J. (1996). Ethics in intercultural training. In D. Landis & R. Bhagat (Eds.), *Handbook of intercultural training* (2nd ed.). Thousand Oaks, CA: Sage.

Parham, T., & Helms, J. (1985). The relationship of racial identity attitudes to self-actualization of Black students and affective states. *Journal of Counseling Psychology, 32*, 431–440.

Pearmain, E. (Ed.). (1998). *Doorways to the soul.* Cleveland, OH: Pilgrim Press.

Pedersen, P. (1997). Do the right thing: A question of ethics. In K. Cushner & R. Brislin (Eds.), *Improving intercultural interactions: Modules for cross-cultural training programs* (Vol. 2). Thousand Oaks, CA: Sage.

Pennington, D. (1990). Time in African culture. In A. Asante & K. Asante (Eds.), *African culture: The rhythms of unity.* Trenton, NJ: Africa World Press.

Pettigrew, T. (1978). The ultimate attribution error: Extending Allport's cognitive analysis of prejudice. *Personality and Social Psychology Bulletin, 5*, 461–476.

Philipsen, G. (1996). A theory of speech codes. In G. Philipsen & T. Albrecht (Eds.), *Developing communication theory*. Albany: State University of New York Press.

Polgreen, L. (2002, July 19). Touring Indian star gets surprise welcome in N.Y. *New York Times*, p. B2.

Puentha, D., Giles, H., & Young, L. (1987). Interethnic perceptions and relative deprivation: British data. In Y. Y. Kim & W. Gudykunst (Eds.), *Cross-cultural adaptation: Current approaches*. Newbury Park, CA: Sage.

Purnell, L., & Paulanka, B. (2003). *Transcultural health care: A culturally competent approach* (2nd ed.). Philadelphia: F. A. Davis Company.

Pusch, M., & Loewenthall, N. (1988). *Helping them home: A guide for leaders of professional integrity and reentry workshops*. Washington, DC: National Association for Foreign Student Affairs.

Rahim, M. A. (1992). *Managing conflict in organizations* (2nd ed.). Westport, CT: Praeger.

Redfield, R., Linton, R., & Herskovits, M. (1936). Memorandum for the study of acculturation. *American Anthropologist, 38*, 149–152.

Remland, M. (2000). *Nonverbal communication in everyday life*. Boston: Houghton Mifflin.

Remland, M., Jones, T., & Brinkman, H. (1995). Interpersonal distance, body orientation, and touch: Effects of culture, gender, and age. *Journal of Social Psychology, 135*, 281–298.

Richmond, V., & McCroskey, J. (2000). *Nonverbal behavior in interpersonal relations* (4th ed.). Boston: Allyn & Bacon.

Richmond, Y. (1996). *From nyet to da: Understanding the Russians* (2nd ed.). Yarmouth, ME: Intercultural Press.

Ridley, C. R., & Udipi, S. (2002). Putting cultural empathy into practice. In P. Pedersen, J. Draguns, W. Lonner, & J. Trimble (Eds.), *Counseling across cultures* (5th ed.). Thousand Oaks, CA: Sage.

Rohrlich, B., & Martin, J. (1991). Host country and reentry adjustment of student sojourners. *International Journal of Intercultural Relations, 15*, 163–182.

Rokeach, M. (1972). *Beliefs, attitudes and values: A theory of organization and change*. San Francisco: Jossey-Bass.

Rokeach, M. (1973). *The nature of human values*. New York: Free Press.

Rosen, R., Digh, P., Singer, M., & Phillips, C. (2000). *Global literacies*. New York: Simon & Schuster.

Rosenblatt, P., Karis, T., & Powell, R. (1995). *Multiracial couples: Black and White Voices*. Thousand Oaks, CA: Sage.

Ross, J., & Ferris, K. (1981). Interpersonal attraction and organizational outcome: A field experiment. *Administrative Science Quarterly, 26*, 617–632.

Rotella, S. (2003, September 13). Soap operas of Argentina make Israelis swoon. *Los Angeles Times*, p. A3.

Rothman, J. (1997). *Resolving identity-based conflict in nations, organizations, and communities*. San Francisco: Jossey-Bass.

Rotter, J. (1966). Generalized expectancies for internal versus external control of reinforcement. *Psychological Monographs, 80*(609).

Rowe, W., Bennett, S., & Atkinson, D. (1994). White racial identity development models: A critique and alternative proposal. *The Counseling Psychologist, 22,* 129–146.

Ruiz, A. (1990). Ethnic identity: Crisis and resolution. *Journal of Multicultural Counseling, 18,* 29–40.

Said, E. (1978). *Orientalism.* New York: Pantheon Press.

"San Diego Wildfires," http://www.msnbc.com/id/4033840 (Retrieved January 23, 2004).

Sapir, E. (1921). *Language: An introduction to the study of speech.* New York: Harcourt, Brace & World.

Schaefer, R. (1990). *Racial and ethnic groups* (4th ed.). New York: HarperCollins.

Schreiber, A. (2001). *Multicultural marketing: Selling to the new America.* Chicago: NTC Business Books.

Schuman, M. (2001, February 21). Out on a limb: Some Korean women are taking great strides to show a little leg. *Wall Street Journal,* p. A1.

Schwartz, S. (1990). Individualism-collectivism: Critique and refinement. *Journal of Cross-Cultural Psychology, 21,* 139–157.

——. (1992). Universals in the content and structure of values. In M. Zanna (Ed.), *Advances in experemental social psychology* (Vol. 25). New York: Academic Press.

Schwartz, S., & Bardi, A. (2001). Value hierarchies across cultures. *Journal of Cross-Cultural Psychology, 32,* 268–290.

Sciolino, E. (2000, September 22). Iran's well-covered women remodel a part that shows. *New York Times,* A1.

Serrano, R. (2002, July 6). Deluge of hate crimes after 9/11 pours through system. *Los Angeles Times,* p. A8.

Shakur, T. (1991). Words of wisdom. On *Jive 2Pacolypse Now* [CD]. New York: Interscope/Jive Records.

Sherif, M. (1966). *In common predicament: Social psychology of intergroup conflict and cooperation.* New York: Octagon Books.

Shoppers on Guam flock to Kmart. (1999, January 2). *The Honolulu Advertiser,* pp. A1, A5.

Simmons, A. (2003, September 21). Giving voice to mother tongues of South Africa. *Los Angeles Times,* p. A5.

Simmons, C., & Wehner, E., & Kay, K. (1989). Differences in attitudes toward romantic love of French and American college students. *International Journal of Social Psychology, 129,* 793–799.

Smiley Face. (1999, May 10). *People Magazine,* 255.

Smith, C. (2003, January 10). International News. *New York Times.* http://www.nytimes.com/2003/01/10/international/europe/10FRAN.html

Smith, P., & Bond, M. (1993). *Social psychology across cultures.* New York: Harvester.

Smith, P., Dugan, S., & Trompenaars, F. (1996). National culture and the values of organizational employees: A dimensional analysis across 43 nations. *Journal of Cross-Cultural Psychology, 27,* 231–264.

Spangle, M., & Isenhard, M. (2003). *Negotiation: Communication for diverse settings.* Thousand Oaks, CA: Sage.

Spines, C. (1998, October). Hey, nineteen. *Premiere Magazine, 11*(14), 62–67, 118–119.

Spitzberg, B., & Cupach, W. (1984). *Interpersonal communication competence.* Beverly Hills, CA: Sage.

Steinfatt, T. (1989). Linguistic relativity: A broader view. In S. Ting-Toomey & F. Korzenny (Eds.), *Language, communication, and culture: Current directions.* Newbury Park, CA: Sage.

Stephan, C., & Stephan, W. (1992). Reducing intercultural anxiety through intercultural contact. *International Journal of Intercultural Relations, 16,* 89–106.

Stephan, W., & Stephan, C. (1996). *Intergroup relations.* Boulder, CO: Westview.

——. (2001). *Improving intergroup relations.* Thousand Oaks, CA: Sage.

Sternberg, R. J. (Ed.). (1999). *Handbook for creativity.* Cambridge, UK: Cambridge University Press.

Stewart, E., & Bennett, M. (1991). *American cultural patterns: A cross-cultural perspective* (2nd ed.). Yarmouth, ME: Intercultural Press.

Storti, C. (2001). *Old world/new world.* Yarmouth, ME: Intercultural Press.

Stringer, D., & Cassidy, P. (2003). *52 Activities for exploring values differences.* Yarmouth, ME: Intercultural Press.

Sue, D., & Sue, D. (1990). *Counseling the culturally different: Theory and practice* (2nd ed.). New York: Wiley.

——. (1999). *Counseling the culturally different: Theory and practice* (3rd ed.). New York: Wiley.

Sullivan, D. (2003, March 3). Personal Communication. San Diego, CA.

Sussman, N. (1986). Reentry research and training: Methods and implications. *International Journal of Intercultural Relations, 10,* 235–254.

Swerdlow, J. (1999, August). Global culture. *National Geographic, 196*(2), 2–6.

Tajfel, H. (Ed.). (1978). *Differentiation between social groups: Studies in the social psychology of intergroup relations.* New York: Academic Press.

Takahashi, C. (2003, February). Musical Masala. *Vibe Magazine,* 92–98.

Tang, I. (2003, March 21). Inside the Shaquille O'Neal taunt controversy. *AsianWeek.com.* http://news.asianweek.com/news/view_article.html?article_id=60812dbc0595245187b40754f042ffc4

Tannen, D. (1994). *Talking 9 to 5.* New York: William Morrow.

Tharp, T., with Reiter, M. (2003). *The creative habit: Learn it and use it for life.* New York: Simon & Schuster.

Ting-Toomey, S. (1985). Toward a theory of conflict and culture. In W. Gudykunst, L. Stewart, & S. Ting-Toomey (Eds.), *Communication, culture, and organizational processes.* Beverly Hills, CA: Sage.

——. (1986). Conflict communication styles in Black and White subjective cultures. In Y. Y. Kim (Ed.), *Interethnic communication: Current research.* Newbury Park, CA: Sage.

——. (1988). Intercultural conflict styles: A face-negotiation theory. In Y. Y. Kim & W. Gudykunst (Eds.), *Theories in intercultural communication.* Newbury Park, CA: Sage.

——. (1991). Intimacy expressions in three cultures: France, Japan, and the United States. *International Journal of Intercultural Relations, 15,* 29–46.

——. (1999). *Communicating across cultures.* New York: Guilford Press.

——. (2004). Translating conflict face-negotiation theory into practice. In D. Landis, J. Bennett, & M. Bennett (Eds.), *Handbook of intercultural training* (3rd ed.). Thousand Oaks, CA: Sage.

Ting-Toomey, S., & Cole, M. (1990). Intergroup diplomatic communication: A face-negotiation perspective. In F. Korzenny & S. Ting-Toomey (Eds.), *Communicating for peace: Diplomacy and negotiation across cultures.* Newbury Park, CA: Sage.

Ting-Toomey, S., Gao, G., Trubisky, P., Yang, Z., Kim, H. S., Lin, S.-L., & Nishida, T. (1991). Culture, face maintenance, and styles of handling interpersonal conflict: A study in five cultures. *International Journal of Conflict Management, 2,* 275–296.

Ting-Toomey, S., & Kurogi, A. (1998). Facework competence in intercultural conflict: An updated face-negotiation theory. *International Journal of Intercultural Relations, 22,* 187–225.

Ting-Toomey, S., & Oetzel, J. (2001). *Managing intercultural conflict effectively.* Thousand Oaks, CA: Sage.

——. (2003). Cross-cultural face concerns and conflict styles: Current status and future directions. In W. Gudykunst (Ed.), *Cross-cultural and intercultural communication.* Thousand Oaks, CA: Sage.

Ting-Toomey, S., Oetzel, J., & Yee-Jung, K. (2001). Self-construal types and conflict management styles. *Communication Reports 14,* 87–104.

Ting-Toomey, S., Yee-Jung, K., Shapiro, R., Garcia, W., Wright, T., & Oetzel, J. G. (2000). Cultural/ethnic identity salience and conflict styles in four U.S. ethnic groups. *International Journal of Intercultural Relations, 24,* 47–81.

Top-five countries with the largest Muslim population, http://www.zackvision.com/weblog/archives/entry/000104.html (Retrieved on January 25, 2004).

Top-five religions in the United States, http://www.gc.cuny.edu/studies/key_findings.htm (Retrieved on January 23, 2004).

Top-seven countries with the highest ratio of cellular mobile phone users, http://www.electronicmarkets.org/files/cms/44.php (Retrieved on January 25, 2004).

Top-ten all-time box office worldwide gross, http://www.imdb.com/Charts/worldtopmovies (Retrieved on March 1, 2004).

Top-ten billboard music singles in the United States, October 3, 2003, http://www.billboard.com/bb/charts/hot100.jsp (Retrieved on October 3, 2003).

Top-Ten countries with the highest divorce rate, http://aneki.com/divorce.html (Retrieved on February 1, 2004).

Top-ten countries with the lowest divorce rate, http://tigerx.com/trivia/divorces.htm (Retrieved on February 1, 2004).

Top-ten countries with the most Internet users, http://www.c-i-a.com/pr1202.htm (Retrieved on January 23, 2004).

Top-ten countries of origin of visitors to the United States, 2003, http://ti-dev.eainet.com/view/f-2003-203-001/index.html?ti_cart_cookie=20040707.210407.18294 (Retrieved on June 1, 2004).

Top-ten most valuable global brands by dollar value, http://www.bwnt.businessweek.com/brand/2004/index.asp (Retrieved on February 1, 2004).

Top-ten study abroad locations, U.S. college students 2002, http://www.iie.org (Retrieved on September 1, 2003).

Top-ten wedding songs in the United States, http://www.weddingzone.net//p-top50t.htm (Retrieved on June 2, 2004).

Top-ten worldwide tourist destinations, 2003, http://www.world-tourism.org/newsroom/Releases/2004/june/data.htm (Retrieved on June 25, 2004).

Tracy, K. (2002). *Everyday talk: Building and reflecting identities.* New York: Guilford.

Training and Development. (1999, November). Training & development annual trend reports: Trendz. *Training and Development, 53*(1), 22–43.

Triandis, H. (1972). *The analysis of subjective culture.* New York: Wiley.

———. (1990). Theoretical concepts that are applicable to the analysis of ethnocentrism. In R. Brislin (Ed.), *Applied cross-cultural psychology.* Newbury Park, CA: Sage.

———. (1994). *Culture and social behavior.* New York: McGraw-Hill.

———. (1995). *Individualism and collectivism.* Boulder, CO: Westview Press.

Tullis, P. (2003, September 21). Ev'rybody's doin' a brand new pose now, C'mon baby, do the yoga motion. *Los Angeles Times Magazine,* 10–15.

U.S. Census Bureau Data Base (2000). Top-ten countries of birth for foreign-born adopted children under 18 in the United States.

U.S. Census Bureau International Data Base, 2000. Top-ten countries with the highest estimated net number of immigrants per 1000 population.

U.S. Census Bureau International Data Base, 2000. Top-ten countries of origin of U.S. immigrants.

U.S. Census Bureau Data Base (2000). Top-ten most racially/ethnically diverse states in the United States.

U.S. Census Bureau Data Base (2000). Top-ten most racially/ethnically homogeneous states in the United States.

U.S. Department of Commerce, Office of Travel and Tourism Industries (2004) Top-ten tourism cities in the United States, 2003, http://ti-dev.eainet.com/view/f-2001-45-561/index.html?ti_cart_cookie=20040307.002823.18497 (Retrieved on February 1, 2004).

Ward, C. (1996). Acculturation. In D. Landis & R. Bhagat (Eds.). *Handbook of intercultural training* (2nd ed.). Thousand Oaks, CA: Sage.

———. (2004). Psychological theories of culture contact and their implications for intercultural training and interventions. In D. Landis, J. Bennett, & M. Bennett (Eds.), *Handbook of intercultural training* (3rd ed.). Thousand Oaks, CA: Sage.

Ward, C., Bochner, S., & Furnham, A. (2001). *The psychology of culture shock* (2nd ed.). London: Routledge.

Ward, C., & Kennedy, A. (1993). Where's the culture in cross-cultural transition? Comparative studies of sojourner adjustment. *Journal of Cross-Cultural Psychology, 24,* 221–249.

Waters, M. (1990). *Ethnic options: Choosing identities in America.* Berkeley: University of California Press.

Watzlawick, P., Beavin, J., & Jackson, D. (1967). *The pragmatics of human communication.* New York: Norton.

Wehrfritz, G. (2000, September 18). Liberated by the Internet. *Newsweek,* 14–19.

Wehrly, B., Kenney, K. R., & Kenney, M. E. (1999). *Counseling multiracial families.* Thousand Oaks, CA: Sage.

Wheeler, L., & Kim, Y. (1997). What is beautiful is culturally good: The physical attractiveness stereotype has different content in collectivistic cultures. *Personality and Social Psychology Bulletin, 23,* 795–800.

Whetmore, E. J. (1991). *Mediamerica* (4th ed.). Belmont, CA: Wadsworth.

Whorf, B. (1952). *Collected papers on metalinguistics.* Washington, DC: U.S. Department of State, Foreign Service Institute.

——. (1956). *Language, thought and reality.* New York: Wiley.

Williams, A., & Nussbaum, J. (2001). *Intergenerational communication across the lifespan.* Mawah, NJ: Laurence Erlbaum Associates.

Williamson, L., & Pierson, E. (2003). The rhetoric of hate on the Internet: Hateporn's challenge to modern media ethics. *Journal of Mass Media Ethics, 18*(3 & 4), 250–267.

Wilmot, W., & Hocker, J. (2001). *Interpersonal conflict* (6th ed.). Boston: McGraw-Hill.

Winters, L., & De Bose, H. (Eds.). (2003). *New faces in a changing America: Multiracial identity in the 21st century.* Thousand Oaks, CA: Sage.

Wiseman, R. (2003). Intercultural communication competence. In W. Gudykunst (Ed.), *Cross-cultural and intercultural communication.* Thousand Oaks, CA: Sage.

Wiseman, R., & Koester, J. (Eds.). (1993). *Intercultural communication competence.* Newbury Park, CA: Sage.

Witmer, D., & Katzman, S. (1997). On-line smiles: Does gender make a difference in the use of graphic accents? *Journal of Computer-Mediated Communication, 2*(4), http://www.ascusc.org/jcmc/vol2/issue4/witmer1.html

Wolf, M. J. (1999). *The entertainment economy: How mega media forces are transforming our lives.* New York: Times Books.

Wood, J. (1997). *Gendered lives: Communication, gender, and culture* (2nd ed.). Belmont, CA: Wadsworth.

Wyatt, T. (1995). Language development in African American English child speech. *Linguistics and Education, 7,* 7–22.

Young, L. (1994). *Crosstalk and culture in Sino-American communication.* Cambridge, UK: Cambridge University Press.

Zelizer, B. (2001). Popular communication in the contemporary age. In W. Gudykunst (Ed.), *Communication yearbook, 24,* 299. Thousand Oaks, CA: Sage.

Zielenziger, M. (2002, December 22). Economy turning many Japanese into shut-ins. *San Diego Union Tribune,* pp. A3, A27.

Zwingle, E., & McNally, J. (1999, August). A world together. *National Geographic, 196*(2), 6–34. ✦

Glossary

accent the inflection, or tone of voice, that is taken to be characteristic of an individual

accommodation the interaction strategies that combine both majority and co-culture views through adjustment and modification of one's behavior

acculturation the degree of identity change that occurs when individuals move from a familiar environment to an unfamiliar one

adaptors the nonverbal habits or gestures that fulfill some kind of psychological or physical need

ambivalent ethnocentrism the confused feelings one has about outgroup members

appropriateness the degree to which exchanged behaviors are regarded as proper and match the expectations generated by insiders of the culture

artifacts ornaments or adornments used to communicate on the nonverbal level

assimilation communication strategies that adopt the majority culture's view

attitude including both cognitive and affective layers. The cognitive layer refers to the willingness to suspend our ethnocentric judgment and readiness to be open-minded in learning about cross-cultural difference issues; the affective layer refers to the emotional commitment to engage in cultural perspective-taking and the cultivation of an empathetic heart in reaching out to culturally diverse groups

attribution the explanation; the act of assigning cause to why people behave as they do

avoiding style involves dodging the conflict topic, the conflict party, or the conflict situation altogether

axiomatic-deductive form emphasizes the importance of starting from general principles or "axioms," and then moving forward to fill in specific details

B

"being-in-becoming" mode living with an emphasis on spiritual renewal and connection

"being-in-doing" e.net philosophy e.net multitrack individuals can fuse the "being mode" value dimension with the "doing" mode value dimension

"being" solution living with emotional vitality and enthusiastic energy

blended family the merging of different family systems from previous marriages

C

chronemics how people in different cultures structure, interpret, and understand the time dimension

co-culture theory Orbe's (1998) theory that African Americans and other minority groups, because of their marginalized position in the larger U.S. society, develop a complex, ethnic/cultural standpoint

collectivism the broad value tendencies of a culture in emphasizing the importance of the "we" identity over the "I" identity, group rights over individual rights, and ingroup needs over individual wants and desires

Colonial ethnocentrism the rights and privileges of groups who are in a dominant power position in a society (whether at political, economic, social class, or societal levels) to impose their ethical standards on nondominant groups or powerless individuals

communication adaptability the ability to change interaction behaviors and goals to meet the specific needs of a situation

communication creativity the ability to break away from habitual ways of communicating and a willingness to experiment with different interaction styles. It is also one of the critical criteria for evaluating intercultural communication flexibility

communicative meaning the intention and goal behind any discourse utterance

compensation exchanges, compensations, or concessions offered by conflict parties for conflict issues they value differently

complementary style a matter-of-fact tone in delivering verbal messages

compromising style a give-and-take concession approach to reach a midpoint agreement concerning a conflict issue *concealment* information guardedness or closedness; lack of disclosure or sharing of exclusive information about either the public self or the private self

conflict communication style patterned verbal and nonverbal responses to conflict in dealing with a variety of emotionally frustrating disputes

conscious competence stage the intentional mindfulness stage in which individuals actively pursue new intercultural knowledge to improve their communication competencies and practice new interaction skills

conscious incompetence stage the troubling realization stage in which individuals have some notions (i.e., attitudinal openness) that they behave incompetently; however, they lack the knowledge or skills to operate adaptively in the new culture

consequences taking into consideration the results that affect all parties who are directly or indirectly involved in a problematic case

content goals the practical, or tangible, issues that are external to the individuals involved

conventional meaning relating to words that refer to the needed coordination between verbal message usage and the expectations or norms of the cultural context

convergent thinking synthesis and analytical problem solving to reach a clearly defined outcome

coping stage the struggles of a couple to gain approval from their families and friends, and the strategies they come up with to deal with such external pressures

cultural communities within a bonded unit, a group of interacting individuals who uphold a set of shared traditions and a way of life

cultural competence skills the cultural knowledge internalized and the operational skills applied in the communicating scene

cultural display rules the procedures we learn for managing the way we express our emotions

cultural distance factors of difference, especially in cultural values, language, verbal styles, nonverbal gestures, learning styles, decision-making styles, and conflict negotiation styles as well as in religious, sociopolitical, and economic systems

cultural empathy the learned ability of the participants to understand accurately the self-experiences of others from diverse cultures and, concurrently, the ability to convey their understanding responsively and effectively to reach the "cultural ears" of the culturally different others in the conflict situation

cultural identity the emotional significance that we attach to our sense of belonging or affiliation with the larger culture

cultural identity salience the strength of affiliation we have with our larger culture

culturally shared beliefs a set of fundamental assumptions, or worldviews, that people hold dear to their hearts without question

culturally shared traditions myths, legends, ceremonies, and rituals that are passed on from one generation to the next via oral or written media

cultural norms the collective expectations of what constitutes proper or improper behavior in a given interaction scene

cultural values a set of priorities that guides "good" or "bad" behaviors, "desirable" or "undesirable" practices, and "fair" or "unfair" actions

culture a learned meaning system that consists of patterns of traditions, beliefs, values, norms, meanings, and symbols that are passed on from one generation to the next and are shared to varying degrees by interacting members of a community

culture shock a period of stressful transition in which individuals move from a familiar environment into an unfamiliar one

D

defensive ethnocentrism a rigidly held mindset and a tendency to create a superior-inferior gap with outgroup members

dialectical tensions conflicts that come from two opposing forces that exist at the same time

differentiation taking an active stance to acknowledge the differing cultural perspectives and lenses in a conflict situation

direct institutional discrimination a community-prescribed endorsement of discrimination

direct verbal style verbal statements that tend to reveal the speaker's intentions with clarity and are enunciated with a forthright tone of voice

disaffiliate distancing, or rebelling against, any existing label that is imposed on an individual as part of a particular racial or cultural group

discourse meaning both the denotative and connotative meaning of a word

dispositional approach a stable or predominant conflict style tendency in handling a wide variety of conflict situations in different cultures

distance of avoidance (i.e., moderate ethnocentrism) attempted linguistic or dialect-switching in the presence of outgroup members, as well as displayed nonverbal inattention (e.g., members of the dominant group maintain eye contact only with members of their group) to accentuate ingroup connection and avoidance of outgroup members

distance of disparagement (i.e., high ethnocentrism) the use of racist jokes or hate-filled speech to downgrade outgroup members

distance of indifference (i.e., low ethnocentrism) the lack of sensitivity in our verbal and nonverbal interactions in dealing with dissimilar others

divergent thinking a fluid thinking pattern; the ability to switch from one perspective to another, connecting unrelated ideas together in a meaningful fashion; and the ability to bring a new idea to completion

"doing" solution involving achievement-oriented activities and concrete, measurable accomplishments

dominating (or competitive/controlling) style emphasizing conflict tactics that push for one's own position above and beyond the other person's conflict interest or need

duties obligations and responsibilities counterbalancing rights and entitlements

dynamic flexibility stage integrating the best of ethical, cognitive, affective, and behavioral layers of identity and communicating in an open-minded, creative manner

E

effectiveness the degree to which communicators achieve mutually shared meaning and integrative goal-related outcomes

emblems gestures that substitute for words and phrases and are very culture-specific nonverbal behaviors

enculturation the sustained, primary socialization process of strangers in their original home (or natal) culture, wherein they have internalized their primary cultural values

e.net identity identification with a new generation of individuals from any age-group, wired to the Internet

ethical absolutism emphasis on the principles of right and wrong in accordance with a set of universally fixed standards, regardless of cultural differences

ethical relativism emphasizing the importance of understanding the cultural context in which the problematic conduct is being judged

ethical universalism emphasizing the importance of deriving universal ethical guidelines by placing ethical judgments within the proper cultural context

ethnic identity a sense of communal belonging and identification with ancestral traditions and practices, especially based on one's beliefs about one's ancestral history and lineage

ethnocentric mindset staying stuck within one's cultural worldview and using one's cultural values as the baseline standards with which to evaluate another's cultural behavior

ethnocentrism the belief that the views and standards of one's own ingroup are much more important than any outgroup's viewpoints, standards, or ways of living

ethnorelative mindset understanding communication behavior from another's cultural frame of reference and the ability to perceive from another's cultural lens

expansion an active search for alternative paths; creative solutions to enlarge the amount, type, or use of available resources (e.g., using existing resources in imaginative ways or cultivating new resources) for mutual gains in the conflict negotiation process

extended family consisting of extended kinship groups, such as grandparents, aunts and uncles, cousins, and nieces and nephews

external locus of control emphasizing external determinism, karma, fate, and external forces shaping a person's life happenings and events

F

face a claimed sense of social self-worth that a person wants others to have of her or him

facework the specific verbal and nonverbal behaviors or actions that we engage in to maintain or restore lost face and to uphold and honor face gain

factual-inductive form emphasizing the importance of presenting facts, evidence, eyewitness accounts, testimonials, and proofs, and from these specific facts, proceeding to draw conclusions or generalizations

fairness equitable treatment on a personal level or on a community-interest level

familism the deep commitment to family ties in the Latino/a family system

fatalism the "being" attitude of some individuals in perceiving their external environment with acceptance and resignation

femininity prescribed gender roles dictating that women should be modest, observant, and tender

feng shui literally, "air" and "water" in Chinese. Used for thousands of years, the philosophy of combining elements to attain good energy within a room, building, or area

flexible intercultural communication emphasizing the importance of integrating knowledge and an open-minded attitude, and putting them into adaptive and creative practice in everyday communication

formal verbal style emphasizing the importance of upholding status-based and role-based interaction that reflects formality and large power distance

functional flexibility stage one can function adaptively, especially on the behavioral level, in using appropriate verbal and nonverbal styles in communicating with dissimilar others

future-oriented time planning for desirable short- or medium-term developments, and setting out clear objectives to realize them

G

gender hierarchy traditional status role differences between males and females—with the male playing the dominant breadwinning role and the female playing the household nurturing role

generational hierarchy showing respect to individuals above you in the family—parents to grandparents, children to parents, and younger siblings to older siblings

gestures culturally specific and significant forms of nonverbal communication

H

haptics the perceptions and meanings of touch behavior

hate crime a crime motivated by hostility to the victim as a member of a group (e.g., on the basis of ethnicity/race, disability, age, religion, gender, or sexual orientation)

high-contact cultures individuals often look each other in the eye directly, face each other, touch and/or kiss each other, and speak in rather loud voices

high-context communication emphasis on how intention or meaning can best be conveyed through the context (e.g., social roles or positions) and the nonverbal channels (e.g., pauses, silence, tone of voice) of the verbal message

high-context communicators individuals who tend to value indirect verbal style, understated or exaggerated conversational tone, and formal verbal treatment, and who emphasize the importance of silence

hip-hop music referred to by some as rap; originating in the inner-city ghettos of the United States in the mid-1970s

horizontal self-construals preferring informal-symmetrical interactions (i.e., equal treatment) regardless of people's position, status, rank, or age

ideals actions that are not required but are still done because it is the right thing to do

identity the reflective self-conception, or self-image, that we each derive from our family, gender, cultural, ethnic, and individual socialization processes

identity-based goals face-saving and face-honoring issues in a conflict episode

identity emergence the stage wherein both partners gain a new sense of security and bravely announce their intimate relationship to their families and ingroups

illustrators nonverbal hand gestures that are used along with the spoken message

independent construal of self the view that an individual is a unique entity with an individuated repertoire of feelings, cognitions, and motivations

independent-self conflict lens an I-identity conflict goal lens, emphasizing tangible conflict issues above and beyond relationship issues; a clear win-lose conflict approach in which one person comes out as a winner and the other person comes out as a loser; a "doing" angle, in which something tangible in the conflict is broken and needs fixing; and an outcome-driven mode, in which a clear resolution is needed

indirect institutional discrimination a biased practice that indirectly affects group members in an unfair or unjust manner, placing them in a disadvantaged position

indirect verbal style verbal statements that tend to soften the speaker's actual intentions and are carried out with a tentative, indirect tone

individualism the broad value tendencies of a culture in emphasizing the importance of individual identity over group identity, individual rights over group rights, and individual needs over group needs

inductive reasoning the importance of proceeding from facts and evidence to make a claim

inflexible intercultural communication stressing the continuation of using our own cultural values, judgments, and routines in communicating with culturally different others

informal verbal style a style emphasizing the importance of informality, casualness, and role suspension in verbal communication

ingroup favoritism principle positive attachment to and predisposition for norms and behaviors related to one's group

ingroups groups with whom one feels emotionally close and with whom one shares an interdependent fate, such as family or extended family, a sorority or fraternity, or people from one's own cultural or ethnic group

intangible resources deeply felt desires or emotional needs, including emotional security, inclusion, connection, respect, control, and meaning issues

integrating (or collaborative) style reflecting a commitment to find mutual-interest solutions, involving a high concern for self-interest and also for the other person's interest in the conflict situation

interaction goal the objective of the meeting (e.g., a job interview meeting is quite different from a chance meeting in a restaurant)

intercultural adjustment the short-term and medium-term adaptive process of sojourners in their overseas assignments

intercultural communication the symbolic exchange process whereby individuals from two (or more) different cultural communities negotiate shared meanings in an interactive situation

intercultural conflict implicit or explicit emotional struggle, or frustration between persons of different cultures, over perceived incompatible values, norms, face orientations, goals, scarce resources, processes, and/or outcomes in a communication situation

intercultural-intimate conflict any antagonistic friction or disagreement between two romantic partners due, in part, to cultural or ethnic group membership differences

interdependent construal of self an emphasis on the importance of fitting in with relevant others and ingroup connectedness

intergroup communication interaction in which individuals belonging to one group communicate, collectively or individually, with another group based on important group membership identity levels

internal locus of control an emphasis on free will, individual motivation, personal effort, and personal responsibility over the success or failure of an assignment

interpretation attachment of meaning to the data received

isolate discrimination harmful verbal and nonverbal action intentionally targeted toward an outgroup member

J

justice impartial treatment of cases by using a consistent set of standards in dealing with similar cases

K

kinesics the study of posture, body movement, gestures, and facial expressions *knowledge* the systematic, conscious learning of the essential themes and concepts in intercultural communication flexibility

L

language an arbitrary, symbolic system that names feelings, experiences, ideas, objects, events, groups, people, and other phenomena

large power distance cultures acceptance of unequal power distributions, hierarchical rights, asymmetrical role relations, and rewards and punishments on the basis of age, rank, status, title, and seniority

layered contextual perspective a belief that the application of ethics can be understood only through the peeling away of different layers of the ethical dilemma—in-depth case-by-case understanding

linear persuasion style style of persuasion in two forms: factual-inductive and axiomatic-deductive

low-contact cultures groups engaging in little if any touching, preferring indirect eye gazes and speaking in a lower tone

low-context communication communication with an emphasis on how intention or meaning is best expressed through direct and to-the-point verbal messages

low-context communicators individuals tending to emphasize direct verbal style, complementary to a matter-of-fact conversational tone, informal verbal treatment, and talkativeness

M

masculinity a male social gender role expectation that men are to be assertive, masculine, and tough, and that they are to focus on task-based accomplishment and material success

meanings interpretations that we attach to a symbol

moderate-contact cultures a blend of both high-contact and low-contact cultures

monotrack focus working on one project at a time on the Internet

morphological rules (or morphology) how combinations of different morphemes, the smallest meaningful elements of a language, make up a word or part of a word (e.g., "new" and "com-er" form "new-com-er")

multiple channels nonverbal messages simultaneously signaled and interpreted through various media, such as facial expressions, body gestures, spatial relationships, and the environment in which people are communicating

multitrack focus tending to do multiple tasks or activities on the Internet

N

nonverbal communication communication without words through multiple communication channels

O

obliging (or accommodating) style a high concern for the other person's conflict interest above and beyond one's own conflict position

organization the second step in the perception process

other-oriented face-giving behaviors attempts to support others' face claims and work with them to prevent further face loss or help them to restore face constructively

outgroups groups with whom one feels no emotional ties, and, at times, from whom one may experience great psychological distance as a result of perceived scarce resources and intergroup competition

P

paralanguage sounds and tones used in conversation and speech behavior that accompany the message

paraphrasing skills verbally summarizing the content meaning of the other's message in your own words; nonverbally echoing one's interpretation of the emotional meaning of the other's message

past-oriented time sense honoring historic and ancestral ties and respecting the wisdom of elderly people

perception the process of selecting cues from the environment, organizing them into a clear pattern, and interpreting that pattern

perception-checking skills skills designed to help ensure that one is interpreting the speaker's nonverbal and verbal behavior accurately during an escalating conflict cycle

personal commitment an individual's desire or intent to continue a relationship on the basis of his or her subjective emotional feelings and experiences

personal family system a democratic family system that emphasizes personal, individualized meanings and negotiable roles between parents and children

personal identity any unique attributes that one associates with his or her individuated self in comparison with those of others

personalism inner qualities of a person that earn him or her respect and social recognition from others

phonological rules (or phonology) the different accepted procedures for combining the phonemes or sounds of a language

positional family system a large power distance family system that emphasizes communal meanings and hierarchical respect, ascribed roles, and different statuses between parents and children; family rule conformity

pragmatic rules (pragmatics) the contextual rules that govern language usage in a particular culture

prejudice an individual's biased feelings and predispositions toward outgroup members in a pejorative or negative direction

present-oriented time sense valuing the here and now, especially the interpersonal relationships that are currently unfolding in front of the individual

private self those facets of the person that are potentially communicable but are not usually shared with others

proxemics the study of spatial arrangement between persons, especially appropriate versus inappropriate physical spatial distance

psychological adjustment feelings of internal well-being and satisfaction during cross-cultural transitions

public self those facets of the person that are readily available and are easily shared with others

R

racial awareness the gradual awakening stage in which the partners in an interracial relationship become conscious of each other's views and societal views on intimate racial relationship matters

racial profiling the singling out of one particular ethnic group in a police investigation

racism feelings of superiority based on biological and/or racial differences, strong ingroup preferences, and solidarity; rejection of any outgroup that diverges from the customs and beliefs of the ingroup; a doctrine that conveys a special advantage to those in power

reframing the mindful process of using language to change the way each person or party defines or thinks about experiences and views the conflict situation

regulators nonverbal behaviors used in conversation to control, maintain, or "regulate" the pace and flow of a conversation

relational conflict goals how individuals define the particular relationship (e.g., intimate vs. nonintimate, informal vs. formal, cooperative vs. competitive) or would like to define it in that interactive situation

relationship expectation how much role formality/informality or task/social tone one wants to forge in the interaction *relationship maintenance* the continuous hard work a couple has to face in dealing with new challenges, such as having children, moving to a new neighborhood, and meeting new social circles

revealment the disclosure of information concerning the different facets of the public self (e.g., interest, hobbies, political opinions, career aspirations) and/or private self (e.g., deep family issues, identity, self-image and self-esteem issues)

rights what one is entitled to as a human being or as a citizen of a country

"Romeo and Juliet" effect the more the respective families are against the intimate relationship, the more the couples want to rebel against their parents and "do their own thing" and, therefore, find each other more attractive

S

SADFISH an acronym referring to these recognizable facial emotions: Sadness, Anger, Disgust, Fear, Interest, Surprise, and Happiness

selection process picking out cues from our cultural environment

self-credentialing verbal mode drawing attention to or boasting about one's credentials, outstanding accomplishments, and special abilities

self-disclosure the deliberate process of revealing significant information about oneself that would not normally be known

self-humbling verbal mode lowering oneself via modest talk, verbal restraints, hesitations, and the use of verbal self-deprecation concerning one's effort or performance

self-oriented face-saving behaviors attempts to regain or defend one's image after threats to face or face loss

semantic rules (semantics) the features of meaning we attach to words

separation communication strategies that emphasize separation, such as intraethnic networking or showcasing the strengths and pride of one's own ethnic group

setting the consideration of cultural context (e.g., the interaction scene takes place in Japan or the U.S.) or physical context (e.g., in an office or a restaurant)

single family a household headed by a single parent

situational approach stresses the importance of the particular conflict topic and/or the particular conflict context in shaping what conflict styles will be used in what types of relationships and in what situations; this means that the individual does not have a consistent or predominant conflict style

situational meaning the physical and social context in which the utterance is made

skills operational abilities to integrate knowledge and a responsive attitude with adaptive intercultural behavior or practice

small-group discrimination a band of individuals from an ingroup engaging in hostile and abusive actions against outgroup members

small power distance cultures cultures valuing equal power distributions, equal rights and relations, and equitable rewards and punishments based on performance

social identities cultural or ethnic membership identity, gender identity, sexual orientation identity, social class identity, age identity, disability identity, or professional identity

sociocultural adjustment the ability to fit in and execute appropriate and effective interactions in a new cultural environment

speech community a group of individuals who share a common set of norms and rules regarding appropriate communication practices

spiritualism the religious and spiritual convictions of many cultural members

stereotypes exaggerated pictures one has about a group of people based on inflexible beliefs and expectations about the characteristics or behaviors of the group

strong (or high) uncertainty avoidance cultures preferring clear procedures and conflict-avoidance behaviors

structural commitment individuals taking into consideration various external social and family reactions in deciding either to continue or to terminate a relationship

symbol a sign, artifact, word(s), gesture, or nonverbal behavior that stands for or reflects something meaningful

symbolic exchange the use of verbal and nonverbal symbols between a minimum of two individuals to accomplish shared meanings

synergistic perspective combining the best of all cultural approaches in solving a workplace problem

syntactic rules (or syntactics) how words are sequenced together in accordance with the grammatical practices of the linguistic community

synthesizers the influence of aspects of both one's parents' cultural backgrounds; to synchronize and synthesize the diverse aspects of one's parents' values into a coherent identity

systems approach integration of both dispositional and situational approaches, recognizing that most individuals do have predominant conflict style profiles because of strong cultural and family socialization conflict scripts

T

tangible resources resources, including money available to spend on a new car, a sound system, or a vacation

traditional family a family structure consisting of a husband-wife/father-mother pair that has a child or children, with a father working outside the home and a homemaker mother

U

unconscious competence stage the "mindlessly mindful" intercultural sensitivity stage in which individuals move in and out of spontaneous, yet adaptive, communication with members of the new culture

unconscious incompetence stage the "mindless ignorance" phase in which individuals have neither culture-sensitive knowledge nor responsive attitudes or skills to communicate competently with the host members of the new culture

V

value content the standards or expectations that people hold in their mindset in making evaluations

values shared ideas about what is right or wrong, what is fair or unfair, what is important or not important

vertical self-construal preferring formal-asymmetrical interactions (i.e., differential treatment) with due respect to people's position, titles, life experiences, and/or age

virtues the commendable qualities of an individual

W

weak (or low) uncertainty avoidance cultures encouraging risk-taking and conflict-approaching modes

worldview one's larger philosophical outlook or way of perceiving the world and how this outlook, in turn, affects one's thinking and reasoning patterns ✦

Author Index

Subject Index